15-941

A

Voice to America

GENERAL LIBRARY
University of
MICHIGAN

OR,

THE MODEL REPUBLIC, ITS GLORY, OR ITS FALL:

WITH A REVIEW OF

The Causes of the Decline and Failure

OF

THE REPUBLICS OF SOUTH AMERICA, MEXICO, AND OF THE OLD WORLD;

APPLIED TO

THE PRESENT CRISIS IN THE UNITED STATES.

"Shall we, upon the footing of our land,
Send fair-play orders, and make compromise,
Insinuation, parley, and base truce,
To arms invasive?"

By Thos. Bangs Thorpe.

NEW YORK:
EDWARD WALKER, 114 FULTON-STREET.
1855.

I0834857

Entered according to Act of Congress, in the year 1855,

By EDWARD WALKER,

In the Clerk's Office of the District Court of the United States for the Southern District of New York.

Dedication.

THIS VOLUME IS INSCRIBED TO

ALL

WHO LOVE AMERICAN INSTITUTIONS,

AND DESIRE TO SEE THEM PERPETUATED

To Bless the Living,

AND

DESCEND IN THEIR PURITY TO FUTURE GENERATIONS.

"Breathes there a man with soul so dead,
Who never to himself hath said—
This is my own, my native land?"

SCOTT.

"Of all the dispositions and habits which lead to political prosperity, religion and morality are indispensable supports. In vain would that man claim the tribute of patriotism, who should labor to subvert these great pillars of human happiness—these firmest props of the duties of men and citizens."

WASHINGTON.

PUBLISHER'S PREFACE.

For some time past, the publisher of this work has entertained the idea of presenting to the citizens of the Union, a volume devoted to national interests. Maturing his plans, he laid them before a number of friends—gentlemen distinguished alike for their patriotism, social standing, and wide-spread reputation—and they were cordially endorsed as the promise, if carried out, of supplying a book really needed at this present crisis.

The gentlemen selected to write the various chapters, were chosen with reference to their ability to treat upon the subjects committed to their especial charge; and the publisher indulges the belief that their labor, careful research and investigation, joined with their conscientious desire to accomplish a work of so momentous interest, will be appreciated by every patriotic and reflective mind.

The subjects treated of concern not only the statesman and politician, but every American citizen, however humble or exalted—whether native or naturalized. They extend over a vast range of valuable facts and historical illustrations pertaining to the rights and immunities of citizens under a republican government. The present anomalous state of political parties throughout the country suggests a reason for the appearance of the work; and in the endeavor to meet this exigency it has been carefully prepared.

As a nation, we are essentially eclectic in character, receiving constant accession to our numbers from all parts of the civilized globe. It is, therefore, of the first importance to the integrity and security of our free institutions, that the balance of power in the republic should be sedulously guarded; that a spirit of nationality should rule in the councils of our government; and that the element of foreign political faith, as well as foreign manners and customs, be carefully precluded from vitiating our national morals,—the proud distinction of a free people consisting in its public virtue, which is the animating and sustaining principle of true democracy. It is not enough that we glory in our boasted liberties,—we must be jealous of their integrity—must learn wherein consists their security, their defences, and their danger.

It was a maxim of one of the "early heroes of liberty," that "none could love freedom heartily but good men; the rest love not freedom but license, which never hath more indulgence than under tyrants." This fact is amply sustained by the testimony of all history. The knowledge which we acquire at our own expense is undoubtedly the most efficacious, but that which we learn from the misfortunes of others is the safest, inasmuch as we receive instruction without pain or danger to ourselves.

The "Voice to America" is not the product of any clique; it enforces the opinions of no one party; it has not been prepared under the auspices, nor has it received the sanction, of any set of men organized for political purposes; but the publisher has been cheered on in his purpose, in the confident assurance that, notwithstanding sectiona lfeeling, and the specious pretences of fanaticism and political partisanship, there is yet a sufficient number of true-hearted Americans, pledged for the defence and preservation of the inestimable privileges conferred upon our common country, under the ægis of a glorious constitution. The book, therefore, goes forth to the world, claiming only the deference due to honestly-expressed opinions. It relies alone, for success, on the truth of its arguments, and the sacredness of its mission.

New York, August, 1855.

CONTENTS.

APPENDIX.

A
VOICE TO AMERICA.

THE UNITED STATES—RETROSPECTIVE AND PROSPECTIVE.

"With America, and in America, a new era commences in human affairs. This era is distinguished by free representative governments, by entire religious liberty, by improved systems of national intercourse, by a newly-awakened and unconquerable spirit of free inquiry, and by a diffusion of knowledge through the community, before altogether unknown and unheard of."

DANIEL WEBSTER.

WHEN the inhabitants of the old Thirteen Colonies arose against the despotic and mercenary aggression of England, they were three millions of people, mostly scattered farmers. They inhabited a strip of the Atlantic seashore—a half-wild territory between the Alleghanies and the ocean—about one thousand miles long, and a hundred and fifty miles wide, and containing only six towns of any size, three of which had less than ten thousand inhabitants, and none over twenty thousand. It is true that they were an enterprising, industrious, honest, intelligent community—a happy and flourishing nation in fact, though not in form. But whatever were the precise point of prosperity to which they had then attained, it was in spite of the discouragements of their supreme government that they attained it; for the agriculture, manufactures, and commerce of the colonies were capriciously controlled and restricted for the advantage of English speculators; and the laws and constitutions of the little republics were constantly attacked and insulted by the placemen of the English administration, for the sake of enforcing arbitrary schemes of government, fit only for tributary slaves. Navigation acts, stamp acts, writs of assistance, prohibitions of the manufacture of iron, the manufacture of cloths, of hats, of every thing which Englishmen wanted to manufacture, and endless other troublesome and unrighteous enactments, perplexed and annoyed the provinces. Yet the new nation, which, under the name of the United States of America, spoke itself into being by the Declaration of Independence, contained all the elements of a healthy, powerful, and vigorous life.

With the fervent sympathy of the majority of the people, but with lukewarm aid or timid indifference from very many; with overwhelming fears and doubts on the part of some of the wisest and best men of the day, and even in spite of the venomous treasons and intestine wars of the Tory population, the new commonwealth agonized through the seven years of the revolutionary struggle, fainting and almost torn in pieces, and achieved what seemed at the moment to be a fruitless independence.

At the end of that war it was indeed a nation in name, and one in form; but it had little of actual national life. It was repeatedly on the extreme verge of falling into fragments—into anarchy; of returning to a monarchical form of government. One hundred and seventy millions of dollars in money had been actually spent in the war, and that when money was worth nearly twice as much as it is now, and when the nation was not one-twentieth as rich as at present. The country had been ravaged through and through: crops had been destroyed, towns and houses burned. The inhabitants were sick, disabled, demoralized, fled; manufactures had been encouraged but little; commerce was stagnant, or even utterly dead; disbanded and immoral soldiers roamed up and down, unable to obtain work, or to get their wages, even in the good-for-nothing continental money, which was worth sometimes three cents on the dollar, sometimes nothing, and of which one hundred dollars were once given for a mug of cider. The central government was everywhere despised and abused—a beggarly, strengthless shadow. It labored under an immense home and foreign debt, which it could not pay; it was an importunate and unwelcome beggar for home and foreign loans,—unsuccessfully, because it could not meet its former engagements; its requisitions upon the States were neglected or refused; it was even bullied in its own hall by a sergeant's squad of unpaid mutineers dunning for their wages, against whom the militia of Philadelphia declined to protect it, except in case of actual assault and battery.

The States quarrelled with each other about lands, or insulted and encroached on the miserable central government. There arose in many of them, within a few years after the termination of the war, home insurrections of their own. The whisky insurrection in Pennsylvania; Shays' insurrection in Massachusetts, with the risings that preceded it; a similar mob in New Hampshire, which, for a time, besieged the legislature and courts of that State; the general disorganization of the western country, and other such tumults, showed the unsettled and anarchic condition of men's minds, as well as their poverty and distress. Wise men, the revolutionary fathers of the country, communicated to each other their apprehensions of the loss of our nationality, almost at its birth. Despondency weighed upon the best of the patriots of the day, and with painful forebodings they speculated upon the probabilities of many republics—of a monarchy—of a retreat beneath the English power.

The native sense of the country, however, was at last aroused to the exigencies of the case, and the people, responding to the call that emanated from the Virginia Legislature, deputed that great and wise assembly which created the Constitution of the United States—a frame of government the nearest perfection which the world has ever seen; by the operation of which the nation was at once invigorated; under which it forthwith sprang out into that unparalleled career of growth, whose constantly increasing speed has already made all the world astonished spectators, and which seems to possess an immortal vigor equal to any emergency.

Within less than three-quarters of a century of national life under this constitution, the United States of America have arisen to a prouder height of physical strength and of moral power, than has ever been occupied by any other nation in the world. The allotted life of a man covers a period equal to the whole existence of our mighty empire. Men are this day alive and well who voted for the adoption of the Constitution, and for Washington in 1789. At the end of the Revolutionary War, we numbered about three millions of people — as many as now inhabit the single State of New York; now we are twenty-five millions. Then we had nine hundred thousand square miles of territory; now we have three millions of square miles—half of North America — three times as much as France, Great Britain, Ireland, Austria, Prussia, Spain, Portugal, Belgium, Holland, and Denmark—a domain as large as the Roman Empire ever was; a territory by the side of which the possessions of the proudest European dynasties are "but a patch on the earth's surface."* European distances are steps to ours; European rivers are brooks. It is as far across the United States from New York to San Francisco as from London to Ispahan, in Persia; from New York to New Orleans is as far as from Paris to St. Petersburg, or from London to Constantinople. The Mississippi is twice as long as the Danube; the Ohio is six hundred miles longer than the Rhine; the Hudson is navigated, within the State of New York, a hundred and twenty miles — a distance greater than the length of the Thames. Nor is this vast expanse in danger of falling apart by its own weight: it is knit the tighter as it expands, by the iron bands of the railroad and the telegraph. Our country extends through every healthy climate. Avoiding the inhospitable wastes of the Arctic snow, and the fever-haunted jungles of the tropic zone, it stretches from the cold and bracing mountain air of New England and Oregon, to the everlasting spring of the sunny South. Within our limits is found every tree of the forest, from the towering pines of Maine, and the more gigantic cedars of California, four hundred feet high; the northern oak, the birch, the beech, and the other hardy woods of its kindred forests, to the live-oak of the south, the cypress, and the magnolia, the orange, the cocoanut, the banana, and the palm. We

* Webster's Letter to Hulsemann.

grow alike the corn, flax, and wheat of temperate regions, and the sugar and cotton, the rice and indigo of the south. From the bosom of the earth we dig all the precious and all the useful minerals: gold comes from California at the rate of seventy-five millions of dollars a year; pure copper is blasted or chopped out from the mines at Lake Superior by the ton together. There is lead enough in Wisconsin to supply the world; iron is piled into mountains in Missouri, and its ores are found in the majority of the States; and the coal of single States—Ohio and Pennsylvania—is sufficient to furnish all the earth with fuel for thousands of years.

Nor are our treasures inaccessible. There is only one of the great divisions of the earth—Europe—which has a greater proportion of seacoast to the square mile than North America. The shore-line of the United States, on the two great oceans and the Mexican Gulf, is eighteen thousand miles. The land is pierced through and through with enormous rivers, upon which we possess forty-nine thousand miles of steamboat navigation, together with thirty-five hundred miles of shore on the sides of the great northern lakes. Five thousand miles of supplementary artificial navigation by canals completes this most enormous amount of internal water conveyance. Within the single State of New York there are three thousand miles of navigable inland waters. Besides the innumerable ordinary roads, we are netted and woven together by twenty thousand miles of completed railroads, and thirteen thousand miles more, now in process of completion. Upon these inland routes a capital of one thousand millions of dollars is invested in the gigantic transfers of our internal trade and travel.

We have not been idle in improving the advantages of our situation. Our wealth and industry—our credit and commerce, both at home and abroad, have enlarged to an immeasurable extent. At the close of the Revolution we had possibly seven hundred and fifty millions of dollars' worth of real and personal estate; now we have at least fifteen thousand millions of dollars' worth, besides fourteen hundred millions of acres of public lands—enough to give a large farm to every man, woman, and child in the nation. Then, our ambassadors were besieging European capitalists and governments for a hundred thousand dollars; now, the nation distributes at once forty millions of surplus revenue; bears four hundred millions of debt without feeling it, and sells the privilege of lending to her at six and ten cents for every dollar that she will condescend to borrow. Then, we had no manufactures; now, we have more than five hundred millions of dollars invested in manufactories, whose annual productions are worth more than a thousand millions of dollars. Our cotton manufactories alone, while the English millmen confess that the business in Great Britain has reached its very utmost capacity of development, are now employing eighty millions of capital, are using thirty-five millions of dollars' worth a year of raw material, and turning out a yearly product worth seventy millions of dollars, and yet are steadily increasing, while we compete with our English rivals in our own market, and all over the world. Then, we had neither commerce nor shipping; now, it is not long since we dismantled a national warship to send her, laden with the superabundance of our rich fields, to stay the famine in Ireland. Of the same overflowing plenty we have imparted to the starving people of Greece, of Madeira, of the Azores. Our cotton crop, besides supplying the immense home demand just stated, is sent across the sea at the rate of eleven hundred millions of pounds a year, and, after being manufactured, supplies the primary human necessity of clothing to all nations, from the tropic to the pole, from the Englishman to the Chinese.

The extent of the shore line of the United States, on the Atlantic, Pacific, and the Mexican Gulf, is about twelve thousand miles. The northern and southern boundaries amount to at least six thousand more; making, in all, *eighteen thousand* miles—equal to three quarters of the distance around the world.

Now we have the largest mercantile marine on earth. Fourteen hundred steamers, measuring five hundred thousand tons, and seventeen thousand sail vessels, registering four and a half millions of tons burden, besides carrying a portion of our enormous mass of internal exchanges, are bringing yearly from abroad three hundred millions of tons of foreign, and carrying away two hundred and eighty millions of domestic merchandise.

These vast totals, indicating such limitless resources and such superhuman energy, and demonstrating only the aggregate of the resources in territory and riches wielded by our population, constituting the greatest force on earth, yet only refer to physical power, and do not by any means give a comprehensive view even of that power.* However important our pecuniary wealth and material power at this present moment may be, as securing to us a high station and commanding influence in the great commonwealth of nations, there are other departments in our national life, of profoundly greater significance. The state of our intellectual, social, and moral development, after all, is of infinitely more importance than our property per head, or our annual revenue. These mere acquisitions may easily depreciate in value. Our vast mass of wealth naturally tends, of itself, to be scattered and lost. It is the mind and the soul which inform and impel the people of our country, which constitute their real character, which alone can determine their lasting prosperity, even in respect to dollars and cents, and which certainly are the only basis upon which can be raised or maintained a collective or individual character which can justify our national pride, or command the respect of strangers.

Our condition in these respects—the intelligence and morality of our native population; the social condition of the nation—is such as to inspire every patriotic heart with an exultation infinitely loftier and purer than any boasts of riches or displays of strength. The right training of our citizens for their duties to God and the State, has ever been a principal object of our government. It is true that the main regulation of this subject, and the direction of the chief expenditure

* The statistics of the machinery employed in manufacturing—a very important and significant item—although actually collected, are kept strangely concealed in the Census Office; nor is there any adequate estimate, yet compiled, of the total machinery of all kinds owned and used in the United States.

for it, rests in the States individually; yet the Federal Government alone, doing what it could constitutionally do, has given outright, for educational purposes, fifty-three millions of acres of land, which, even at the minimum Government price, are worth nearly seventy millions of dollars. Of public funds alone, besides the much greater amount paid by individuals, there are paid for education annually, in the United States, at least seven and a half millions of dollars. There is no child so poor or vile as to be excluded from a good school education; and if any children miss it, the fault is that of their parents or themselves. In our schools are taught, not only the rudiments of literature, but pure morals, and the elements of a just and manly character. Entire freedom in true and right thought is encouraged; and the result of our school systems, which are confessedly the best extant, is such as fully to uphold their claim to superiority. In those parts of the country where they have reached their completest development, only one native in four hundred is unable to read or write. In the far northern State of Maine, there are more children at school, in proportion to the population, than in any other state, kingdom, or country whatever. In the whole United States, the proportion of school-going youth is only exceeded by that in Denmark, where attendance is enforced by law.

The tone of our national life throughout is such as to maintain the intelligent independence and self-controlling activity, which our citizens learn in their childhood. No policeman, or spy, or uniformed soldier prohibits our people from discussing the measures of government. We are not holden by force to follow the commands of hereditary despots. We consider and inquire to our heart's content what we would have the government do, and then vigilantly watch its execution. No such broad political freedom was ever heard of before, either in Greece or Rome, in Switzerland or England. The diffusion of current information, and of intercourse among our citizens, has increased to a corresponding extent. The fecundity and ability of our newspaper press is without parallel. The best and brightest talent of the day is increasingly employed in this business. In 1775, there were thirty-five newspapers in the whole country. That number is now more than equalled in each of four single towns, and in two of them it is tripled. In the whole country there are twenty-two hundred newspapers, circulating a hundred and fifty millions of copies annually; and of periodicals of all kinds, more than twenty-seven hundred, circulating nearly four hundred and thirty millions of copies a year. A single American monthly circulates more copies than all the magazines of Great Britain together. Our Post-office Department, which, upon its re-establishment after the Revolution, enumerated about seventy-five post-offices, along a few coast-routes of some two thousand miles, upon which it was thought remarkable that the mail came through from New York to Philadelphia in three days, now numbers twenty-five thousand post-offices, and sends its mail-bags over two hundred and twenty thousand miles of roads. Seventy years since, steamboat speed was impossible; and railroads were not even conceived of in dreams. Now our letters hurry along the water, in steamboats, at twenty miles an hour, and fly across the land, by railroad, at fifty miles an hour. But that is not enough for our restless people. It will not do to wait for time, or to measure space. So forty-two thousand miles of telegraph bring Maine and Louisiana—New York and St. Louis, within moments of each other, for the merchants who cannot let their messages lag along on lightning trains. Nay, the intervening space of the Atlantic Ocean is to be annihilated. The wires are now being prepared for the ocean line, between Newfoundland and Ireland; and the unreasonable philosopher, Faraday, not content that messages will be delivered in New York three hours *before* they are dispatched at Liverpool, is grumbling in England because there is to be an actual delay of two minutes.

The same keen and disciplined, but tremendous energy which has driven us so swiftly onward in our career of material prosperity, and which is yet surging hither and thither across the continent in accumulating waves, has operated alike in all departments of human action. Not only have we excelled in the mere organization of human industry and the gathering of riches, but Americans have stood pre-eminent in every domain of original thought, in every sphere of labor, physical or mental. It would be too long a story to enumerate the daring of our exploring seamen; the exhaustless fertility and practical adaptedness of our myriads of inventors; the triumphs of our mechanics, who have surpassed the world in making whatever can be made, that requires beauty, strength, or skilful handling. Their enormous clippers dash through the billows of every sea, and their engineers go abroad to construct monster railroads for foreign powers. Their brass clocks tick within the households of every nation, from England to China; their pistols are arming the officers and soldiers of all civilized troops.

In science and literature, even more than in such conquests over the material world, has our career been rapid and our attainment glorious. In all those departments of literary labor which are related to the present needs and future progress of humanity—in theology, ethics, law, politics, political economy, education, natural sciences, history, romance, poetry—we are at least fully abreast of the very foremost.

Even in the fine arts, hitherto always the latest blossom of civilizations which have been refining for centuries, we have risen up suddenly to the highest position. Our sculptors and painters are rivalling the modern masters of artistic Italy, amidst the very shrines of the muses, and the homes of the arts.

In all the realms of thought, both elegant and profound, we have quietly surprised the elder nations out of supercilious contempt and thorough ignorance, into admiring acknowledgment. A quarter of a century ago, the assumption was coolly and currently made throughout Great Britain, that English writers were sure of the monopoly of the American market for an indefinite period. Since English authors were good enough, why should we meddle with pen, ink, and paper, as long as we could be busy in raising raw material to support the manufacturing monopolies of Manchester and Leeds? It was taken for granted that we could not write either prose or poetry worth reading.

"We have changed all that." The works of Story and Kent, and in general our Reports of Decisions in Law, Equity, and Admiralty, are authority in English courts. Dwight and Edwards in Theology, Prescott and Bancroft in History, Sparks and Irving in Biography, are text-books on both sides the Atlantic. Within the last twenty years, more than one thousand editions of American books have been published in England, numbering at least six millions of copies, and six and a half millions of volumes. Single American books have circulated outside of the United States, in ten and twelve languages, in fifteen and twenty and twenty-five successive editions, to the amount of half a million, a million, and a million and a half of copies.

"Who reads an American book?" jeered Sydney Smith, a quarter of a century ago in the Edinburgh Review. The question of the clerical satirist must now be, to have any force—Who does *not* read American books?

Such statistics tell a proud story for our country. But it is not merely in science, philosophy, or elegant literature, that American thought is moulding the opinions of the world. Ever since the publication of the Declaration of Independence our statesmen have been confessedly, for breadth and depth of thought, and for power of reasoning, the ablest of the age. Were there three such men outside of the United States as Daniel Webster, Henry Clay, and John C. Calhoun? Our public policy has put us at the head of the world's progress in international law. We have taken the lead in asserting a righteous equality among the great commonwealth of nations. We compelled England to discontinue kidnapping sailors by her piratical system of impressment; we first stipulated by treaty not to allow of privateering in time of war; we have successfully asserted the principle that free ships make free goods. Austria, at the imperative demand of our Executive, sulkily releases American citizens, imprisoned on suspicion. We first are moving to destroy the stingy monopoly, held by Denmark, of the entrance into the Baltic Sea. Is it not a conceded fact that the European nations, at the very farthest, cannot do better than to take a lesson in government from our Republic? Is it not our example which is stinging and goading the restive democrats of Europe into their desperate revolts and crushed, but not conquered, revolutions? Have the despotic kings and emperors of that Continent more than one thing to fear? is there more than one ghost at their banquets? They are haunted by American Freedom—if by naught else.

Reformers and revolutionists, tyrants and their victims, alike look westward. Kossuth exhausts all the magic of his eloquence to engage us for his dear, fallen Hungary; Russia is our very good friend—for the time being—and would not grieve us for the world; Englishmen look to our administrative forms for examples to be imitated by the imbecile red-tapists of Downing-street. Blackwood's Magazine at last admits that the truth of our power and progress fully equals all the statements which have heretofore been considered "extravagant gasconade;" the Westminster Review terms our Republic "the pole-star to which the eye of struggling nations turns," and, in a long article, compares our effective and economical governmental methods with the expensive follies of Victoria's administration; the Edinburgh Review, which has heretofore spoken so bitterly and scornfully, concedes the full reality of our physical prosperity, and our present success in literature and art, and foretells for us a splendid future in each and all.

Hitherto, the energies of our republic have been expended in developing the immense resources of our extended territory. We have taken no position amongst the nations; our name, in fact, was scarcely mentioned. But the Russian war has summoned us to Europe; American diplomacy has made monarchs thoughtful; the United States have come to be regarded, not merely as a great nation, but as one to be courted and feared—a government capable of arbitrating in the affairs of the Old World, whose public opinion is respected, and whose favorable decision is regarded as a great moral power. Already, Europeans give us the possession of this entire continent. They apply the term *American* only to us. A Mexican, a Canadian even, is never, by them, called American; that name they consider ours alone. Europe, in fact, embraces the Monroe doctrine. Every month sees our influence increasing. Steam communication between the two continents has reached an unparallelled perfection, and yet is insufficient to meet the demands of our business men. A fortnight, a week, a day, nay, an hour, is too long to obtain information—ere long, the submarine telegraph will put America and Europe in momentary communication. All things tend to give our country an immense preponderance in European affairs—a preponderance which is now beginning to be felt, and is deprecated by the despots and tyrants of the Old World.

Such have the United States been—such they are to-day. What they will be a century from this time, is a question which it is beyond the power of human prescience to answer, except by estimate or conjecture. Of our future, some few elements may be considered capable of reasonably reliable prophecy. That every ten years of our future growth will surpass any preceding ten, is proved by our progress hitherto. The last decade of our physical and intellectual progress shows an advance greater than that of the preceding twenty years, and greater than any other fifty years. For territory, within the coming century we may have the entire continent of North America; for population, we shall have one hundred millions of people, not of an effete and overgrown stock, like that hideous monster, the Chinese race, but a people of vigorous youth, foremost in the blessings of freedom, and still marching onward, in the pure light of civilization, towards the highest human development.

The Anglo-American is the king of men. He possesses all the powerful and commanding nature of the Anglo-Saxon, the clear, cool head, the sober, calculating mind, the regard for law, the obstinate adherence to justice; but fused and fired by the pure bright air of America, and yet more by the wide freedom of American life, into the go-ahead and tireless energy, which endures no delay and brooks no opposition. The Anglo-American is the controlling type, the leading element of our future population.

America in 1950 promises to be, what the folly of the misproud Celestial so sillily calls his stolid people—the Central Nation. Already we stretch forth our hands to Europe and to Asia, and control the commerce of two oceans, and modify the politics of two continents. Europe, inspired by our example, already smokes and groans in the rising ferment of revolutions. We have opened the heretofore closed doors of distant Japan. American commerce and American civilization are striding inland, up the vast streams of the great Asiatic rivers and across her tremendous steppes. Even our missionaries among the heathen are driven by the logical results of Protestant Christianity to become founders of States and the promoters of independent political action. The Christianized kingdom of the Sandwich Islands, was converted and liberalized by Protestant missionaries. A Christian civilization has gone from us to commence the work of enlightening Africa, and has made a firm lodgment within the small but vigorous Republic of Liberia. Our missionary stations among the North American Indians, in Turkey and Armenia, in China, have been the centres of a light which has illuminated first the souls and then the minds of the barbarians, and which is gradually transforming them into self-governing and dignified communities. We have joined the Atlantic and the Pacific by railroad; we shall repeat the junction by telegraph and by canal. Throned between two oceans, we shall control the mercantile exchanges of the world, and with them the civilization and the welfare of mankind. It is not for us to rule with the barbarous violence of conquest. It is not for us to force a prostrating commercial system upon tributary millions by war, to steal colonies everywhere, to speckle the world with our garrisons, and then to boast that the drum-beat of our army ever greets the rising sun.

For us there is a safer, a surer, a nobler road, to a more desirable and enduring empire. Our destiny is to show the nations what is the greatest amount of national and individual happiness and prosperity which is possible under laws free and enlightened, and with a people self-governed and self-controlling. In the quiet and unaggressive fulfilment of that destiny we wield the lever which shall move the world.

A free and lofty humanity, seeking all that is good by every means that is right—such is the ideal of man and his life, which became practicable in our empire for the first time. That ideal life satisfies all aspirations. Men will come to us to enjoy those privileges under our broad banner for a time, but, ere long, they will assert their right to enjoy them at home. Before a century has passed, the United States of America will stand peerless in strength and beauty, the pride and excellence of the whole earth; the refuge of the oppressed; the apostle of all truth; the freest, noblest, happiest, purest among the nations; the crown and culmination of human progress; the full expression of human development, under the conditions of a national existence based upon the eternal truths of Christianity,—maintained by laws enacted by the wide consent of all, restricting not one hair's breadth the rightful activity or happiness of any—invigorated and intensified by the untrammelled play of those infinite powers which God has given to man, and which are as comprehensive as the universe of matter and of thought in which he exists.

THE ANCIENT REPUBLICS:

A GLANCE AT EARLY CIVILIZATION.

"Out of history we may gather a policy no less wise than eternal, by the comparison and application of other men's forepast miseries with our own like errors and ill-deservings."

SIR WALTER RALEIGH.

THE records of past ages are the inheritance of the present. They are a study fertile in interest and value. They form the great text-book, to which all make their appeal. It is in the classic ages we seek for the most splendid triumphs of art—the purest models—whether in sculpture or poetry, in philosophy, science, ethics, or law. We gaze, through the dim vista of centuries, with deep and solemn interest upon the ruins of those grand and colossal states and empires which successively swayed the destinies of the world—the Assyrian, the Egyptian, the Grecian, and Roman. We are not only amazed at their magnificence and splendor, but we are curious to know the secret sources of their rise, progress, and decay. It is thus that "history is philosophy teaching by example."

The Germans, who are distinguished for their love of antiquarian research, yet fail, with all their zeal and perseverance, to derive all the advantages of which the study is susceptible. Their deductions, Coleridge compares to the stern-lights of a ship, illuminating merely the past; the true uses of history—its warnings and teachings—are comparatively forgotten. May not every government read, in the experience of the ancients, its dangers, its destiny, and its duties? And especially to every republican government, are not the fall of the classic republics, and the sanguinary revolutions of France, full of admonitory interest? Let us extract the moral which the eventful story of the free States of antiquity suggests. A vast amount of labor and learned research has been expended upon the history of the ancient republics, but comparatively little is written or known concerning their social economy, which formed the great moral lever of society. We propose to take a brief survey of the causes which superinduced the overthrow of these renowned States. We shall avail ourselves of the best recorded testimony, and the best judgments of historians and political economists. If it be an admitted maxim of liberal government, that the safety and happiness of the whole community is the true and only end of all government; and if this is the basis of the republican form, and the converse of it, the despotic—who among us is not fired with a generous enthusiasm as he pores over the details of the heroic virtues, and lingers over the philosophic maxims of the sages of antiquity? Who does not glory in their brilliant though brief successes, or watch, with the sympathy of suffering friends, their decline and fall? The world is on the side of liberty, and the history of its progressive development comprehends the history of the race. The advocate of freedom is, therefore, the friend of humanity. But it must not be forgotten that between true liberty and unbridled license, there exists as wide a distinction as between virtue and vice. The latter is the bane of the former; they have ever been antagonistic in their influences.

A mysterious system of causes has crystallized society into cycles, in each of which some particular idea has become the dominant principle. These cycles are illustrated by the early idolaters of Canaan, who had their Iconoclast in Abraham; by the sophists of Athens, and their Aristophanes; those of Rome, with their Lucian; the knights-errant of modern Europe, with Cervantes; the religious bigots of the sixteenth century, with their polemical and philosophical scribes.* Coleridge observes that "the Jewish theocracy was itself but a mean to a further and greater end; and that the effects of the policy were subordinated to an interest far more momentous than that of any single kingdom or commonwealth could be." Liberty, civil and political, has also had its confessors and noble army of martyrs, and

* Dem. Rev., 1842.

the history of its heroic progress is filled with illustrious names and deeds—Pericles, Cicero, and Cæsar; Tell, Wallace, and Washington; Cromwell, Mirabeau, and Napoleon. These were, in the language of an old dramatist, the planets of the ages in which they lived, and illustrate their times. It was for her sacred cause that the ever-memorable events of Thermopylæ, of the Punic wars, of Marston Moor, and the American war of Independence were enacted,—the last named of which has this proud distinction: that it is guiltless of wantonly shedding the blood of the innocent; and was triumphant alike over tyranny and despotism, and the lawless passions of victors. Taking a bird's-eye view of history, we see Cæsar, the pagan, preparing the way for Christianity; Charlemagne, the barbarian, for civilization; and Napoleon, the despot, for liberty—yet presenting the anomalous character of the popular patron of aristocratical power.

The study of history is one of political and social progress. In the earliest ages, society was in a crude, chaotic condition, equally removed from the luxuries and refinements, as well as the amenities and courtesies which characterize it in modern times. We discover the germ of popular or republican power in Greece and Rome. There was yet wanting in these republican States the great essential of free institutions—self-government. The intellectual force of Grecian character kept in check the revolutionary tendency of the fickle populace, while in Rome the intellectual refinement of Greece tended rather to emasculate than invigorate the body politic. The histories of these States—Greece and Rome—are, therefore, those of our instructors in the arts and sciences,—guides in literature and patterns of intellectual excellence, rather than the models of political or social ethics. The history of the mediæval ages—which forms the connecting link between the remote past and the present—although comparatively barren of instructive teaching, is necessarily replete with interest, being that of our more immediate ancestors, from whom we have derived our language, laws, and customs. The feudal system of the Middle Ages, with all that may be justly urged against it, for its severe exactions upon popular freedom, was yet a necessity of the times, while it superinduced a love of heroism, patriotism, and virtue. A romantic interest invests that long period of the world's eclipse; for although the populace surrendered themselves to the thraldom of superstition and ignorance, it was the proud era of Papal pomp and magnificence,—of gorgeous cathedrals, splendid pageants, cloistered learning, and the chivalrous exploits of the knights-errant. Society, however, was in servile subjection. Two classes—lords, or feudal barons, with their vassals, or serfs—constituted its great distinctions. Feudalism accomplished nothing for popular progress. Amidst the brilliant constellation of genius which at length dispelled the lingering darkness, came forth the great spirits of Liberty. Then came the great revolutionary eras of modern times—the English, the French, and the American. These tended, in each instance, to determine the true sources of power, and to reveal the long-hidden truth, that freedom is the birthright of the race. It was the American "Declaration of Independence" which gave the full solution of the problem, and assigned it a place in the common heart. It was that modern "Magna Charta" which conferred upon the model republic of the nineteenth century the full immunities and privileges of freemen.*

The great religious revolution originating with Luther and his

* "It is as a great, solemn *political act*, that it demands our highest veneration. What had the world ever seen that was equal, that approached to it? Go to antiquity—to Greece, to Rome—travel over France, Spain, Germany, and the whole of modern continental Europe,—all was comparative gloom; political science had not risen. Go to the isles of the sea—to Britain, then the freest of nations; and Englishmen would proudly point you to their Magna Charta, as their most valuable birthright, and the greatest bulwark of liberty which any nation had raised. It was so. And yet how does it dwindle in contrast with our Declaration of Independence, which was a greater era in the history of mankind, than Magna Charta was in the history of England! The latter was a concession, extorted by armed barons from their sovereign. It was what is called a *charter* from the king, as the fountain of all right and power. He was their lord and master—the ultimate owner of all the soil in the kingdom; and this was a *grant*—forced, it is true, but still a *grant*—from his grace and favor, allowing the exercise of some rights to his subjects, and consenting to some limits to his royal prerogative.

"The former is not a grant of privileges to a portion of a single nation; it is coadjutors, however, gave to the world the first grand impulse towards freedom, by bursting the shackles of ignorance and superstition. Up to the middle of the seventeenth century, the nations of Europe were at a low state of civilization. A new era then dawned upon mankind, by the discovery of the Western continent; and there the spirit of religious and civil liberty found its temple and its home. There Liberty had a most bold and adventurous priesthood—men of heroism and virtue, the pioneer-missionaries of the cross.

"The Puritans were men whose minds had derived a peculiar character from the daily contemplation of superior beings and eternal interests. Not content with acknowledging, in general terms, an overruling Providence, they habitually ascribed every event to the will of the Great Being, for whose power nothing was too vast, for whose inspection nothing was too minute. To know him, to serve him, to enjoy him, was with them the great end of existence. They rejected with contempt the ceremonious homage which other sects substituted for the pure worship of the soul. Instead of catching occasional glimpses of the Deity through an obscuring veil, they aspired to gaze full on the intolerable brightness, and to commune with him face to face. Hence originated their contempt for terrestrial distinctions. The difference between the greatest and meanest of mankind seemed to vanish, when compared with the boundless interval which separated the whole race from him on whom their own eyes were constantly fixed. They recognized no title to superiority but his favor; and, confident of that favor, they despised all the accomplishments and all the dignities of the world. If they were unacquainted

a DECLARATION, *by a whole people*, of what before existed, and will always exist—*the native equality of the human race*, as the true foundation of all political, of all human institutions. It was an ASSERTION that we held our rights, as we hold our existence, by no charter, except from the KING OF KINGS. It vindicated the dignity of our nature. It rested upon this 'one inextinguishable truth, which never has been, and never can be wholly eradicated from the human heart, placed as it is in the very core and centre of it by its Maker: that man was not made the property of man; that human power is a trust for human benefit, and that when it is abused, resistance becomes justice and duty.'"—*Sprague.*

with the works of philosophers and poets, they were deeply read in the oracles of God. If their names were not found in the registers of heralds, they felt assured that they were recorded in the Book of Life. If their steps were not accompanied by a splendid train of menials, legions of ministering angels had charge over them. Their palaces were houses not made with hands; their diadems crowns of glory which should never fade away! On the rich and the eloquent, on nobles and priests, they looked down with contempt; for they esteemed themselves rich in a more precious treasure, and eloquent in a more sublime language,—nobles by the right of an earlier creation, and priests by the imposition of a mightier hand. The very meanest of them was a being to whose fate a mysterious and terrible importance belonged; on whose slightest action the spirits of light and darkness looked with anxious interest; who had been destined, before heaven and earth were created, to enjoy a felicity which should continue when heaven and earth should have passed away. Events which short-sighted politicians ascribed to earthly causes, had been ordained on his account. For his sake, empires had risen, and flourished, and decayed. For his sake, the Almighty had proclaimed his will, by the pen of the evangelist and the harp of the prophet. He had been rescued by no common deliverer from the grasp of no common foe. He had been ransomed by the sweat of no vulgar agony—by the blood of no earthly sacrifice. It was for him that the sun had been darkened, that the rocks had been rent, that the dead had arisen, that all nature had shuddered at the sufferings of her expiring God!

"Thus the Puritan was made up of two different men—the one self-abasement, penitence, gratitude, passion; the other proud, calm, inflexible, sagacious. He prostrated himself in the dust before his Maker; but he set his foot on the neck of his king. In his devotional retirement, he prayed with convulsions, and groans, and tears. He was half maddened by glorious or terrible illusions. He heard the lyres of angels, or the tempting whispers of fiends. He caught a gleam of the Beatific Vision, or woke screaming from dreams of everlasting fire. Like Vane, he thought himself intrusted with the sceptre of the millennial year. Like Fleetwood, he cried, in the bitterness of his soul, that God had hid his face from him. But, when he took his seat in the council, or girt on his sword of war, these tempestuous workings of the soul had left no perceptible trace behind them. People who saw nothing of the godly, but their uncouth visages, and heard nothing from them but their groans and their whining hymns, might laugh at them. But those had little reason to laugh who encountered them in the hall of debate, or in the field of battle. These fanatics brought to civil and military affairs a coolness of judgment, and an immutability of purpose, which some writers have thought inconsistent with their religious zeal, but which were in fact the necessary effects of it. The intensity of their feelings on one subject made them tranquil in every other. One overpowering sentiment had subjected to itself pity and hatred, ambition and fear. Death had lost its terrors, and pleasure its charms. They had their smiles and their tears, their raptures and their sorrows, but not for things of this world. Enthusiasm had made them Stoics, had cleared their minds from every vulgar passion and prejudice, and raised them above the influence of danger and of corruption. It sometimes might lead them to pursue unwise ends, but never to choose unwise means. They went through the world like Sir Artegle's iron man Talus with his flail, crushing and trampling down oppressors—mingling with human beings, but having neither part nor lot in human infirmities; insensible to fatigue, to pleasure, and to pain; not to be pierced by any weapon, not to be withstood by any barrier.

"Such we believe to have been the character of the Puritans. We perceive the absurdity of their manners. We dislike the sullen gloom of their domestic habits. We acknowledge that the tone of their minds was often injured by straining after things too high for mortal reach; and we know that, in spite of their hatred of Popery, they too often fell into the worst vices of that bad system—intolerance and extravagant austerity; that they had their anchorites and their crusades, their Dunstans and their De Montforts, their Dominics and their Escobars. Yet, when all circumstances are taken into consideration, we do not hesitate to pronounce them a brave, a wise, an honest, and a useful body."*

But we ask—Where are the free nations of antiquity?

> "Gone, glimmering through the dream of things that were,
> A school-boy's tale, the wonder of an hour."

It has been said that no civilized nation has, at any period of its history, so completely thrown off its allegiance to the past, as the American. The whole essay of our national life and legislation has been a prolonged protest against the dominion of antiquity. This disregard of ancient precedent is quite consistent with the intrepid daring and sagacious policy of the revered founders of our national institutions. It would be impossible to institute any analogy between the governments of the ancient republics and our own; yet we should be willing to profit by the voices of antiquity—be warned by its errors, and incited and sustained by its virtuous examples.

* Macaulay.

SPARTA AND ATHENS.

"Unrivalled Greece! where every power benign
Conspired to blow the flower of human kind."
THOMSON.

"The taste, love, and intuition of the Beautiful stamped the Greeks above all nations."
BULWER'S ATHENS.

GREECE, with her matchless schools of learning and philosophy, her arts and civilization, lustrous with the triumphs and trophies of her splendor, has for twenty centuries ceased to exist, save in the imperishable monuments of her intellectual glory and a few broken columns of her once superb temples, her Parthenon, some of the beautiful creations of Phidias, as well as the classic Vale of Tempé, the rugged defiles of Thermopylæ, and the towering heights of Areopagus. We naturally ask whence did this mighty people derive the elements of their greatness? Some, by a fanciful conceit, have suggested that it was in part superinduced by the influences of climate and the scenery by which they were surrounded; that the physical geography of Greece—a combination of sea and mountains—served to make it the cradle of a bold and free people; or, as Wordsworth apostrophizes it—

"Two voices are there: one is of the sea,
One of the mountains: each a mighty voice.
In both from age to age thou didst rejoice:
They are thy chosen music—Liberty."

Such a theory is, however, manifestly untenable, as the abortive attempt, in modern times, to resuscitate Athens sufficiently attests.

"'Tis Greece, but living Greece no more!
So coldly sweet, so deadly fair,—
We start, for soul is wanting there!"*

Leaving the solution of the problem with the ingenuity of the curious

* Byron.

in such speculative matters, we shall probably content the reader by a rapid survey of the geographical limits of the Hellenic States, together with an outline sketch of their rise, progress, and decay. Greece, bounded on the north by the Cambunian mountains, which separate it from Macedonia, on the south and east by the Ægæan, on the west by the Ionian sea, extended two hundred and twenty geographical miles in length by one hundred and forty in breadth. In its salubrity of climate, variety and fertility of soil, it possessed advantages unequalled by any other country of similar extent. Situated in the vicinity of the three quarters of the world, on three sides washed by the sea, and abounding with commodious ports and harbors, its advantages for commerce and navigation were scarcely less conspicuous. It was divided into Northern Greece, comprehending Thessaly and Epirus; Central Greece or Hellas, which included Attica with its Marathon, Megares, Bœotia with its Thebes, Platæa, and Chæronea; and the southern peninsula, or Peloponnesus, containing Arcadia, Achaia with its twelve cities, and Laconia with its Sparta. Its jurisdiction also extended to groups of islands adjacent in the Ionian and Ægæan seas, as well as more extensive separate islands.

Greece was originally peopled by several insignificant races of barbarians: among them two principal tribes claim our notice—the Pelasgi and the Hellenes. These were of Asiatic origin, but of different dialects. The Pelasgians settled in the Peloponnesus about 1800 B. C. Although rude in their origin, they are supposed to have made some advances towards civilization, since they founded the ancient states Argos and Sicyon; and to them are attributed those marvellous monuments termed Cyclopian. They spread towards the north, founded Attica, made settlements in Thessaly, and existed as a people for one hundred and fifty successive years.

The Hellenes—subsequently so called from Hellen, one of their chieftains—originally the weaker of the two tribes, made their first appearance in Phocis, near Parnassus, under Deucalion. They afterwards invaded Thessaly, expelled from thence the Pelasgi, and subsequently drove them to Arcadia. The gradual spread of the various branches of the Hellenic tribe over Greece was effected by several migrations; after which they preserved the settlements they had already obtained, until the later migration of the Dorians and Heraclidæ, about 1100 B. C.

Besides these original inhabitants, colonies at the same early period came into Greece from civilized countries,—from Egypt, Phœnicia, and Mysia. Much of their early attainments in domestic civilization is to be traced to these foreign sources, as well as their mythological and religious rites and observances. These, however, became in their adoption less Egyptian, Asiatic, or Thracian than Grecian. To their religious system, in part, is to be ascribed their progress towards polished refinement. The ancient minstrels or bards contributed to this end, by their dissemination of moral and religious sentiment, diverting them from a love of barbarous warfare to the advantages of civilized life. The oracles of Delphi, Dodona, and Olympia were no less powerful to the same end. The necessity of consulting these sanctuaries naturally led men to regard the oracles as the common property of the nation; and thus these various tribes, who had been hitherto strangers, met in peace; and hence arose spontaneously the first idea of a commonwealth and a confederacy.

It was at Delphi that the most important and the most protracted of these political reunions—that of the Amphyctions—occurred. It adopted the principle that none of the cities belonging to the league should be destroyed by the others. We now discover the germ of the chivalric spirit of the nation, and the development of its youthful vigor in the heroic ages. A love of daring adventure and heroic exploit, not only individually but also in confederate bodies, led them beyond the limits of their fatherland. These emprises of valor being rehearsed by their bards, they thus acquired a national poesy such as no other people possessed, and such as contributed to the fuller development of the national genius. At this juncture, when the combined Hellenic nations were ripe for some grand military expedition, came the memorable siege of Troy. The most important result of that war was the kindling of one common national spirit—a spirit which even survived all the domestic feuds and animosities. This expedition, which lasted ten years, and was crowned with such signal success, caused the Hellenes to regard themselves ever after as one people.

The Trojan war was quickly followed by tempestuous times,—internal strifes, and incursions from the ruder tribes of the North, shook Greece during an entire century. The Dorians with their allies strove to possess themselves of Peloponnesus, and, after repeated attempts, at length the Heraclidæ succeeded in revolutionizing the Hellenic States. The territories of Argos, Sparta, Messene, and Corinth were wrested from the Achæans, who had hitherto inhabited them. The Achæans expelled, in their turn, the Ionians, and formed the settlement called Achaia; while the fugitive Ionians were received by their former kinsmen, the Athenians.

But among the consequences of this migration of the Hellenic races must be reckoned likewise the establishment of Greek colonies in Asia Minor—an occurrence of the highest import to their national development. This colonization, commenced by the Æolian Hellenes, was soon followed by the Ionians, and even the Dorians. Among the effects of these migrations and wars was not only an interruption to the progress of civilization, but even almost entirely the annihilation of it; yet in this universal movement the foundation was laid of that constitution of things which afterwards existed in Greece.* The tribes which had migrated, as well as those which had been expelled, remained at first under the dominion of their hereditary princes, some for a longer, others for a shorter period. In the two centuries, however, immediately subsequent to the migrations (B. C. 1100–900) republican constitutions took the place of hereditary clanship in all the Grecian countries, the distant Epirus excepted. These republics continued to exist amid the various revolutions which happened, and the love of political freedom became from this time the national sentiment. In this newly-constituted order of things, each city with the territory around it formed a separate state, and framed its own constitution; hence there arose as many free states as cities. Although

* Heeren's Researches.

thus parcelled out into a number of petty states, there existed a certain unity among the Hellenic race, a certain national spirit: this was produced in part by their custom of attending the national festivals and games; and this union was further promoted by the Amphictyonic council, from which originated Grecian ideas of international and judicial law. Even at this early period Sparta and Athens became distinguished for their superior constitutions and laws. These two cities in fact constitute a leading essential in subsequent Grecian history. We now approach a revolutionary era in the government of Sparta. The Achæans were previously governed by princes of the house of Perseus; the royal power was now divided between the families of Procles and Eurysthenes. Soon the Dorians acquired the conquest of many of the cities of the peninsula, and the Achæans became for a time their bondsmen. The Spartans, however, ultimately usurped authority over the whole country, which they continued to retain. The records of the two following centuries, to the time of Lycurgus, are filled with a series of belligerent engagements on the part of the Spartans with their neighbors, the Argives. Lycurgus gave to Sparta about the year 800 that constitution to which she was principally indebted for her subsequent splendor. His laws were not written, but conveyed in apophthegms, which were confirmed by the oracle of Delphi. The principal object of the laws of Lycurgus was to insure the existence of Sparta, by creating and supporting a vigorous and uncorrupted race of men. His grand maxim was, "that children were the property of the State, to which alone their education was to be intrusted."

With the view of equalizing the two extremes of great wealth and great indigence, he divided the lands into equal lots, proportioned to the number of the inhabitants. This partition of the territory met with violent opposition from the opulent, as might have been expected; but such was the commanding influence of this great man, that he triumphed over all opposition. He also appointed public tables, at which all citizens were enjoined to eat together without distinction. The diet was simple, and each had to contribute his quota for the repast. On these occasions of public feasting, the conversation was restricted to topics wholly of an instructive kind. Xenophon observes, "they were schools not only of temperance and sobriety, but also for instruction." Soon after the time of Lycurgus, the Spartans increased greatly their territory by their wars with the Messenians; and although a long interval elapsed before the former made any further attempts at invasion, yet on the deposition of Demaratus, Cleomenes, his former colleague, was compelled to bear a part in the Persian war. That struggle, together with the idea of supremacy in Greece, which had now taken its rise, introduced a series of political relations before unknown.*

It was at this epoch that the seeds of strife were sown between the rival republics of Sparta and Athens.

The history of Athens during this period, observes Heeren, is rendered important rather by domestic revolutions, which gradually tended to convert the State into a republic, than by external aggrandizement. The situation and peculiarities of Attica, rendering it less exposed than other parts of Greece to the attacks of wandering hordes, favored the tranquil growth of national prosperity. The history of Athens, as a State, begins properly with Theseus (temp. 1300 B. C.); although certain institutions, such as that of the Areopagus, the division of the people into nobles, husbandmen, and mechanics, may be traced to the colony of Cecrops. The last king was Codrus, who by a voluntary sacrifice of his life rescued Attica from the inroads of the Dorians, in 1068. The period of the Archons lasted till the year 752 B. C. From that time until 682 no remarkable events occurred, except the internal commotions which were occasioned by the oppressive exactions of the aristocratic party. From this state of anarchy Athens was rescued by Solon; a man to whom not only Athens, but the whole human race, are deeply indebted. He effected the happiness of his country, by remodelling the constitution of the State.

Solon not only aimed to invest the administration of government

* Heeren's Researches.

with the best intelligence and prudence of which he could avail himself; but his code for private life was no less deserving commendation. Unlike Lycurgus, he regarded polity as subordinate to morals. Yet the reader need not be reminded, that the social condition of Greece, as compared with that of the modern ages, had little, indeed, to boast. Plato, Socrates, and other eminent philosophers and sages, not only tolerated, but were even the avowed apologists of polygamy, and its train of vices. The legislation of Solon was soon disturbed by the factious tyranny of Pisistratus, who obtained by force of arms the government of Athens. This usurpation was again succeeded by the return of Alcmæonidæ, who, aided by a Spartan army, took possession of the city in 510. This resulted in a modification of the Constitution. Clisthenes, with a view of quenching party spirit by a new combination of the citizens, increased their elective powers.

A struggle with the Spartans and the allies, who sought to re-establish monarchy in Attica, soon ensued; and yet the glorious success of the republic, in this her first effort in the cause of liberty, gave fresh impulse to the national spirit. It was that which induced Athens to unite with the Asiatic Greeks in the cause of freedom, and which provoked the vengeance of the Persians; and yet, but for that daring encounter, Greece would probably never have achieved that greatness and renown which have signalized her in the history of the world.

It is, perhaps, sufficient for our purpose thus to sketch the outline history of Sparta and Athens—the two most important of the Grecian States; the others being of subordinate interest. Greece derives her importance among the nations of antiquity, not only from her brilliant successes in arms, her love of art and letters, and her liberal institutions, but also from her numerous colonies. These spread along the shores of the Mediterranean and the Black seas. The history of early civilization, therefore, owes much to the efforts of Greece, for she carried her influence east and west, far and wide. This gives us the clue to the sources of her opulence, supremacy, and splendor. These colonies, numbering over a hundred, had each its own peculiar form of government,—showing a wonderful variety of political views among these people. "Of the Greek colonies, the most ancient, and in many respects the most important, were those along the western coast of Asia Minor, extending from the Hellespont to the boundary of Cilicia. Here, ever since the Trojan war, which first made these countries generally known, the Æolians, Ionians, and Dorians had planted settlements. These were the most important for trade. Here likewise, in the native country of Homer, the father of Grecian civilization, of Alcæus, and of Sappho, poesy, both epic and lyric, expanded her first and fairest blossoms; and hence, too, the Mother Country herself received the first impulse of moral and cultivated tastes."*

When almost all the Grecian States and colonies submitted to the Persian yoke, Sparta and Athens alone boldly resisted it. The ever-memorable battle of Marathon proved not only the superiority of Athenian heroism, but was also the preservation of Grecian liberty. After the fall of Miltiades, the history of Athens becomes that of eminent generals or demagogues: Themistocles and Aristides were the real founders of the power of the Commonwealth. The former, in successfully accomplishing what Miltiades failed to achieve, made Athens also a mighty maritime power. While the rival State was thus advancing in power, Sparta suffered from the insanity of one of her kings, Cleomenes, and the arrogance of another, Leotychides. To Themistocles belongs the glory of frustrating the second Persian invasion of Greece, under Xerxes. However weak might have been the national leagues, separately,—being bound together by common interests and animated by the controlling spirit of the Grecian deliverer, they were irresistible. The great naval victory of Salamis does not reflect greater glory upon the Greeks, than did the gallant action of Leonidas with his three hundred Spartans: yet, as the plan for the conduct of these engagements originated with Themistocles, the pre-eminent merit of their success is to be alone ascribed to his

* Heeren's Ancient Researches.

statesmanship and military skill. Further successes by the battles of Platæa on the land, and of Mycale at sea, ending in the destruction of the Persian fleet, expelled forever from the shores of Greece that mighty foe.

Sparta at this time acquired a temporary ascendency, yet soon the command was transferred to Athens; and not only was this the occasion of jealousy between these States, but it also had a decided influence on all the subsequent relations of Greece. Then follows about half a century of eminent prosperity to Athens: far different was it with Sparta; there rude customs and laws arrested the development of genius; there men were taught to die for their country, while in Athens they learned to live for it. The loss of Themistocles was supplied by Cimon, who protracted the war against the Persians in order to maintain the union of the States; while the death of Aristides and the banishment by ostracism of Cimon, concurred in elevating Pericles to the head of affairs, who for forty years swayed Athens, without either being archon or member of the Areopagus. His administration was evidently of the democratic character, as that of his predecessor was that of the aristocratic.

The idea of a perfect equality among the Grecian States is proved to have been chimerical, since the minor independencies were swayed by the more powerful; and even between these—Sparta and Athens—an almost uninterrupted strife for supremacy existed. Sparta was now doomed to be abased before the great Theban general, Epaminondas. In her distress, Sparta formed an alliance with Athens; while Thebes entered into a compact with Persia. A sanguinary struggle between Sparta and Thebes left Greece but an independence proceeding from enervation; yet at the very time of the growing power of Macedonia under Philip, she madly plunged into another devastating civil war of ten years' duration, known as the Phocian war. "The treasures of Delphi circulating in Greece, were as injurious to the country as the ravages which it underwent. A war springing out of private passions, fostered by bribes and subsidiary troops, and terminated by the interference of foreign powers, was exactly what was requisite for annihilating the scanty remains of morality and patriotism still existing in Greece."*

The very first advance of Philip was a premonition of the fate of Greece, although the eloquence of Demosthenes warded it off until the second invasion. The battle of Chæronea was the commencement of the Macedonian ascendency over the Grecian republics. The history of Greece, from the accession of Alexander of Macedon until the final subjection to the Roman power, it is scarcely necessary to detail. At the decease of Alexander, Sparta had been humiliated by defeat; while Athens remained the first State in Greece. Frequent revolutions, civil commotions, and State intrigues and crimes, mark her declining career. While Greece was thus passing into her decadence, Roman strategy and Roman valor were striving for the transfer of the supremacy. Rome, taking advantage of the disorder caused by the frequent factions and feuds which occurred between the Achæans and Sparta, or Messene, conquered Macedonia; and at the sack of Corinth, the light of Grecian freedom finally vanished.

Of all the great nations of antiquity, none, perhaps, boasts of such a rapid and brilliant career as Greece; and her decline was as strangely sudden. It may well be asked, whence came the efflorescence of Grecian mind in the age of Pericles? What was the element of power that caused a handful of Greeks to overmaster the proud chivalry of the Persians? what the mighty spell which made the Hellenic arms the terror of the surrounding nations,—and won such brilliant triumphs at Marathon, Salamis, and Platæa, as to fill all Greece with the exultant shouts of Liberty, and blazon the scroll of history with the records of heroic glory? Yet was her triumph as brief as it was brilliant. In a single generation, Grecian Liberty reached its culmination, and in another century, its overthrow. The conflicting and diversified character of Grecian society suggests a clue. Hers was a social amalgam: all the gradations of wealth and poverty, as well as liberty and oppression, were among its elements. Hence feud and faction, as well as military despotism, were among

* Heeren.

the disturbing causes of the public weal. It has been eloquently said, that Attic wisdom, Theban hardihood, and Spartan valor, could not combine to save her; that very army which Greece had bred and nourished, to reduce oriental pride, was turned, vulture-like, upon herself. Thus Greece, with her battlements and towers, her glorious triumphs in arts and arms, is hurled headlong from her giddy height,—a parricide,—at once the shame and pity of the world!

> "When Greece with Greece,
> Embroil'd with foul contention, fought no more
> For common glory and for common weal;
> But false to freedom, sought to quell the fire,
> Broke the firm band of peace and sacred love
> That lent the whole irrefragable force,
> And as around the partial trophy blushed,
> Prepared the way for total overthrow."*

The Commonwealths of Greece were generally the scenes of popular commotion,—the tyranny of one part of the people over the other, or of usurping demagogues over the whole. Pericles, the noblest, perhaps, of his class the world has ever seen, was yet a demagogue. He sacrificed the last conservative institution of Athens for the advancement of his own political power,—the dictatorship. "It cannot be denied that the Athenian democracy abused its absolutism, and that the Athenian State made an unjust use of its supremacy over the allies; and thus viewed, there is some truth in the assertion of Isocrates, that the dominion of the sea was the source of all the misery of Athens and Greece. But it is not fair to confine our views to the abuse: what form of government, or what State, ever effected so much in the same space of time for humanity, as Athens and its democracy, during the brief period of their meridian glory? Pericles, Phidias, Polygnotus, Sophocles, Socrates, Plato, Demosthenes, were the children of the democracy; and truly great must the public spirit of that nation have been, which could foster, encourage, and develop the genius capable of achieving their mighty deeds."†

* Thomson. † Taylor's Nat. Hist. of Society.

Although the age of Pericles was the age of glory to Greece, yet it was then, as Pliny remarks, that Greece lost her freedom; for then she lost her virtue, and with it her love of art. Shall we not heed the admonitory teaching of an eminent classic historian,* when he affirms that the occasion of the Peloponnesian war—the direst civil calamity that befel Greece—was the *alleged* mutual rupture of the thirty years' league between Athens and Lacedæmon; but that the true cause was, the jealousy of the latter at the growing superiority of Athens. Intestine feuds are the most implacable and deadly in their influence and effects, and therefore most sedulously to be guarded against in a confederacy of free States. A spirit of rivalry or jealousy, resulting from differences of opinion and local interest, are among the evils to which they are exposed. The vaulting ambition of Pericles for territorial acquisitions, is an illustration of this.

Webster, referring to Greece, observes: "Political science seems never to have extended to their contemplation of a system, which should be adequate to the government of a great nation upon principles of liberty. They were accustomed only to the contemplation of small republics, and were led to consider an augmented population as incompatible with free institutions." They sought to erect systems of more perfect civil liberty, but the light of the moral and mental world of their time was not to be compared with that when our forefathers did the same.

The Peloponnesian war was succeeded by those protracted disasters and civil commotions which tended to reduce and exhaust the Greeks, and to destroy that bond of union once the palladium of their strength and glory. It was at this crisis that Philip of Macedon, taking advantage of their disorder, made himself master of all Greece, by his conquest at Chæronea.

Grecian history has been presented in three aspects: that of Themistocles, in which the statesman was subordinate to the general; that of Pericles, in which the general was subordinate to the statesman; and that of Demosthenes, in which the statesman acted inde-

* Thucydides.

pendently of the general. The first is distinguished by its love of military glory; the last, by its marvellous displays of Grecian eloquence—for it was the age of the ten famous Athenian orators:

"Those ancients, whose resistless eloquence
Wielded at will that fierce democracy,
Shook the arsenal, and fulmined over Greece
To Macedon and Artaxerxes' throne."*

The golden age of Grecian heroism, art, and eloquence, was from the era of Solon to that of Alexander. From the reign of Alexander to the extinction of taste in design and excellence in execution, not a single name is recorded worthy of note, as meriting comparison with the masters of the Grecian republic. The same applies with equal force to the Augustan age of Rome. Homer's great epic was designed to exhibit the ill effects of division in a confederate power. Virgil, on the contrary, flattered the oppressor of his country's liberty, in his adulation of Augustus.

It is evident, therefore, that political liberty may consist with the culture of the arts. Even the rugged Spartans delighted, for a time, to embody and perpetuate their heroic achievements, by the chisel of Bathycles; and the sacred inclosure of Amyclæ is no less memorable as the depository of the earliest creations of Grecian sculpture.

It has been said there are few who, if asked in which of the States of antiquity they would choose their own lot to have been cast, would not name Athens—since nowhere was there so much good, because nowhere was there so much freedom. Yet that freedom was constantly jeopardized, both by oligarchical conspirators, and by the tyranny of the sovereign people. The glories of Marathon and Salamis are obscured when we remember that the same victories which rescued the Athenian freeman but riveted the fetters of the Athenian bondsman. These two factions destroyed her greatest man, Socrates. The altar of Athenian liberty is overthrown, and its ashes poured out, because it burnt with alien fires. Grecian polity differed from that of

* Milton.

our own times. It was far less expansive and comprehensive, pertaining merely to cities, rather than States or territories. We possess little in common with the politics of the ancient free States. Their circumstances were widely dissimilar to ours, while theirs was a pagan and ours a Christian faith. Nor can the virtues or the vices of their age excite any other than a philosophic interest. Yet, allowing for this difference of circumstances and condition, there is exhibited much that is suggestive and admonitory to be gleaned for the advantage of modern times.

Chenevix observes: "It was in Greece that mankind began the new career which had a much greater affinity to true civilization than any condition of society that could have been previously conceived. It would be unjust to say that Asia, though luxurious, was not civilized; but the characteristics of civilization in that continent were so weak as to give but little tincture to the general mind. In Greece, the best mode of social progress became predominant, and may be traced in every province of thought, as sensuality gave place to intellect, and men found that the powers and faculties of each might be useful to the whole community." The great conservative principle or characteristic of civilization, as opposed to luxury, is combination,—the conviction that more may be obtained by unity of design and concert of action, than by the divided wills of multitudes, however numerous. He continues: "The difficulties which the Greeks had to overcome sufficiently taught this lesson, and turned their social career into the path of true civilization. It was thus that they became the parents of European advancement, and that the legacies which they have bequeathed remain at this day among its richest treasures.

"Since the independence of the United States, the North Americans principally followed the path which had been traced out by their British forefathers; and they were induced to continue in it because they had many difficulties to oppose. But those difficulties, as in ancient Greece, bespoke abundance more than poverty; and promised such easy fertility and greatness, that it may be questioned, notwithstanding the remembrance of past examples, whether civilization or luxury will finally predominate. But this much may safely be conjectured: Should the social improvement of the United States terminate in luxury, their luxury, like their vanity, will be much more European than Asiatic."*

Another authority remarks that history abounds in proofs that almost all the good which nations have possessed is to be attributed to social progress; nearly all the evil, to luxury. "It was by the corruption of civilization and the ascendency of luxury, that the fall of Greece was caused,—that the armies which had triumphed under the banners of intellect, were defeated when summoned away from their pleasures. It was because the influence of Lycurgus over the small republic of his birth had banished from it all the means of sensuality, that the power of Sparta, her domestic tranquillity, her good order and virtues, lasted from the time of her lawgiver till the Achæan league; that, during five centuries, she was paramount in Greece, by her abstinence. It was immediately following the Periclean age—which was that of Grecian luxury—that her moral decline commenced, in the age of Philip, or corruption, when her fall was completed. By civilization she made conquests; by her luxury she was herself overthrown."

Bancroft observes: "The democracy of Athens, with all the imperfections in every part of its public service, with the abuses attending its finances, and the corruption which finally turned the elective franchise into a source of personal revenue, maintains its dignity in the eyes of the world; for there the elements of civil liberty were first called into action. No tongue can adequately praise many of the results of that State; and it would also be difficult to display the deficiencies in its organization, and the gross injustice of its foreign policy. Our own confederacy does not more surpass the Grecian in the extent of territory over which its liberties are diffused, than in the excellence of the details of its laws."

The admirable maxim of Isocrates is worthy the attention of mod-

* Chenevix on Nat. Char., 1832.

ern times, because it requires, as the foundation of national prosperity and obedience to law, the establishment of the religious principle, as the surest guarantee for both. His advice to Demonicus respecting a citizen was: "First exercise piety towards God, not only in sacrifices, but also in the preservation of oaths; for the former indeed may be an indication of abundant wealth, but the latter is a proof of integrity of character." The growing influence and contending interests of political parties in their struggles for ascendency, may superinduce the corruptions and treacheries which tarnish our national glory and jeopardize our national stability; and thus we are in danger of re-enacting the political immoralities and crimes of the ancient republics—repeating the history and calamities of those splendid yet mournful examples of the past. The prerogatives of the Federal government must be maintained inviolate—the majesty of its authority supreme. In the multiplication of its constituent States there is great tendency to a reduction of the central constitutional power. In the desire for increasing territorial acquisitions, and a thirst for military renown, the harmony of the confederacy may also be fatally disturbed, and anarchy usurp its place. An instance of this we have seen in the history of the Grecian republics. Severe and onerous military services were sustained by the warlike and heroic citizens of those ancient States, in consequence of this fostering, by the government, of an excessive desire for military power and conquest. A military despot is surely no friend to national or civil liberty; and wherever the demagogue can take advantage of such social disorder, he is sure to do so. It may be well to repeat the warning given to us in the brilliant but terrible example of Athens,—it teaches us that an insatiate lust of territory marks the overthrow of a free State.

According to the political creed of Aristotle, the Grecian State was antecedent to the individual citizen. He therefore possessed no inherent personal rights, and was only allowed such immunities as were conferred by the State itself. Our commonwealth acknowledges an opposite rule. Both extremes are equally fatal to the liberties of a democracy; the one tending to an oligarchy, the other to lawless despotism.

Bulwer remarks: "As in despotisms, a coarse and sensual luxury, once established, rots away the vigor and manhood of a conquering people, so in this intellectual people (the Athenians) it was the luxury of the intellect which gradually enervated the great spirit of the victor race of Marathon and Salamis, and called up generations of eloquent talkers and philosophical dreamers from the earlier age of active freemen, restless adventurers, and hardy warriors. The spirit of poetry, or the pampered indulgence of certain faculties to the prejudice of others, produced in a whole people what it never fails to produce in the individual: it unfitted them—just as they grew up into manhood exposed to severer struggles than their youth had undergone—for the stern and practical demands of life; and suffered the love of the Beautiful to subjugate or soften away the common knowledge of the Useful. Genius itself became a disease, and Poetry assisted towards the euthanasia of the Athenians."

The fundamental essentials to the security of a free State, are religion, virtue, and intelligence in its individual citizens. This is the palladium of her strength, and the augury of her greatness and glory. These three great weapons of our strength will form the surest bulwark of our defence against the evils which may menace our national security, arising from the incessant influx of foreign immigration and foreign political influence. Before the vestal purity and celestial light of virtue, the shades of ignorance, superstition, infidelity, and crime will flee away. With the true light of Divine revelation for our guide, and the ample experiences of the past for our instruction, we may, and we assuredly ought to present to the world, not a mere problematical experiment, but an accredited and actual illustration of the great fact of a mighty nation of self-governed freemen—a spectacle "grander, vaster, and more majestic than any thing ancient statesmen ever dreamed of." Is such a brilliant immortality to be conferred upon these United States?

With the lapse of centuries, the lustre of Grecian intellect has lost none of its splendor. It still towers in Olympian grandeur over all the boasted achievements of intervening ages. Her proud trophies have defied the assaults of time; and, whether in sculpture, eloquence, or in song—in military prowess, heroic virtue, or in her love of liberty—her name has ever been a watchword on the earth. Not only was Greece the home of the graces, but it was here that Freedom first erected her mountain-throne. It was the triumph of mind that gave the pre-eminent glory to Greece; and Greece was the glory of the earth. What a galaxy of great men she gave to the world—Pericles, Epaminondas, Socrates, Aristotle, Demosthenes, Homer, Plato, and Alexander—Titans among the race! What a wealth of learning have they bequeathed to mankind! Classic Greece was the great academy of science and song—our storehouse of philosophy, ethics, poetry, sculpture, æsthetics, and architecture, as well as civilization and refinement. She was the first of the nations of antiquity to assert the supremacy of intellectual empire. It is not surprising, therefore, that her very name should have become talismanic, and that her sages, philosophers, and poets should still be regarded as our models, and their wisdom deemed oracular. Poetry still recognizes her great high priest in Homer, Philosophy her Socrates, History her Thucydides, Eloquence her Demosthenes, Art her Phidias, Justice her Aristides, and Heroism her Leonidas. While, therefore, we do homage to Attic models in art, poetry, ethics, and philosophy, shall we neglect the warning which her political errors and immoralities suggest?

THE FALL OF ROME.

'Alas! the lofty city! and alas!
The trebly hundred triumphs."
CHILDE HAROLD.

The seven-hilled city of the Cæsars — once the capital of the world,—the most potent and the most opulent of the nations of antiquity,—with her august pageants, her gorgeous temples, her triumphal arches, her Coliseum, her Forum, and all her colossal achievements in arts and arms, is numbered with the past. All that remains of her eminent glory, is a splendid ruin — a mighty and majestic shrine, attracting pilgrim feet from all parts of the earth. Her towering greatness, with her almost superhuman virtues and crimes, lives only on the scroll of history—a sublime illustration of human power and human weakness. Of all the voices of the past, Rome's eventful story is the most marvellous, the most memorable, and the most eloquent.

"Rome! thine imperial brow
Never shall rise.
What hast thou left thee now?
Thou hast thy skies!
Thou hast the sunset's glow,
Rome! for thy dower—
Flashing, tall cypress bow,
Temple and tower!"

The history of Rome exhibits a strange compound of conflicting elements of human character. It abounds with instances of the generous and the heroic,—the cruel and the base,—the patriotic and the perfidious. Hers were the extremes of wealth and poverty—of ignorance and learning. Rome was the scene of the direst calamities and the most brilliant triumphs. At one time devastated by a fearful plague, which continued for more than two years, destroying, in a single day, some two thousand human beings; at another, the city was in great part consumed by fire, kindled by lightning,—while these calamities were followed by famine. The history of her government is, for the most part, one of despotic cruelty, strategy, and crime—most of her rulers being corrupt and treacherous; yet were there among them men of heroic and noble virtue.

The topography of Rome may be thus briefly described: Situate on the bank of the Tiber (about seventeen miles from the sea, and near its junction with the Arno), the city was built on seven hills, or insulated heights, divided by little valleys. These hills are the Capitoline, Palatine, Cœlius, and Aventine. The others (Quirinal, Viminal, and Esquiline) are promontories, jutting out towards the Tiber. The Capitoline being so precipitous that it formed a natural fortress, it became the citadel of Rome.

A reference to the map of Italy will best exhibit its physical geography. It will be seen that, like Greece, Italy is made up of numerous valleys, pent up between high hills, each forming a country and political community to itself. There is the Apennine range, stretching from the southern extremity of the Alps across Italy, to the edge of the Adriatic, thus separating Italy proper from Cisalpine Gaul. Between them and the Alpine semicircle which forms the northern boundary, is inclosed a wide plain, open only on the east to the sea. One great river flows through its whole extent, being fed, from the north and south, by numberless streams. Of course, this well-watered plain was filled with flourishing cities, and often contended for by successive invaders. The geographical features of Italy proper strikingly accord with its political divisions. "It is *not* one simple ridge of mountains, leaving a broad belt of level country on either side, but, as it were, a backbone, thickly set with diverging spines of unequal length, running out from the main ridge, some parallel to the backbone itself; in which latter case, the interval between their base and the Mediterranean has been broken up by volcanic agency; *e. g.*, Vesuvius, and the Alban Hills, ten miles from Rome."* We thus perceive the force of the remark of Napoleon, that Rome was the spot best suited to be the capital of its empire.

The early history of Rome, like that of Athens, is based upon tradition, made up in part of poetic fiction. The line of demarcation between what is mythical and purely historic truth, it is difficult to determine. This is, however, less essential to our purpose, since we have to do with the later times of the Republic. During the first two centuries or more subsequent to its foundation, the city of Rome was under the rule of governors, or kings, of limited power and prerogatives. Its constitution originally somewhat resembled that of England about the times of the three first Edwards. The governing body consisted of the three classes or tribes, divided into thirty curiæ, ten in each tribe. Their assembly was called *Comitia Curiata.* Besides this general body of citizens, there was a select council, called the Senate, originally comprised of one hundred chief men of the Ramnes. After the union of the Sabines, one hundred of the Titienses were admitted; and though the Luceres always had votes in the general Comitia, yet they had no representatives in the Senate till the time of Tarquinius Priscus, who added a third hundred, called Patres Minarum Gentium. The reign of this monarch is the Etruscan period of Roman history. The buildings above and under ground, the religion, the games then introduced, have all of them an Etruscan stamp. The next king, the sixth, was Servius Tullius, who belonged neither to a royal nor patrician family, and who promoted Latin and Grecian customs. He revised the constitution, having brought together, in some degree, the Populus and the Plebs, and made all of them vote according to their property, in classes and *centuries.* The last king was Tarquinius Superbus, who, with his family, was banished; and with him ended the monarchy, having lasted, according to the legends, two hundred and twenty-five years. Then followed the establishment of the Republic, at the head of which were two

* Arnold.

consuls—L. Junius Brutus and Tarquinius Collatinus. The consular government was annually elected.

The struggle for liberty, in which the new Republic was engaged with the Etrusci and Latins, contributed to arouse that republican spirit which subsequently became the main feature of Roman character. The party which had deposed the ruling family, now took wholly into their own hands the helm of state; and the oppression of these aristocrats became at length so galling, that, after the lapse of a few years, it gave rise to a sedition of the Plebs,—the consequence of which was the establishment of annually elected Presidents of the People (*Tribuni Plebis*). Just previous to this (temp. 508 B. C.), took place the first commercial treaty with Carthage, in which Rome appears as a free State, although not as yet sovereign of all Latium. The political constitution of Rome received further development in the contests which now arose between the popular presidents and the hereditary nobility. The Tribunes, instead of confining themselves to the defence of the people from the oppression of the nobles, soon began to act as aggressors, which subsequently resulted in a complete equalization of rights. An illustration of this state of things is afforded by the trial of Coriolanus.

The more equitable distribution of the lands obtained by conquest, among the poorer classes, was suggested by the ambitious attempts of Cassius. The well-known code of the "Twelve Tables" confirmed the ancient institutions, and was in part completed by the adoption of the laws of the Greek Republics, especially those of Athens. Yet, as the commissioners appointed to draw up the laws were exclusively Patricians, an occasion was given for usurpation, which could be frustrated only by a sedition of the people. By the laws of the "Twelve Tables," the legal relations of the citizens were the same for all; yet that code contained little or nothing in relation to any peculiar constitution of the State, while the government not only remained in the hands of the aristocracy, who were in possession of all offices, but the prohibition of marriage, according to the new laws, of Patricians and Plebeians, interposed an insurmountable barrier between the two classes. The consequence of this was, renewed attacks by the people upon the privileged Patricians, especially as the power of the popular leaders was now not only renewed, but even augmented—the only limit to their authority being their unanimity of decision.

New dissensions arose between the Patricians and Plebeians, one of the causes of which was the exclusive participation of the former in the consulship, of which the Tribunes demanded the abolition. This right of admission was not, however, extended to the Plebeians till after a struggle annually renewed for eighty years. Meanwhile, Rome was engaged in petty wars with the neighboring federate cities. These contests continued almost uninterruptedly, and arose out of the oppression, real or imaginary, which she practised upon them. The cities sought every occasion for asserting their independence; and the consequent struggles must have depopulated Rome, had not that evil been diverted by the policy of increasing the complement of citizens in admitting the freedmen, and not unfrequently even the conquered, to the enjoyment of civic privileges.* Little as these feuds, abstractedly considered, deserve attention, they become of high interest, inasmuch as they were not only the means by which the nation was trained to war, but they also led to the foundation of that senatorial power, whose important consequences will be exhibited hereafter.

The last of these wars was that against Veii, the richest city in Etruria. The siege of that place, which lasted nearly ten years (404–395 B. C.), gave rise to the introduction, among the Roman military, of winter campaigning, and of pay. Thus, on the one hand, the prosecution of wars more distant and protracted became possible; while, on the other, the consequences were, increased taxation. About this time, Rome was reduced to ashes by the Gauls, who pressed out of Northern Italy through Etruria, and possessed themselves of the city, the Capitol only excepted. One of the chief heroes of this period was Camillus, the deliverer of Rome, who laid a double claim to the gratitude of his native city, by overruling, after

* Heeren.

his victory, the proposal of a general migration to Veii. Scarcely was Rome rebuilt, ere the former feuds revived, springing out of the poverty of the people, induced by the oppressive military taxation. Licinius, the Tribune, at this juncture having decreed that no individual should hold more than a certain amount of the national lands, the people became eligible equally with the nobles to the office of consul. The dictatorship, censorship, prætorship, and even the priesthood, quickly followed, as a matter of course. Thus political equality was conferred upon the Plebeians, with the Patricians; and the differences between them ceased, for a time, to form opposing political parties.

We now approach the true heroic age of Rome. This was introduced by the Samnite war—an engagement far more important than any in which Rome had previously been involved. In former contests her object had been to sustain her supremacy over her immediate neighbors; but in these latter wars, which continued for half a century, she opened a way for the subjugation of Italy, and laid the foundation of her future greatness. In this period commenced the practical illustration of the leading ideas of Rome upon the political relations in which she placed the States and cities she subdued. After the subjection of the Samnites, Rome, wishing to confirm her dominion in lower Italy, became entangled in war with the Tarentines, who secured the alliance with Pyrrhus. In the first two battles with this foreign prince, Rome was unsuccessful. In a subsequent engagement at Beneventum, he was defeated, and compelled to evacuate Italy, leaving a garrison at Tarentum. That city soon afterwards fell into the hands of the Romans, whose dominion became thereby extended to the extremity of lower Italy.

The early expedient of Roman colonization served the double purpose of relieving the capital of its pauper population, and of peopling her captured cities, as well as forming garrisons. This colonial system took its rise in the Samnite war, and ultimately embraced the whole of Italy. Connected with it was the construction of military highways, of which the *Via Appia*, constructed B. C. 312, was one, and which, to this day, remains the lasting monument of Roman greatness. These colonies were not invested with the privileges of Roman citizenship; they possessed their own civic government, but had no share in either the *Comitia* or magistracies of Rome. They were obliged, however, to furnish tribute and auxiliary troops, and were in other respects amenable to the Roman præfects or magistrates.

The constitution of Rome was at first essentially democratic, inasmuch as it conferred an equality of rights and immunities both for the poor and the opulent. It was yet a democracy so modified by ingeniously contrived expedients, that, even considering the warlike character of the people, it seemed well defended against the evils of military despotism on the one part, and popular discord on the other. Without specifying in detail its various features, it may suffice to state that it produced a senate, which at this epoch was the first political body in the world. It is remarkable that the constitution was in great part the result of experiment, no complete charter having ever been written.

The memorable war which took place between Rome and Carthage, and which lasted twenty-three years (B. C. 264–241), although it cost her much, was the first step in her splendid series of triumphs. Considering its important consequences, with the great heroes enlisted on both sides, as well as the vastness of the struggle, an interest attaches to it, surpassing that of any other age. The occupation of Messina by the Romans gave rise to this war; it resulted in driving the Carthaginians from Sicily. Thus the conquest of Carthage gave its pre-eminence to Rome. No monument of Carthage—the stupendous rival of the Romans—now remains to point out the ancient splendor of that Republic. That city, originally founded by a Tyrian colony about eight centuries prior to the Christian era, became the capital of a powerful Republic, which continued upwards of seven centuries; during which time it controlled the commerce of the world. Her interval of peace, which lasted seventy years, was the epoch of her glory—she was then the most renowned of the independent States of antiquity; but the love of conquest was the procuring cause of her ultimate overthrow.

When the Carthaginians resolved to have provinces instead of factories, and garrisons instead of colonies, a large force became necessary in order to keep possession of the conquered lands. From the time that a nation of merchants becomes a nation of princes, and exchanges commercial pursuits for territorial possessions, it abandons its proper strength for alien weakness, and fixes the limits of its own duration. The spirit of party and faction scarcely appeared in Carthage, until after the Republic had yielded to the trial of conquest, and the passion for territorial aggrandizement. The strength of Carthage in the war with Rome depended merely on its mercenaries and its money: it was founded on sand and gold-dust; when the tide of fortune turned, both were swept away. There were, however, other elements of social demoralization among the Carthaginians, which tended in no small degree to their overthrow. Their religion allowed the horrid rites of Moloch: they attempted to propitiate their deities by human sacrifices. The immolation of infants was carried to a fearful extent, even by their infatuated mothers. To a flagrant and undisguised disregard of female honor has been ascribed this frequency of infanticide.*

The conquest of Carthage inspired the Romans with arrogance, and although, ostensibly, her constitution remained unchanged, by it the power of the Senate acquired an undue preponderance. An illustration of this was seen in her invasion of Sardinia, in the midst of peace. Rome's maritime power was also extended in the Adriatic, and at the same time she formed her first political relations with the Grecian States. In the mean time Carthage was endeavoring to atone for the loss of Sicily and Sardinia, by extending her Spanish dominions. Rome at this time numbered, in all Italy, an army of eight hundred thousand men. While Hannibal, who had the command in Spain, was meditating a descent upon Rome, the preparations she made for defence show that it was not believed

* Dr. Cooke Taylor.

possible that he could execute his enterprise by the route which he took.

The results of this war were, the destruction of the naval power of the Carthaginians, and, notwithstanding her immense loss, a great increase of the territorial dominion of Rome. Rome now presented the fearful spectacle of a great military Republic. Flushed with the brilliancy of her achievements, she became a nation of warriors, and to this cause may be ascribed her aspirations after the dominion of the world. It demanded the most dexterous and sagacious policy on the part of Rome to frustrate the powerful alliances formed against her. The Roman Senate at this epoch usurped almost unlimited control—despotic and oligarchical—and yet it was the embodiment of the highest political wisdom. Notwithstanding the remonstrance of the Tribunes, war was declared against Philip of Macedon. The Roman arms were led to conquest in the east, by T. Quintius Flaminius. He gained his victory more by strategy than by feats of arms. As he had already gained over the Achæan league, this brought Greece into a state of dependence upon Rome. A system of espionage was carried on by Rome, not only in the West, but also in the East, over Greece. The fall of Carthage and Macedonia sufficiently exemplifies the political rapacity of Rome.

The ambassadors or Roman commissioners were skilful in diplomacy and intrigue. By an artful policy, Rome procured the banishment of her most formidable foe, Hannibal, from Carthage, and thus prevented his projected league with Syria and Macedonia. A contest then arose between Rome and Antiochus, who, at the battle of Magnesia, was compelled to accept conditions of peace, and which reduced him to a state of dependence.

Within ten years, Rome had laid the foundation of her sway in the East, and she soon became sovereign arbitress of the world from the Adriatic to the Euphrates. The internal condition of Rome had now become grossly immoral, and her political system no less corrupt. Venality and perfidy obtained the mastery, and with reckless disregard of honor, she devastated all the States that opposed the way to her universal dominion.

The civil broils under the Gracchi, to "the first use of power which the emperors made," Mr. Merivale observes, "was to control the fiscal tyranny of the proconsuls and publicani. The revolution of Drusus and the Gracchi opened the spoils of the world to the Italians; but those of Julius and Octavius closed them again, and restored them to their rightful owners. The luxuriance of Roman oppression flourished but for a century and a half; but in that time it created, perhaps, the most extensive and searching misery the world has ever seen. The establishment of imperial despotism placed in the main an effective control over these petty tyrants; and notwithstanding all the crimes by which it won its way, and the corruptions which were developed in its progress, it deserves to be regarded, at least in this important particular, as one of the greatest blessings vouchsafed to the human race."

Sallust forcibly remarks that the Roman manners were precipitated at once to the depth of corruption, after the manner of a resistless torrent. The era from which the rapid degeneracy is to be dated, was the destruction of Carthage; yet, it cannot be doubted that the atheistical tenets attributed to Epicurus, tended in no small degree to accelerate the subversion of Roman virtue and Roman liberty. A firm belief in the Divine superintendence of affairs is the true guarantee of public and private virtue as well as of liberty. It was Atheism that slew a million and a half of people during the first French Revolution. It was not Voltaire alone who blighted all France with the curse of infidelity; France had previously ignored the Sabbath, desecrated her temples, and banished her priesthood. It is evident from the lessons of all history, that the Supreme Governor of the world holds nations as well as individuals to a strict moral accountability.

The historical student, in comparing the Athenian Republic with the Roman, will at once perceive the characteristic differences of the races. The polished Greek preferred the polite arts of life, while the sturdy Roman yielded to the instinct of his nature in love of martial exploits. With the former, genius and learning were the cynosure; with the latter, the ensanguined trophies of war. Except during the age of the Republic, the records of Roman history boast of few illustrious names in literature. It was then that public virtue was sustained by public education; it was then that the heroic fame of the Roman matrons passed into a proverb. No wonder that rhetoric and poetry should then have attained such rare excellence; or that the populace even should have been fired with emulation of literary distinction; or that Sallust, and Cæsar, Cicero, Lucretius, Virgil, Horace, and Livy, became the master spirits of the age. It will be also remembered that the laws of the "Twelve Tables" of the Decemvirs or ten Commissioners, were the product of the Republican intellect of Rome.

Though the temples of Rome are in ruins, these "Tables," which Cicero declared, "contained more wisdom than the libraries of all the Philosophers," are preserved intact, through the lapse of twenty centuries, since they form the basis of the law and the jurisprudence of the civilized world.

The fate of the Republic seemed now to depend upon the success of her Liberator—the elder Gracchus. In his effort to establish a yeomanry—the last expedient for reconciling the ceaseless discords between the politicians and plebeians—he became the victim of the brutal fury of the former. "The election day for tribunes was in mid-summer; the few husbandmen, the only shadow of a Roman yeomanry, were busy in the field, gathering their crops, and failed to come to the support of their champion. He was left to rest his defence on the rabble of the city, and though early in the morning great crowds of the people gathered together, and though, as Gracchus appeared in the forum, a shout of joy rent the skies, which was redoubled as he ascended the steps of the Capitol, yet when the patricians, determined at every hazard to defeat the assembly, came with the whole weight of their adherents in a mass, the timid flock, yielding to the sentiment of awe rather than of cowardice, fled like sheep before wolves, and left their defender, the incomparable Tiberius, to be beaten to death by the clubs of senators. Three hundred of his most faithful friends were left lifeless in the market-place. In the fury of triumphant passion, the corpse of the tribune was dragged through the streets, and thrown into the Tiber."* The deluded nobles flattered themselves into a belief that they had accomplished a victory; that the senate had routed the people, but it was the avenging spirit of their fearful wrongs, that had struck the first deadly wound into the bosom of Rome. The blood of their victim, like that of other martyrs, but cemented his party. A succession of fearful insurrections ensued, and the soldiers of the Republic became the captives of their bondsmen, whose numbers had prodigiously increased.

Such were the horrors of this civil war in Sicily and Italy, that it is said a million of lives were sacrificed, and that Sicily suffered more from its devastations than during the Carthaginian war. Two evils seemed to have resulted, unbridled license among the wealthy, and the most degrading servitude of the bondsmen. It was now that Roman citizens, by their own vote, consented to the degradation of becoming paupers, their extreme poverty requiring that they should be fed from the public table. Discarding the pursuits of agriculture and the industrial arts, the public treasury had to be supplied by plunder of foreign countries, and thus Roman virtue and Roman valor were exchanged for piracy and pillage. At this crisis the demagogue Marius became the chieftain of the oppressed poor. The streets of Rome and the fields of Italy again became the scenes of massacre, and the oppressed bondsmen witnessed the fearful destruction of their oppressors.

They triumphed over Sylla, the leader of the opposite party, who, to gain influence, conferred freedom upon ten thousand of their number. The subsequent insurrection of Spartacus failed, however, of its proposed result, for, when in sight of the Alps, the immense emigration, which had already defeated the armies of four Roman generals, fell a snare to its lust of plunder, and was thus overthrown. The defeat of

* Bancroft's Miscellanies.

Spartacus took place at a moment when the Roman state was in jeopardy from foreign enemies, and from the fiercest domestic distractions. It was then that the haughty tyranny of her nobles was at its greatest height, and when the degradation of its industrial classes was most insupportable. It was at this juncture, when the last glimmering light of liberty had vanished, that the dark reign of despotism began.

Thus we see that oriental luxury was the parent, first of civil, then of political despotism, and the train of its vices appear to us through the lapse of time, in all their monstrous deformity. The reign of Roman luxury was gigantic in crime, for it would sacrifice ten thousand gladiators with as much unconcern as the Spaniards exhibit at a bull-fight.

"Despotism now became the government of the Roman empire. Yet there was such a validity even in the forms of liberty, that they were still in some degree preserved. Two centuries passed away, before the last vestiges of Republican simplicity disappeared, and the Eastern diadem was introduced with the slavish customs of the East. Up to the reign of Diocletian, a diadem had never been endured in Europe. Hardly had this emblem of servility become tolerated, when language also began to be corrupted; and, within the course of another century, the austere purity of the Greek and Roman tongue, the languages of Demosthenes and of Gracchus, became for the first time familiarized to the forms of oriental adulation. Your imperial highness, your grace, your excellency, your immensity, your honor, your majesty, then became first current in the European world; men grew ashamed of a plain name, and one person could not address another without following the customs of the Syrians, and calling him rabbi, master."*

Previously, Roman citizenship constituted by far the smallest portion of her inhabitants. Her dependencies and allies were treated, with very slight exceptions, as aliens, who were denied the right of voting, &c. Herein consisted her safety, and her deviation from the

* Bancroft's Miscellanies.

rule is proved to have been fraught with ruin. The same cause will ever insure like results.

"The universal record of history teaches that all republics which have risen and fallen, owe their destruction to foreign influence—unseen at first,—permitted till too strong for resistance,—at last fatal."*

During the greatest successes of Cæsar, just after his defeat of Pompey at Pharsalia, the Senate was crowded with aliens and soldiers, instead of Roman citizens. Michelet remarks, the victory of Cæsar bore all the character of an incursion of barbarians into Rome, and into the Senate. In the commencement of the civil war, he had given the right of the city to all the Gauls between the Alps and the Po, and he raised to the rank of Senators a whole host of Gaulish Centurions in his army, as well as soldiers. Thus the conquerors of Pharsalia came to stammer out Latin by the side of Cicero. Thus that body, once so august, was now under the control of the thrice-elected Dictator. This Senate decreed a general celebration of his various victories, during forty days. A bronze statue of him was to be set up in the Capitol, inscribed "the demigod !" His triumphant processions, one for Gaul, another for Egypt, a third for Syria, and a fourth for Numidia, bore him four times, in the highest state which mortal could sustain, up to the temple where his image testified to immortality, while to all classes of the people, revellings, games, and fastings, were continued with unsparing prodigality. His fifth and last triumph was that obtained over the sons of Pompey, of Munda. The Senate still continued to lavish upon him every kind of extravagant homage, even acknowledging him as the Julian Jupiter, and ordaining a temple and a priesthood to be consecrated to his worship. So fell the liberty, and so trembled the religion of Rome. There was now but one man for those "that talked of Rome," to praise as their sovereign, and to confess their deity.†

Thus by their vices were the Roman people brought to servitude, not as they were unwilling, but as if bondage had become more acceptable to them than liberty.

* Gov. Gardner of Mass.

† Elliot's Liberty of Rome.

"But what more oft, in nations grown corrupt,
And by their vices brought to servitude,
Than to love bondage more than liberty?"

The almost superhuman influence which Cæsar exerted as Emperor was, however, destined to a swift annihilation. His work of massacre and spoliation had ceased, and now the retributions of Providence were to follow. The story of his subsequent career to its end is already familiar to the reader. With the accession of Octavius Cæsar, who assumed the title of Augustus and Emperor, may be said to have ended the greatest commonwealth the world has ever seen, and the commencement of the greatest monarchy. The empire of Rome was extended over the whole globe; in Europe, it comprised Italy, Gaul, Spain, Lusitania, Greece, Illyricum, parts of Britain and Germany;—in Asia, Armenia, Syria, India, Asia Minor, Mesopotamia, and Media;—in Africa, Egypt, Numidia, Mauritania, and Libya. But it was under the tyranny of her prætorian guards that the liberty of Rome was sacrificed. There is a voice which yet speaks to us from Marius, and Sylla, and Philippi.

The ruin of the free classes of Rome, and the consequent depopulation of the empire, appears to have been the specific malady of the state, and under which it suffered dissolution.* Gibbon forcibly portrays the skepticism and its usual accompaniments, which obtained among the higher ranks of Roman society. "It was indifferent to them what shape the folly of the multitude might choose to assume, and they approached with the same inward contempt, and the same external reverence, the altars of the Libyan, the Olympian, or the Capitoline Jupiter."

The Abbé Lamennais asserts, "that in such a frame of society, the human mind had nothing to rest upon. Despoiled of its faith, and even of its opinions, it was drifted upon an ocean of uncertainty and doubt. There was no more of paganism—no more of philosophy, unless you call by that name those idle vagaries with which the Romans amused their leisure in the gardens of their villas, or under the porti-

* Michelet.

coes of their palaces, but from which proceeded no guide to the conscience, no fixed rule of conduct. They descanted upon their gods only to doubt their existence—on their duties, to elude them—on death, to determine how life could be enjoyed most; and the whole was terminated by abandoning themselves, heedlessly, to the current which carried, pell-mell, the wrecks of social order, men, institutions, and the empire itself." Montesquieu, and other reliable authorities, do not essentially differ in their opinions.

Last, but greatest of all the causes that rendered the Roman people incapable of existing any longer as a Republic, that made their subjugation to the rule of some military adventurer inevitable, was the universal spread of irreligion and profligacy.* This is disguised, or lightly passed over by some modern writers; but no one can become familiar with the classics, without having it perpetually forced upon his notice in a thousand different forms; no mistaken delicacy should prevent us from dwelling and reflecting on the facts. They teach the great moral, that, to preserve freedom, piety and virtue must not be suffered to decay. The Romans, whose foreign conquest and domestic concord Polybius witnessed, believed firmly in a future state of rewards and punishment; hence, as Polybius remarked, came the probity that honorably distinguished their nation. The Romans of Cæsar's time had learned to look on such ideas as vain and ridiculous.

Among the Roman virtues, not the least conspicuous, was her sublime patriotism. It was this that added such august dignity to the Roman character; but, with the loss of her virtues, came the fall of the great commonwealth.

No people has ever been destroyed unless internal division has first prepared the way for an invader. Nationality is of too strong a power to be seriously affected by external attacks: its foes are in its own household, and cliques and feuds are its most dangerous enemies.

The armies of Joshua found the Canaanites an easy prey, for that ancient people were split up into numerous principalities and tribes,

* Merivale.

though of common origin, language, and customs. Their several kings or chieftains could resolve on no settled action against the invader; internal jealousies prevented a united action, and the several nations were annihilated in detail.

Carthage, the mistress of the world when Rome was yet in its infancy, flourished peacefully so long as concord and unity influenced her citizens in the common good, but faction wrested victory from her brow, persecuted and banished the immortal Hannibal, and left her palaces in ruins at the feet of her conquerors.

Rome, eternal Rome herself, felt the terrible evils of division. Against such treason to the Republic, Cicero thundered in fearful eloquence, denouncing the Catilines and anarchists of the age who sought to divide a united people. It was by such divisions that Cæsar and Pompey destroyed the Republic, and left it the prey of emperors.

Feuds and civil war delivered Italy to the barbarians, and the rival houses of the Arsini, Colonna, Medici, &c., plunged her in mediæval darkness. Poland shone among the nations, and drove back the Moslems from the walls of Vienna, for she was then moved by one principle, and patriotism had an existence in her midst. But an evil day came, and her nobles forgot their country, and thought but of their own selfish interests. Then, what the mighty Turkish power had failed to injure, trembled before a northern invader; Poland was still the same nation, the same heroic people; but her soldiers were slain, and her scythemen annihilated, because the bond of union, the common action, was now no more.

History has graven on the granite columns of Time the incontrovertible maxim, "Union is Strength." Ambition and Tyranny have divined its import, and embraced the only course which could affect it. That course is, *Diviser pour regner:* (Divide, in order to reign.) It is only by such a policy that liberty can be attacked; she is safe against all foreign enemies; storms will pass harmlessly over her; but dissension will induce rancor, and rancor, anarchy: thus the State is quickly left to bemoan its loss of freedom, when it sees itself the prey of ever-changing tyrants.

The loss of a firm national character, or the degradation of a nation's honor, is the inevitable prelude to her destruction. Behold the once proud fabric of a Roman empire, an empire carrying its arts and arms into every part of the eastern continent; the monarchs of mighty kingdoms, dragged at the wheels of her triumphal chariots; her eagle waving over the ruins of desolated countries: where is her splendor, her wealth, her power, her glory? Extinguished forever. Her mouldering temples, the mournful vestiges of her former grandeur, afford a shelter to her muttering monks. Where are her statesmen, her sages, her philosophers, her orators, her generals? Go to their solitary tombs and inquire. She lost her national character, and her destruction followed. The ramparts of her national pride were broken down, and Vandalism desolated her classic fields.*

Thus has the mighty mother of nations fallen—with all her pride of beauty, her majestic power, her intellectual greatness, and her sublime patriotism!

> "Ah, eloquence, thou wast undone,—
> Wast from thy native country driven,
> When tyranny eclipsed the sun,
> And blotted out the stars of heaven!"

Yet the world ceases not to do homage to her lost virtues, as well as her triumphant exploits in arts and philosophy; and in all coming time, will there be found admiring multitudes who will delight to gaze up into those bright blue skies, which inspired the muse of Virgil, to linger amid the ruins of her Forum, so memorable for the stupendous eloquence of Cicero, and to bend before that Temple of Liberty, in which Rienzi vowed to her protection in her last asylum.

> "Her ruined columns stand sublime,
> Flinging their shadows from on high;
> Like dials which the wizard Time
> Had raised to count his age gone by."

Other great cities of past ages may attract us—Thebes, Babylon,

* Maxcy.

Persepolis, and Nineveh—but Imperial Rome awes us with a solemn sense of her mighty mind, as well as her magnificence. It is the *genius loci* of the great capital that invests it with such deep and absorbing interest. "It is because she was the lawgiver of the nations; parent of institutions that give civility and development to society; inventress of the arts that establish right through reason; source of that social wisdom which is civil power,—that the all-imperial city sits throned in the ever-during reverence of the mind, girt with a divinity invisible, perhaps, to the frivolous, but irresistible to the thoughtful minded."

ITALIAN LIBERTY IN THE MIDDLE AGES.

"The sea, that emblem of uncertainty,
Changed not so fast, for many and many an age,
As this small spot."

When the irruption of the Teutonic tribes into the Roman Empire had plunged Europe in barbarism, the first attempt at the establishment of order and government was the creation of the feudal system.

"The establishment of the feudal system had a powerful and striking influence upon European civilization. It changed the distribution of the population. Hitherto, the lords of the territory, the conquering population, had lived united in masses more or less numerous, either settled in cities, or moving about the country in bands; but, by the operation of the feudal system, these men were brought to live isolated, each in his own dwelling, at long distances apart."*

No system has been so powerful in checking democratic liberty as feudalism. Leaguing with the throne or the Church, as circumstances rendered necessary, it consolidated power, and became, as it were, an integral part of government. The people, ignored by it, were only used to add *vis inertiæ* to the pretensions and encroachments of their oppressors.

But one country refused its adoption. Whilst the rest of Europe was developing feudality, Italy barred its progress beyond the Alps, and created those asylums of individual liberty, the various Republics, which it is now our intention to examine.

The Italian Republics of the Middle Ages demand the serious attention of our citizens, suffering, as they did, from like attack with ourselves, and succumbing eventually beneath those evils which

* Guizot.

equally affect us, and which, if unchecked, will ultimately prove our ruin. The Italian commonwealths are worthy the love and esteem of our citizens; for they preserved all that then remained of democracy, and shielded liberty from destruction during the most critical period of European affairs. We do not propose to give a history of all or any of these States, but, glancing at their origin and prosperity, to study those causes which destroyed freedom, and thus, from the misfortunes of Italy, to inculcate a warning to America.

The municipal government which Rome had established throughout the empire, had taken deep root in Italy, and having flourished during many centuries, offered a firm barrier to the progress of feudalism. This system had existed too long for Italy to unite as one nation. Each large city had a government peculiar to itself; and the smaller towns which sprung up around them, entering into alliance for mutual defence, formed the nucleus of a republic.

Venice seems to have been one of the earliest States which developed the republican form of government. The hordes of Lombards which devastated Italy in the sixth and seventh centuries, succeeded in establishing their power in the north and south, but failed on the Lagunes, at the extremity of the Adriatic. As early as the time of Attila, these marshes had been the refuge for the rich citizens of various towns, fleeing from the Huns and other barbarous tribes.

> "A few in fear
> Flying away from him, whose boast it was
> That the grass grew not where his horse had trod,
> Gave birth to Venice."

In course of time, a large population found a home on the various islands, supporting themselves by the making of salt, fishing, and the commerce of the various rivers whose mouths form the Lagunes.

> "Like the water-fowl,
> They built their nests among the ocean-waves."

The barbarians, not possessing any vessels, left these refugees unmolested; and they maintained their independence under the administration of tribunes, named by the inhabitants of the various islands. Each island formed a separate State, and thus jealousies and disputes arose, until, at length, they united themselves into one republic, electing an assembly and a chief, to whom they gave the name of Doge. In 809, during a war with Pepin, they made choice of the island of the Rialto as their capital, and, twenty years later, transported thither the body of St. Mark, whom they chose as their patron saint.

In the south, the republics of Gaeta, Amalfi, and Naples had successfully resisted the attacks of Lombards and Saracens, and covered the Levant with ships of merchandise. To Amalfi is due the glory of the invention of the mariner's compass, the establishment of the order of the Knights Hospitalers of Jerusalem, and the preservation of the pandects of Justinian. Naples and Amalfi both succumbed to the Normans, under Roger II., in the beginning of the twelfth century.

"When, towards the end of the eleventh century, the Western world took up the dispute with the Saracens for the sepulchre of Jesus Christ, Venice, Pisa, and Genoa had already reached a high point of commercial power. These three cities had more vessels on the Mediterranean than the whole of Christendom besides. They seconded the Crusaders with enthusiasm. They provisioned them when arrived off the coast of Syria, and kept up their communication with the West. The Venetians assert that they sent a fleet of two hundred vessels, in the year 1099, to aid the first crusade. The Pisans affirm that their archbishop, Daimbert—who was afterwards Patriarch of Jerusalem—passed into the East with a hundred and twenty vessels. The Genoese claim only twenty-eight galleys and six vessels. But all concurred with equal zeal in the conquest of the Holy Land; and the three maritime republics obtained important privileges, which they preserved as long as the kingdom of Jerusalem lasted."*

Such was the prosperity of the Italian Republics when Frederic Barbarossa determined to abolish their freedom, and render Italy an

* Sismondi.

integral part of the German Empire. The small towns quickly perceived that their only safety was in joining some one of the great cities, and making common cause against their oppressor. Thence arose the Guelph and Ghibeline parties, which distracted the peninsula with civil war during several centuries.

The two party-cries, which seem to us insufficient to account for the sanguinary proceedings which desolated Italy, represented two important principles. The Emperors of Germany were determined to vanquish the democratic institutions of the Italians, and, by granting certain immunities to different cities, obtained their assistance against the Guelphs, who asserted their independence of the Emperors, and found a willing ally in the Papacy, then in the height of the struggle to rid itself of the temporal power.

Notwithstanding the civil commotion which threw the entire country into one camp or the other, Italy presented a magnificent picture at the close of the thirteenth century. The authority of the popes and emperors having become suspended, numerous petty independent republics had arisen: the country was filled with cultivated plains and valleys, the proprietors advancing capital and sharing the harvests; immense canals were constructed for purposes of irrigation, of which the *Naviglio Grande* of Milan still bears testimony to the science and perseverance of seventy-eight years. The cities began to construct and perfect those wonderful works of art, which the lapse of six centuries still sees drawing the steps of travellers to Florence, Genoa, and Venice: the towns were surrounded with fortifications, and the streets paved with flag-stones. Magnificence and taste combined to raise and beautify the palaces of Italian citizens, at a time when the nobles and princes of the rest of Europe thought but of security and defence. Sculpture, both of bronze and marble, flourished under the chisels of the forerunners of Michael Angelo; the "Gates of Heaven" of the Baptistery at Florence were cast, whilst Cimabue and Giotto revived painting, Casella, music, and Dante gave to the world his glorious poem. History was studied, and written with elegance and truth by Giovanni Villani and others, whose records bear testimony to the flourishing state of their country, and its happiness under the blessings of self-government. The manufactures of Italy, particularly in stuffs and arms, excited the astonishment and cupidity of the northern nations; the Tuscan and Lombard merchants trafficked in the East and West, bartering their goods to the people, and lending money to the nobles at large interest: the banking and monetary system of Europe was established by them. The laboring classes were in similar prosperity; each gained largely, and spent but moderately, for manners were yet pure, and luxury had not as yet affected virtue.

But this prosperity was doomed, and the dissensions of the various republics soon surrendered liberty to the uncontrolled power of such despots as the Visconti and the Medici. War broke out in 1282, between Genoa and Pisa, which continued with various success until the year 1284.

The history of Florence, "that land where the poet's lip and the painter's hand are most divine," presents more objects of importance than any other republic of the Middle Ages. Previous to her subjection to the Medici, she was free, active, and independent, the protectress of Italian liberty, the nurse of art and science. There was an immeasurably greater degree of democratic liberty in her midst than elsewhere. Venice was an oligarchy, whilst a powerful aristocracy predominated more or less in the other republics.

"Florence was the Athens of Italy. The genius displayed by some of its citizens,—the talent and intelligence in business to be found even in the mass of the people,—the generosity which seemed the national character, whenever it was necessary to protect the oppressed to defend the cause of liberty,—raised this city above every other."*

Discord broke out, however, in 1378; the lower orders demanding a more complete equality with the higher classes. The constitution became at this time entirely democratic; the people were sovereign, and the nobles were excluded from the government. The seeds of anarchy and oppression were, however, in her midst,—the citizens

* Sismondi.

were divided into twenty-one different corporations of arts or trades, from seven of which, termed *arti maggiori*, the magistrates might alone be chosen. From these sprung the Albizzi and Ricci, rival houses, and eventually the Medici, who, from popular leaders, became the absolute sovereigns of the republic.

The disputes between the higher and lower orders of the citizens broke out with renewed intensity in 1378. The poorer classes of artisans flew to arms, and made themselves masters of the city. A carder of wool, Michele Lando, marched at the head of the people, carrying in his hand the gonfalon or national standard, when suddenly the citizens proclaimed him gonfalonier. He restored peace and security to the State, and ordained that in future the chief magistracy should consist of three members of the major arts, three of the minor, and three of the *ciompi* or wool-carders. But this state of order and freedom did not long exist: in 1381 the people were deprived of power, and the family of Albizzi then directed the republic for fifty-three years. This house governed the State prosperously; Florence attained an unexampled degree of prosperity, setting a limit to the ambition of the powerful Gian Galeazza Visconti, Ladislaus, king of Naples, and Filippo Maria, duke of Milan.

"No triumph of an aristocratic faction ever merited a more brilliant place in history. The one in question maintained itself by the ascendency of its talents and virtues, without ever interfering with the rights of the other citizens, or abusing a preponderance which was all in opinion."*

The family of the Medici having obtained the leadership of the people by advocating popular doctrines, now intrigued to build up the fortunes of their house, and Cosmo de Medici became the rival of the Albizzi. Driven from the city in 1433, he was recalled the following year, and the Albizzi expelled.

Had there been any patriotism in the Italian nation at this period—had any common course of action or policy existed, or union of the different republics been effected—Italy could have cleared the Penin-

* Sismondi.

sula of foreign armies, and driven the French, Germans, Spaniards, and Swiss, with countless Condottieri, beyond the Alps. The great republics of Milan, Venice, and Florence, could not, however, consent to this forgetfulness of rivalry, and the two latter refused to admit Milan into such a union. Italy, therefore, soon became a prey, not merely to foreigners, but to her own citizens, and the various republics fell into the hands of those rich families, whose only object was self-aggrandizement.

Cosmo de Medici resolved to effect that, in which the family of the Bentivogli had been successful in Bologna,—the subjugation of the State to his rule, and that of his descendants. In this he eventually succeeded, and henceforward we can no longer regard Florence as a republic, but as a duchy,—glorious, magnificent, and powerful, it is true, but a State in which democratic liberty did not exist, even in name, where the pride of a dominant family was the first, the only consideration. Florence had been the least selfish of all the Italian republics: she had opposed the oppressive power of the German emperors, assisted her weaker neighbors against their tyrants, and been the guardian of liberty, generally, in Italy. But she fell, because in an evil hour she followed a selfish policy, and forgot the good of the whole in her private jealousies.

There was a gleam of hope, however, when, in 1494, Florence expelled the Medici, after they had governed the city during sixty years. Three parties aspired to power. The *Piagnoni*, headed by the famous Savonarola, a monk, who demanded a democratic constitution; the Arabbiati, who aspired to hold the same aristocratic power as that formerly held by the Medici; and the Bigi, the partisans of the Medici, who kept studiously in retirement. These three parties became so evenly balanced in the *balia* or national council of 1494, that "Savonarola took advantage of this state of affairs to urge that the people had never delegated their power to a balia, which did not abuse their trust. 'The people,' he said, 'would do much better to reserve this power to themselves, and exercise it by a council, into which all the citizens should be admitted.' His proposition was agreed to, and a general council was formed, and declared sovereign on the 1st of July, 1495; it was invested with the election of magistrates, hitherto chosen by lot, and a general amnesty was proclaimed, to bury in oblivion all the ancient dissension of the Florentine republic."*

But the popular voice proved inconstant, and Savonarola's influence quickly gave way to that of the Arabbiati, who arrested him, and put his partisans, the Piagnoni, to flight. Pope Alexander VI. dispatched messages to Florence, ordering the monk to be put to death, with his two disciples, Buonvicino and Marruffi, and they were accordingly burned alive, after suffering those excruciating tortures which preceded their execution.

With the aid of the Spaniards, in 1512, the exiled Medici returned to Florence; but they had lost every republican feeling, and all sympathy of the Florentines. Their only object was to raise money for themselves, and for those Spaniards who had assisted them in regaining their tyrannical power. In 1569, Pope Pius V. granted the title of Grand-Duke of Tuscany to Cosmo de Medici, a youth of nineteen: seven grand-dukes of that family reigned in Florence, the last of whom, Gian Gastone, died in 1737. Thereafter, Florence, once the first on the scroll of liberty and fame, was scarcely mentioned in Europe.

The little republic of San Marino, which has existed as an independent State since the fifth century, contains, at the present day, but four thousand inhabitants. Whilst her once powerful and magnificent neighbors no longer exist, and, what is remarkable, under the very eaves of the Vatican, she still preserves her laws and freedom. San Marino has its nobles and plebeians, from whom the legislative council of sixty members is chosen by universal suffrage. There is also an Upper Chamber, called the Council of Twelve, two-thirds of whom are renewed every year; and two *capatini*, who form the executive. A supreme magistrate, who is invariably a stranger, administers justice, and is elected for three years. The revenues are about $6,000, and the armed force consists of forty men. The Republic pays great attention to letters, and supports a college which contains some fifty

* Sismondi.

students. The Italian traveller, M. Valery, informs us the usual complaint is heard about the aristocracy, for it appears that a few rich families have managed to keep all political power in their own hands. Another complaint is of a still more serious character—non-resident strangers, unnaturalized, have become possessors, by purchase, of the greater part of the little State. The republicans of San Marino must obviate such a crying treason, or they will soon cease to exist as a separate nation.

Florence, the brightest gem in Freedom's coronet, fell from her high estate, because she kept not guard over liberty. It was an easier struggle to vanquish the aristocratic Venice and Genoa, with the many minor States, which followed their baneful examples; but all alike are now fallen, and the mailed hand of foreign despotism holds Italy in chains. In looking back upon the glorious era of the Italian republics, the mind is almost lost in admiration of the power exerted by these small commonwealths; of their intense love of liberty, when the rest of mankind were sunk in comparative slavery, and their glorious monuments in literature and the arts, at a period when Europe was in mediæval barbarism. But a foe existed in their midst, and the very principles which have worked the ruin of all other republics compassed their destruction. Shall not Italy be a warning to other lands?

Neither the military hordes of the German emperors, the fearful thunders of the Vatican, the impetuous onset of the Gallic knights, nor the ceaseless ravages of the marauding Condottieri, could have prevailed against Freedom, had the Italians remained true to themselves. But union did not exist—union had almost become impossible: the sacred name of Liberty was used as a mere party-cry, and every man's hand was against his fellow. History declares with all the majesty of divinity, for her voice is but the fulfilment of prophecy, that conflicting principles and ceaseless agitation cannot exist in a community without destroying its vitality. Nay, the language of inspiration speaks in tones that man dare not gainsay—"A house divided against itself cannot stand."

THE ANGLO-SAXON RACE AND FREEDOM.

"If there be any thing in the supremacy of races, the experiment now in progress will develop it."—DANIEL WEBSTER.

NEXT to the divine instinct of religion, and scarcely less holy, is love of country and of the family to which we belong. Blood is the first and closest bond of life, endearing us, not only to our brethren, but to the generous soil which is our common heritance. We know not how it attracts us in sympathy, feeling, and disposition; but its potency is none the less indisputable. It has been correctly remarked that the *family* is the first state. Next to occupying the same land, the best guarantee of fellowship is speaking the same tongue. Further bonds of union are established when our brethren share the same belief with us, worship at the same altars, meet at the same time and places to perform the ceremonies of religion and settle the graver affairs that agitate the whole community, and, generally, when they feel and act as the members of one family or race can alone feel and act if they would strengthen the circumstances of blood and common language. A people that is a stranger to such emotions, occupies no position in the world's history, but becomes merely an instrument in the hands of other and more earnest nations. A distinct and sacred nationality is essential to the development of patriotism, as the latter is essential to the growth of virtue and freedom.

The American is a branch of the great Anglo-Saxon family. This we hear every day. It is one of those trite definitions which trip from the tongue on the smallest provocation. How many are there who know any thing at all of the Anglo-Saxon family? How many are there who appreciate to its full extent the truth and glory of the assertion? The number *has* been small, we believe, but it is swelling into magnificent proportions. The day is at hand when twenty millions of free-born sons of America shall rejoice in the boast that they *are* Anglo-Saxons;—that day when the surging of turbulous foreign races shall provoke dignified and decisive reprimand.

Where there are many conflicting elements of discord, it is not easy to mention a subject of national importance without eliciting ridicule and sarcasm. Anglo-Saxonism is particularly successful in this respect. It is a theme which can scarcely be broached in general society, without calling forth some silly sneer. Surrounded on every side by a mixed population, the American almost loses his own identity; but it is for a moment only. The "time that tries men's souls" leads him instinctively back to the great fountain-head of his being, and he feels at once the race to which he belongs. We purpose in this chapter to devote ourselves, firstly, to a consideration of the Anglo-Saxon race *en masse*, and secondly, of that branch to which we belong. We will preface our remarks with what a writer* of the 5th century says of the Anglo-Saxons of his day: "They overcome all who have the courage to oppose them; they surprise all who are so imprudent as not to be prepared for their attack. When they pursue, they infallibly overtake; and when they are pursued, their escape is certain. They despise danger; they are inured to shipwreck; they are eager to purchase booty with the peril of their lives. Tempests which to others are dreadful, to them are subjects of joy. The storm is their protection when they are pressed by the enemy, and a cover for their operations when they meditate an attack." It will be perceived how little the characteristics of the race have changed, and how much we inherit in this present day from our early ancestors, especially in the particulars of overcoming opposition, despising danger, and laughing at the fierce threatenings of the ocean.

The Anglo-Saxon race is undoubtedly of Scythian or Gothic origin. A portion of this great family invaded Britain early as 300 years

* Sidonius, Bishop of Clermont.

before the Christian era, whilst it was in possession of the Cimmerians or Celts. The Anglo-Saxons of that early day, who were called Belgæ, from Belgic Gaul, whence they came, did not assimilate with other tribes more readily than they do now. The Celts had to abandon their advantage, and at the time of Julius Cæsar's invasion it was the stern courage and inflexible bravery of the Gethæ's descendants, not the Cimmerians, that opposed his imperial legions. Pinkerton supposes that the interior of the island was still in the possession of the Welch or Britons, as they were called. All memory of the Celts or Cimmerians who preceded the Welch in their occupation of Britain was unknown to the Roman and Saxon writers.

The genuine Anglo-Saxons, however, whence the present race is descended, did not transport themselves to Britain until the fifth or sixth century. They came from the Cimbric peninsula (now Denmark), and were branches of the great Saxon confederation which had extended itself from the Elbe to the Rhine. The Anglo-Saxons, Lowland Scotch, Normans, Danes, Norwegians, Swedes, Germans, Dutch, Belgians, Lombards, and Franks, have all sprung from this great Saxon confederation,* and may all be distinguished by the terms Scythian, German, or Gothic. Their first appearance in the world's history was in that cradle of nations—Asia. Here they multiplied and extended their area of operations for several centuries.† Amongst themselves their general appellation was Scolati; among the Greeks, Scuthoi or Nomades. They are better known, however, as Getæ or Goths. The more advanced of the tribes were known to the Romans as Germans.

We will here deviate for a moment to explain the meaning of these various designations, and whence they are derived. Pliny speaks of the Scythians as Sacassani, which was probably a corruption of Sakai-suna, or Sons of the Sakai, afterwards abbreviated into Saksun or Saxon.‡ The name is supposed to come from the same root as the Anglo-Saxon word *seax*, a sword. In the Persian book of Kings the same people are called *Ssakalib*, or *Ssaklib*—sword-

* Pinkerton. † Herodotus, Strabo. ‡ Miss Chandler.

lips;—the name being suggested in all probability by the Saxons' fondness for that weapon, a fondness which the Anglo-Saxons of the present day do not fail to manifest whenever they have an opportunity of getting to close quarters with an enemy. That they were a warlike people is beyond doubt; for even the Roman name, German, is derived from the old German *ger*, a spear, and *mann*, a man. After leaving Asia the Saxons adopted a new name and abandoned their Scythian one. They called themselves Teutons, from Teut, Tuisto, Tuisco, or Thiusco, who is said to have been one of the founders of the race, and who was worshipped after his death as a god. The modern name *Deutsch* is derived from this, having passed through the modifications, Dutsch, Dietsch, and Teutsch.

A Scandinavian branch of the family settled in Scotland about the same period that the Belgæ emigrated to Britain. The members of this section of the Saxon stock are known in history by the name of Picts, or Caledonians. They are said to be the ancestors of the Lowland Scotch and the Northern Irish—races that are distinguished from their Celtic countrymen by superiority of intelligence, industry, and firmness of character.

We have thus briefly traced the origin of the Anglo-Saxon family, and have shown whence it came. We will now prove that from earliest time to the present it has been the consistent champion of freedom, loyalty, and devotion. It cannot be disputed that the Anglo-Saxons were from the first, and are to the present day, fond of what is delicately termed "annexation." They were ever ready to purchase booty, as the learned Sidonius remarks, with the peril of their lives. A brave people cannot resist the temptation of adventure, and the peril which it involves is, perhaps, its greatest attraction. A notable illustration may be found in Jonathan's love for Cuba. If that island could be acquired quietly and as a matter of course, no one would trouble himself about it. But it is otherwise; and the Anglo-Saxon principles of overcoming difficulties and vanquishing opposition manifest themselves. Those writers who recommend Jonathan to wait until Cuba, like a ripe pear, falls into the lap of her

American lover, display but little knowledge of the Anglo-Saxon character. Independently of this restless force of character, however, there is the moral element, which governs and controls its action.

If the Anglo-Saxon were a mere marauder, he would rest content with acquisition and pillage. But he does not do so. The land he has fought for, he cherishes. It is thereafter *his* land; a part of himself, and to be regarded from the elevation of his freedom-loving, noble mind. He may have acquired it by the sword, but he retains it by the law, and by a man-to-man faith and affection. Wheresoever the Anglo-Saxon pioneer goes, he fights first; then builds his chapel, his courthouse, his schools, and his stores. He does not labor to forget civilization, but to exclude barbarism. All the Roman writers expressed their astonishment at the moral sternness and rectitude of the Teutonic character. The reverence with which they treated woman was even a matter of surprise. Tacitus says: "They think their women possess something inherent and foreseeing." Is it not just occasion of pride, that in our day this chivalric feeling still remains, and forms a proverbial characteristic of the American character? Wherever Freedom is found, there is woman emancipated. England is the freest country in Europe, and there the position of woman is little inferior to what it is in our own land. Among the ancient Britons (or Celts) marriage was unknown. Men and women lived together promiscuously, like beasts of the field. The Anglo-Saxons, on the contrary, viewed the custom with abhorrence, and were strict in the observance of the marriage vow. Some of their earliest laws, at least the earliest of which any record is known to exist, relate especially to the crime of adultery. It was looked upon as most heinous, and received the severest punishment of the Anglo-Saxon code. In religion, the same wide difference existed between the two races. The Celts adhered to their Druidic worship, and abandoned their souls to the charge of the priests. The Anglo-Saxons, on the contrary, prayed to their mythological gods with individual fervor, and were content to manage their own conscience, and let others do the same. For a while the Romish religion gained the ascendency in Europe, and Celt and Saxon alike obeyed its tenets. But later, ere the voice of Luther shouted sternly through the darkness of Popery, the Anglo-Saxon Wickliffe had proclaimed liberty of conscience. The Celts, on the contrary, adhered to the old traditions; and even in this day of generally diffused theological knowledge, the Celtic races are obedient to the blind dictates of the Holy See.

Thus we perceive, that to the earliest Anglo-Saxons we are indebted not only for the lasting characteristics of our race, but for that inherent reverence for the gentler sex, and toleration of religious opinion, which characterize the American people of the present century. But this is not all. The Anglo-Saxons loved fair play, and could understand no trial that was not based on general principles of equity and justice. In the reign of Ethelred, the following law was passed: "Let there be gemoto in every wapenlace; and let twelve of the eldest thegres go out with the gerefa, and swear on the relics which shall have been given into their hands, that they will condemn no innocent man, nor screen any that is guilty."* In other words: "Let there be courts in every district, and let the sheriff summon twelve men to try all prisoners;" our own prized trial by jury! If we had inherited nothing but this boon from our ancestors, it would be sufficient to endear the race to the present and to all after generations.

If our space permitted, we could dwell on the memorable deeds of famous Anglo-Saxons. But we have proved sufficient to satisfy the skeptic, that Freedom is not a new word, but an old idea, derived and retained from the earliest pages of their history. We will add to these remarks the final sentence of King Alfred's will. It needs no comment. "It is just that the English should forever remain as free as their own thoughts."

Turning to our own history, we find that the Anglo-Saxon element

* Sharon Turner.

has ever been the potent one. Our present greatness and our future progress alike depend on it. The singular purity of the Anglo-Saxon stock, particularly in the Eastern States, has been a matter of surprise with some writers; a moment's reflection, however, explains the circumstance. Oppression or intolerance of any kind was so inimical to the character of the Anglo-Saxon, that it became unbearable. Always preferring a certain to an uncertain remedy, he detached himself from the land of his birth, and sought, on the shores of America, a home, free and filled with promise. Privation, sufferings, and hardships were, to his sturdy nature, mere items arrayed against a grand total. The future nerved him for the present, and he had unbounded confidence in his own inherent will. The New England colonies were founded by such men; stern almost to fierceness, but patient, brave, and elevated in their social and moral thoughts. The counties in England whence they came were chiefly those which refused the domination of the Danes and Normans. Additions were afterwards made from the north of Ireland and the Scotch Lowlands; but, as we have before intimated, these were either Anglo-Saxon in their origin, or Pictish—a kindred Gothic race. The last fifty years have witnessed the influx of hordes of Celts and of inferior German tribes. The effect has been trouble and annoyance. We must look to the pure American stock, and to the pure American stock only, for the remedy of these evils. It is indisputably true, however, that at this moment New England is more Anglo-Saxon, if possible, than Old England. "The names found in a few pages of a Boston Directory, or in the columns of advertisements in a newspaper, if compared with the same number of English names, taken equally at random, will show the far greater proportion of Anglo-Saxon names with us."* According to an eminent historian,† the old Puritan stock leavens the national character to the extent of two-thirds of its aggregation. The other third could, we opine, be traced to the same Anglo-Saxon fountain-head, if necessary.

The heading of this chapter intimates that the Anglo-Saxon is the

* Miss Chandler. † Bancroft.

only race capable of sustaining freedom. We base that opinion on the facts we have adduced, and on the additional one, that America is the only country in the world that *has* sustained institutions perfectly free.

The history of the Anglo-Saxon race affords abundant material for the reflective mind. It exhibits in an unusual degree the fact that the national characteristics of a race do not change.

It may be objected that scarcely any modern people has not been modified or changed by amalgamation with foreign blood, whether by conquest, immigration, or otherwise; and in confirmation of this the English are sometimes cited. But the truth is, the Anglo-Saxons never settled among the Celtæ—as the Franks among the Gauls—but drove them out, and, receiving continued accessions of their countrymen from the shores of the Baltic and adjacent islands, repeopled the conquered territory. The unhappy Britons (Celtæ) in their memorable appeal to Ætius, the Roman patrician, forcibly describe the kind of settlement the Teutons were making. "The barbarians," they say, "on the one hand, chase us into the sea; the sea, on the other, throws us back upon the barbarians; and we have only the hard choice left us of perishing by the sword, or by the waves."*

The Danes in the reign of Egbert and later, to the accession of Canute, were but tribes of the Angles or Saxons, differing only from those already settled in England in the fact of being more civilized. To the same race also belonged the Normans; but these latter never intermixed with the conquered in the same manner as the Danes. Introducing the feudal system into England they became a species of *caste*, and kept themselves aloof from the mass of the vanquished. Eventually the Norman stock became much thinned during the long and bloody wars of the Roses. What remains of it in the English aristocracy has become so softened in its characteristics by contact with the people, that, except in the class distinctions of the feudal system, it is no longer a separate element of the population. Even this last fragment of Norman *caste* spirit is rapidly passing away.

History assists us in drawing certain conclusions from the ex-

* Bede.

perience of the world. In briefly recording the prominent events attending the career of the race from which we are descended, it is impossible to overlook the fact that the Anglo-Saxon race absorbs, but does not assimilate with other races;—borrows nothing from their sentiment; derives nothing from their nationality. What it was a thousand years ago it is to-day; Civilization and Education have not modified, but intensified its characteristic aspirations for Freedom and the Institutions of Freedom. The same unconquerable energy; the same indomitable courage; the same inflexible determination to *accomplish* destiny, individualize the Anglo-Saxon people of to-day, as on the advent of the race under the victorious banners of Hengist and Horsa. The genius of the people has always been manifest; their susceptibility for the highest achievements of the human body or intellect, undeniable. Wherever they have penetrated, Freedom, Religion, Arts, Sciences, and Literature have found a home. Colonization, which has been a ruinous experiment with every other nation, has prospered with the Anglo-Saxon, and for this reason: The latter retain, no matter what the difficulty of doing so, and cherish, their nationality. It is never laid aside or forgotten for one moment, and always rises superior to the circumstances by which it is surrounded. The colonization of other nations has failed for the reason, that the colonists, lacking force of character, have been too anxious to assimilate with the people amongst whom they settled. The Spanish, French, Dutch (Hollanders), &c., have at various epochs in the world's history made successful attempts at settling on distant shores, but after the small end of the wedge has been inserted, the leverage has been thrown away by a degenerate imitation of the worst characteristics of the people amongst whom they settled. The Anglo-Saxon stands alone in that repellent force which, concentred in itself, throws off all inferior bodies, but ever widens with opportunity to embrace what is most desirable and advantageous. In a word, it looks forward, never backward; upward, but never downward. What is beneath it, it passes by; what is above it, it aspires to, strives for, and achieves!

We have remarked that the Anglo-Saxon absorbs other races, and this too, without suffering any apparent deterioration. Its characteristics have not changed, because the infusion of one race with another of stronger and better defined characteristics results in a general assimilation of the infused with the people amongst whom they settle, unless a spirit of *caste* prevail. Thus the Franks, after driving out the Romans from Gaul, soon lost their national characteristics, and became blended or lost in the immense majority of the Gaels. Thus, also, innumerable races may assimilate with the American, if, in their earnestness for what is desirable, *they imitate the characteristics of the Anglo-Saxon.* But if on the contrary they retain a spirit of *caste*, establish clanships or race distinctions of any kind, as the Tartars in China, assimilation is impossible. The national spirit will eventually drive them out. Before long the Tartars will cease to exist in China. The present revolution numbers their days.

In all strongly individualized lines of descent, there is a persistency of type which is not affected by an admixture of foreign blood. At the revocation of the Edict of Nantes, thousands of French refugees settled in England, but the controlling majority obliterated their national peculiarities, and few traces now remain of their origin. Races preserve their characteristics, but individuals assimilate. They are absorbed into the dominant race—particularly if it be Anglo-Saxon.

The important consideration of race cannot be too vigorously impressed on the American mind. No other country in the world is so besieged with opposing elements of caste, sect, and foreign nationality. In the pulpit, in the senate, in the street, and in the home circle, we find representatives of other races than our own. In the majority of cases these representatives have imbibed a certain amount of American sentiment, sufficient perhaps for an easy passage through politics or society, and are consequently in process of absorption. But too frequently we find them tenaciously adhering to Old World doctrines of government, religion, and social life. It may not be easy to abandon a life-long theory, but it should be no more difficult than abandoning the land of one's birth. When the latter becomes imperative, the former should be absolute. The American, by attaching due importance to every circumstance of race, learns precisely whence freedom sprang, and inversely to appreciate his own glorious birthright, and to guard against encroachments from inimical sources. No sentiment that is not thoroughly Anglo-Saxon can he entertain, for it is his Anglo-Saxon principles that make him what he is. Montesquieu remarks in his "Spirit of Laws"—"The English (by which of course is meant the Anglo-Saxon race) are the people who have best known how to preserve in full vigor those three great things (principles), religion, commerce, and liberty." This important avowal from such a philosopher should be studied word for word, and justified from the pages of history; as indeed it is briefly vindicated in this chapter. If we ask ourselves why it is so, we shall find that it is because in religion the Anglo-Saxon is always sincere in obeying his own conscience without extraneous dictation. Piety is an instinct with him, not a sensual gratification, as in Southern lands; or an intellectual exercise, as in Northern ones. He has no dependence on any one but God and himself; and needs no mediator but his own conscience. It is for the simple reason that the Anglo-Saxon is no hair-splitting doctrinarian that he has preserved his free religion. Speak to him about his faith, and he may hesitate in its exact definition; but speak to him of his conscience, and he knows precisely what you mean. If we would learn the secret of his success in preserving and fostering commerce, we must turn to that other source of his greatness—his faith and confidence in the transactions of his fellow-man. He does to others as they should do to him. He begins by inviting confidence, and ends by securing it. The American people is the most trusting on the face of the earth, and the most enterprising for that reason. The low vice of trading nations—*meanness*—is unknown to him. He is shrewd enough in securing a good bargain, but he forfeits nothing of his integrity in doing so. The advantage he obtains is strictly a commercial one; bought at no sacrifice of independence or morality, but such an advantage as he would appreciate in others, if they could gain it over him. The same characteristics are the features of his political history. He is free, loves freedom, appreciates it, and asks every one to come and share it with him. A little less confidence in the miscellaneous guests he has invited to his home might be desirable. It would be well if he noticed the peculiar characteristics of races, and remembered that they were inevitably the result of local circumstances, which, although they may be changed or removed, are for the most part difficult to eradicate.

But these things the American should never forget:

That the Anglo-Saxon race is the only one which has proved itself capable of sustaining free political institutions;

That the representation of the people, of the *whole people*, is of Teutonic origin, and can be traced up to the earliest time of the race;

That the government of the Anglo-Saxons (and also of the Danes and Northmen) was never monarchical; the chieftainship was never hereditary. A chief had power only in the field. The battle over, he was but a simple warrior, claiming no immunity and no superior portion of the booty taken in battle;

That the chief was chosen by universal suffrage. Alfred the Great came to the throne not in virtue of his birth—though *de facto* king of the Heptarchy, he was not so *de jure*. The Saxon constitution never thought of divine or hereditary right: that absurd fiction was the result of tyrannous combination and Rome;

That the Representative system is purely Anglo-Saxon. It was *not* instituted by Edward the First, but merely revived by him after it had long lain in abeyance. The king was struggling against his Norman barons, and in his necessity claimed the assistance of his Saxon people;—they remembering former constitutional rights re-demanded and once more obtained them. This national assemblage of the representatives of the people was called in the legal Norman French of the time, *Parler le ment*, signifying to *speak one's mind*. Thus freedom of thought and speech was a recognized right among the Saxons. The feudal system strove in vain to ignore it. No other race in history has had any thing similar to this right. The republics of ancient times were merely the aristocracy governing the *plebs.* The nearest approach to it, however, was found in the immunities enjoyed by the citizens of the Free-towns of Europe in the middle ages, as Antwerp, Bremen, Lubeck, &c.; but even here the suffrage was limited, and lay in the hands of a few.

And, lastly, an American should demand from every foreigner, as an equivalent for the hospitality extended to him, a full recognition of the supremacy of this same Anglo-Saxon race. There is nothing degrading in the admission, for it is justified in the existence of the very freedom he comes hither to enjoy; and it is essential, because until he *does* acknowledge it, he is scarcely likely to imitate its virtues, its heroism, and its veneration for the institutions of freedom. Every man who comes to America with the intention of cherishing his own nationality, is an enemy to the Constitution, and abuses a hospitality which should be sacred. The existence of a population thus disposed must be pernicious and dangerous. It is calculated to lessen the love of the American for his own home, and to render the nation less imposing and distinctive in the eyes of foreign powers.

There cannot be a doubt that Providence has selected the Anglo-Saxon race to spread the blessings of liberal institutions throughout the world. It is the only one, of modern times, which has been able to colonize with success, and firmly establish its character, its language, and its customs upon the new territories. What the English have gained by the rights of discovery, or the aggressions of war, America seems destined to organize and perfect. It is therefore that our country displays to the world a power and a success characteristic of no other age or clime; a liberty, of which the Grecian and Roman philosophers never dreamed, and which, next to Christianity in effulgence, shines through the earth as the light of suffering humanity. But this freedom is the victory, the hard-earned conquest, of centuries of struggles against oppression. Men of other races, individuals of other peoples, have declared the great principles of freedom—have, in thousands of instances, died in their defence—but the nations to which these men belonged have made no universal response, but left them exceptions, and not characteristic examples. Not so with the Anglo-Saxon; the race has acted, and its heroes have embodied, only what its heart cordially responded to—what was the very instinct of its nature.

THE HEROES OF THE FOUNDERS OF LIBERTY.

"The present age is benefited by the experience of the past. We have in fruition what thousands hoped for, and vainly suffered to possess."—GOETHE.

THE wisdom of king Solomon will ever be perpetuated in the one declaration, "There is nothing new under the sun." Homer remarks that we always take the liberty of thinking ourselves wiser than our ancestors. Whatever we do, whatever idea illuminates our mind, whatever progress we attempt, the conclusion always is, that we are by so much abandoning the past and approaching a future more radiant and ennobling than any preceding epoch of the world's history. It is doubtful, however, whether civilization, like the emblem of eternity, be not in the form of a circle; whether we do not simply diverge from a point, to converge to it afterwards. Modern philosophy embraces the idea that the earliest era of man's existence was the most perfect; and that what we lost then, is but now being slowly recovered.

Be that as it may, there can be no reasonable doubt that the modern idea of freedom is of very early inception. All freedom, indeed, is the result of long agitated reform, based at first on an individual *idea*, permeating afterwards as a *principle*, and accomplished finally as a *necessity* of the times. Reforms usually commence with argument, and end with bloodshed. The comparative few who think, appeal to those who feel, and the two constitute leaders and revolutionists.

There is no error more common than that which attributes to the principles of the war of American independence an original character. Many well-informed men entertain the belief that in the Declaration of Independence were conveyed startling and entirely new ideas of liberty, and that the men who achieved it were indebted solely to the inherent greatness of their natures for a civil and political triumph, whose equal has yet to be found in the world. Whoever has studied the history of the world—its constant yearnings for religious and political freedom—and observed the slow but certain progress of reform, needs scarcely to be told that this is an error. The American war of independence consummated a preconceived idea; gave vitality to a principle which has from time immemorial occupied the attention of thinkers. It was not a sudden, unexpected dispensation of liberty; it was not a patriotic suggestion of the moment, but the accumulated result of centuries of effort.

Wherever reform begins, revolution must, sooner or later, follow. It will be objected, that England is an exception to this rule. It must be borne in mind, however, that the best revolutionary spirit of England—that is, the spirit most tenacious of prerogative—left the mother-country for America in the sixteenth and seventeenth centuries. It was the strong, stubborn Saxon spirit that had risen in rebellion against the idiotic misrule of James, which first scaled the rocks of Plymouth Sound, and explored the inviting banks of James River. Congenial natures followed, and England rapidly lost the foremost men of her time,—men who had been the centre of all reforms, and who brought with them the most elevated opinions of the century. In speaking of America as a new land, it should always be borne in mind that, practically, it is as old, if not older, than any nation of Europe. The mere consideration of centuries is of little importance. Intelligence and civilization are the characteristics which stamp manhood on a nation's brow. The Chinese in their chronologies go back far beyond the period when we are taught to believe the world was created. It is said that in their school-books it is customary for the teacher to insert a pencil-mark opposite the year in which the world is popularly supposed to have been made. But notwithstanding their extensive line of progenitors, the Chinese are the youngest, the least informed, most frivolous people on the face of the earth.

GENERAL LIBRARY
University of
MICHIGAN

THE HEROES OF THE FOUNDERS OF LIBERTY.

The progress of humanity may be likened, says an eloquent writer,* to the successive necessities of repairing the ancient homestead of our fathers. We are unwilling to disturb the old framework, and yet the decay of parts imperatively calls for repairs. But every attempt to add and beautify, by comparison, discovers defects, and the skill of the mechanic and artist stands in permanent requisition. The homestead of our American forefathers was found too seriously dilapidated to admit of repairs. It was vacated, and a new one erected on the Atlantic shores of wild America. But the men who erected that homestead were no untutored pioneers. They knew precisely the defects of the old homestead, and avoided them—falling, however, for a time, on others equally great and pernicious. Their new house was, in all important respects, put in order with the best of all judgments—that which had been tutored in bitter experience.

The perfection of earthly happiness is freedom, and that, as we have before asserted, is the slow result of gradual reform. If we penetrate the darkness of remote antiquity, we find minds of a superior order striking initial blows at the root of tyranny and oppression. In Dr. Abbot's Egyptian Museum (New York) there is a remarkably curious illustration of this fact. A rude artist of the earliest Egyptian period (3000 years B. C.), caricatures the priesthood for their low, fox-like cunning and rapacity. This exceedingly curious work of art is executed on a tile, and was doubtless in its day a missile of some weight. Thus we perceive that there were religious reformers even in the days of the first Pharaoh. It is not unreasonable to suppose that there were political reformers also.

The men who have made sacrifices in the holy cause of Freedom,—particularly those who come from the same stock as ourselves,—are assuredly worthy of our best remembrance. To them we are indebted for the prosperous consummation of a free country. They are not only our lineal ancestors, but the parents of our best and most noble thoughts. Without their example and their spirit, we should be, even now, a colony, cursed with Church, State, and

* History of Democracy, Vol. I. page 34.

UofM

man-worship, and all the other imbroglio of monarchism. Unfortunately, the limits of our work prohibit any thing like a complete sketch of the antecedent heroes of political liberty. The most we can accomplish is to select a few names, and present them as finger-marks along the track of history, for the admiration of the reader. Our endeavor will be to make them, as far as possible, the representatives of their class and epoch, and briefly but explicitly to set forth their claims to the consideration of the law-abiding people of this country.

Our sketch is to illustrate the growth of those institutions which we now enjoy in America. To do this with any thing like elaborateness, would compel us to epitomize the general history of the past. Political heroes obtain their greatest attraction from the circumstances in which they were placed; and, indeed, would not be interesting to a general reader, in the absence of such connecting information. Hence the necessity for dwelling with some detail on events which were of vital importance to the early founders of American freedom. The antecedent history of America begins, of course, with the Saxons. In this chapter we have commenced with Alfred the Great, for it is only subsequent to the reign of that monarch that Freedom began to be modernized.

For the record of an able, patriotic, liberty-loving man, and the people's beloved ruler, we cordially turn to the life of an early hero. Instances of unselfish loyalty to constitutional liberty are so scarce, that this model man may well be venerated. His merits were not of a class order; he was good not merely as a king,—which would scarcely concern us,—but as a citizen. In private as in public life, he practised what he professed: "so happily were all his virtues tempered together, so justly were they blended and so powerfully did each prevent the other from exceeding its proper boundaries."*

Alfred the Great, youngest son of King Ethelwolf, was born in Berkshire, England, in 819. At an early age he was taken by his father to Rome, where he remained twelve months, but without ac-

* Hume.

quiring any kind of knowledge, save perhaps an insight into the avariciousness of Romish priests, of which he afterwards made good use. Pope Leo the Third, perceiving in the boy something of promise more than was usually manifested, went through the playful operation of giving him the royal unction. This consisted, so far as we have been able to discover, in muttering a few prayers, accompanied with some theatrical ceremonies, in return for which the recipient was expected to make liberal grants of money and land—a common sort of exchange in days of bigoted superstition. Ethelwolf, Alfred's father, returned to England to find his kingdom torn to fragments by the ravages of the Danes. The incursions of these desperate marauders continued with unabated fury to the day of his death. If you can imagine a noble steed pursued by a band of remorseless wolves, sometimes giving them battle with success, at others fleeing from them with apprehension, you will have a good idea of the condition of England in the year 800. Ethelwolf died, and was succeeded rather summarily by his sons, Ethelbald, Ethelbert, and Ethelred. It was during the reign of the latter that Alfred gave the first indication of his patriotism. Ethelred had unjustly deprived him of a large patrimony, and beside this, kept him from a throne which had been bequeathed to him by the will of his father, Ethelwolf. Either of these reasons was sufficient, in those days, to attract a band of eager warriors to his standard. The national danger, however, was from the continued irruptions of the Danes. To put a stop to these, Alfred eagerly seconded all the efforts of his brother Ethelred. The nation's welfare, and not the individual's right, was consulted for the first time in that rude age.

Reading and writing in those days were accomplishments of a high order, and were seldom essayed except by members of the priesthood. It is said that Alfred's enthusiasm for learning was first aroused by hearing the Saxon bards repeat their wild lyrics. Himself a poet, as he afterwards abundantly proved, he at once estimated the incomparable advantages of an education. He soon learnt to read, and proceeded then to acquire a knowledge of the Latin language. The

Roman poets and philosophers fired him with noble emulation, and contributed in no small degree to the formation of a character naturally heroic. In the midst of his studies, he was called to the throne. His first enterprises, like those of his predecessors, were, of course, directed against the common enemy—the Danes. They were prosecuted with varied success. At one time, Alfred had so hemmed them in, that they were glad to come to terms with him. A treaty was entered into, by which the Danes stipulated to depart from the country; but the Danes were not remarkable for keeping their treaties, and in this and other instances behaved perfidiously. Fresh hordes came over to the assistance of their brethren, and Alfred found himself deserted, or surrounded by men who were too broken-spirited to be available against a foe so savage and uncompromising. Under such circumstances, he thought it best to retire for a while from the contest, and await a more propitious moment to free his country from the insatiate locusts who infested it. In the meanest disguise, he sought refuge from the fury of his enemies. He concealed himself under a peasant's habit, and lived some time in the house of a neat-herd who had been intrusted with the care of some of his cows.

The Danes, discovering no traces of Alfred's whereabouts, concluded that he had left the country, or was dead. After a time, they gave up the pursuit. It was then that the fugitive king began to collect some of his followers, and to hope seriously for an opportunity to free his country. He ordered his subjects to hold themselves in readiness against the enemy, gave them intelligence of his retreat, and succeeded in gaining information of the strength and position of the Danes. He was determined not to lose this final opportunity by any rashness or false estimate of the power he had to cope with. In order more fully to inform himself of the latter, he entered the camp of the chief Dane, disguised as a harper. He was an admirable musician, and, it is said, possessed much native humor. By the exercise of skill and wit, he succeeded in passing unmolested through every quarter. Shortly afterwards, he led his troops against the enemy, and was completely successful. The Danes begged for peace. Those who were already in the country he allowed to remain, on condition that they and their king should embrace Christianity. Firmly established on the throne—which he filled for twenty-nine years—he devoted himself to the glory and honor of his country, the propagation of religion, and the dissemination of knowledge. Centuries after his death, he was known and spoken of as "England's darling." The wonderfully balanced intellect of this great man, his holy impartiality in all matters submitted to his judgment, and the manifest love of freedom evidenced in his whole career, entitle him to the fond appellation. Speaking of Alfred, Gibbon says: "Amidst the deepest gloom of barbarism, the virtue of Antoninus, the learning and valor of Cæsar, and the legislative genius of Lycurgus shone forth in that patriot king."

Alfred was a pious, God-fearing man. He loved learning and those who possessed it. Necessarily, the clergy or bishops were the receptacles in which it lay. But, with singular clearness of vision, Alfred hesitated to increase the power and influence of the bishops. During his reign, they enjoyed fewer privileges and far less political power than they had possessed in other reigns. Alfred preferred making concessions to the people, rather than to the priests. The truth is, that Alfred, whilst he venerated religion and its ministers, had none of that superstitious awe which usually accompanies inferior minds. The liberality of Alfred's views, and his constant distrust of the temporal power of the Pope, lead us to agree with Dr. Pauli, that he felt and thought more as a German than a Roman Catholic, and that in his character were already to be traced the rudiments of those opinions which afterwards showed themselves in the independence of Protestantism.

During the reign of Alfred, and for the first time in England, the work of practical and political reform was commenced. The admirable institution of trial by jury was put into execution on a thorough basis. There were courts of appeal also established, at which twelve freeholders swore to administer impartial justice. Lest corruption should reach even the presiding magistrate, there was an annual meeting appointed for the inspection of police, for the inquiry into crimes, the correction of abuses in magistrates, and the obliging of every person to show the district in which he was registered. There was still another appeal in default of justice in these courts, namely, to the king himself. He was overwhelmed with petitions from all parts of England, for the people rightly estimated the privilege of appealing to a man of such strict impartiality. He was indefatigable in the dispatch of these causes, but finding that his time would be entirely consumed by their adjudication, he conceived the happy idea of obviating the difficulty by correcting the ignorance or corruption of the inferior magistrates. He took care to have his nobility instructed in letters and the laws;* he chose the earls and sheriffs from among the men most celebrated for probity and knowledge; he punished severely all malversation in office,† and he removed all the earls whom he found unequal to the trust. The better to guide the magistrates in the administration of justice, he collected a body of laws for their study, which long served for the basis of English jurisprudence, and was the origin of what is now denominated the common law.‡ The result of these admirable precautions was perfect security to the individual, and a greater amount of freedom than had ever before been enjoyed. So exact was the character of the inhabitants, and so unfailing the arm of justice, that it is said that Alfred, by way of bravado, hung up golden bracelets by the wayside, confident that no man would touch them.§ Under his beneficent rule, learning and literature took firm hold of the minds of the people. He was himself an ardent student, and contributed in no small degree to the enlightenment of the age in which he lived. That he might have time to attend to his multifarious duties, he divided the day into three equal portions: one was employed in sleep, and the refection of his body by diet and exercise; another, in the dispatch of business; a third, in study and devotion.‖ Thus, although he often labored under great bodily in-

* Asser. † Le Miroir de Justice. ‡ Hume.
§ William of Malmsbury. ‖ Hume.

firmity,* this martial hero, who fought in person fifty-six battles by sea and land,† was able during a life of no extraordinary length to acquire more knowledge, and even to compose more books, than most studious men. He died in the vigor of his age, and the full strength of his faculties, A. D. 901, after a reign of twenty-nine years and a half.

In presenting to our readers this sketch of the life of one of the most interesting heroes of history, we do so in the belief that it is instructive and gratifying to trace to such a noble Saxon fountain-head, the first indications of a political liberty which has since culminated so practicably and sublimely in the American descendants of this same Anglo-Saxon stock. It is contrary to our intention to take the history of England as our only key to political freedom. Other nations have furnished their quota to the general aggregate. But it cannot be too often impressed, or too tenaciously remembered, that all the solid practical fundamental principles of freedom which prevail among us, have been transplanted from the mother country. Whatever may be the political jealousies which irritate the two nations—America and England—and they are aggravated enough, there can be no justification of national hatred. The English trace all their political freedom to the Germanic element. We must do the same. The life of Alfred furnishes us with an illustration of the necessity for this justice. To that illustrious hero we are indebted for the restitution of trial by jury, and the condensation of a legal practice, now familiarized to us by the title of Common Law.

The necessity for reasonable brevity prohibits our dwelling on the successive acquisitions of political freedom by the people. Only the prominent triumphs can be glanced at.

The Saxon rule in England terminated with the death of Harold—the last of the Saxon kings. Feudal or Norman rule succeeded. The Normans, a tribe of Northern Germans, after they had subdued the provinces of the Roman Empire, established the feudal as the best system of government. Great change of circumstances rendered it necessary for them to deviate from many of the established customs

* Asser. † William of Malmsbury.

of their native Germany, but they retained all those which were compatible with their new situation.

The feudal government was simply a confederacy of independent warriors. The chief or head of this confederacy was chosen from the rest on account of his valor; his glory and strength consisted in the number of suffrages he could thus command. Under certain conditions of society the feudal system of government was undoubtedly beneficial, especially when based, as was the Germanic, on theoretical principles of liberty, which after all have only been more practically applied in after generations. On the acquisition of fresh territory by the chief, it was customary to apportion it out among the nobles who had assisted in its conquest. The conditions imposed on the latter were, that they should hold these grants in trust for the crown. If military service were needed, they were required to repair to the field with a certain number of retainers. The peculiarity of their tenure rendered it necessary for the nobles to maintain a large retinue. In process of time these military establishments became immensely powerful. The nobles erected fortresses, castles, and other improvements, and thus in an indirect way acquired a kind of hereditary right to the lands which they merely held in trust. At length this hereditary claim became recognized, and all that was asked from the nobles was occasional military assistance when it was needed, and at other times the payment of some trifling dues. Thus the authority of the sovereign gradually decayed, and each noble, secure in his own territory, became too powerful and too dangerous to be turned out by an order of the sovereign. The interests of the nobles being reciprocal, there was no possibility of obtaining a combination against any one of the body. But, on the other hand, there was a certainty of a strong combination against the sovereign if he sought in any way to encroach on the privileges of the nobles. Such an instance occurred in the reign of King John, and resulted in the humiliation of the monarch and the triumph of the nobles. There is an old saying, that when rogues fall out honest people get their rights. In the case of the Magna Charta this was signally illustrated.

This important document, to which the Anglo-Saxon race owes so much of its freedom, renders it necessary for us to introduce that contemptibly weak prince, King John, to our readers as one of the heroes of political liberty. He was the instrument wielded by the strong arm of right, and although paltry and insignificant in himself, was important to the triumph of the moment. In dignifying King John even with this importance, we feel some reluctance. But he was the man who conceded, who had the power to concede the Great Charter. The barons who extorted that great national boon from him, were in no respect greater heroes than he. They were actuated by purely personal motives, exactly as he was. The concession of the Great Charter affords another illustration of the truth of the dogma, that "out of evil cometh good."

King John, having disgusted his people with his cowardice and duplicity, succeeded in offending the Pope, for which piece of pleasantry he was excommunicated. In those days of superstition and Pope-worship, an excommunication from Rome was a grave calamity. For a while John tried fiercely to retaliate, but he was already so odious with his people, that he could obtain but little sympathy. He was compelled to bow submission to the Papal supremacy. With the usual instincts of a coward, he was not content with submission. He thought it necessary to conciliate. Amongst other monstrous things, he assigned his kingdom to the Pope, and relinquished all claims to ecclesiastical power. Having secured, as he imagined, the powerful influence of the Pope, he determined to revenge himself on his barons, imagining, with perfect justice, that they were not well disposed towards him. Contemptible natures always nourish some idea of revenge, if at any future time they think they may have an opportunity to gratify it. Petty persecutions and gross outrages were the weapons used by John. The barons rebelled. The king desired to know what they wanted. They sent a schedule containing a list of their principal demands. It was no sooner showed to the king than he burst into a furious passion. He asked why they did not demand from him his kingdom, and swore that he would never grant them liberties, which, if granted, would make him a slave. Neither daunted by the fury nor the oath of the king, the barons forthwith levied war against him. The besieged him in his castle, and drove him to such straits, that he was at length left with a poor retinue of seven knights. He was compelled to submit at discretion.

Between Windsor and Staines, in England, is a green spot called Runnymede: it has changed but little since the days of King John, and the Englishman points to it with reverence as one of the shrines of political liberty. It was there that King John met the Barons, and signed and sealed the famous deed called the Great Charter. We need scarcely refer to this document at length. It is sufficient to say, that it restored many Saxon laws and usages (which had, under the Norman rule, sunk into abeyance), and for the first time extended equal rights to the vassals as to the lords. It is generally esteemed the foundation of modern political liberty, and was so considered by the early founders of our own republic, who made repeated reference to it in time of trouble. At all events, it has remained for some centuries the most quotable text of Liberty, and to the present day serves as the basis of more comprehensive legislation.

Nations, like individuals, experience emotions of gratitude. Give them something they can value, and they will prize it thankfully for centuries. The Magna Charta was a great boon; unquestionably radical in its day, sufficient in its operations, and liberal in its provisions. For several subsequent centuries nothing more was asked. The people were content to enjoy what they had, and to prepare themselves for more. It is in these periods of civil rest that consummate ideas of political freedom dawn in the future of history. Men have time to think. They arrive at certain fixed principles of justice and liberty. When the time comes for enunciating these principles, they have acquired all the weight and importance of privileges, and must inevitably be conceded as such. Thus, after the signing of the Magna Charta by John, we find a period of thoughtful repose. The ideas promulgated in that instrument were fermenting in men's minds. Many heroes—lacking only the stamp of success—

essayed with untimely zeal to extend the area of popular freedom. The lives of these men afford ample material for the biographer, and instructive lessons for the world. Our limits prevent any special reference to these worthies. Details must be sought in the contemporary works of history. To the dispassionate republican, there will always be an attraction in the lives of men who have striven for liberty, even if the means they adopted were erroneous, and provoked by hate and party zeal. William Wallace, Jack Cade, Monmouth, Wat Tyler, and others, were men who raised a bold front against oppression, and thus achieved a niche in the many-colored Pantheon of Liberty.

Notwithstanding the concession of the Great Charter, Liberty had two fundamental difficulties to contend with for a long time. First, the feudal despotism of the nobles; and secondly, the gradual increase of the Papal power. As an illustration of the former, we may refer to the well-known incident of Lord Warren, who, when questioned as to his title to certain lands, drew his sword, and said *that* was his title, let who would dispute it. As an illustration of overspreading Papal power, we have the exhibition of a great emperor,* clothed in sackcloth and barefooted before the palace of the Pope, standing there for three bitter winter days, suing for mercy. These incidents furnish us with an insight into the real possession of power in those days, and indicate quite clearly the shoals and quicksands on which the frail bark Political Liberty was likely to strand. Against these two evils then, Feudal and Papal power, the popular energies were long directed. Men's thoughts invested them with a thousand hideous shapes, and made them more horrible and momentous than they really were. In process of time it became quite plain, that whatever advanced the authority of either was, on the whole, unfavorable to the interests of mankind. Any thing of a contrary tendency was watched and examined with the greatest anxiety, for it gave the hope of future improvement.

It is unnecessary to dwell on the evils of an aggravated feudal

* Henry IV. of Germany.

system, or how they were slowly removed. It is sufficient for us to mention the establishment of privileged or free cities, communities, and corporations, which, in course of time, fostered a thriving commerce, and benefited the poorer class of the people, by drawing them off from the retinues of the nobles. As these towns and cities increased in importance, so did the inhabitants. They became materially leagued with the Crown, and the power of the Barons was thus assailed from without. In addition to this, the number of retainers being diminished, their absolute power and political importance began slowly to crumble.* In the war of the Holy Sepulchre, and afterwards in the wars of the Roses, the feudal Barons were decimated and nearly exterminated. As they disappeared, the lower and middle classes obtained more importance and consideration. As for the Papal power, that melted slowly but surely away in the brightening light of knowledge.

In the interval which we are now bridging, liberal ideas were beginning to be entertained with some earnestness. There was a constant struggle between prerogative and privilege, for the people began to entertain a dim perception of their rights. Many concessions were already made, and society settled down into well-defined limits, to break beyond which would be dangerous. Burgesses were summoned by Leicester, at the close of the reign of Henry III. (1265), to attend a parliament in London. These burgesses were selected from an order of men who, up to that time, had been always regarded as too mean to enjoy a place in the national councils. It was Leicester's policy to anticipate this concession, which the urgency of the people had already made inevitable. In the reign of Edward the III., the knights of the shire and the burgesses emerged into a separate house, and became what is now called the House of Commons. A vital principle began to animate the mass—the principle of self-government. Intelligence, spirit, and dignity inspired men with a knowledge of their own importance.

In the reign of Elizabeth (and indeed in several earlier ones), we

* Smith's Wealth of Nations, 3d Book.

and the monarch jealous of the privileges of the Commons, and claiming a royal prerogative in matters which the latter had taken under their especial charge. Whatever concerned the royal prerogative was considered by Elizabeth as forbidden ground, and she included within this description every thing that related to religion, to her particular courts, and to the succession to the crown; she insisted, in her own words, "that no bills touching matters of state or reformation in concerns ecclesiastical should be exhibited."* Pretensions of this character were not likely to pass current with men who already had a clear perception of their own rights and their own power. It was evident that a collision must sooner or later take place between the queen and her "faithful commons," for notwithstanding Elizabeth's remarkable popularity, there was a stern class of thinking men who remained proof to her blandishments, and thought more of liberty to the people than gallantry to the queen.

Such a man was Peter Wentworth. In this uncompromising but loyal old Puritan, we have a perfect type of the stock which peopled the Eastern portions of our own country. Fearless, clear-headed, honest, and loyal, he was not only capable of asserting the privileges of the house, but of impressing others with the exactness of his definition of them. The event which drew Wentworth out was a commission issued by the queen, directing the speaker to stop a discussion in the house, and giving orders that in future "no bills concerning religion should be preferred or received into that house, unless the same should be first considered and approved of by the clergy." This interference on the part of the queen elicited a speech from Wentworth, in which he maintained that the house was assembled to make or abrogate such laws as were for the surety, safe-keeping, and enrichment of the noble realm of England. It was necessary for this purpose to preserve such advantages by free speech: without this it were a scorn and mockery to call the parliament a place of free speech. It was nothing but "a very school of flattery and dissimulation, and so a fit place to serve the devil and his angels in, and to glorify God and benefit

* Cobbett.

the commonwealth. Waxing still more bold, he went on to say, "that to avoid everlasting death and condemnation, with the high and mighty God, we ought to proceed in every cause according to the matter, and not according to the prince's mind." In a similar strain of independent protest and argument, the patriot dwelt on the message of the queen, giving the house and her majesty some sound advice and admonition. It was not altogether acceptable to either, for, before Wentworth had finished, the house stopped him. He was sequestered for said speech, and had to answer for it before a special committee. All that passed is singularly noble. "I do promise you all," said the intrepid patriot, "if God forsake me not, that I will never during life hold my tongue if any message is sent wherein God is dishonored, the prince perilled, or the liberties of the parliament impeached." Wentworth was committed to prison; a fate which did not surprise him. In his examination before a committee, he observed: "I do assure your honors, that twenty times and more, when I walked in my grounds, revolving this speech, to prepare against this day, my own fearful conceit did say unto me that this speech would carry me to the place whither I shall now go, and fear would have moved me to put it out. Then I weighed whether in good conscience, and the duty of a faithful subject, I might keep myself out of prison, and not to warn my prince from walking in a dangerous course. My conscience said unto me, that I could not be a faithful subject if I did more respect to avoid my own danger than my prince's danger: herewithal I was made bold, and went forward, as your honors heard; yet when I uttered these words in the house, that there was none without fault—no! not our noble queen; I paused, and beheld all your countenances, and saw plainly that those words did amaze you all. Then fear bade me put out the words that followed, for your countenances did assure me that not one of you would stay me of my journey. But I spake it, and I praise God for it."

Wentworth was committed to the Tower, but Elizabeth was far too politic to allow such a man to become a martyr to the cause of popular freedom. After a month's incarceration she remitted the sentence. The toadies of the house held forth hugely on the divine leniency of the queen, with which Wentworth may or may not have been impressed. Certain it is, that eleven years afterwards he was so dissatisfied with further encroachments on the privileges of the house, that he prepared in writing a series of tough queries, which he handed to the speaker. One of these was couched in the following words: "Whether there be any council which can make, add to, or diminish from the laws of this realm, but only this council of parliament." It was reserved for another century, in which other men of Wentworth's calibre were the actors, to answer this vital question. Much trial and tribulation were undergone before the people's indignant negative was recorded in the bloody scrolls of history. To that period we will now hasten.

The most momentous political occurrence of the sixteenth century was that which provoked the document called the Petition of Rights. This was the commencement of that memorable epoch, since denominated the English Revolution, and which, resulting in the execution of Charles the First, and the Protectorate of Oliver Cromwell, effected in a remarkable degree the early characteristics of this country. It was in this epoch that the word Puritan was first used. It stood for the appellation of three parties, all of them opposed to the intolerance of King Charles's reign. There were the political Puritans, who maintained the highest principles of civil liberty; the Puritans in discipline, who were averse to the ceremonies and Episcopal government of the Church; and the doctrinal Puritans who rigidly defended the speculative system of the first reformers.*

During two preceding reigns, the English people, as we have seen, had been gradually imbibing sentiments of enlarged political and religious freedom. Elizabeth, with a tact for which she was remarkable, conceded what was necessary. But imbecile James lacked the talent and the inclination to appreciate the wants of his people. In the midst of difficulties, dissensions, and civil commotions, and at a

* Hume.

time when practical common sense was especially demanded, he wrote and published an elaborate work on the divine right of kings. The object of this ridiculous production was, to prove that kings could do no wrong; that their prerogative was from Heaven; and that any encroachment on it was flagrant heresy! James's parliament soon became refractory. Public disapprobation increased with fearful rapidity. The king endeavored to get on without a parliament, and succeeded for a while in raising funds for the State exchequer. But there was great indignation, and the grievances of the nation were all converging to a crisis. King James died on the 27th March, 1625. Under his weak rule, the spirit of liberty had grown strong, and had become equal to a great contest.*

Charles I. succeeded to the throne. He was unlike his father in many respects; but he was false, imperious, obstinate, narrow-minded, ignorant of the temper of his people, unobservant of the signs of the times,† and firm in the determination to protect what he conceived to be the prerogatives of the Crown. The spirit of reform had grown strong and muscular, but he thought he could strangle it with his weak hands. Failing in this, he tried, as the next best thing, to chastise it. Parliaments were assembled at the king's pleasure, and dissolved the moment they were found to be intractable. In consequence of the extreme difficulty with which the king raised supplies, he determined to resort to the illegal process of imposing a forced loan on the kingdom, thus subverting the entire object and usefulness of the House of Commons. Great numbers resisted this unjustifiable imposition, for which they were immediately thrown into prison. Foiled in his purpose, the king had once more to assemble parliament, and as a necessary consequence, one of the first discussions was on the late illegal proceedings of the Crown. The result of their discussions was, the document called the Petition of Right, so called because, although drawn up in the usual strain of a humble petition, it had all the force of a law on the king's endorsement of his concurrence. This document, which is justly considered the

* Macaulay. † Ibid.

second Great Charter of English liberty, was drawn up by Sir Edward Coke in the eighty-third year of his age. It was the last act of a brilliant judicial career, and is a lasting monument to Coke's patriotism and genius. It provided that no tax or loan might be levied except with the concurrence of parliament; that no man might be imprisoned but by legal process; that soldiers might not be quartered on people contrary to their will; and that no commissions be granted for executing martial law.* A few days after the receipt of the petition, the king returned an evasive answer. A discussion immediately ensued in the House of Commons. Among the eminent men who took part in it were Sir John Eliot, John Hampden, and John Pym; heroic names that adorn the brightest pages of political history.

Sir John Eliot spoke with dignity and fervor. "His mind," says Lord Nugent, "was deeply imbued with a love of philosophy and a confidence in religion, which gave a lofty tone to his eloquence." The effect of the debate was so seriously damaging to the king, and particularly to his pampered minister, Buckingham, that he could no longer withhold his consent to the Petition of Right. He gave it with surly remorse, but with a mental reservation that he would be avenged on the men who had extorted it from him. He again dissolved parliament, and determined to rule in his own right, without their aid or assistance. Two days later, he committed Sir John Eliot and other members to the Tower, on a charge of high treason. Servile courts sustained him in this flagrant breach of privilege and violation of the Petition of Right. But he was inexorable, and Eliot remained in prison—doomed to die a martyr in the cause of political liberty. After two years of wearisome confinement, his health began to fail. He petitioned for the privilege of a temporary release, that he might recuperate his sinking energies. But the king demanded concessions from him which, as an honest, high-purposed man, he could not make. Another year, passed in suffering and cruelty, terminated his life. He died in November, 1632. The vengeance of

* Goodrich.

the king continued even after his death. One of Sir John Eliot's sons petitioned for the privilege of interring the body in a distant county. The king replied, "Let him be buried in the parish where he died." Truly, Charles was one of those monarchs destined by Divine Providence to hasten revolutions.

All the promises of the king were violated; the Petition of Right forgotten; persecutions and exactions of the worst kind inflicted, particularly with regard to the Puritans. The king, who was a zealot for Church discipline, looked upon the Puritans with all the concentrated bitterness and hatred of his treacherous nature. They were forced to fly from the country. They were whipped, imprisoned, scourged, and mutilated. "But the cruelty of the oppressor could not tire out the fortitude of the victims. The mutilated defenders of liberty again defied the vengeance of the Star Chamber,—came back with undiminished resolution to the place of their glorious infamy, and manfully presented the stumps of their ears to be grubbed out by the hangman's knife."*

John Hampden was a member of the House of Commons, and, like others before referred to, opposed the assessment of the forced loan. That he did so from the highest patriotic motives, is beyond question. The sum at which he was assessed was a mere trifle, and he was a man of wealth. For this contumacy he was imprisoned. After the passing of the Petition of Right, he was released; and we do not find him taking an active part in public affairs, until the government—that is, the king—again attempted an unwarrantable exaction. A writ was issued, commanding the city of London to man and equip ships of war for his service. Similar writs were issued, not only for the seaboard counties, but the inland ones. This excessive abuse of authority created the greatest excitement. No precedent could be found, in the legislation of any other king, for such an oppressive system of taxation.

Buckinghamshire—of which county Hampden was a native—was assessed for a ship of the value of four thousand five hundred pounds.

* Macaulay.

The individual portions of this assessment were necessarily small, but every shilling subscribed towards the aggregate was the recognition of a pernicious principle. Hampden at once refused to pay his portion, and determined at all hazards to bring the matter to a crisis. Before this time, "he was rather of reputation in his own county, than of public discourse or fame in the kingdom; but then he grew the argument of all tongues, every man inquiring who and what he was that durst, at his own charge, support the liberty and prosperity of the kingdom."*

Hampden, as the representative of the people, tried the question of the illegal assessment, in the Exchequer Chamber, before all the judges of England. The fear of court displeasure possessed the bench; only four of the judges had sufficient courage to declare in Hampden's favor, although the law was clearly on his side. The remaining eight were in favor of the writ. Thus, so far as the law was concerned, justice was denied to Hampden, and, through his person, to the people. The result of this decision was, to place at the disposal of the Crown the whole property of the English nation.† A defeated man receives but little consideration from a despot. Hampden was not long in discovering that his person was scarcely safe from the fury of the king. Opposed to violence, and desiring, of all things, to save his country from the miseries of civil war, he determined to flee to a distant land, where, at least, he would be beyond the reach of oppressors. Beyond the Atlantic ocean, a few persecuted Puritans had founded a settlement, in Connecticut. Thither he determined to flee. He secured passage in a sailing vessel, and completed his arrangements for permanently vacating the land of his birth. Among others who arrived at a similar determination, were Oliver Cromwell and John Pym. This illustrious trio, so soon destined to convulse society, were on the point of sailing, when an order from the king intercepted the vessel. It seems that, although the king did not care to crush Hampden whilst public feeling was in its present state, he was yet unwilling to let him escape. He had sufficient penetration

* Clarendon.

† Macaulay.

to know that the fearless nature of the man would soon display itself, and he was content to wait.

In the next parliament, Hampden took his seat for his native shire, and thenceforth devoted himself entirely to the affairs of the nation. He was now unquestionably the most popular man in England. The king affected respect for him, but hated him bitterly. A message was sent to the House for fresh supplies. It was couched in the usual language of promise. Redress for grievances was the boon. The Commons had experienced the king's treachery, and were determined, in this case, to get what redress they needed *first.* On the next day, with an angry speech the king dissolved parliament. Such an act indicated, with very impolitic clearness, that the king expected the Commons to do precisely as he wished, or he would not allow them to sit at all.

The necessities of the king, after a most inglorious campaign in Scotland, compelled him to assemble parliament once more. On the 3d of November, 1640, the Commons met. It is a memorable day in history, being the first of what is now universally known as the Long Parliament—a parliament which, as Macaulay forcibly expresses it, was destined to every extreme of fortune: to empire and to servitude,—to glory and to contempt; at one time the sovereign of its sovereign,—at another time, the servant of its servants, and the tool of its tools. The first session of this memorable parliament was spent in actively redressing public grievances. All those who had assisted in subverting the laws, including the judges who had officiated on Hampden's trial, were tried. The prime minister, Strafford, was executed; and other prominent characters, to escape a similar fate, fled the country in alarm.

The conduct of Hampden during this crisis was moderate, manly, and peaceful. He was opposed to extreme measures, apprehending a reaction. He seemed disposed to soothe rather than excite the public mind.* The king, humiliated and crest-fallen, had taken refuge from obloquy in Scotland. Hampden was dispatched by the

* Clarendon.

parliament to visit him there. During his absence, measures of an extreme character were enacted, and what Hampden had wisely dreaded came to pass. A reactionary party sprung up, formed of men who thought that enough had been done, and that possibly too much might be attempted. Encouraged by these new manifestations, Charles returned. All that was now necessary for the permanence of his crown was, that he should abstain from treachery, from violence, from gross breaches of the law.*

This was expecting too much from a man so abject, cowardly, and treacherous. With his usual volubility he promised every thing, and with his customary duplicity, violated all his promises. Without the slightest intimation of displeasure, he impeached several of the leading members of the house. Hampden and Pym were of course among the number. Such an instance of perfidious tyranny was unparalleled. The House of Commons refused to surrender their members, maintaining that the impeachment coming from the House of Peers was unconstitutional. Not to be defeated in his purpose, the king, accompanied by two hundred soldiers of his guard, made a descent on the house with the intention of seizing the contumacious members by force. They had been previously warned of their danger, and had fled to a populous district of London, where they were sure of the sympathies of the citizens. A proclamation was issued by the king, directing that no person should harbor the fugitives, but it came too late. The spark had been ignited, and the explosion followed with fearful rapidity.

The tramp of armed citizens was heard in every corner of the great city. All the societies turned out in battle array. A careful watch was kept on every approach leading to the neighborhood in which Hampden and Pym lay. Every one, from the youngest apprentice to the oldest merchant, was on the alert to avenge the insult offered to their liberty. After a short delay the members were invited, in defiance of the king's proclamation, to attend their seats in the House of Commons. The immense population of London turned

* Macaulay.

out *en masse* to escort them in triumph past the windows of the palace. "On the 11th January," says Macaulay, "the Thames was covered with boats, and its shores with a gazing multitude. Armed vessels, decorated with streamers, were ranged in two lines from London Bridge to Westminster Hall. The members returned by water in a ship, manned by sailors who had volunteered their services. The train bands of the city, under the command of the sheriffs, marched along the Strand, attended by a vast crowd of spectators, to guard the avenues to the House of Commons, and thus with shouts, and loud discharges of ordnance, the accused patriots were brought back by the people whom they had served, and for whom they had suffered." On the day preceding this great demonstration, the king fled. The excitement was not confined to London only. Throughout the provinces the people were agitated in a like manner. Buckinghamshire dispatched a deputation of four thousand freeholders to defend the person of their beloved representative, and other counties did the same. The crisis had indeed come.

It was evident that the king could no longer be trusted. The only way to prevent his doing injury to the liberal cause, was to deprive him of the power. A fearful struggle was inevitable. The king was already in the field with a numerous retinue.

Hampden was a man who loved peace, so long as peace could be honorably maintained; but he was not a man to be daunted by the flashing of hostile swords. He had been the consistent advocate of moderation. Whilst the laws could be appealed to for redress, he was content to depend on their efficacy. Finding them utterly useless, he prepared to leave his country. Foiled in this endeavor, he boldly faced the evils of the day. Almost exacting a representative privilege, he took on himself the grievances of his countrymen, and battled for them with unflinching valor. Thus when recent events had made civil war imperative, we find Hampden stepping into the foremost place with unconscious activity and bravery. He placed a large portion of his fortune at the service of parliament; raised, armed, and, at his own expense, equipped a regiment of Buckinghamshire cavalry, and took his place at their head as colonel. Military discipline—usually so obnoxious to civilians—fell on him like a garment. He was ever on the alert, and never missed an opportunity that might be improved by intrepidity and activity. It is not easy to do full justice to the admirable rapidity of Hampden's movements. He was constantly in the saddle, and really seemed ubiquitous. A lampoon aimed at him by a political opponent is immensely funny at his incessant journeys between Windsor and the House of Commons. He was constantly hurrying from the field to the house.

It would be an endless task to recapitulate these events of the civil war in which Hampden took a conspicuous part. It must suffice that wherever there was an opportunity for displaying an unselfish patriotism, there he was found. Unhappily his career of usefulness was not destined to be of long duration. On the 18th of June, 1643, Hampden gathered his men at Chalgrove for the purpose of cutting off the retreat of a band of cavaliers who had been on a foraging excursion. A fierce conflict ensued. In the charge, Hampden received his death-wound—inflicted by two bullets in the shoulder. With head drooping and hands leaning on his horse's neck, he rode faintly from the field of battle. After several days of intense physical suffering, the shadows of death thickened round his pillow. With invincible fortitude he dispatched what public business most demanded his attention. When his last national duties were discharged, he calmly prepared himself to die. He asked for the consolation of the Holy Sacrament, and it was administered to him. When the hand of death lay coldly on him, he murmured short prayers for the cause in which he perished. "Lord Jesus, receive my soul—O Lord, save my country—O Lord, be merciful to"—. In that broken sentence passed away a man whose every act was one of unselfish patriotism and unconscious virtue; a man whose life is of such refulgent brightness, that time will in vain seek to dim its lustre.

John Pym, who was intimately associated with Hampden in all the important events of this epoch, was born of good parents in Somersetshire, in the year 1584. He received his education at Oxford, and at an early age received an appointment in the office of the Exchequer. He was distinguished for his eloquence, and knowledge of the common law. He served in several parliaments during the latter part of the reign of James I., as member for Tavistock, and in all those held in the reign of Charles I. He distinguished himself by his zeal in defending the rights of the people against the aggressions of royalty. In 1626 he was one of the principal managers of the impeachment against Buckingham. After the opening of the Long Parliament, Pym took an active part in the vigorous legislation of that tribunal. He classed the grievances of the nation under three heads: Privilege of Parliament, Religion, Liberty of the Subject. The termination of this consideration resulted in the impeachment and execution of Strafford. The latter was at one time attached to the popular side, but became an apostate to the court. When he had determined on acting thus treacherously, he sent for Pym, and endeavored by specious arguments to win him to a similar line of conduct. Pym listened to him impatiently for a while, then turning on him furiously said, "You need not use all this art to tell me that you are going to be undone: but remember, that though you leave us now, I will never leave you while your head is upon your shoulders." He kept his word too.

To appreciate the services of Pym, it is necessary to realize the peculiar characteristics of the age in which he lived. Government was subverted by the treachery of the king, and the unscrupulous co-operation of his minions. In the effort to restore the privileges of parliament, and thereby the liberty of the subject, great personal courage and invincible integrity were demanded. By intimidation or by corruption, all the reformers were silenced, that were capable of ignominious silence. Only those who entertained genuine sentiments of patriotism,—men who recognized danger as an element of their success,—were able to withstand the alternate bullying and flattery of the court. A conspicuous member of the House of Commons, like Pym, excited peculiar hatred. His life was in constant danger. Any one of the many high-handed outrages of the king might have placed Pym's head upon the block. But he did not swerve from the path of duty. Threats and bribes were alike unavailing. With fearless energy and burning eloquence, he denounced the oppressors—never once looked back, but with eyes sternly fixed on the future, righted what was wrong. The impeachments of the Long Parliament were conducted mainly by Pym; and in consequence, more than an ordinary share of danger attended his proceedings. For these and other reasons, he is justly estimated one of England's worthies, and one who in no slight degree contributed to the establishment of political liberty.

The hostilities between the soldiers of the people and the soldiers of the king, now assumed the grave form of a civil war. Charles, as we have already stated, sought refuge in the camp of the Scots—a people thoroughly enamored of monarchical institutions, but influenced, at this crisis, by considerations of a religious character. Had Charles possessed the tact to conciliate their Presbyterian spirit, or even to abandon some of his own Episcopalian dogmas, he could undoubtedly have depended on the valor and loyalty of his Scotch adherents. As it was, they basely sold him to the parliament.

At this stage of civil discord, there appeared a man who must ever absorb attention. Suddenly emerging from pursuits of a quiet agricultural character, Oliver Cromwell darts through the pages of history like a fierce meteor. It is only of late years that his real character has begun to be understood. The patient industry and impartiality of Carlyle have been effectual to rescue the memory of this great hero from the obloquy with which it had so long been covered.

Oliver Cromwell was born at Huntingdon, England, in 1599. He was descended of a well-born family. "I was by birth," said Cromwell, in one of his speeches to parliament, "neither living in any considerable height, nor yet in obscurity." Oliver's education was commenced at the grammar-school of his native town, and completed at Sydney Sussex College, Cambridge. He appears to have been wild and roystering during the youthful portion of his life. In 1620 he returned home, was married, and took up his position as the respectable head of a household. About this time he became oppressed by convictions of conscience almost amounting to insanity. He sat about retrieving some of his former errors; made himself bankrupt by paying back sums of money he had formerly won at play; and declared that he was ready to make restitution to any whom he had wronged. The persecuted Puritans found a welcome refuge beneath his roof. In the third parliament of Charles I., he sat as the representative of his native town; and although not a prominent actor in the events of that period, was a keen and anxious observer of what transpired.

After the parliament had been dissolved, Cromwell returned to St. Ives (a town in the vicinity of Huntingdon), and for five years was a grazing farmer. His demeanor was characterized by religious severity. There is now no reasonable doubt for supposing that it was insincere. "He had certainly materials enough for reflection. Not to speak of the inward conflicts of his own mind—conflicts arising from the views of truth he had been recently led to take—deep, earnest, heaven-born impulses—society round him was raging like a volcano. * * * * The writs of ship-money had been issued, and Hampden had stood resolute in its refusal. The thunder-storm was rising."*

The moment for action arrived, and Cromwell, feeling himself inspired for great actions, did not longer hesitate. When the attempt to seize the five members was made by Charles, he rushed at once to the rescue. His influence, his purse, his sword, were at the nation's call. He was appointed captain, and, soon after, colonel of the sixty-seventh troop of the parliamentary forces. But he was dissatisfied with the troops. "They were," he complained, "old decayed serving-men, and tapsters, and such kind of fellows." To organize a different corps was with him a simultaneous thought and action. The members of this corps were men who, stimulated by similar religious zeal as Cromwell, were prepared to understand and appreciate his acts. "I had rather have a plain russet-coated captain," he said,

* Triall.

"that knows what he fights for, and loves what he knows, than that which you call a gentleman, and is nothing else." The terrible "Ironsides" was the corps thus raised.

It is impossible for us to follow Cromwell in his military expeditions against the royalists and other enemies of his country. Wherever he appeared, victory crowned the day. His activity and decision were marvellous, and in every kind of military tactic, it is doubtful if England has ever had his superior. Charles was decapitated, and Cromwell appointed Protector. Under his administration, popular freedom received much invigorating support. Indeed, it must be a matter of surprise with all dispassionate thinkers, how he could have accomplished so much, surrounded as he was by jealousies, hatreds, and intimidations. He appointed for judges the most upright and distinguished men,—among others Sir Matthew Hale. He never interfered with the courts of justice. In religion, he was as tolerant as any man living in that age, and belonging to the Puritan party, could be. He promoted the arts and sciences, and helped, by decisive legislation, to lay the foundation of a great nation. Usurpers must be tyrants, but whilst they tyrannize, they try to conciliate. If Cromwell were "a scourge of God," Charles had prepared the nation for its infliction; and if Charles was a mild tyrant, Cromwell was moderate as a despot.* Charles was beheaded to insure justice to the people, and Cromwell would have met with a similar fate, but for his superior justice, vigor, and forethought. The hypocrisy of Cromwell has been a standing theme with historians. But there is no reasonable ground for supposing that he acted otherwise than from conscientious conviction. The publication of his most private letters indicate clearly, that what he professed in public, he believed in private. A charge of hypocrisy is a common way of assailing the reputation of a Puritan, particularly by men who believe in the possibility of wearing religion like a garment, for decency's sake. He must be strangely constituted who, while reading Cromwell's letters, and there viewing his private life, can discern nothing in him but

* History of Democracy.

unmingled dissimulation.* The present age is doing him justice, spite of kings, queens, and houses of lords. His memory is cherished, and he may yet be invoked when the country which gave him birth is convulsed in the throes of civil war and revolution.

One of the sincerest republicans of Cromwell's epoch, was that illustrious man who afterwards wrote the sublime poem of "Paradise Lost." John Milton was Latin secretary to the new council of state, and in every official act proved that he was the consistent advocate of political liberty. To an extent he was a hero in the cause. That sad calamity with which he was afflicted in the latter years of his life, is said to have been produced by the severe devotion with which he applied himself to the composition of a work entitled "Defensio pro Populo Anglicano." Salmasius had written a defence of monarchy, and particularly of Charles I., under the title of "Defensio Regis." Milton's work was a reply to this, and exhibited so much learning and fervid eloquence, that his opponent was completely overwhelmed. Close application, midnight toil, and intense study were necessary for the composition of this able defence of popular rights against monarchical pretension. Milton was frequently told by his physicians that it would result in blindness, but he was far too earnest to heed their warning advice. Total loss of sight was the result. He was not cast down even with this calamity. The moment he had recovered from the first shock of its intensity, he set about writing another *defence of the people of England.*

On the death of Cromwell, Milton employed his pen with great vigor to check the prevalent feeling in favor of the Restoration. Unable to do so, he sought refuge in the house of a friend. In the act of indemnity which followed, his name found no exception. With many others he was given into the custody of the sergeant-at-arms. After a while he was released. In impoverished circumstances, he sought the tranquil pleasures of poetic studies. To his withdrawal from the political arena we are indebted for that lasting monument of sublime genius, the "Paradise Lost."

* Triall.

Before quitting this prolific period of effort and achievement, it may be profitable to refer to an invaluable document obtained after much trouble from the government of Charles II. We refer to the Habeas Corpus Act: arbitrary imprisonment became impossible after its passage. By this act it was prohibited to send any one to prison beyond sea. No judge, under severe penalties, was permitted to refuse a prisoner a writ of habeas corpus, on the issuing of which the jailor was required to produce in court the body of the prisoner (whence the name), and to certify the cause of his detention and imprisonment. If the jail lie within twenty miles of the judge, the writ must be obeyed in three days, and so for greater distances. Every prisoner must be indicted the first term after his commitment, and brought to trial in the subsequent term. And no man, after being discharged, can be recommitted for the old offence.* The general freedom of the subject is thus secured. No man could be incarcerated on mere suspicion or caprice. Cause had to be shown why he was detained, and he had an early opportunity of appealing to a jury for his discharge. The Magna Charta, the Petition of Right, and the Habeas Corpus Act, completed the English Constitution, and gave an impetus to popular liberty, which has been gaining in momentum from that day to the present. The Constitution of the United States is based on the principles of these three great documents. The struggles which wrenched them from the iron claw of prerogative, must always be interesting to the American, forming as they do the antecedent history of his own country.

All that is necessary for the completion of this chapter is the addition of one more great political triumph; need we say—the American Revolution? The student of history, if he seek to trace and connect the great chain of Anglo-Saxon triumphs, lights on this naturally as the last and greatest of them all. It is a necessary sequence; a point at which the mind rests, and expatiates with confidence and delight. In the Declaration of Independence is epitomized all those incontrovertible truths, which are at once the wealth and the glory of the Anglo-Saxon race.

* Hume.

In dealing with the preceding topics, we have been compelled on several occasions to refer to the peculiar religious characteristics of the times, and in glancing hastily at our history, we are confronted with the same difficulty. The Puritans, as they were called, were men who stamped the age with a peculiar individuality. They were not only men who thought, but men who *felt* with the keenness of thought. The grievous oppressions of the Star Chamber were not secret wrongs with such men, but intolerable public calamities, which it were well to flee from. Their consciences, as well as their bodies, were endangered. The Puritans everywhere fled, preferring the dangers and vicissitudes of a home in the wilderness, to the emasculate freedom of their own native homes.

Arrived in the new land, they were under no apprehensions concerning their individual liberty. With no kingly foe to oppress them, they were secure—at all events for the present. Their danger lay in the possibility of religious dissension. It was for their religion they were obnoxious at home; they had been persecuted for it, and if they now strove with more firmness than liberality to preserve it, some excuse can surely be made for them. The Puritans on board the Mayflower, before landing, united upon a compact in which they solemnly covenanted with each other to combine into a civil body politic, for their better ordering and protection, and to enact, constitute, and frame such just and equal laws, ordinances, acts, constitutions, and offices, from time to time, as should be thought meet and convenient for the general good of the colony. These just and equal laws would scarcely be considered so in the present day, but they had the advantage of simplicity. The social compact thus entered into has generally been looked upon as an extraordinary document. It marked with boldness a circle of freedom, and recognized the great principles of justice and equality.

The government of the colonists resembled a theocracy in its form. Every thing was subservient to the Church. Deficiencies in the legal code were avowedly to be remedied by "the Word of God," and public questions were more often determined from the pulpit than the bench. Nothing approaching liberty of conscience was permitted. It was denounced as compaction with the devil. In 1648, these acts of the Puritans appear to have been a little grievous. Some of the colonists petitioned the session for their rights "as English subjects," and the petitioners expressed their opinion that the Puritan government was an ill-compacted vessel. In return for this piece of criticism, the petitioners were fined, and told, bluntly, to mind their own business for the future. Political authority was entirely absorbed by the Church, and was hurled from the pulpit with fierce ardor. Every man who had the temerity to claim equal political liberties, was persecuted in the courts, and denounced in the churches. Indeed, the church-members generally appear to have been pursued in a most remorseless manner.

The early settlers in Virginia were, at first, merely speculators,—and singularly unfortunate they were in their speculation. When, however, the tide of emigration began to flow steadily towards their shores, they were recuperated with some of the best blood of the old country. It was a complaint in that colony that too many "gentlemen" were sent there. In the first vessels dispatched by the London company, there were but twelve laborers, four carpenters, and a few other mechanics. The remainder of the one hundred and five passengers were "gentlemen." The Virginians were Episcopalians, disposed to be moderate and accommodating. But they too, like their brethren of Plymouth, thought a great deal of their consciences. The first extant laws of Virginia relate more to the moral well-being of the inhabitants, than their worldly prosperity. Virginia, together with Maryland and the West India islands, adhered to the cause of the king. Irritated by this, the government fitted out expeditions against those places, and required from them an engagement to be true and loyal to the commonwealth of England, as now constituted, without king, and without House of Lords. In Massachusetts, after the Restoration, a different difficulty was experienced. It took the worthy Puritans of that State a period of twelve months to make up their minds whether or not they should proclaim King Charles II.

When they had concluded to do so, they published an ordination prohibiting all unseemly or disorderly demonstrations of joy.

In a theological point of view, we find strange contrarieties in the history of America, not the least being the palpable intolerance which, for nearly a century, tyrannized over the hearts and minds of its inhabitants. But, on the other hand, this same history is the most consistent in the world, so far as unhesitating resistance to royal prerogative was concerned. The settlers looked on their various charters as the fundamental justification of all their acts. "They contented themselves with the powers conferred upon them by their respective charters, without looking beyond the seal of the royal parchment for the measure of their rights and the rule of their duties."* They would on no account consent to an appeal to England, not even during the Commonwealth. All they would consent to, was to send out commissioners to explain why they had not paid their debts. They preferred settling every other difficulty amongst themselves, "on consideration that if we should put ourselves under the protection of parliament, we must then be subject to all such laws as they should make; in which course, though they should intend our good, yet it might prove very prejudicial to us."†

No kind of political concession was ever made by the Puritans, either to the king's commission, when headed by Laud, or, subsequently, to the commissioners sent out by the Long Parliament. In 1672, when a custom-house was attempted to be established, the Bostonians quietly evaded its exactions, and refused, in the most contemptuous manner, to pay any kind of attention to Randolph, or his customs either. The ridiculous dilemma in which the latter found himself, compelled him to return to England. He returned later, armed with greater powers, and encountered the same resistance—as, in turn, did the colonial governors appointed by the home government. The Puritans were, from first to last, thoroughly intractable. They denied the justice of English prerogative, and fought for every inch of privilege in the sternest manner. They would not admit that

* John Quincy. † Winthrop.

England had any thing at all to do with them, and distinctly asserted that there was not the shadow of pretext for her interference in American affairs. The same spirit, in the American Revolution, inspired the courageous hearts of the citizens of all the colonies; and the result was — the triumph of freedom in the New World. The sacrifices suffered, and the blood spilt by the HEROES OF THE FOUNDERS OF LIBERTY had, at the appointed time, produced their fruits.

THE BOUNDARIES OF COUNTRIES—HOW ESTABLISHED.

> "Westward the Star of Empire takes it way,
> The four first acts already past,—
> A fifth shall close the drama with the day;
> Time's noblest offspring is the last."
>
> BISHOP BERKELEY.

NATURE fixes her limits to all things. Her laws are too deeply engraven on the world, to be transcended by any power less than her own. Man may be impelled by ambition to compass certain ends, but these impulsive sallies are harmoniously governed by the requirements of Nature; and what at the first promised only antagonism and consequent confusion, is found in the end to be tranquilly obedient to the most comprehensive and beautiful laws.

To one who will sit down reflectingly, with the world's map before him, it will be apparent that Nature has from the beginning fixed boundaries to every country; and furthermore, that these boundaries are unalterable. It is useless attempting to set aside her suggestions; they are immutable. Whatever hint she has thrown out, carries with it all the authority of a law. Her finger points to no great fact in the formation of the world, that is not of itself, sufficient to give shape to all human histories, and color to the events of a long procession of centuries.

The countries of Asia lie separated, either by long chains of towering mountains, stretching away from point to point, until one is completely walled in, and the rest walled out; or by vast deserts, uninhabitable by man, trackless, bare of vegetation, destitute of animal life, and altogether desolate. Across these wastes, invading forces in any great number would hardly come. Surrounded by them, a nation may repose in all the security of massive walls and armed forts. They are as fixed boundaries for a country, as if the population had caused them to be placed there. Large inland seas offer a like security, as, for instance, the Persian Gulf, lying between Arabia and Persia; the Red Sea, between Arabia and Africa; the Caspian, between Circassia and Tartary; or the Japan Sea, dividing the peoples of two monstrously overgrown empires.

Asia, however, is thoroughly cut up into principalities and dominions by her lines of mountains—the Great and Little Altai, separating the colossal power of Russia from the vast Chinese Empire; the Himalaya, keeping the Chinese Empire in turn distinct from India; the Beloor mountains, lifting their shoulders between the same empire and Tartary the Independent; and the Hindoo Koosh, drawing the line between Tartary and Afghanistan. The whole face of that quarter of the world has been thus accurately parcelled out to those who dwell upon it.

In Africa the truth is no less plain. The Barbary States can extend no further south than to the great Desert of Sahara; Soudan, beginning with the southernmost limit of the desert, stops at the barrier interposed by the Mountains of the Moon; the countries along the western coast reach into the dim confines of Ethiopia, where all is unknown in that land of the Sun.

Europe, peopled by a great variety of races, obeys minutely these physical laws. Her nations are so many, that smaller boundaries are necessary, and become objects of grave political consideration. As civilization advances from the East, it seems to grow correspondingly jealous of its rights and privileges; rivers, lakes, channels, and mountains are impressed into her service. Behold the Alps, lofty and grand, walling in the independent little region called Switzerland, a name that invariably summons the word Liberty to the tongue. There are the Pyrenees, eternal bounds for both France and Spain; the Scandinavian chain, parting Norway and Sweden as naturally as if that were the single purpose of their erection. There stretch along the Carpathians, hemming in Austria from Prussia and Russia.

We need but to glance at the course of the immortal Rhine, to believe, with the great Napoleon, that nature intended it for the eastern limit to France. The Danube, with its numerous mouths, forms a natural boundary to Turkey and her Principalities against Russia and Austria. The Rhine again performs its part in dividing one petty German kingdom from another; and the Tornea completes the work for Sweden, against Russia, which the Gulf of Bothnia seems to have left unfinished. A narrow channel alone separates England from France—two nations whose boast it is that they combinedly stand in the front of the world. Denmark is hemmed in by a couple of channels, from both Norway and Sweden. Sweden, in turn, rests secure against Russia, with the Baltic and the Gulf of Bothnia interposed between them.

In all these national divisions, the hand of Nature is but too apparent. Her suggestions must everywhere be obeyed. Whoever deliberately opposes *them*, thinking by the force of his own will to change these natural limits, is surely throwing himself upon a stone that will in the end grind him to powder.

Poor Poland! she has no boundaries at all! An open plain, she became the prey of nations stronger than herself. She has no mountains to keep imperial Russia back; none to hold in check the rulers of Prussia; none to shut out the cruel forces of the more cruel House of Hapsburg. She encamped on a broad plain; and there was she stealthily surrounded and set upon by three robbers with crowns upon their brows, and her nationality, bleeding and dying, torn limb from limb. Yet let us hope that Poland *has a future*, and that the morning of her resurrection is approaching.

"Plains are the proper territories of tyranny. There the arms of a usurper may extend themselves with ease, leaving no corner unoccupied in which patriotism might shelter or treason hide. But mountains, glens, morasses, and lakes set *bounds* to conquest; and amidst these is the impregnable seat of Liberty." This is lamentably true in the case of Poland. On the other hand, the freedom that has lived through the storms of so many years, amidst the mountain-heights of

Switzerland, proves the justice of the observation. And where have men, single-handed, as it were, offered such bold, resolute, and defiant opposition to all the usurpations of tyranny, as in the mountains of Scotland? The tales of her heroes make one's blood tingle with admiration. The names of Wallace and Bruce, engraven on the heart of every real lover of freedom, will live till the "last syllable of recorded time." Their examples will never die, but the spirit of Freedom which breathes through them, will move forward in silence, but with power, till the whole globe is finally encircled in its blessed embrace.

On this Western continent, nations have as yet hardly settled themselves in their natural positions. As it is a comparatively new field of operation, so must many things that are esteemed fixed in the Old World, continue for a long time in a state of transition. Principles may be established, yet, from their very nature, they may keep all persons in a state of perpetual activity. Such are the principles of popular liberty—offering freedom to every man, opening grand fields for the exercise of his various powers, and inciting him to continued exertion.

The original thirteen States lay stretched along the Atlantic coast. In their front was a vast ocean; in their rear an almost impenetrable wilderness. Little did the early settlers think that small beginning was to result, least of all to result so speedily, in the subjugation of a broad continent to the purposes of a high civilization. Their first thought was for their own protection. They sought to command an independent subsistence. In industry, in heroic resolve and action, in energy and persistent endurance, no people ever lived who were their superiors. In taking wise thought for themselves, they seem never to have forgotten the great and distinctive principles on which their political system was founded. It was self-preservation; but that involved something far more lofty than mere selfishness. Periling their lives and fortunes in defence of their convictions, they did not forget, in the flush of success, the cause on which their very lives depended. To men actuated by such principles, ordinary natural boundaries could offer but trifling impediments in the work upon which they were engaged. The spirit of their principles was expansive, perpetually enlarging its limits. Our fathers settled the whole of the immense tract extending from Maine to Georgia. Every imaginable tie held together the people at the extremes of the Union, equally with those who were neighbors. The purpose that pervaded all hearts alike, and cemented the union which a common interest had been instrumental in forming, was one that readily leaped the widest streams, and found its way over the highest mountains. It was no more to be controlled by the limits of natural bounds, than the silent and mysterious passage of light could be checked by the impotent ordering of man.

If now we direct our attention to the map of the United States, we shall see that Nature had apparently set no limits to the growth of this nation, save perhaps the Mississippi River, the Rocky Mountains, or the Pacific Ocean. Our march was still westward, in obedience to the inexorable law. Forests fell, as if by magic, before the ringing axe of our sturdy pioneers. Broad fields lay extended in the sunlight, where, but a short time before, wild beasts found their coverts and hunted their prey. Acre after acre waved with the bending wheat and rye, and gleamed with the yellow gold of ripening corn. Cabins dotted the hillsides, and mill-wheels flashed in the running streams. Hamlets grew and thickened. Villages everywhere gave a new life and light to the landscape. Towns and cities sent up their busy hum, and the air was alive with the sounds and voices of intelligent and independent industry.

In an incredibly short time, State after State was added to the confederacy, wheeling into the ranks with all the order and precision of a military manœuvre. Each remained an independent power, yet materially contributed to the strength of the confederacy. The troubles that were so readily imagined for us, as a consequence of such rapid and unexampled growth, all dissipated like dew before the morning sun. Those who watched our course with critical eyes, could not understand that the very spirit of our institutions begat *harmony*, and not *discord;* that it had no relation to conquest, nor even to a selfish ambition, but that it exerted itself rather upon the convictions and feelings of men, than upon either their will or their power of resistance. It appealed only to men's volition, never to their obstinacy. It sought only to win over, never to compel. The first fruit of such a spirit could not fail to be peace.

We kept growing at the same unparalleled rate continually. We reached the Mississippi and the Mexican Gulf. Here, said some of our wisest statesmen, we will rest. "Thus far, and no farther." But the great coil of events in our national history was only beginning to run out. It would be a long time before we should come to the end. The spirit of enterprise, the highest characteristic of the American people, was nowise content to rest here. The great Mississippi poured itself into the Gulf; but why could it not wash States on *both* shores as well as on *one?* Was that turbid current a sufficient limit for the energies of free culture and free institutions? The indomitable men of the nation said No, and forward went the work of settling and civilizing an entire continent.

Texas was with us, and became a part of us. We founded a great and powerful State on the Pacific shore, as if to be a new inducement to draw us over the mountains and deserts that lay between. Oregon claimed a place by our side, her people and ours being one in sympathy, as they were in blood and education. And the great Western and Northwestern Territories were finally partitioned out, receiving their names and forms of government. The inquiry was next made,—Are not the *Rocky Mountains* a natural division for the country? But the question seems suddenly to have answered itself. Already we have *crossed* the Rocky Mountains. We have *conquered* them. They are no longer impassable. We have friends, neighbors, sons, brothers, who inhabit that far-off land. The very *ideas* of boundary, which they once so naturally excited in our minds, have fallen away upon a nearer acquaintance with them, and now hardly exist at all.

This age of steam and lightning, of discovery and perpetual application, is performing incredible things in bringing distant places and people together. It seems almost to keep abreast with sympathy itself in the race. The spirit that vitalizes it, tunnels mountains, bridges our widest rivers, leaps deserts at a single bound, and stops only with the vast ocean itself. Our brethren in California and Oregon are not more distant from us to-day, than were the early settlers of Ohio but thirty years ago. Nothing could have worked such a revolution but a radical change, or progressiveness, in ideas. Distance itself has not diminished, but its effects have been reduced in estimation. We are put in closer communication this day with our brethren on the far-off Pacific shore, than we formerly were with the pioneers on our Western frontiers. Nothing has wrought this great change but our own efforts. Our energy and enterprise have accomplished all. And what yet remains undone, the coming years will certainly behold completely realized.

Perhaps with different institutions, some such natural barrier as the Rocky Mountains present, would fix a final limit to their progress. Under forms of government that hold men as mere *subjects*, such an obstacle might prevail; but under ours, wherein each man is considered a *citizen*, such a chain of mountains but creates an additional spur to enterprise. Educated to the most liberal and comprehensive habits of thought, our minds seem only to expand with the contemplation of these things, and our ideas sympathize with the geographical magnitude of our rivers, plains, and mountains. Freedom may perch upon the summits of that rocky chain, and descend thence into the broad valleys on either side; but monarchy would be unable to breathe so pure and bracing an atmosphere. They may stand as landmarks,—scarred, whitened, and time-honored; but never need they stand as limits either to civilization or the living spirit that holds us together as a mighty people. On to the ocean! There can be no natural boundary but its shore. There this great Republic rests; there its ships anchor. We are ready to accept no confines, save those vast oceans that wash with their never-sleeping waves our eastern and western coasts!

In time, greater things are destined to be accomplished. New

Mexico is ours; shall not the whole empire of Cortez be ours, not by force, or conquest, or fraud, but in obedience to the same laws that have extended our institutions across this continent? Will not that enfeebled and enervate nation in time awake to the real blessings of self-government, of industry, of enterprise, and of free institutions? And Central America,—is there any hindrance to her many petty powers throwing aside their differences, and coming peacefully and hopefully under the influence of this large family of States? Cuba was plainly intended by nature as the key to the great valley of the Mississippi, and will yet be knocking at our doors, for the day cannot be far distant when she will be *free*.

On the north, we see no reason why the great lakes interpose any boundary between ourselves and Canada. We see not why all will not yet become UNITED AMERICA. We are not able to understand why an imaginary parallel of latitude should keep the spirit of free thought back, dooming it to a tract that has been bounded and surveyed by the *dictum* of a purely arbitrary power. The new reciprocity treaty is a long step in the direction desired. The Provinces on the east are separated only by lines that may be easily wiped out, but not at all by any such great and deep differences in sympathy as divide nations. Their natural interests are in common with our own. Their modes of thinking continually assimilate to ours. Their pursuits require the same perseverance and courage in order to attain like results. And it can hardly be questioned that the logical course of events will in due time bring them also, peacefully and voluntarily, into this extended federal compact. Our boundaries are wide apart, and contain territory enough to sustain a countless population. Under free institutions like ours, all may rise to the level of their true destiny; individual selfishness and usurpation cease, and nothing but wishes for the common good be in the ascendant. Who can clearly predict the condition of our country in the far-off future? We are alive with hope,—a hope that blazes with a brighter and still brighter illumination, lighting us along on the broad pathway of *realization*.

ROMANISM AND FREEDOM.

> "By the patriot's hallowed rest,
> By the warrior's gory breast,
> Never let our graves be prest
> By a despot's throne."
> PIERREPONT.

The advocates of Romanism claim that she is the patron of learning and of freedom!—the encourager of free thought, free opinion, and free expression; and there are some favorite examples quoted to maintain this monstrous proposition. The Magna Charta, the very groundwork of freedom, is held up as the fruit of Catholic liberality, and so continually announced in our Legislative Halls, from the stump, and in flaming editorials. Unfolding the page of history, we find that John, king of England, engaged in a controversy with the Pope, which resulted in the king's yielding up his possessions to the Holy See, and receiving them back as a vassal. The proud Barons, who at the time possessed no defined rights, could not brook the insults and degradation which were heaped upon them through the weakness of their king, and solemnly demanded, for their protection, what is now known as the Magna Charta. In the struggle between the lords and the crown, the Pope took part with John against the Barons, and brought the whole of his temporal and spiritual power to defeat their demands. Against them Pope Innocent, from the Council of Lateran, thundered his bulls of excommunication:—"We will have you to know, that in General Council we have excommunicated and anathematized, in the name of the Father, and the Son, and the Holy Ghost, in the name of the Apostles Peter and Paul, and in our own name, the Barons of England, with their partisans and abettors, for persecuting John, the illustrious King of England, who has taken the cross, and is a vassal of the Roman Church, for striving to deprive him of a kingdom, which is known to belong to the Roman Church."

The example of France, which has in modern times shaken off a tyrannical monarchy, and made approaches towards republican institutions, has been held up as a testimony that Romanism favors liberty. The French people always resisted, more perseveringly than those of any other Catholic country, the assumptions of Popery; to France, the world is indebted, not only for Catholics imbued with a true spirit of Christianity, but also for some of the most powerful writers against the assumptions of the Holy See. The Kings of France ever contended for the right of appointing their own Bishops, and it was only under monarchs most deeply imbued with Romanism that France found her greatest tyrants. Of late years, as the light of true liberty has made encroachments upon the domain of despotism, it has modified the illiberality of darker times, and one of the first fruits of the late popular revolutions in that country was the separation of Church and State, and protection to every religious belief. But France, liberal as her people naturally are, is yet too much under the influence of Roman supremacy to be quoted as an example of religious toleration.

It seems but yesterday that Rome herself woke from her long night of slavery, and declaring herself free, her spiritual and temporal despot, the Pope, fled from her walls, and took refuge in Gaeta. The regenerated Romans offered to receive the Pope as their spiritual head, but resolutely insisted on the abolition of his temporal power, and that of his tyrannical cardinals. The overture was scorned, and the work of their subjugation to despotism was assigned to France, and, in spite of her Republicanism, the lingering slavery of priestcraft was so wrought into the blood and bones of her rulers and her soldiery, that she accepted the work, marched her armies on Rome, bombarded and carried the city by assault, and crushed the new Republic and the liberals of Italy in the dust.

Maryland, settled under the auspices of Cecil Calvert, a Catholic, and by its charter granting popular liberty and religious freedom, has been held up as an example of Catholic toleration. The wily Bishop, the innocent layman, and the designing politician, can never sufficiently eulogize the liberality that characterized that Colonial government, where, in times of universal intolerance, men could live unmolested in the enjoyment of the rights of conscience. If this were the result of the direct interference of the Roman Church, had it been voluntarily suggested by Lord Baltimore, then it certainly would have been an illustrious example, and would have stood out a monument of light from among the accumulated darkness. But history shows, that neither the Church nor its adherents in any way favored the cause of liberty, so far as the early settlement of Maryland was concerned.

If Lord Baltimore had been a Protestant nobleman, a Protestant prince would have granted him a charter for a Protestant province. If the king had been a Catholic, a Catholic proprietary would have procured a charter for a Catholic province. This course of action characterizes the history of the period. The luminous and beautiful exception of Maryland to the spirit of colonization of the seventeenth century was owing to the happy coincidence of a wise and energetic statesman receiving a charter from a Protestant monarch jealous of his faith, and both statesman and monarch compelled to pay deference to the progressive doctrines and political strength of the Independents of England, who were then preparing the way for successful revolution, and the final triumph of universal liberty, in these American States.*

The claim that Romanism is in favor of free thought, free expression, and free opinion, is never urged by her votaries out of the United States; the policy of doing it in this country, however, sometimes becomes insupportable, and the leading Catholic presses occasionally break forth in the following natural language:

"No good government can exist without religion—and there can

* See History of Democracy in the United States, Maryland, p. 199.

be no religion without an Inquisition, which is wisely designed for the promotion and protection of the true faith."*

"For our own part, we take this opportunity to explain our hearty delight at the suppression of the Protestant chapel in Rome. This may be thought intolerant; but when, we ask, *Did we ever profess* to be tolerant of Protestantism, or to favor the question that Protestantism ought to be tolerated? On the contrary, we HATE Protestantism—we DETEST it with our whole heart and soul, and we pray our aversion to it may never decrease."†

In the United States toleration is claimed as a Papal virtue, because it is known to be harmonious with public sentiment. Upon the Continent of Europe all is different, and Romanism becomes the strong right arm of despotism, and the enemy of every thing that is free. Not the supporter of tyranny by inference of its enthusiastic devotees, but by the powerful precepts of its written laws, sanctioned by all the solemnities of tradition, and all the massive machinery of the Church. Of the doctrines of the Council of Trent it is decreed, "If any one shall presume to teach, or to think differently from these decrees, let him be accursed." As late as 1832, the Church, through Gregory XVII., in its famous Encyclical letter, pronounces, "From that polluted fountain of indifference flows the absurd and erroneous doctrine, or rather raving, in favor and in defence of liberty of conscience, for which most pestilential error, the course opened by that entire and wild liberty of opinion, which is everywhere attempting the overthrow of civil and religious institutions, and which the unblushing impudence of some has held forth as an advantage to religion." "From hence arise those revolutions in the minds of men, hence this aggravated corruption of youths, hence the contempt among the people of sacred things, and of the most holy institutions and laws; hence, in one word, that pest of all others most to be dreaded in a State, unbridled liberty of opinion."

The establishment of the Inquisition in the sixteenth century was

* Boston Pilot. † Pittsburg Catholic Visitor, 1848.

for the avowed purpose of putting down free thought, free expression, and free opinion. Under its sway, enormities were committed which make humanity shudder. Under its administration John Louis Vivis, a Spaniard of great learning and reputation, bewails the fate of moderate and charitable Catholics even in Spain; what must have been the fate of avowed Protestants who came under its condemnation? Says Vivis, in a letter to Erasmus, dated May 18th, 1534, "We live in hard times, in which we can neither speak or be silent without danger." In the forty-three years of the administrations of the first four Inquisitors-General, which closed in the year 1524, they committed eighteen thousand human beings to the flames, and inflicted inferior punishments on two hundred thousand persons more, with various degrees of severity. It was this work of the Inquisition in Spain, with a knowledge that the Spanish and French monarchs meditated the extension over all Christendom of the Inquisition, that seated Elizabeth firmly on the throne of England, and secured that political toleration that led to the brightest triumphs of the Reformation.

Popish devotees are made to believe, and Protestants are constantly told, that the Inquisition was not established by the Catholic Church, and therefore the Church is not to be held accountable for any of its acts; yet we find Saint Liguori, one of the most reverend of the Fathers, says,—

"Pope Paul III. established the General Inquisition at Rome, in the year 1542, by his Bull 34, commencing with the words '*Licet ab initio.*'"—(*Ligor. de Prohib. Libro*, p. 238.) "In the General Congregation," continues the Saint, "of the holy Roman and Universal Inquisition, held in the Apostolical Quirinal Palace, before our MOST HOLY LORD, Lord Benedict, by Divine Providence the fourteenth Pope, and before the most eminent and most serene doctors, the Cardinals of the Holy Roman Church, *specially deputed* by the holy *Apostolical See, General Inquisitors* against heretical pravity."—(*Ligor. de Rom. Pont.*, Dec. iii, p. 85.)

The fact that the Romish Church assumes to be infallible, of necessity makes her intolerant. Her arrogant claim of supremacy above all governments of the earth in things spiritual, must also of necessity make her an enemy to free thought and action. The truth of this position is clearly set forth in the Rhemish Testament, which urges that "the blood of heretics is not called the blood of saints, no more than the blood of thieves, man-killers, and other malefactors, for the shedding of which, by order of justice, no commonwealth shall suffer."—(*Rhem. Test., Annot. upon* Rev. xvii. 6.)

"Experience teaches," says Cardinal Bellarmine, "that there is no other remedy for the evil but to put heretics to death; for the Church proceeded gradually, and tried every remedy. At first, she merely excommunicated them; afterward she added a fine; then she banished them; and finally she was constrained to put them to death."—(*Bellarm. de Laicis*, lib. iii. c. 21.)

Finally, as an utter refutation of the claim Romanism makes to free thought, free expression, and free opinion, we quote the language of the General Council of Lateran, which says, "Let the secular powers be compelled, if necessary, to *exterminate* to their utmost power all heretics denoted by the Church."—(*Gen. Coun. Lat.*, A. D. 1215.)

Such are the assumptions of this mighty religio-political organization, which, under the mild ægis of our Republican institutions, sends forth both its deceived and its knowing disciples, to teach the people of America, that it cherishes the fundamental principles of Republicanism, denying for the time its most ancient doctrines, denying its practice through centuries, and seemingly holding in contempt the intelligence of the American people, by claiming attributes so utterly opposed to its practices and precepts. That the Jesuitical foreign priest who was born under the system, nursed in its iniquities, who has no home, no ambition, no future, no glory that does not centre in Rome, should be willing to load his conscience down with mental reservations, or being so utterly corrupt, from his early education, to know nothing as right but the building up of his Church;—that such a man should claim any thing and every thing for Papacy, that would palliate the opposition of the American mind to its despotic and liberty-crushing requirements, is not strange; but the terrible influence of Papal power is more awfully illustrated than in any other case, when it can make a free and independent native-born citizen, educated and enlightened, and accustomed in his early life to think and act for himself, suddenly cease to have a mind of his own, suddenly deny the truths of history, suddenly discard the lessons of his own experience, and the accumulated testimony of ages, and declare that in the Romish Church there is free thought and free expression, and support it by sophisms upon history, that upon examination by the light of truth are dissipated, and leave the advocate in the condition of a person who willingly lends himself to deceptions of the grossest kind, or who, if sincere, must be passed upon as incapable, from ghostly influence, of announcing the truth.

No historical fact can be produced which will show that the Pope of Rome has aided in any cause that might properly be termed one of freedom, or that any of his official councils, or any acknowledged councils of the Church, have ever done any thing to enlighten the people, and encourage them in the principles of self-government. The present Pontiff may be presumed to have as enlarged views as any of his predecessors, yet he is as far removed from encouraging republican ideas as the most bigoted prelate of the dark ages. He represents, in this matter, not himself, but his Church; and acts only in accordance with the spirit and dictates of the great religio-political institution of which he is the head. Pius IX. blessed the Czar of Russia, and the newly made Emperor of Austria, because they aided in restoring him to his throne, from which he had been driven by the republicans of Italy. At the same time he cursed Piedmont and Belgium, because they asserted that the civil power was superior in civil matters to the power of the priests, and attempted to escape from some of the galling usurpations of Rome. Pius entered the hospitals, filled with wounded republicans who had fallen in the attempt to give liberty to the people, and poured out upon them his especial maledictions. To the wounded French—those hireling troops who had been employed to stifle liberty—he dispensed his blessing, and loaded them with rosaries, medals, and crosses of honor. Such was his treatment to the men who had cruelly shot down his own subjects—his own people! The bones of the martyrs of liberty were left to decay upon the surface of the ground; and, in this nineteenth century, travellers were disgusted in witnessing this savage cruelty, allowed almost under the very walls of the Vatican. We repeat, that Pius IX., in these enormities, represents the principle of his Church; and were he to act more liberal—more in accordance with the spirit of the age—he would cease to be Pope; for Romanism and freedom will ever be at war.

EFFECTS OF ROMANISM AND PROTESTANTISM ON CIVILIZATION.

"The prosperity of a country is founded upon the intelligence of its inhabitants. This intelligence is dependent upon an enlightened religious belief; for the highest civilization is the result of the purest Christianity."

THREE centuries ago, the people of the continent of Europe became divided by the Reformation; those of the North embraced Protestantism, those of the South remained Romanist. The great powers sided with Rome; the second-rate embraced the new faith. The former held command over the most fruitful domains of the Old and New World, and swayed the sceptre of ocean. Literature, science, and the arts were theirs. The latter, in comparison, had received but little from Nature, and commerce and manufactures were scarcely known amongst them. Such was the position of affairs in the sixteenth century. Let us now examine the transformation which these respective countries have undergone.

At the period of the Reformation, Spain was the first among the nations of Europe. By comparing its former with its present state, we shall discover how much it has lost; and this loss is owing, if not entirely, at least in part, to its religious faith. Never was a nation so completely under the influence of Romanism as Spain. She presented a brilliant picture in the sixteenth century; for the conquest of Grenada had raised her to the pinnacle of wealth and prosperity. While the nobility gave themselves up to the profession of arms, the other classes enriched their country by assiduous labor. On all sides, irrigation, canals, and reservoirs distributed water over the remotest and most barren tracts. Agriculture was especially honored, whilst industry and commerce added to the general prosperity. The development of trade was equal to that of industry. A minister of Philip the Second, asserted, in an assembly of the Cortes, that at the fair of Medina del Campo, in 1563, business was transacted to the amount of one hundred and thirty-two millions five hundred thousand dollars. A multitude of trading vessels set sail every year from various ports, conveying to Italy, Asia Minor, Africa, and the East Indies, the products of the national industry. Sculpture, architecture, painting, and music were enshrined in her midst. The drama, epic and lyric poetry, and history found worthy interpreters, names which will live forever. The palaces of the Spanish ambassadors were in foreign countries the resort of the most elegant society; and France, Italy, England, and Germany sent their youth to Madrid to acquire Castilian manners and politeness.

Towards the close of the fifteenth century, Spain, victorious over the Moors, became the discoverer and mistress of the New World. What a magnificent *present!* What a glorious *future!* All peoples looked to her as first amongst the nations, and sovereigns trembled at her power.

What was the condition of England at the period of the Reformation? One-half of the land was the property of the clergy; the remainder belonged to the nobility. Sixty-five thousand priests and monks supported immense establishments by the moneys levied on the people. The land was cultivated to a comparatively small extent, the gross agricultural product being under forty millions of dollars. Her trade was small, compared to that of many nations on the continent, and commerce was scarcely known in her ports. Manufactures were obtained from other countries, and education of the people had not yet commenced. Everywhere feudalism and priestcraft were triumphant, and divided the nation for their mutual benefit.

England, under the benign influences of the Reformation, from a fourth-rate power, soon took her station at the head of the nations of the earth; and peoples once her superiors became dependent upon her for protection and aid. Her ships whitened every sea, and her drum-beat greeted the rising sun around the world. Her capitalists have covered Europe with railroads, and she has made laws to millions in Asia. She has her colonies in Africa, America, and a rising empire in Australia. What the United States are effecting in the Western Hemisphere, she is accomplishing in the Old World.

Within eleven years, Spain effects the subjugation of Grenada, discovers and conquers America, and establishes THE INQUISITION! At the summit of prosperity in the fifteenth century, behold her in the nineteenth! See that spectacle of agony which cannot come to an end; that all-pervading confusion to which no term can be assigned; the certain and progressive ruin of a nation that, for a whole century, dictated laws to Europe; that inhabits the richest and most fertile soil, perhaps, under heaven—but a nation so disheartened that it feels itself perish, and watches its own decline with the resignation of a fatalist!

The clergy possess nearly one-third of the entire surface of Spain. As a consequence, one-twelfth of the inhabitants earn a livelihood by smuggling, robbing, and begging; and it has been estimated that three million Spaniards wear no shirt from want of money to purchase one. There are forty classes of vagrants, each class with a specific, recognized name. There is an assassination for every four thousand of the population. Education is scarcely known, and there is but one pupil to every three hundred and fifty inhabitants. Internal navigation, agriculture, and manufactures are at a stand-still. Such is modern Spain, once the first, now the last of nations! What is the cause of this? what the origin of such utter misery and helplessness? Tyranny, answers the politician; Romanism, says the Protestant; the Inquisition, replies the historian. But these three are one. Tyranny and the Inquisition!—foul offspring of blighting Romanism!

During the past year, the Queen of Spain having presented to the Pope a magnificent tiara of diamonds, the Pontiff returns an allocution to the "Catholic Sovereign," and the gift of the body of St. Felix! Thus has it ever been. Spain parts with her wealth to Rome, and receives in return bones, putrefaction, and rottenness! But Rome has borne sway there too long. The Spaniards are now rising against this frightful spiritual and civil tyranny; the dupes and tools of the priesthood have fled the country like malefactors, and the sovereign herself obeys the dictates of her subjects. Rome is no longer to hold Spain as her property, to farm and pillage it to benefit the Papal treasury. She has fattened on it too long, and has left it, poor, weak, uneducated, superstitious, low in civilization, the prey of countless factions. But Spain is ridding herself of the cause of her misery—may we not hope, *forever?*

We address to the reader's conscience this twofold question: First, is it not true that Spain, favored with the finest climate, placed at the head of Europe, enriched with a world, but remaining Romanist, has continued to decline and grow poorer, sinking at last into ignorance, misery, and immorality? Secondly, is it not true that England, with a sterile soil, a cloudy sky, and starting from the lowest rank among European nations, but having embraced Protestantism, is now prosperous, enlightened, moral, and at the head of the civilized world?

We find the relative influence of the two creeds fully developed in the Republic of Switzerland. The Protestant cantons are more populous than the Romanist, and carry on a far greater trade. The latter are obliged to keep many holidays besides Sundays, and thus agriculture is much neglected. The Cantons of Zurich, Basle, Geneva, Glaris, and Neufchatel, *all Protestant*, are distinguished above the rest for their industry and manufactures. The people are not so well educated in the Romish as in the other cantons. There are but twenty-two presses in the former to eighty in the latter. Ten Protestant journals are printed to three Romanist. In the Papist cantons, ignorance and misery go hand in hand, and distress the eyes of the traveller. The taste for processions, pilgrimages, and other acts of devotion introduced by the monks, has encouraged a spirit of idleness which is the bane of trade and agriculture, and augments the numbers of the poor. In the cantons where the peasants bow the neck to the yoke of the clergy, men have lost all their energy, all elevation of mind. Servile and taciturn as slaves, they have forgotten their rights, and know nothing beyond the performance of a mechanical and unreasoning obedience. The Canton du Valais is celebrated throughout Europe for its filth, superstition, and wretchedness. "Mangè pas les puces et les Prètres" (eaten up by lice and priests), is the proverb applied to its inhabitants throughout Europe. The population is behind the other cantons even in regard to agricultural operations and the management of cattle. They are inferior in education, knowledge, and science; and are specially idle, negligent, and dirty. In the villages, at every door are seen horrible crètins, sickly, wretched, languishing, with an enormous head, lost in an immense goître, their faces swollen and livid, the eyes sunk under the thick and heavy lids; the flabby cheeks, the half-opened lips, with the tongue hanging out, and a filthy saliva round it. Some, scarcely covered with rags, lie warming their limbs in the sun; others, seated on the laps of half-crètinized old women, resign their beards and heads to their inspection, or moodily count their beads, muttering Aves and Pater Nosters. Medical men are decided that the causes of this deformed idiocy, crètinism, are moral as well as physical; the neglect of education leads to their imbecility.* Children are left to themselves, and exist like beasts. They wallow in the mire, seizing and devouring all they find there. In winter they pass whole days stretched in a room warmed by a stove. Drunkenness is the prevailing vice, and the population is universally superstitious, insensible to their own interests, intractable and obstinate.

Romanism had a hard battle to fight in Germany at the time of the Reformation. The North, represented by Prussia, became Protestant; the South, under the influence of Austria, remained Romanist. In the latter, two powers, the government and the clergy, have united in working the nation to their mutual advantage. The clergy, at first, strove to govern both the people and the nobles; but

* Raoul Rochette, Vol. III. p. 392. Lautier, Vol. II. p. 204.

these resisted, and took the place coveted by the clergy. The civil power is therefore master, only it reigns in the nation by the means and tutoring of the Church. A compromise exists; the Church is the instrument, the Government is the hand; but the instrument acts according to its own aptitude, so that a harmonious concurrence exists between the two powers. Rome has fashioned Austria, although Rome obeys Austria, and the two forces have successfully enthralled the nation, by depriving it of liberty and education. Freedom of thought does not exist: there are twelve offices for the revision of books, and as many censors, at Vienna, Prague, and Milan. The advance of industry is stopped by an exaggerated prohibitive system; her commerce in nowise answers to the extent of her monarchy, and her internal trade is scarcely half developed.

There is no individual liberty; the subject is a simple tenant; he cannot be more. The lords judge between their own subjects; they may even judge in their own cause. Up to 1846, except in Hungary, no peasant might emigrate, buy, sell, make a will, or marry, without authorization; he was, in fact, a minor, kept under by perpetual legislative guardianship.

Gallicia, a country possessing all the elements of wealth, has remained barren, and frightful indigence bears sway. In the wretched and repulsive-looking villages, narrow huts, formed of branches of trees rudely kept together with osier bands, and covered with straw and clay, surround a church. The other provinces of the empire are in similar condition; religion and misery go hand in hand. There is, as we before observed, no liberty of thought, no liberty of commerce, no individual liberty; but instead, drudgery for the peasants, beating for the soldiers, humiliation for officials, and a villainous system of secret police.

The different professions are enrolled to serve as spies, as also are the hackney-coachmen. Servants are called upon to tell what they know of their masters and households; door-keepers, tradesmen, and clerks render the same service. One-half of the people are spies upon the other half.

Thanks to this abominable tyranny and vile superstition, Austria is falling daily in opinion; the distrust and discontent which the government excites, germinate like fertile seeds, and will one day bear bitter fruits.

Whilst Austria extinguishes the light of knowledge and forbids liberty of thought, Prussia, on the contrary, governs by means of that light and liberty.

Prussia is a state in which instruction is very generally diffused and watched over with the greatest care: the number of schools increases annually. There is no country where science and learning are more encouraged, or cultivated with greater success, and the inhabitants have reached a high degree of moral and intellectual attainment. The government pays the greatest attention to public education, and the advancement of the arts and sciences. Freedom is granted to all religious denominations.

The result of Luther's reformation in Germany was liberty of thought and opinion. No distinction was made between theological and philosophical truth, and public disputations were held on all subjects without opposition. Nowhere has the human mind been permitted to expand or express itself more freely than in Northern Germany: Liberty of thought and Protestantism are there united by strong ties, and German Philosophy is the daughter of the Reformation. The language even has felt the benefit: Protestants were the first to write it with intelligence, and this pure style is, in the countries subject to Austria, called *Lutheran German.*

Agriculture is improving, manufactures increase, and trade flourishes. In fifteen years, Prussia has expended a capital of fifty-four million dollars in roads and railways. Throughout the country, beautiful villages spring up on every side; the houses are well built, and almost concealed by the thick covering of vine leaves. The villagers universally wear bright, happy countenances, and their courteous manners and picturesque costumes all bespeak the contentment and comfort which reign among them.

Such is Germany. In the South, Austria and her band of Romish

States career in the darkness of material despotism, without consciousness of the noble destiny of man.

In the North, Prussia, and her company of Protestant nations, blessed with increasing liberty, bask in the bright light of knowledge, in ceaseless speculations after God and immortality.

Romanist Belgium and Protestant Holland having been alternately united and separated, cannot be so entirely different from one another as the countries we have already compared. During the last half century alone, Belgium has been successively under the rule of Infidel France, of the Protestant Netherlands, and of its own Romanist government. These powers have each left an impression, and thus have modified the contrast which strikes us so forcibly elsewhere.

In the eighteenth century, Belgium passed under the dominion of the French, then much irritated against priestcraft; Belgians must in a measure have shaken off the same yoke, and lost some of their prejudices. If this were not an advance in good, it was at least a step out of evil.

But it was especially from 1815 to 1830, under a Protestant government, that Belgium received abundantly the treasures of freedom and civilization. Agricultural colonies were established, and flourished; institutions for the poor were founded; a general increase of population and comfort ensued, and commerce received a great development.

The advantages on the Romanist side, as regards soil and climate, are very considerably in favor of Belgium in comparison with Holland. The former has a fertile soil, generously endowed by nature; a ray of sunshine covers it with abundant crops; it possesses mines of lead, copper, iron, alum, sulphur and calamine, quarries of marble, freestone, limestone, &c.

In Holland, instead of these natural riches, we find water! water everywhere. While Brussels, the capital of Belgium, rests upon a rock, Amsterdam is built in the midst of the floods, on thirteen million stakes. What have the Belgian Catholics done with their fertile land in comparison with what the Dutch Protestants have made of their marshes?

Belgian agriculture is, at the present time, greatly below that of Holland. Travellers are struck with the wisdom with which the Dutch cherish every thing which tends to the improvement of that science. Their laborers enjoy an amount of comfort which contrasts strongly with the poverty of Flanders; their dwellings are well kept, their clothes are clean and substantial; all things bespeak ease and prosperity. There are scarcely any paupers amongst them, whilst in Belgium they form a seventh of the population.

Since 1830, educational and scientific institutions have greatly fallen off in the latter country. What the Priesthood could not control, they willingly allowed to decay; they direct, at least partially, all primary instruction, not only as to religion and morals, but in every branch of education. In Holland, they take not the slightest part in public instruction; they do not even visit the schools; sectarianism is not allowed to enter, but the master is charged to teach his pupils the rules of morality and the truths of the Gospel.

The preponderance of the Romish clergy in Belgium is a bad omen for the future; all things converge towards a moral and intellectual subjugation: the Jesuit system of education is greatly dreaded, for it aims at nothing less than the extinction of all free-will and spontaneous action. Belgium has greatly retrograded since her disruption with Holland, whilst the latter has steadily progressed in freedom and civilization.

Romanists are fond of citing France as proof positive of the civilizing influence of their faith: but France is not Papal; if she be any thing in ethics, she is *Deist.* We admit at the same time that some provinces, like Brittany, for instance, are really under the influence of the Popish clergy. We shall compare these districts with those localities in which Protestantism has many adherents. The Huguenots in France were in a similar position to that of the Irish Romanists. Both were persecuted by their respective governments. We know to what depths of misery the Irish Papists sank;

their neglect of agriculture, their idleness, their frightful poverty Is the same sight offered to us by the equally persecuted Protestants? Gradually excluded from court employments, and from almost all civil posts, they applied themselves to agriculture, trade, and manufactures. The vast plains they possessed in Béarn, and the Western provinces, were covered with rich harvests. In Languedoc, the cantons peopled by them became the best cultivated and the most fertile, often in spite of the badness of the soil. In Guyenne, they took possession of almost the whole wine trade. In the two governments of Brouage and Oleron, a dozen Protestant families had the monopoly of the trade in salt and wine. The wealth of Alençon passed through their hands; and the Protestants of Rouen carried on an immense commerce, especially with the Dutch. Those of Caen sold to the English and Dutch merchants the linen and woollen cloths manufactured in Normandy. It is to the Protestants that France owes her commerce at Bordeaux, La Rochelle, and the Norman ports. In fine, nearly all the silk, cotton, linen, and paper manufactures were supported by them, and their tanneries in Touraine were renowned throughout the whole of Europe.

This magnificent prosperity was annihilated by Romanism at the Revocation of the Edict of Nantes. England, Holland, Germany, and Denmark all received the flying Huguenots. The American colonies were largely benefited by the refugees. The uncultivated banks of the James River were by them transformed into fields covered with rich harvests. All Virginia admired the flourishing state of their model farms in the environs of Mannikin. In the State of New York, the founders of New La Rochelle, recoiled from no fatigue that might render productive the virgin land on the shores of the East River. Men, women, and children unceasingly labored until they converted a wilderness into a smiling landscape; and in South Carolina they reared magnificent plantations on the banks of the Cooper. The agricultural colony on the banks of the Santee surpassed all others in the same province, although the refugees were unaccustomed to that kind of labor.

The Revocation of the Edict of Nantes, in 1685, had its reaction in the fearful atrocities of the French Revolution of 1792. But a great Protestant element exists still in France, and we can compare their comparative prosperity with that of the Romanists. In Paris, the average personal tax paid by all the inhabitants is six dollars and twelve cents; the average paid by the Protestants is seventeen dollars; that is to say, the fortunes of the Paris Protestants are, at the present time, nearly three times that of their Romanist countrymen. Throughout the length and breadth of France, the Protestant departments are the most industrious, most wealthy, and pay the highest taxes to the government. The six departments which supply the primary schools with the largest amount of pupils, are those containing the largest number of Protestants. The six departments numbering the smallest number of pupils are precisely those which are exclusively Romanist populations.

The Reformed Faith is making progress throughout France. At the same time, we must not ignore the fact that in many parts of the country Romanism is very powerful, especially with the court. Services rendered necessarily demand favors in return. Hence the decree placing education in the hands of the priests. The occupation of Rome is oft-times cited as a proof of Gallican support of the Holy See, but there were far too grave political reasons to prompt such a procedure for us to suppose that the French Government was, and is guided by mere faith, or reverence for a system which the Napoleons have always made subservient to their own purposes. As a nation, France is simply Deist; and to this state has she been reduced by centuries of priestly domination and Romish superstition.

In no country do the effects of Romanism and Protestantism so strike the observer as in Ireland. Here, as elsewhere, the fruitful South has fallen to the lot of the former, and the Reformation displays its power in the comparatively barren North. The effect upon the Irish of the bad direction which the priest gives to their minds, is a prostration of their moral force, annihilating all their intellectual faculties, and blunting even the consciousness of misfortune and desire to put an end to it. Ireland is peopled with poor; mendicity seems almost the national characteristic. The Irish beggars are the Lazzaroni of England.

The Romish population of Ireland live in huts, the walls of which are made of mud and flints, or of old and almost rotten planks; the roof is composed of a layer of clods, spread over the laths. Generally, no windows are to be seen. Light enters only by means of the door, or a hole made in the roof, which serves as a chimney. In this same damp shed live, pell-mell, two, three, and sometimes four generations of human beings. The sow seems a member of the family—lying in the corner, surrounded and petted by the children. In these miserable abodes the Irish Romanists pass their lives, except when engaged in agrarian outrage, or resistance to the laws of the land. For centuries have they existed in this manner; and when patriotic individuals attempt a reformation of so horrible a state of things, the priests denounce the philanthropists from the altar, and cause their deluded congregations to lie in wait to assassinate them. Such is Papal Ireland!

The Irish of the North, living under the same laws, "tyrannized (?) over by the same government," show exactly a contrary picture. They devote themselves to manufactures and trade, and their linens surpass all others. The growth and manufacture of flax was commenced by Protestants, and has been maintained by them ever since. Belfast is a remarkable example of the prosperity of the Protestant towns of the North. There are special hospitals for the blind, deaf and dumb, fever patients, lunatics, the feeble; with asylums for penitent girls, liberated convicts, domestics out of place, and women out of work. There are sixteen Protestant chapels to two Romanist; and the inhabitants are almost all Protestants, and merchants. The houses are well built, large, and convenient. Lovely villages are scattered through the country, well-built cottages stand in the midst of gardens profuse in flowers, the inhabitants are well dressed, and an air of contentment and happiness pervades every thing.

As it is in prosperity, so is it in education and morality. Three-fourths of the criminals of Ireland are Romanists, and education is scarcely known among them. In order to remedy such a frightful state of crime and ignorance, the English Government has lately established schools and colleges, where religion as a study is rigorously excluded; thus endeavoring to supply the wants of a mixed population, and eventually end sectarianism. Rome anathematizes these institutions, naming them the "Godless colleges," and denounces from the altar those enlightened parents who permit their children to frequent them.

There is not an election in which we do not find instances of priests threatening from the altar those who voted for a Protestant candidate. The fearful riots which result from this interference are only quelled by the intervention of an armed force. Everywhere the Romanists are deficient in knowledge and wealth. They are the uneducated, the miserable, the servants of their own land. In short, turn where you will, the result is the same. The difference between Romanism and Protestantism is known by the appearance of every parish, every village, every house and cottage in the land.

Italy! Italy! Mistress of the World! the glory of Europe! She had decked herself with the master-works of the human mind, like a queen adorning her brow. Michael Angelo was her architect; Raphael, Titian, and Da Vinci were her painters; Dante, Petrarch, and Ariosto sang her praises. For her, Genoa and Venice unladed their rich argosies; emperors and kings were her willing vassals. Italy, possessing in her bosom the Infallible Head of the Church; Italy, enjoying the pure influence of Romanism, and never suffering from heresy,—surely Italy must give high proofs of the blessed influence of the Papacy; but the Eternal City! Imperial Rome! is in ruins! Half her streets are deserted; wretchedness and filth reign triumphantly. The glory of the City of the Sea, Venice, is gone; Genoa is fallen; Florence is in tears! Italians are distracted and desolate, the prey of ever-changing tyrants!

It is to Popery alone we must attribute the shame of the actual state of Italy. It is the work, the legitimate offspring, the exclusive pupil of the Papal power. Whatever Popery is able to accomplish, has been accomplished in Italy. No opposition has been offered there. On the contrary, Popery has been enthroned; princes and people have bowed before it, as an idol; and the Head of Romanism, armed with a triple tiara, held as infallible. The Roman Caiphas, accepted as vice-God, has prepared and consummated this tremendous ruin.

But there is a bright ray of hope for this glorious country of the past. Sardinia is waking up to liberty, and manfully striding on in the road to freedom. Rome is in agony; her ministers fume, her Pontiff threatens excommunication and interdict. But bravely do Sardinia's king and people bear such Middle-Age threats; and the secularization of the property of the Church, the appointment of bishops by the government, the annihilation of the monasteries, all go bravely on. Italy's salvation is in the North; and we trust ere long to see a magnificent empire rising up, embracing Sardinia, Lombardy, and the lesser States, and setting free the city of Rienzi—Eternal Rome herself.

But in order to appreciate the struggle between modern Romanism and Protestantism, we must leave Europe. Here they are both embarrassed in their movements by too many old established customs and prejudices. Providence has given them a vast arena, where each, being surrounded by its own deeds, will be judged by them alone. The Church of Rome and the Reformation have each, in America, a world in which to try their civilizing power,—a duel which has heaven and earth for witnesses. America is a country of the future. She is a virgin, fertile, and extensive land. She has not, by degrading laws, closed the doors upon truth. Neither has she proscribed error; all forms, religions, governments, are admitted. Truth, eternal truth, will alone prevail.

A magnificent armament, under the banners of imperial Spain, arrives in South America. The strength and chivalry of Europe land amidst wondering spectators. They march from victory to victory. Untold treasures fill the coffers of the Church. Rome, in intoxication, sings countless Te Deums.

A few men land, one by one, on the shores of North America; poor, humble, and unknown. They bring with them but one book—the Bible. They open it on the strand; and begin forthwith to build up the new city, on the plan of the book recovered by Luther.

Hearken to the sound of the axe. The emigrant fells the primeval oak in the virgin forests; the sweat inundates his brow. With toil and trouble he builds an unknown hut, near a running stream. The traveller scarce deigns to turn his head towards this humble dwelling, where the noise of the axe and hammer mingles with the chant of a psalm. But if, a few years later, he pass again by the same spot, he sees, by a sort of social miracle, in the place of the hut, a mighty empire rising from the earth. The poor emigrant has conquered a world!

In this immense arena the lists are opened between two religions. The doctrines of the Council of Trent have received, for the display of their strength, South America. There the founders are not isolated individuals, but on the contrary, according to Romanist principles, an association already formed. A powerful empire, with all its resources, comes to take possession of the soil. Rich valleys and fertile plains seem to demand the living energy which would give birth to new empires. In order that the trial may be more decisive, Romanism alone is allowed to approach these shores. The civilization of the natives, which might have embarrassed her actions, disappears. Nothing remains but mighty nature, who, in her solitude, invites man to crown her with vast ideas, projects, innovations, kingdoms, gigantic as herself. But man remains motionless, bound by an invisible force.

Throughout the entire continent of South America, it is impossible to enforce the observance of the most simple law or police regulation. The insolence of the inhabitants renders them hostile to every kind of control. Morals are in a state that makes us blush for humanity; manufactures are scarcely known; commerce languishes, or is in the hands of foreigners; society is utterly demoralized, and anarchy reigns supreme. From the Isthmus to the Horn, wherever Rome has planted her Faith, civilization flies. Revolution succeeds revolution, but no good results from the change. South America is one vast moral charnel-house. Mexico, even, which should receive some beneficial influence from the neighboring states, is paralyzed by the priesthood, in alliance with despotism. Cuba, the brightest jewel in the bosom of ocean, for which nature has done so much and man so little, is ground down and cursed by this overwhelming spiritual tyranny. Priestcraft pillages her, and military despots put her to death. Rome, wherever supreme, reduces society to chaos.

What a magnificent contrast in the Protestant North! Forests have given place to fruitful fields; cities spring up on every side; railroads stretch to remotest points; commerce brings to her the wealth of the old world; Science bridges her rivers, works her roads and canals; the Arts enshrine themselves in her midst; and Literature carries her glory into far-distant climes. Her Faith and her Progress are one and inseparable; the dignity and independence of man, his self-reliance, have wrought this. Protestantism settled her finest States—it breathes through and animates her constitution; her forefathers were the everlasting enemies of Rome and tyranny. Instead of ignorance, we find education more diffused than in any other part of the world; a school is as necessary to a village as houses; and every succeeding year strives to surpass the last in improving instruction.

The mind fails to grasp the FUTURE of such a people. When we see the progress accomplished in so short a period; plenty everywhere and misery nowhere; churches, schools, towns, manufactories, rising on all sides, as if by enchantment; forests cleared away almost as soon as discovered; a hardy population, active, persevering, eager for knowledge, and ever advancing, we are almost tempted to give history the lie, when we think how much has been done in so short a time.

Romanism, opposed to all social and commercial progress, is defended by its subjects with the specious remark that the change proves nothing against the Church, because man is not made for this world, and, therefore, it makes but little difference whether he be free, happy, prosperous, or otherwise, so long as he is an acceptable member of the Papal communion. This is the favorite argument to make the Irish people contented with the misery they suffer by the priest-ridden degradation in their native land. Another class of the defenders of the Papacy admit the commercial and social degradation of Papal nations, but assert that their decline in temporal prosperity is due to the change of the great routes of navigation. It is true that America and England obtained access to the East Indies around the Cape of Good Hope, but this route is, and was, open to Spain, Portugal, and all Romanist countries. No recent discoveries have altered the route to South America; nearly the whole of that trade was hers, for her colonies, eleven times the area of the mother country, were equal to India in fertility; rivers were more numerous and mineral productions far superior. England, and in fact the whole of Europe, could never reach the South American Continent as quickly as Spain, for the north-east trade-winds were in her favor, and those nations would always be compelled to take a southern course to reach the Gulf of Mexico. Portugal and Spain obtained a vast continent, besides possessions in the West Indies and North America. No change in navigation could possibly affect the development of these immense acquisitions; but, as we have seen, ill government and superstition have left them a wilderness, and the very name of Spain an execration.

But granting, for the sake of argument, that the carrying trade has been transferred, surely the loss of commerce cannot have plunged Spain, Portugal, and Italy into such moral debasement and political annihilation as they are now suffering. The asserters of so monstrous a proposition would make us believe that no country can prosper without commerce, which is palpably ridiculous. But if their argument be correct, why should Protestant Holland differ so materially from the above-mentioned countries? She has lost the greater part of her commerce and colonies, yet we see no such moral debasement, no such reducing of man to the level of the brute as we find with them.

Protestantism found the world in medieval barbarism; feudalism and tyranny triumphant; mankind in slavery and ignorance. She has disenthralled the people, blessed them with literature and science, raised them to the virtue and dignity of MEN. Under her benign auspices they have learned the blessings of liberty, the charms of intellect, the triumphs of free government. She has given them a world, and taught them how, from a primeval forest, to carve out the glories of a rising empire, the terror of despotism, the star of hope to all nations. She has burst the barriers of three thousand years, and opened China to commerce and the West. She has forced Japan to obey her behests, and carried her faith into the polar zone. She has invented railroads, telegraphs, steam-engines, and countless appliances to benefit humanity. Her myriad presses carry heaven-born thought into far-off climes; she commands the ocean, and commerce is obedient to her. Man, disenchained man, stands forth as sovereign of the universe, a being after the image of God.

THE RIGHTS OF CONSCIENCE.

"The small voice within
Heard through gain's silence, and o'er glory's din:
Whatever creed be taught, or land be trod,
Man's conscience is the oracle of God."
BYRON.

THE American mind declares itself in favor of the right of every man to worship God after the dictates of his own conscience. It acts upon the constitutional dictation, that "no religious test shall ever be required as a qualification to any office or public trust under the United States." That in the first article of the Amendments of the Constitution it is declared, "that Congress shall make no law respecting an establishment of religion, or prohibiting the free exercise thereof." Leaving every individual free to establish his own standard of qualification, and to vote for or against those who hold certain religious principles, or political views, as each one may see right in his own eyes. The war the American mind wages is for the freedom of religious opinion; it only opposes the tyranny of priestcraft—a tyranny which educates its slaves that the Church is infallible, superior in authority to the civil power, and that unquestioned obedience is the highest duty of the layman. The American mind demands that the people of this country, whether native or alien, be brought to consider principalities and powers as entitled to consideration, only as they are creations of the Constitution and the laws. That they be imbued with the spirit of independence, and regard the principle of equality as an article of living political faith; that they obey no authority, recognize no titles, save those which emanate from the civil power; that they admit no right to command on the part of any Church, and no duty of obedience on the part of the laity; that they see no peculiar sanctity in priestly robes, unless accompanied by the superior sanctity of those who wear them; that all deference to Church dignitaries is but the voluntary homage of the heart to exalted virtue; that there is no divinity hedging in a king, and a mitred bishop, even of the See of Rome, is but a man, entitled to respect only as a man, and to extraordinary consideration, only as his Christian graces shine with a lustre superior to those of common men.

The Pope of Rome claims to be the vicegerent of God, and infallible; that all power on earth, spiritual and temporal, is given him by Divine appointment; that all countries and governments belong to him, and are either subject to his will and command, or in a state of criminal rebellion; that all authority in Church and State which does not profess to be under him, and act in strict conformity to his commands, is unlawful and wicked; that all religious opinions different from the dogmas of the Romish Church are heretical, and that those who profess them are heretics with whom no faith should be kept, whether plighted by contract or by oath; that it is the highest duty of all Romanists to extirpate this heresy and these heretics by sword, fire, and fagot; and by the same means to bring the political authorities to submit to the Pope in all things, and every human being to profess, and conform to the Romish faith; and to these ends they intend to devote their time, their labor, their energies and powers, and even expend their lives, which would be glorious martyrdom. It is because of the entertainment of such a belief that Romanism is opposed, and the influence of foreigners, who blindly and passively consent to such doctrines, dreaded; for all modern history teaches us, that the fairest portions of the earth have been ravaged with fire and sword to sustain these monstrous doctrines of a religio-political institution.

It is true, that Romanism has not attempted for many years, save in its recent manifestoes against Sardinia, to assert its political and temporal power outside of the Papal dominions; but still, in its constitution and principles, it adheres to these and all its other assumed powers. It has renounced none, nor will it do so. None of her exemplary children repudiate any of them, and if they did, they would be brought to recant by priestly visitation, or else have the spiritual thunder of excommunication denounced against them. For no higher offence than simply refusing to violate the most sacred enactments regarding church property existing in the State of New York, the trustees of the church of St. Louis, Buffalo, and its entire congregation, were placed under ban. The Bishop of the diocese published the pains of excommunication against them, and held their names up to infamy and reproach. The marriage sacrament was refused, and the priest forbidden to minister at the altars.

The assertion of the full extent of the assumed power by the Papal Church only slumbers, because the condition of human affairs—the light, liberty, and moral power of the world, will not suffer it to be put into execution. It is not the advance and elevation of principle, of morals, and Christian charity in that Church, and among its priesthood, which has purified it for the time being of these enormities. Let the state of the world favor it, and other Gregorys and Innocents would arise to enforce the powers of the Papacy in their utmost amplitude, and their most inexorable spirit. She believes that she is to be coeval with man, and ultimately to have his whole and perfect obedience. She has seen the great flux and reflux of her authority through many centuries, and she is looking forward patiently through other centuries in confidence, when her strength in full tide is to come to her again. Ever watchful, the priesthood, for whom mainly this wonderful edifice has been constructed, and been progressing to perfection in its way for fifty generations, will patiently bide their time; and when it comes, if come it ever does, they will move with a policy, a courage, and a perseverance to command success; and the grandest and most awe-inspiring scenes of the Papal drama will be again reenacted on the theatre of the world.

But whether it is the destiny of man to revolve back to Papal supremacy in all his affairs or not, that is the consummation to which the whole priesthood devote themselves, their time, their energies, and their lives. That is their one great object; compensating and supplying the subjects of their affections, hopes, and ambitions; taking the place of wife, children, friends, and country; wealth, social position, station, honors, fame, and distinction in the arts, sciences, politics, and war. This ascendency, now partially lost, is their glorious tradition, and to regain it is the permanent, immutable, ever-present policy of the Papacy in all its parts. That the Pope is a hierarch, and they a portion of the hierarchy, is a part of the education, mind, soul, and personal identity of every member of the priesthood; and not less so, that the business and ends of their lives and labors is to expend themselves according to times and circumstances, for the restoration of the authority and splendor of both; and never to be disheartened or discouraged, whether or not there be any perceivable result. These are objects for which, in this country, the foreign priests especially labor. They summon every Papist, upon his reaching our shores, to his fealty, and hold them united and faithful to their religion, their priest, and their sovereign hierarch. They get possession of all the children they can, by means of schools, and their parents, where even but one of them is a Romanist, and they attend and keep these children from the cradle to the grave.

The dying find it to the interest of their eternal welfare to give the Church liberally of their worldly treasure; and thus in every country it absorbs within its coffers a large share of the wealth of its devoted congregations. With signal flexibility and cunning it has addressed itself to the ruling power, and paid it court adulation, or used other means to win it; and when won, it may do what it will, on condition that it becomes subservient to the peculiar views of this priesthood and its hierarchy. They know that in our country the main-spring of political power is the ballot-box, and the object of their unceasing efforts is there to collect and consolidate strength. The members of all other sects divide in their politics and votes, but foreign Romanists never, and the priest thus has in his hands their absolute will, and it becomes a matter of calculation how this tremendous engine of power can best be used to build up, not the interests of America nor the happiness of the people, but the ever-absorbing pretensions of the Papal Church.

The possession of this voting power is denied, and so is every working principle of the Church denied, where a frank acknowledgment would operate against its interests; but the fact that our most unscrupulous office-seekers are constantly paying court to the priests, and in every possible way endeavoring to build up the interests of their Church, tells its own tale, for where the carcass is, there will be the buzzards also, and where there are votes to be purchased, there will be the demagogue and the trading politician.

But the organs of the Papacy printed among us, occasionally thrown off their guard by some unexpected success, sometimes let us into their plans and future aspirations. We occasionally have the boldest avowals of the intention of usurping our government, of destroying our liberties, and shaping every thing to the standard of priestly ambition. Denying, as all true Americans do, the Divine right of any human being to govern, the chief organ of Romanism therefore ridicules the permanency of our institutions, and breaks out in the following rhapsody:—

"Are your free institutions infallible? Are they founded on Divine right? This you deny. Is not the proper question for you to discuss, then, not whether Papacy be or be not compatible with Republican government, but whether it be or be not founded in Divine right? If the Papacy be founded in Divine right, it is supreme over whatever be founded only in human right, and then your institutions should be made to harmonize with it, and not it with your institutions. The real question then is, not the compatibility or incompatibility of the Catholic Church with democratic institutions, but is the Catholic Church the Church of God? Settle this question first. But in point of fact, democracy is a mischievous dream, wherever the Catholic Church does not predominate, to inspire the people with reverence, and to teach and accustom them to obedience and authority. The first lesson for all to learn, the last that should be forgotten, is—to obey. You can have no government where there is no obedience; and obedience to law, as it is called, will not be long enforced, where the fallibility of law is clearly seen and freely admitted. But is it the intention of the Pope to possess this country? Undoubtedly. In this intention he is aided by the Jesuits, and all the Catholic prelates and priests. That the policy of the Church is dreaded and opposed by all Protestants, infidels, demagogues, tyrants, and oppressors, is also unquestionably true. Save then, in the discharge of our civil duties, and in the ordinary business of life, there is, and can be no harmony between the Catholics and Protestants."*

"The time has come when Catholics must begin to make their principles tell upon the public sentiment of the country. Heretofore we have taken our politics from one or another of the parties which divide the country, and have suffered the enemies of our religion to impose their political doctrines upon us; but it is time for us to begin to teach the country itself those moral and political doctrines which flow from the teachings of our own Church. We are at home here, wherever we may have been born; this is our country, and as it is to become thoroughly Catholic, we have a deeper interest in public affairs than any other of our citizens. The sects are only for a day; the Church forever. We care little how the elections go, for that is a small affair; but we can never, as Catholics, be indifferent to the moral principles which enter into the laws and shape the public policy of the country."*

These extracts, so characteristic of the arrogance of the Priest, avow most distinctly all the ambitious designs imputed to the Roman priesthood. The proposed discussion of the great practical political questions is announced, that this country itself may be taught the moral and political doctrines which flow from the teachings of the Church, and may become thoroughly Roman—all other sects being for a day, and that Church forever; and that our Republican institutions may be altered to conform to the Papacy, by its principles

* Brownson's Review.

being made to enter into the laws and to shape the public policy of this country—all this is here boldly avowed; and also that every Jesuit, Prelate, and Priest, who is faithful to his religion, will aid the Pope, their hierarch, to possess himself of this country. The means by which they expect to achieve all this, is by the slow and cautious movements, the profound dissimulation and arts, which have ever characterized the operations of this priesthood, to get possession of the political power by controlling the ballot-box. Whether they ever succeed or not, that is their sleepless effort; and so subtle are they in their operations, that thousands are unconsciously made their agents who would never knowingly submit themselves to any such purposes of mischief. The priesthood are encouraged by their own strong faith, that, if they do not succeed in this century, their successors may in the next, for their system is, never to relinquish a foothold gained. They do not build humble cabins or perishable houses for their services; their edifices, composed of granite and iron, are planted deep in American soil, their names indicate promised supremacy, and the States in which they are erected are called, with arrogant assumption, "provinces of the Holy See."

Whatever may be the result of these great projects, the future can alone reveal, but their prosecution is utterly opposed and hostile to the design, spirit, and practical ends of our system and institutions.

In carrying out this vast plan of aggression, no respect is paid to the laws of any country that interfere with the general plan. The ends justify the means. Thus we see the Grand Council of Bishops sitting in Baltimore in 1829, solemnly passing the following as a fundamental rule of the Church:—

"Whereas lay trustees have frequently abused the right granted to them by the civil authority, to the great detriment of religion and scandal of the faithful, we most earnestly desire that in future no church be erected or consecrated, unless it be assigned by a written instrument to the Bishop in whose diocese it may be erected for the Divine worship and use of the faithful, wherever this can be done."

Now these Bishops, mostly foreigners, inflated with the idea of their infallibility, thus deliberately demanded, wherever it could be done, the violation of the whole spirit of our constitution and laws, and have acted upon this treason ever since, and would probably have carried it on under the secrecy of their movements, had it not been dragged to light by the appeal to the civil laws of some few independent trustees, who denied that their Bishops must rule them in temporal matters.

So persevering, indeed, are these Bishops, that in the State of New York, even before the special law confining church property to the ownership of trustees had been fairly spread upon the statute books, Bishop Hughes dedicated in Brooklyn, the church of "St. Mary, Star of the Sea," and in his sermon announced to his congregation, that that very church did not in its titles conform to the civil laws of the land! and that the Trustee system was "uncatholic and heretical;" and the inference in the minds of his congregation of course followed, that no faith was necessarily to be kept with such laws.*

The American has no hostility to the Roman Church as a system of religious faith, notwithstanding he conscientiously dissents from its essential dogmas and doctrines. He makes no war against the religion of any sect. It is only in its political phases, and its spiritual connection inseparably blended with them, that he opposes the Church of Rome. To that extent, all true lovers of liberty have the constitutional right to animadvert upon it. Its efforts to connect itself with the politics of the country, not for the sake of office; but for the purpose of controlling the officers to its own will and advantage; to imbue them with the spirit and doctrines of its peculiar faith,—these are the things, so comprehensive in their hostility to our system of civil and religious freedom, to which alone the American expresses his determined hostility. The union of politics and religion, of Church and State, have ever proved themselves to be the direful curses of man; and in every pulsation of the heart,

* See Tribune of Monday, April 30, 1855, and other New York daily papers, for Report of Bishop Hughes' Sermon upon the occasion of consecrating the church known as "St. Mary, Star of the Sea," Brooklyn, New York.

in every ray of reason, in every emotion of the soul, the true and patriotic American, will make war against every and any religious association, which seeks to bring about an alliance so much to be dreaded.

Our ancestors came to this New World to enjoy, themselves and their posterity forever, perfect civil and religious freedom, and the right of inquiry, thought, and the expression of opinion upon subjects, short of invasion of the rights of others, unfettered as the winds of heaven. The divorce of Church and State, of politics and religion, of temporal and spiritual affairs, they have provided for in our constitutions, and it was intended to be absolute, complete, and forever. In the scheme of the hierarch of Rome and his emissaries—spread and spreading over the face of this country, to revolutionize silently and stealthily this order of things—they now have at their command an immense army of voters, perfectly trained to do their bidding. At every election, local or general, this mighty force is made to act with a view, present or remote, to the grand objects of those who control it. The certain and promptest way to get large accessions—accessions which, in another generation, may give them the mastery at the polls—is, to permit no restriction upon emigration, or upon the faculty of the immigrant to vote and exercise a full share of political sovereignty. All attempts to put upon them any restriction will meet the inflexible opposition, the anathemas of every Roman priest, and probably of almost every Romanist in America.

All this host of foreign Romans, now here and coming, are brought up to the confessional, at least once a year, to make a full avowal of their sins, by whispering them into the priest's ear, and whoever omits it is to be excommunicated, and if he die, is not to be allowed Christian burial. This is the function of the priesthood, which brings up before it all the liegemen of the Papal empire, and bows all in utter subjection and submission to it. When the noviciate for the first time, with convulsive excitement, breathes into the ear of the ghostly father the deep and criminal secrets of the heart, the soul is enslaved forever; a chain of adamant is thrown around it, and that chain is held by this priest. Even then he may grant or withhold absolution and forgiveness. Such are the mighty spells which Romanism brings over all her sons and daughters; and those who work them, control not only their acts and conduct, but their thoughts and emotions. And how often is this puissance of the priesthood exhibited strikingly in our country. Bands of rude and stormy foreign Romanists, who have traditionary feuds, are loitering in the same neighborhood. They meet in bloody affray. The civil officer of the law interposes and is unheeded. He calls to his aid a large constabulary force, which is laughed to scorn by the infuriated mob. The military is summoned to uphold the civil authority, and blank cartridges are fired among the combatants, but no more regarded than the whistling of the winds. At length death-dealing bullets begin their fatal office, and men fall, but the fight still rages. Lo! the priest makes his appearance, the contending mass of men pause at once, and give attention. He speaks a few words, the tempest of excited passion ceases, and savage men are subdued as children under the rebuke of an invisible power. These men all vote; but is it not the madness of folly to say, that their wills, when under such control, are represented at the polls?

There are numerous Romanists, natives of these States, who possess every element pertaining to good citizens, men who are every way able to assume the responsibility of self-government, and discharge with honor every political privilege imposed upon them; but these men, educated in this country of light and liberty, of the Bible and free schools, are not representatives of the Romanists of Europe. The immigrant is radically imbued with the spirit of decayed dynasties; he was never taught that he had rights and an individuality. On the contrary, his whole history has been one of humiliation; he was made to feel that he formed an insignificant part of a great all-grasping institution, claiming the whole earth's sceptre, spiritual and temporal. The trembling worshipper at the foot of a hierarchy, and the Pope a hierarch. Such are the notions the Romanist immigrant brings to our land, and, under the guidance of the priests that foster him, cherishes while here as his life's blood. It is the influence of this false education (profanely called religious) against which the true American declares eternal war.*

"Among lukewarm partisans and ardent antagonists, a small number of believers exist, who, in defence of their faith, are ready to brave all obstacles, and to scorn all dangers. They have done violence to human weakness, in order to rise superior to public opinion. Excited by the effort they have made, they scarcely know where to stop. They look upon their contemporaries with dread, and recoil in alarm from the liberty which their fellow-citizens enjoy. They are at war with their age and country, and they look upon every opinion which is put forth, as the necessary enemy of their faith."†

Such men, in demanding liberty of conscience for themselves, deny it unto others; and the step is rapid from intolerance to persecution. But our Constitution, in guaranteeing perfect religious freedom to all, will not justly be charged with abjuring its principles, if it compel these bigots to award the same deference to the opinions of others, which they enjoy for their own.

The determination on the part of any Church to force its faith upon another—the tendency to proselytize at all hazards—is certain to lead to a state of anarchy in which liberty cannot exist. When such views are openly avowed and acted upon by any creed, it becomes necessary, for the safety of others, either to prevent its residence in our midst, or so to fence about and confine it within the strict bounds of legality, as to render it incapable of mischief. Religion is a question on which we cannot legislate; it is a matter concerning the individual, not the mass. But if the creed of any party attempt to control temporal affairs by means of a so-called

* At the last celebration of St. Patrick's day in New York city, the Irish guests (intoxicated with zeal by an inflammatory speech of one of the several priests present on the occasion) announced themselves as supporters of American freedom and the hierarchy. It would be difficult to imagine one mind supporting two things more directly antagonistic; yet the announcement was perfectly consistent with the gentlemen's *ideas* of American liberty.

† De Tocqueville.

spiritual power, the Constitution of our country is only carrying out its high and holy mission, by restraining their ambitious views with wholesome and necessary coercion. The framing of laws to bring about this coercion, however, would not only be difficult, but almost, if not quite, impossible. It is, therefore, necessary that the citizen should have correct opinions, and that the desired effect should be produced by the force of public opinion, rather than by written laws.

RELIGIOUS TOLERATION.

> "True religion
> Is always mild, propitious, and humane;
> Plays not the tyrant, plants no faith in blood;
> But stoops to polish, succor, and redress,
> And builds her grandeur on the public good."
>
> MILLER.

THE opposition which exists in the mind of every American against oppression, causes a dislike to any and every institution, no matter what may be its name, that is the support of the oppressor. In looking over European countries, the larger portion of their inhabitants are found to be sunken into the lowest depths of ignorance and semi-barbarism. They have no defined rights, and are the uncomplaining servants of aristocratic rulers. Upon one subject alone they seem thoroughly instructed, and that is, to render slavish obedience to the priests, and the ceremonies of the Roman Church. Hearing a service on the Sabbath-day conducted in a dead language, and studiously debarred from all the ordinary channels of information so common in America, their minds are literally in the chains of ignorance, and to keep them there confined is brought to bear the whole machinery of the Roman Church. One of the most vital principles of our government is religious toleration; the American, whatever may be his creed, shrinks from any imposition upon the conscience, and hence it is that the grossest abuses may creep into our body politic, if profanely sanctioned by the garb of religion, and for that reason it is difficult and delicate to discuss the causes of this European degradation, because it is at once urged by the Jesuit and the demagogue, that any determination of the citizens of this country to make a distinction between the political and religious character of the

Roman Church, is an attack upon the rights of the conscience, and at once the cry of persecution is raised. Whatever may be the excitement, the work has to be done; it is the duty of the true Romanist as well as the true Protestant to examine this subject dispassionately and come to a perfect understanding, for upon it rests at this moment, more than upon any other thing, the perpetuity of our free institutions.

The enthusiastic lover of liberty has heretofore argued, that under the bright rays of religious toleration, the minds of our most ignorant naturalized citizens would insensibly be enlightened, and that the most bigoted would gradually become converted to charity, and that the beauty of our political system would thoroughly absorb their affections, to the exclusion of any fondness for anti-republican sentiments and oppressive political institutions. But, so far from this being the case, the experience of the last few years develops the melancholy fact, that men born in this country, and deservedly honored for their general intelligence, can sometimes, under the severe discipline of Romish institutions, be brought to support them with all the enthusiasm and Jesuitical casuistry that characterizes the uneducated European or the designing ecclesiastic. It is but recently that a gentleman of national reputation, in making a defence of the Pope and his authority upon the floor of Congress—a gentleman who is possessed of great knowledge and a keen sense of truth when treating of civil or general matters—boldly announced that the Pope had no political power, that he never meddled himself with governments, but confined his authority to religious matters alone. But even while the echoes of his voice were vibrating in our national Capitol, the news from the Italian States announced, that the Pope, finding he could not arrest the progress of liberal opinions in Sardinia, had issued a "Bull," releasing all Romanists of that kingdom from allegiance to their civil rulers!

We find also that gentlemen in our various Legislatures, who ordinarily love the truth and respect the lessons of history, proclaiming that the Roman Church is the friend and encourager of free institutions, while they know, and often from personal observation too, that the people of the Papal States are the most degraded, and the farthest removed from freemen, of any other government of the world; and that in all Papal countries, oppression and decay are paramount, just in proportion as they acknowledge the influence of the Romish power.

To the ingenuous American mind, these strange misrepresentations of history for the purpose of defending the Roman Church are hard to understand, and they can only be accounted for on the principle, that that Church seizes upon the imagination and the will of its adherents, and blinds them to the plainest truths, and makes them unresisting instruments for the propagation of the most pernicious errors.

In no Romanist country is there any real religious toleration; seven-eighths of our emigrants are brought up and educated to believe that such toleration is an unpardonable sin. Sunken in poverty, and suffering from the severest oppression, they leave their native countries and seek a home on American soil; but, do they leave behind them the errors of their early education? Are they forever freed from the presence and baleful influence of their political priests? Certainly not. So far from this being the case, we find the Jesuit follows in their footsteps, and, taking advantage of the freedom of Protestant institutions, manages to exert a power over the minds and consciences of our immigrant population, as perfect as if they lived under monarchical governments. The American, perceiving this evil, and noticing its political character, denounces it from the stump, through the press, and attempts to counteract it at the polls; instantly the cry is raised by the wily Jesuit and the office-seeking demagogue, of religious intolerance, and people, who never breathed one breath of Christian charity, who, as an act of religious faith, denounce all who differ from them as heretics and heathen—people who are prepared, at any moment they can grasp the power of the State, to punish freedom of thought with imprisonment and death, go forth in the highways and byways denouncing American citizens, who desire to protect the purity of their institutions from the evils of this foreign influence.

In America alone is enjoyed in the fullest sense the right to worship God according to the dictates of the conscience. Americans conceived and put in practice such toleration; but while it is freely enjoyed here by the Romanists, and demanded as a right, still it is not accorded to Americans in Romanist countries, and this illiberal spirit finds advocates and meets with justification in the organs of Romanism, and the gross inconsistency seems to be unnoticed.

The Island of Cuba is the resort of hundreds and thousands of our citizens, either as mariners, merchants, or invalids; among the latter are many who visit the island to die, and yet to this day there is no Protestant chapel, nor clergymen to give spiritual instruction. Any attempt to hold Protestant service calls forth the interference of the police; and it was only recently that an English Bishop, visiting Havana, was denied the privilege of celebrating religious service in the house of the British Consul.

There is no American Protestant chapel in Mexico, and it would be impossible to establish one.

In Italy, the central country of Romanism, with the exception of the Pope-denounced kingdom of Sardinia, no religious service could be held by an American Protestant minister, unless it were in the house of the American Consul, and under the American flag.

In Romanist Spain and Austria, the war upon Protestants amounts to a total exclusion under all circumstances.

In Portugal, the penal code, promulgated as recently as 1852, punishes with imprisonment and fine all who engage in acts of worship not of the Romanist religion.

American Protestants are exposed to insult and maltreatment in Mexico, Central America, all South America, Cuba, Porto Rico, Spain, Portugal, Austria, and nearly all of Italy, if they do not kneel when they meet a procession bearing "the Host," although they may conscientiously deem the act idolatrous, and contrary to the word of God. The records of every year are filled with details of outrages perpetrated, for the reason above given, upon Americans travelling abroad.

The right, in many Romanist countries, of quietly depositing in the mother earth the remains of the dead, is denied to American Protestants, and the living have had to carry the deceased many hundred miles, to find a resting-place under the ægis of less bigoted governments. Where the privilege is granted, it is attended, as in some parts of Italy, with the degrading condition that the burial shall take place at unseasonable hours—and American Protestants have been unceremoniously thrust into the earth as if they were brute beasts, to avoid exhumation and insult from the imbruted populace, who were thus inflamed against the religion of the deceased by the bigoted priests.

A few years ago, a highly respectable American merchant had the misfortune to lose a beloved wife, whom he had taken to the Island of Cuba for the restoration of her health. Abandoned by all the people who surrounded him, he was compelled in an obscure spot to dig a grave with his own hands, and with difficulty succeeded in procuring the help of two negroes, to assist him in the melancholy task of consigning all that was once so cherished to its mother earth; and yet these Africans, pagan-born and besotted in ignorance, had been taught to fear for their lives, if it were known to the authorities they had assisted in the "burial of a heretic!"

Mr. Wise, late U. S. minister to Brazil, states, that Mr. Tudor, our Chargé to that government,—the successful negotiator of a treaty of amity and commerce, and the representative of the greatest Republic in the world,—was indebted to the British legation for a sanctuary for his corpse, and but for this charity, the Romanist government of Brazil would probably have spurned the body of Mr. Tudor from its dominions, the hatred of heretics extending even into the grave. Mr. Wise establishes himself in his new residence, he has his family around him, he has been accustomed to advocate and to grant religious toleration. He is the minister plenipotentiary of a great nation, and should command respect; but the Sabbath comes, he hears the bells chiming for church, dismay seizes upon him and his household, and he exclaims, in the true sense of his deprivation, "Where am I and my family and American friends to attend Divine worship? There is no ground here consecrated for us! We are reminded on this Lord's day of our homes in our own blessed, happy land of universal tolerance in religion, but here, by treaty in a land of commercial friends, we have no religious allies, and are indeed 'strangers in a strange land!' If their God is our God, their country is not ours to worship in!"

In all Protestant countries, Romanists enjoy the liberty of religious worship. Everywhere they may fill not only magisterial, but even political offices. O'Connell, the champion of that Church, was a member of the British Parliament! Examples of the same liberality can be found in the governments of Prussia, Holland, Sweden, Denmark, and the United States. Toleration is the fundamental spirit of the organic law. Not an example can be quoted where the religious worship of the Romanist Church is impeded in a Protestant country, as that of the Protestant is, in Rome, Naples, Florence, Milan, Madrid and Lisbon, and the South American States.

The mass of the people of France are tolerant, but the Roman clergy are restless under their loss of power, and watch with unceasing energy to restore their fortunes by giving their influence to the usurper of the nation's liberties. Napoleon III. found the priests his most willing tools, and the first to forgive his falsehoods and his perjuries.* Their political influence was bought at the price of the imperial recognition of their religion; the effect is already felt. Without any repeal of fundamental laws, Protestantism is discouraged, its schools under various pretexts successively suppressed, and its publications prohibited.

In Austria, all Protestant meetings require the sanction of the police; the government thus prevents them, without appearing to

* "May he (Louis Napoleon) be blessed, this man of God, this great man, for it is God who has raised him up for the happiness of our country."—*Bishop of Chalons' Address to his Clergy, September*, 1854.

prohibit; and those persons who have presumed to publish or propagate the Bible, have been banished at the instigation of the Romish clergy.

In Spain but one religion is professed, and none other is permitted in any shape. To be a Spaniard implies necessarily to be a Romanist. He who dares to forsake that faith is by law banished, lest the poison of his heresy should spread contagion, while those who have tempted him from his early faith are liable to imprisonment. Hitherto the traveller was looked upon as an exception; but as Spain decays in political power, as she sinks into contempt among the family of nations, Papacy grasps her soul more firmly, and her priest-ridden government decrees, that even the "traveller" is no longer permitted "to profess any but the Romanist religion;" and the American Protestant, while residing in Spain, must hide his religious sentiments, and, when dead, must be cast as some foul thing into an obscure, and, by the Spanish people, what is considered a dishonored grave.

Tuscany is notorious, and Naples infamous for its intolerance. The Madiai persecution, which roused the sympathy of the Protestant world, and yet found defenders among the foreign Papists of this country, is but a single instance of many, that, in spite of the secrecy of Jesuit police, and the depths of Italian dungeons, find their way before the judgment-seat of enlightened Christendom. Naples, where nature appears in its most glorious forms, and where man alone is base,—Naples, which in days of yore coped with the haughty Pontiffs of Rome, the decrees of the Council of Trent, and trampled upon Papal Bulls,—now lies prostrate in the dust. Violent, bigoted, and profligate, her people violate every precept of morality, yet observe every ceremonial of religion. They are the degraded vassals of intolerance, without alleviation, and without hope.

At last we penetrate into the "imperial city," and reach Rome itself. If other countries have admitted unjustifiable Papal claims, if other countries have harbored the Inquisition, it was here the haughty thunders were launched. Here intolerance reigns supreme. Here it had its birth, here it has made its throne. Here it was that

Gregory XIII. rejoiced over the slaughter of the Huguenots, and ordered a *Te Deum* to be sung, with illuminations for the people, and, for the benefit of posterity, a medal in brass commemorative of the glorious event! Here it is, in our own day, where the Pope, in a studied allocution, congratulates Christendom because Spain relapses into the intolerance of bygone centuries. When New Grenada, not a year ago, by decrees established a free press, free education, and tolerance in religion, from Rome comes another allocution, condemning such fearful approaches to "hated liberty," which are denounced "as horrible and sacrilegious war against the Romish Church;" and her citizens are stimulated to open rebellion against their rulers by the Pope's annunciation, that he "declares utterly null and void all the aforesaid decrees, which have been enacted by the civil power." The Pope knows, "That wherever religious liberty exists, it will, first or last, bring in an established political party; wherever it is suppressed, the Church Establishment will, first or last, become the engine of despotism, and overthrow, unless it be itself overthrown, every vestige of political liberty."*

The cause of this intolerance is fundamental with the Roman Church; it cannot alter its character without losing its individuality. Styling itself "Infallible," its claims cannot be set aside. Its intolerance, its ministers say, arises from *authority;* it is therefore legitimate, and to yield would be sacrificing to licentiousness. Nor do the advocates of Romanism claim the virtues of liberality so much admired by the true-hearted American. They are willing to enjoy the advantages of liberty, and shelter their institutions under the broad folds of our tolerant flag. The Jesuits themselves, a proscribed class of political priests even among most of the countries devoted to Romanism, find here a foothold, and, from the unsuspicious character of our people, scarcely call forth an observation to their ulterior designs, of sapping our liberties and changing the character of our institutions. Yet all this toleration on our part meets with no response

* Justice Story.

from the Romanist hierarchy or people. The hierarchy hate and fear it; the lay members, if they cherish any admiration, dare not express it. Hence we find that no minister at Washington representing a Romanist country acknowledges the superior Christian liberality of our government, nor has it ever been officially reciprocated or commended. The Romanist journals published in America never advocate religious toleration; on the contrary, they threaten, if their cherished doctrines gain the ascendency, that toleration will cease; and special care is taken by the priests, who are with few exceptions foreigners, to cultivate and encourage among our immigrant Romanist population, the same bitter hostility to the "heretic" that characterized their chief education in their native land. The American, in consideration of these facts, finds no difficulty in distinguishing between the abuse of the name of religion, and religion itself. He strips the matter of its complications, and, giving to the conscience full liberty, opposes political tendencies and practices calculated to destroy our Republican institutions; he opposes a political system despotic in its organization, anti-republican in its tendencies, and at utter war with the simplicity of our whole government.

It is only as a hierarchy, as a religio-political institution, having vast political projects, and organized for political action, and because its principles, purposes, and operations are utterly inimical to popular and American constitutional liberty, to all civil and religious freedom, that the true American stands up in opposition to it. Until American Romanists call their general councils, and purge their system of its interior and harsh ecclesiastical despotism; until they join together as a body, and demand the same toleration for American Protestants abroad, that Romanists everywhere receive in America; until they announce to the Pope and the world that his supremacy is only spiritual, and out of his Papal dominions in Italy, he, nor his priests, have right to interfere in politics or temporal affairs; that they owe him or his hierarchy no duty or obedience incompatible with their full and perfect allegiance to the United States, or any of the States, or that is hostile to any of the principles of their governments; that they are opposed to, and will ever resist the union of Church and State, and any mixing of their affairs; until they bid, and will compel their priesthood to cease their meddling with the government and politics of the country, with a view to shape its laws and policy for their ulterior purposes, and to desist from their efforts to control the entire Romanist vote of America;—Until these things are done, no native American, no true friend of liberty, wherever born or whatever be his religion, can conscientiously cease his opposition to this great religio-political institution; for the very spirit of self-preservation requires, that war be waged as much upon an aggressive religious power, as upon an aggressive civil power, for both are equally hostile to our Republican institutions.

Religion is a question between man's conscience and his God. No government can interfere with it, except to guarantee perfect freedom to all, in the exercise of that faith which each has seen fit to embrace; or to prevent a persecuting system of proselytism, which history shows us has been the characteristic of every religious sect in all ages. A government guaranteeing toleration to every Church, has the right to compel them to tolerate each other.

Religion is perfectly distinct from, and cannot possibly be any part of, political government. The former regards not the present world, but looks to a future state. The latter regulates the affairs of time, but leaves untouched those of eternity. There is an impassable gulf between them—one that mankind can never bridge. When the attempt has been made, it has invariably met with a calamitous issue.

"In Europe, Christianity has been intimately united to the powers of the earth. Those powers are now in decay, and it is, as it were, buried under their ruins. The living body of religion has been bound down to the dead corpse of superannuated polity. Cut the bonds which restrain it, and that which is alive will rise once more."*

Shall such be the result in our country? This is the question which Americans have to answer, and to answer ere it be too late. Let them arise and tell the priestly hierarchies that when they

* De Tocqueville.

attempt to subjugate the temporal to the spiritual power, and, by means of uncontrolled influence over the minds of their followers, peril the peace of the community, hinder the operation of the laws, and, by their acts, proclaim the Constitution a dead letter, toleration becomes impossible; for toleration would then be treason to the country.

THE BIBLE THE CHARTER OF LIBERTY.

> "Out from the heart of nature rolled
> The burthens of the Bible old,
> The Litanies of nations came
> Like the volcano's tongue of flame;
> Up from the burning core below
> The Canticles of Love and Woe."
>
> EMERSON.

THE BIBLE is the charter of human liberty, and in the teachings of that sacred volume are to be found the glad tidings that all men are free and equal, not only before each other, but in the sight of God. So long as the Scriptures were confined to the few, so long as its pages were closed to the multitude, so long the world rested in darkness, and oppression existed throughout all lands. From the time of the invention of printing, and the consequent circulation of the Bible, do we date the commencement of those struggles against despotism which finally resulted in the establishment of our free government.

It cannot be controverted, that the Bible was the cause of the early revolutions that startled kings from their thrones, and shook the foundations of the Vatican. It taught men the rights of the citizen, and these led them to examine the claims of rulers. It questioned traditions and authorities, and rejected them if not in accordance with the humble but sublime teachings of Christ. Finding that the Creator looked upon all men with equal favor, all laws not in conformity with this principle were pronounced unauthorized and unjust. The inculcation of the direct confession of sins to the Throne of Grace, swept away at a blow the assumptions of priestcraft, and made man responsible for his actions to his own conscience and his God. Multitudes, who before the reading of the Scriptures were debased, made self-reliance the prevailing feature of the age. The light that poured into the civilized world, overwhelmed society with new views and aspirations. Every page of the sacred volume strengthened the minds of the reformers, and shed a lustre over the memories of the martyrs who had through all time died in defence of liberty. The very foundations of society rocked to the centre; the divine right of kings, and the profane assumptions of priests, were scoffed at.

In England, and on the Continent, the standard of rebellion was raised, and thousands, filled with new-born zeal, fearlessly asserted the glorious promises of man's regeneration. The triumphs of humanity, of civilization, and of Christianity, which are the boasts of the nineteenth century, would have been unknown, and the pall of the dark ages would still be upon us, were it not for the free circulation of the Bible. This great truth has always been acknowledged with the greatest solemnity by our Revolutionary fathers. Washington and his compatriots entered upon no serious duties, without the reading of the Scriptures, and an humble acknowledgment of dependence upon Divine Wisdom for instruction in council, and strength in the hour of battle. In all hours of suffering, in the darkest days that tried men's souls, it was the encouragement held forth in the sacred volume that kept our sires from despondency, and strengthened their arms in the noble thought, that their cause was sanctioned by the God of battles. The original demands of the men, whose sufferings and martyrdom form so large a page in the early struggles for human freedom, was, that the Bible might be made free, and that its teachings might illume the hearts and consciences of all men.

The question, then, comes home seriously to every conscience, Can our present form of government exist if the Bible be excluded from the public eye? Are those persons who fear its influence, and do all in their power to suppress its circulation, friends to liberty? Are those of our citizens who consent to be deprived of the Bible, and avoid its pages as if they were possessed of contagion, capable of self-government? We can imagine individuals who may be good citizens without the enlightenment of the precepts of the Holy Book, but we cannot conceive of a nation prospering without sensibly feeling and acknowledging their influence. Man is a religious being, and upon that immortal principle rests the security of all human rights; he must therefore either have his morals cultivated by his own intelligent pursuit of good from the fountain of truth, or he must consent to put himself in ecclesiastical servitude, and have his conscience controlled by others.

The American is distinguished from all other people, because he thinks for himself, and thus displays the possession of the very essence of self-government. He reads the Bible, learns from its precepts the distinctions between right and wrong, that all men are equal in the sight of Heaven, that he must love his neighbor as himself, and that he alone is responsible to God for his acts. This high state of intellectual and moral culture never was obtained in perfection except under American institutions, and the accomplishment of it was heralded as the greatest triumph of humanity from the bondage and oppression of ages.

Any doctrine, therefore, that teaches the suppression of the Bible, must be inimical to liberty—must be treason to the preservation of the Republican character; and whether it is advocated by the avowed skeptic, or more dangerously urged under the guise of religion, in both cases the pernicious tendency is the same. Infidelity would strike at the foundations of all liberty, by destroying the authority which sanctifies its existence: religion, falsely so called, would accomplish the same object, on the ground that the individual is not in matters of conscience capable of deciding for himself.

The country has been agitated about the reading of the Scriptures in our public schools. The Romish priests have protested against such an enormity, and the usefulness of the noblest institution of our country has been impaired and imperiled, in the effort to drive the book from the teacher's desk. In many cases our American populations have yielded to the assumption, that certain American children could be injured by hearing its Divine precepts, instead of taking the position, that children reared in such bigotry were in the hands of those who neither sympathized with nor understood our institutions; for it is certain beyond contradiction, that those who persist in such strange exclusiveness have still lingering in their minds a reverence for absolutism not in accordance with universal liberty.

Charles Carroll of Carrollton, a Romanist, and one of the signers of the Declaration of Independence, is constantly quoted as an evidence of the liberty-loving spirit of his Church. That he was a patriot and loved his country there cannot be a doubt; but when he associated himself with Washington, Franklin, Jefferson, and other fathers of the Revolution, he surrendered, at the very commencement of his political career, the identity of Romanism on the altar of universal toleration, else he could not have participated in the stirring and glorious scenes enacted around him. Had he retained the spirit, if he ever possessed it, that would banish the Bible from the public eye, he would have solemnly protested against the reading of the Scriptures at the openings of the convention that adopted the Declaration of Independence, and if it had been persisted in, he would have thrown up his seat and his solemn duties, and retired in indignation, announcing to the astonished patriots about him, that he was afraid to hear that book read in his presence—that in so doing he would be disobeying the orders of his ghostly father;—it was because Charles Carroll did not thus act, because he repudiated such control of his conscience, that he did sign the immortal Declaration of our Independence, and engraved his name upon a monument that will cause it to be remembered with honor as long as virtue is cherished among mankind.

The Council of Trent decrees, "That no Bible shall be held or read except by priests—that no Bible shall be sold without a license, except upon the pains and penalties of that mortal sin that is neither to be forgiven in this world or the next."* By the priests of the

* See Father Paul Sarpis' History of the Council of Trent.

Romish Church it is, therefore, denied to their congregations, and innumerable instances have occurred of the Bible being seized and publicly burned in this country when found in the possession of Romanists. In Europe, in Piedmont and Tuscany, imprisonment and persecution are even now meted out for such a crime.

Some years ago a society termed the Christian Alliance was formed in the city of New York, the object of which was to circulate the Bible without note or comment, in the prevailing language in different Papal countries. The labors of this society produced the greatest consternation at Rome, and in 1844, Gregory, the then reigning Pope, fulminated a bull against this association, of which we give a single extract:—

"Moreover, venerable brothers, we recommend the utmost watchfulness over the insidious measures and attempts of the Christian Alliance, to those who, raised to the dignity of your order, are called to govern the Italian churches, or the countries which Italians frequent most commonly, especially the frontiers, and parts whence travellers enter Italy. As these are the points on which the sectarians have fixed to commence the realization of their projects, it is highly necessary that the bishops of those places should mutually assist each other zealously and faithfully, in order, with the aid of God, to discover and prevent their machinations.

"Let us not doubt but your exertions, added to our own, will be seconded by the civil authorities, and especially by most influential sovereigns of Italy, no less by reason of their favorable regard for the Papal religion, than that they plainly perceive how much it concerns them to prostrate these sectarian combinations. Indeed, it is most evident from past experience, that there are no means more certain of rendering the people disobedient to their princes than rendering them indifferent to religion, under the mask of religious liberty. The members of the Christian Alliance do not conceal this fact from themselves, although they declare that they are far from wishing to excite disorder; but they notwithstanding avow that, once liberty of interpretation attained, and with it what they term liberty of conscience among Italians, these last will naturally soon acquire political liberty."

Here is palpably revealed the natural connection and alliance between the political despotism of the Papal See, and the oppressors of the people of Europe. The only object of the Christian Alliance was to give the Holy Scriptures to the people of Italy. How quick it excited the fears of the Pope, how conscious was the prevailing power at Rome, that wherever the light and power of that volume was admitted, that religious liberty, and rebellion against the assumptions of crafty priests, would follow, that the civil and religious despots were the natural enemies of the Bible, and hence was invoked the aid of those hated enemies of mankind, the ruling sovereigns, to aid in the work of suppressing the sacred volume.

The last official act known to the world of Gregory XVI. was dated May 8th, 1844, in which for the second time he expresses his dread of the circulation of the Scriptures. With more elaboration than is usual in such documents, the Pope points out all the dreaded evils, and renews his orders to his subordinates, to assist each other in zealously carrying out his decrees. Among other things his Holiness says,—

"Subsequently, when heretics still persisted in their frauds, it became necessary for Benedict XIV. to superadd the injunction that no versions whatever (of the Bible) should be suffered to be read but those which should be approved of by the Holy See, accompanied by notes derived from the writings of the Holy Fathers, or other learned Catholic authors."

"As for yourselves, my venerable brethren, called as you are to divide our solicitude, we recommend you earnestly in the Lord, to announce and proclaim, in convenient time and place, to the people confided to your care, these apostolical orders, and to labor carefully to separate the faithful sheep from contagion of the Christian Alliance, from those who have become its auxiliaries, no less than those who belong to other Bible societies, and from all who have any communication with them. You are consequently enjoined to remove from the hands of the faithful alike the Bibles in the vulgar tongue which may have been printed contrary to the decrees above mentioned of the sovereign Pontiffs, and every book proscribed and condemned, and see that they learn, through your admonition and authority, what passages are salutary, and what pernicious and mortal. Watch attentively over those who are appointed to expound the Holy Scriptures, to see that they acquit themselves faithfully according to the capacity of their hearers, and that they dare not, under any pretext whatever, interpret or explain the holy pages contrary to the tradition of the Holy Fathers, and to the service of the Catholic Church."

"Let me know, then, the enormity of the sin against God and his Church which they are guilty of who dare associate themselves with any of these societies, or abet them in any way. Moreover, we confirm and renew the decrees recited above, delivered in former times by apostolic authority, against the publication, distribution, reading, and possession of books of the Holy Scriptures translated into the vulgar tongue."

Without commenting upon the spectacle here exhibited, of the assumed infallible head of the true Church denying the Holy Scriptures to the mass of mankind, or attempting in any way to dispute the authority for so doing, every true American, whatever may be his creed, must ask the question, "Could our peculiar institutions flourish under such a system? and are those persons, in this country or Europe, proper citizens for a republic, who will submit to such dictation?" It cannot be disguised, that liberal principles, and the behests of the Pope, here meet in eternal opposition. One or the other power must give way. On the continent of Europe, wherever Romanism has undisputed sway, the Bible is indeed a proscribed book. In many Italian states, and almost under the very shadow of the dome of St. Peter's, families are imprisoned for being found with the sacred volume in their possession; delicate women are incarcerated in dungeons, and their husbands and brothers consigned to the lingering death of the galleys.

A few examples of Bible burning have been afforded even in our glorious country, and "the faithful" have quietly yielded up the volume, to be consigned by the Jesuit to the flames. Thanks to our institutions no civil punishment has followed, but what have been the more terrible denunciations of the Priest upon the guilty the world will never know. This is the spirit that the American wars against—he cannot find it sanctioned by any commendable toleration, because it is sanctioning wrong. He cannot believe it to be in accordance with any religious sentiment, for the conscience enlightened by reason revolts at such tyranny—the question then again recurs, Are individuals capable of self-government who will yield up unresistingly, and from any plea, or by the dictation of any power, this most sacred right of reading, not only the Holy Scriptures, but any book of morals that has made its impress upon the world.

The Sacred Scriptures are not only the Divine revelation of a life to come, and the Guide for the life present, but also the great Conservator of morals, and the basis of all true social virtue and happiness. In the quaint words of Jeremy Taylor, the Bible is "the ligature of souls, and the great instrument of the conservation of bodies politic." Montesquieu justly observes, that "the principles of Christianity deeply engraven in the heart, would be infinitely more powerful than the false honor of monarchies, the human virtues of republics, or the servile fears of despotic states." We know, and, what is better, we feel inwardly that religion is the basis of civil society, and the source of all good and of all comfort.* All history conclusively proves, that wherever the Bible was possessed by the people, virtue and civilization advanced;—wherever it was not, the converse was no less true. A spurious civilization may exist without the faith of Christianity, but it is a civilization that opposes no check to idolatrous superstition and cruelty, and the most flagrant immoralities and crimes.

The moral effects of the Bible are illustrated in the history of the Jewish race; since their superiority over the heathen nations is mainly

* Burke.

to be ascribed to their possession of the Divine Oracles. Since the introduction of Christianity, the influence of its Divine precepts on society is still more marked, in mitigating the horrors of war, in suppressing the iniquitous and sanguinary rites of heathenism, and the gladiatorial combats, which, according to Lipsius, sometimes cost Europe from twenty thousand to thirty thousand lives in a month.

But the influence of the Bible is to be sought for, not so much in the councils of princes, as in the debates or resolutions of popular assemblies, in the conduct of governments towards their subjects, or of states and sovereigns towards one another, of conquerors at the head of their armies, or of parties intriguing for power at home (topics which almost alone occupy the attention, and fill the pages of history), as in the silent course of private and domestic life, and in the yet more private regulations of the heart.* Here have ever been its great triumphs. The fact of its inculcating self-government renders the Bible the great essential in a state where the people are invested with the sovereign power.

The presence of the Divine Oracles sanctified the councils of our patriot fathers alike in times of war and peace. It was to the Bible that they made their appeal in all emergencies, in the tented field and in the legislative hall. It was to this fact that we may ascribe the noble testimony of history, which asserts that our Revolutionary struggle was unstained by a single crime. It was to the same source that we trace the pure patriotism and self-sacrificing heroism and faith of the revered founders of our free institutions; and it is in a like jealous regard and cherishing love for the Bible, as our national text-book of civil and religious liberty, as well as of Christian faith, that we confidently rest all our hope for the prosperity and perpetuity of our great Republic. Shall we lightly esteem so precious a boon? Shall we ever forget that it comes to us with the sacred insignia of Divinity, baptized with the blood of ancient saints and worthies, and all fragrant with celestial Truth? Shall we forget that it has passed through the

* Paley's Evidences.

fires of persecution all unscathed, and that its soul-entrancing truths sustained confessors and martyrs who suffered to the death to transmit to us, their descendants, the inestimable treasure? Can we be free, we would again ask, if we suffer ourselves to be deprived of the Scriptures? and are those friends of liberty and free institutions who would proscribe their circulation among the people?

THE PRINCIPLES AND PERILS OF OUR COMMON EDUCATION.

Education is the cheap defence of nations."—EDMUND BURKE.

THE wisest must govern. This truth has been the basis of all the governments in the world, from the Patriarchs to the Presidents. It is a text upon which a whole circle of sermons has been preached. It has supplied the arguments of the absurd monarchist, Filmer; the aristocratical aspirations of Thomas Carlyle; of the ravings and reveries of all the red republicans in the world. In the rude times, when men were gathered into tribes, the old men, as wisest, ruled the band; not very stringently, but with all the authority of the tribe. This primitive mode of governing has descended down, among savages, to the Wittenagemote (" witty men's meet," " wise men's meeting") of the Saxons, and to our Indian contemporaries.

Monarchs, whether autocratic or constitutional, usurping or hereditary, have asserted the same principle. Great rulers, such as Julius Cæsar, Oliver Cromwell, and Napoleon Bonaparte, who grasped supreme power because they knew they could use it; and petty tyrants, who abused it because the people were supine and ignorant, have asserted the same claim—the right of the wisest to govern.

The feudal governments of Europe are set on a like foundation. The wealthy and (so-called) noble aristocracy—whose power, and whose intention to keep it, are alike and almost equally represented by Alexander the Autocrat, and Victoria the constitutional Queen—make appeal to this principle in their very name. An "Aristocracy" is, literally, a Best Government—a Government by the Wisest.

Not that these rulers have always deliberately claimed that they, individually, were wisest among men; but they have done it for themselves as *officers*, in their formal documents. They say, "In our wisdom;" and, "Of our free grace and mere motion," and such things. These forms at least defer to the common consent of mankind that the wisest ought to govern, by taking the name of wisdom; just as vice acknowledges the supremacy of virtue, by pretending to *be* virtue. Republics—Greek, Italian, Swiss, German, French, American—have alike proclaimed the same universal maxim, with so loud a voice that we need not stop to repeat their words.

The only difference amongst all these different rulers has been in their answers to the question, Who *are* the wisest? The king, the emperor, the holy czar—say the monarchists. The king and his nobles—say the feudalists. The nobles, said the oligarchic Venetians. The people said, and still say—The people. So say we. But precisely at this point is a common and enormous omission. "The people ought to govern," is the loud cry of all our politicians. But there can be no reason *why* they ought to govern, unless that they are wisest—because they are wise enough to govern. It is with the nation as it is with the individual. When a man is old enough, knows enough, to take care of himself, then he *may* take care of himself. Until that time, he is under more or less restraint. And a nation not wise enough to govern itself, will as surely work out its own destruction, as an inexperienced boy in the sole charge of a great estate would unwisely waste and lose it.

Our politicians happen in fact to be right. But that is only because our people have been wise enough to govern. The presumption has always been, that each voter has been intelligent enough and upright enough to be intrusted with the power. The exceptions have been so few as to serve only to prove the rule. But of late years, the exceptions have increased so rapidly, especially by immigration of ignorant and immoral foreigners, that this presumption of intelligence can hardly any longer be said to exist. The politicians continue to cry, "Let the people govern!" But the trouble is not now lest the people shall *govern*. *That* they will always do. They will never, in this country, suffer the sceptre to pass out of their hands. But the trouble now is, to keep them wise enough to govern *well*. They are not in the case of the boy who is not old enough to manage his estate; but they are in the case of the man who is in danger of ruining his estate by falling into evil courses.

The American Republican theory is *not* merely that the people should govern; it is, first, that *the people are the wisest;* and second, and only by virtue of this wisdom, comes the other truth which we hear so often, The people must govern.

For abundant proof of our position, let us look to the practice and precepts of those founders of the Union and fathers of American liberty—the first settlers of the thirteen colonies. In the early times of the various colonial commonwealths, only members of churches were admitted, in some of them, to the exercise of the electoral franchise, for the declared reason that the body of the people ought to consist of honest and good men. Decent and reputable conduct as members of society was also a recognized requisite of those admitted to vote. The written constitutions, and the whole spirit of the frame of government of all the early colonies, is conclusively in point. The strong, clear-minded men who established them, saw plainly the absolute necessity of admitting none to the freeman's privilege of governing the State, except such as were duly qualified in intellect and morals for that high responsibility. They set their standard of qualification higher than would now be endured. They required, until public sentiment compelled a change, both the ownership of property, that the voter might the more sensibly feel the effects of his own governing, and church-membership, that he might be approved a man of pure heart and life, and as one not about to endanger their peculiar semi-theocratic institutions. That their application of the principle was extreme and mistaken, may be allowed; but the demonstration is not less conclusive, but rather more so, of the strength and clearness of their conviction that only *safe* men—well-qualified men—should conduct the affairs of the State.

Since this is our theory, and has been our practice, as it ought to be, is in some measure, and as we hope it will be again, evidently it is the very profoundest and most absolute necessity of the State, if it desires to be a righteous, prosperous, and happy State, to foresee its future, and to secure to itself the means of a prosperous and progressive life, by raising up well-trained citizens for the next generation. The nation, during one generation, must prepare the next; just as a provident man of business during one season is making arrangements for his investments and enterprises during the next; or as a farmer, while cultivating one crop, makes that crop help prepare for the next, and thus preserves and improves the value and productive power of his land.

The children of the present age are the nation of the future, and properly educating them for wise and right action as men, is not only the very greatest responsibility of our adult generation, but it is also a necessity as plain and indispensable as that a man should preserve his life now, in order to be alive next year. The training of the children is the whole basis of our republic; the one thing needful, without which all our other pains and trouble for perpetuating our Union must come to naught; the primary source and condition of all that is desirable in our peculiar national life, if any such we have.

The American common-school education is the essential condition of all that is valuable in our American citizenship and polity. It is consistent with them; a part of the same machine—as one particular wheel is of its own engine, and of no other. It differs from other common-school educations, precisely as our people differ from other people, and our institutions from other institutions. American school education, as fostered and enforced by our government, is intended to train citizens fit to uphold our State; men wise enough to govern. They must be intelligent; possessed of minds free, active, stored with the fundamentals of knowledge, and with as much as possible of the superstructure. Yet they must be so trained, morally and religiously, as to keep their intellects and their passions subject to their regard for right, Christianity, and the law.* They need the widest freedom, that they may manage and discuss their political business with the confident courage which distinguished the founders of the republic. They need the utmost wisdom, that they may make few mistakes themselves, and may profit by the examples of others. They need the most thorough and deeply-founded conviction of the supremacy of God and the sanctity of His great laws, and of the moral and human laws based thereon, in order that they may not pass from freedom to riot; that their own stability as law-abiding, honest, and upright citizens may be sufficient to guard and guide them in the wide freedom of our constitution, and to bring them to the strenuous support of that constitution when attacked or violated by the ignorant or the wicked.

That such is the true relation of our common-school training to the State, seems proved by the mere statement of the case. That such was in fact its scope and purpose, and that they have ever been so regarded by our wisest men, needs little proof. The histories of the early settlements, and the documentary evidence of their records, are alike conclusive of the question. The fact is notorious, that the education of the young engaged a very large share of the solicitude of the first Americans. The Virginians established, in 1621, the first free school in America. The first in Boston was set up in 1635.

It is repeatedly declared in the records of the colonies, that it is the legal duty of all parents and guardians to give religious and other instruction to the children under their care, and to train them up in some learned profession or other employment profitable for themselves *and the commonwealth.* In 1642, it was declared, by solemn enactment, that all children must be educated, and that it was "barbarism" not to have a knowledge of the principal laws of the State.

Indeed, recognition of the absolute and fundamental importance of *education, enforced and paid for by the State*, raising the scholar to that standard of moral and intellectual ability and acquirement

* For relation of Christianity to the State, see Girard will case. Also, Webster's Works, Vol. VI. p. 133, &c.

which prepare him for safe and reliable citizenship, are conclusively evident in the earliest legislative records of the New England States. The same solemn recognition is embodied, in one form or another, in all the State constitutions, from Maine to California, at this day. A monument of the same belief also remains, in the power which has from the beginning been granted to the selectmen, of apprenticing, for labor and education, all children neglected by their parents or guardians. This regulation has, most unfortunately, fallen into very general disuse; but its importance and meaning are none the less evident.

Such is our American idea of common education: a careful and thorough training for all purposes of government and self-government. A comparison with it of the character of European education, and of its results upon the population subjected to it, will serve to exhibit contrasts seldom considered, but extremely important.

The greatest difference between the two systems arises from the difference in their objects. Americans are free, and the freedom of our American law must be made up for by a corresponding increase in the exercise of self-control by the individual. Therefore, it is a principal and direct object of our education, to train our youth to independent and careful thought. They think on public business, and manage public business—an employment which demands the widest intelligence. They are trained to feel it not only a privilege, but a duty, to take a direct and active interest in the government of their country.

But it is an equally direct object of the European educational systems—more especially of the Continental, but measurably also of the English system—to *prevent* the people from examining the government or its measures, or from concerning themselves at all with them. The Prussian school-system—the most liberal on the Continent—has of late years been found too liberal for the purposes of the Government, and has been gradually shorn of its best features, until now it is, like all the rest, merely an adjunct of despotic power; a great machine, from which are turned out ready-made subjects—not ready-made men. The reading-books of the schools of the Austrian dominions are arranged to teach submission to tyranny. In them the children read, in so many words, that subjects must behave towards their sovereign like faithful slaves towards their master, because their sovereign *is* their master, and has power over their property as well as over their lives. Intelligent consideration of political matters, or any consideration of them, would shake the seats of the kings; and for self-preservation's sake, therefore, they carefully keep such matter of investigation as much as possible out of the people's hands. More than that: lest they acquire too free a habit of thought elsewhere, they not only prohibit a direct training for the duty and habit of governing, but they prevent the study in a free manner of any thing else. Lest scholars should learn the intelligent study of politics, they are prevented from the intelligent study of any thing. They are not taught to think for themselves for their own good, but only to believe what is taught them, in order to subserve the bad purposes of others. Intellectual debasement always brings moral and social debasement along with it. The victims of this education for ignorance are not only miserably besotted in mind, but brutishly savage and heathenish in manners. Their whole character is the natural consequence of such training in youth. Mutual confidence and helpfulness, the reliance of our citizens upon the kindness and honesty of others, the social friendship and good fellowship which are the very texture of so much of our daily life, are things unknown in Europe, and strange and incomprehensible to Europeans travelling here.

In Europe, everybody distrusts everybody. It was a principal reason for the transitory insecurity of the many constitutional governments established in Germany and elsewhere, in the years 1848–50, that, of the numerous little cliques of politicians and theorists who were at work, none trusted any other; nor did any man trust his fellow. There is none of that feeling which causes our minorities to submit peacefully to the measures of the majority, and even to assist, in good faith, their support and full accomplishment. A Eu-

U of M

ropean nation would almost necessarily pass from the excitement of our Presidential elections, into an armed revolution. The eagerness with which the Irish and Germans gather into exclusively national armed bands in this country, their promptness in rising into mobs, their brutal fights among themselves, are plain indications of the passions which boil in their minds, very near to overflowing.

Thus far it has been shown:

1. How our peculiar American education is the basis of our peculiar American nationality and freedom.

2. How the aims of American education and European education are diametrically opposite.

It remains to consider:

1. What the actual influence of foreign population is upon our schools; and,

2. What measures are needed to secure our schools in their proper condition.

1. *The actual influence of foreign population upon our schools.*

Considering the character of most European training, and its influence upon the minds of its victims; considering also their besotted subservience to their Romish priests, or else the rampant infidelity and lawless, riotous, and licentious tendencies of those not so subservient, it is easy to see how little community of thought and feeling can subsist between the two classes of people, European and American. The Europeans are studiously kept ignorant and servile, and are deformed with the vices which accompany servile ignorance. They are bigoted, false, selfish, cunning, and revengeful. They are governed by fear; and, like passionate children, they seize every occasion to violate laws which are only kept over them by force, and to indulge the passions which are only subdued by terror. How can such men coalesce with our law-making, law-abiding, and self-controlling men? Our laws are so free that only such men as ours can properly use or safely endure their freedom. Our thoughtful people see that their own self-control must make up for the absence of stringent laws, a standing army, and the heavy pressure from above of despotism and an armed and disciplined aristocracy. Liberal laws, *and a correspondingly careful self-government by the individual*, are the distinguishing dignity and prerogative of our freemen. But the very freedom which we use to increase our moral power of governing ourselves, the foreigner seizes as an opportunity to indulge his ingrained antipathy to law, his ferocity, and his appetites. Our population is so intelligent as to recognize the necessity of a universal Christian and democratic education, without regard to sects. The foreigner, under the control of Romish priests, regards it even as his duty, to insist upon the exclusive propagation, in all schools where he can secure it, of *his* special sectarianism, or his own atheism, if he has renounced the Romish Church.

The character of the actual educational operations of our foreign population has, in fact, been precisely such as we have shown that it must be. In Detroit, in Cincinnati, in New York city—wherever they could muster strength enough to hope for success—they have begged, bargained, and bullied to get their hands upon the money of the State, for the propagation of their religious dogmas. Failing in that, they have, by the like means, attempted to destroy in our national schools their national significance and value, by driving out from them *all* religious instruction or influence. The demands of the atheistical Germans have been of a similar character. More than one meeting of these people has formally resolved that the legal enforcement of the observance of the Christian Sabbath, and the giving of any religious instruction in schools, ought to cease; and with besotted blindness, while making these absurd demands, they have also called upon the Government to provide everybody with property and labor. This is a like treachery with that of those villains who ask a night's lodging, and then set fire to the house, for the sake of plunder.

The liberal grants by the British government to the College of Maynooth, while they have had no effect in mollifying the Irish priests' opposition to popular education in Ireland, have acted as a stimulus to the preparation of Jesuit priests for this country, who, headed by Bishop Hughes and his confederates, are, as we all know, constantly interfering with the operation of our school-system, and endeavoring, under the plea of religious scruples, to secularize them and destroy their usefulness. We also suffer from the outside influence of Austria, where, in 1829, was instituted "the Leopold Foundation," the direct object of which was to supply money for the support of foreign teachers for American children. From this propagandist society have been received the immense sums of money that have been paid for Romanist teachers, and for schoolhouses, in communities entirely Protestant; and to Austria we must look for the solution of the oft-repeated question among our Protestant rural populations, "How do the Romanists manage to get funds to pay for their buildings and support their priests?"

What the result of the success of this speckled army of disorganizers and bigots would be, it requires no prophet to foretell. Every professedly religious body, would grasp at the State funds with the intensely bitter, selfish, and spiteful rivalry of sectarian quarrelers. The strongest would snatch the most, and would try to secure all. American free common-school education—that invaluable institution which has been, and is, the life-blood of the Union, the nucleus and source of all our liberty and all our happiness—would be bandied about, like a bone in a pack of snarling curs. The keystone of the State would be knocked out of the arch; and the solid architecture of the iron men who founded our commonwealth would be demolished, to make room for the crude fancies and foggy dreams of infidel German metaphysicians—the most visionary and unpractical of men—or for the cunning machineries of a subtle priesthood, striving to rear the Inquisition and convents of the Romish Church on the ruins of our State. At the very best, our young men and young women would have passed the forming years of their lives in a discipline calculated to develop intellect, but to smother morals and religion together. All the strength of our republic would be sapped. Like the image in Nebuchadnezzar's dream, whose feet were part of iron and part of clay, we should totter upon a failing and incongruous basis. The first stone thrown at us, would prostrate our country in irremediable ruin.

2. *What measures are needed in order to preserve our schools in their proper condition?*

Only the religious belief underlying and interweaving all the thoughts and habits of our people, co-operating with intellectual elevation and habits politically discreet, have held us together hitherto. The elements of disunion are to-day fermenting more deeply and dangerously than ever. Questions of policy, and of sectional prejudice, have agitated the nation quite enough for its health. If these questions are to be determined without any other judges than cunning intellect and unbridled passion, the death of our Union is at hand. If they are to be determined by men believing and seeking to practice right and justice, the Union may yet endure. But if they are to be so determined, it can be in no other way than by the graduates of our common schools, brought up under an education based upon Christianity, and teaching freedom of body, heart, and mind, democracy, and, above all, Christianity, without sectarianism.

There is no doubt what is necessary for the security of our education and of our country. It is high time that the distinctive Christianity of our State polity, and the Christian and political character of our public-school education, were re-established and restored to their former footing, there to be maintained. Trial by jury is an excellent custom. Taxation according to representation is a very true principle. Popular election and the ballot-box are the best possible mode of choosing rulers. But neither custom, principle, nor machinery will help a rotten nation. Unless we are able to handle our instruments, we shall turn out but a bungling piece of work. These good things are only good by virtue of skill in the hands of the user. Unless we know how to use our blessings well, we shall turn them into curses. Our common schools are the only medium of the requisite education. These must be kept American in spirit, American in practice, American thoroughly, everywhere and always. The fanatics or the fools who would destroy our liberties by ousting from our schools the sources and preservatives of those liberties, with a wisdom like that of a man who should burn his own home over his head to warm his fingers, must be rebuked and silenced. Our schools must remain public, free, democratic, unsectarian, and Christian. There is room for no hesitation about the matter; the case is urgent. As surely as we trifle with this blind giant, Ignorance, he will repay us with such a destruction as Sampson brought upon the Philistines. He is even now feeling about to grip the pillars of our State. Having them once in his grasp, he will overthrow our national edifice, and crush us among the falling fragments.

Perhaps the most significant, comprehensive, and useful measure which could be taken in order to the accomplishment of the purposes set forth in this chapter, would be an educational qualification for voting,—the requirement that every voter should read intelligibly, in English, our State and National Constitutions. This single requirement, of reading, is probably the best, although, of course, very imperfect, as all such tests must be. Any such test must be capable of quick and easy application, and must also determine the possession of an essential requisite. Reading is a ready mode of estimating a man's literary acquirements. A more elaborate inquiry would be so tedious in the application, as to be practically inconvenient. Ability to read can be proved in a moment. And one who can read, is able to use the most extensive and important source of information in the world, namely, printed matter.

The enforcement of such a rule would be attended with many advantages. It would shut out from the polls the most degraded and dangerous class of voters, native or foreign. The men who are most easily bought or fooled would not then be worth buying. Immigrants would be under a strong temptation to learn English, and to learn to read; of which two attainments the first would be of great value in assimilating them to our own people, and the second as a main step forward in their progress towards intelligent freedom. A most important benefit, also, to be derived from the operation of this educational test, would be its effect upon our schools. The children of foreigners, now the most ignorant and inaccessible of our youthful population, would at least learn to read. Their fathers would also learn, in order to vote; and as much as they learned themselves, so much it is safe to conclude that their children would be greatly benefited. Education, moreover, would thus once more be definitely recognized and significantly honored by the State; and the possession and exercise of political power would once more be publicly declared conditional upon the possession of the ability to use such power. The declaration would not be very perfect; the test proposed is not. But probably it is the best that circumstances will admit of. Its adoption would, at least, make a renewed and important public assertion of our hereditary State policy, namely, the restriction of the governing power to those fit to use it.

The principle of demanding that religion, though free from sectarianism, should be carefully excluded from our common-schools, is not of American origin. "Education, without religion," says a great authority, "merely transforms an ignorant brute into a clever fiend." True religious feeling is the basis of all useful education. It is the wholesome check upon that power which man acquires through the acquisition of knowledge. "Knowledge is power, but it is neither wisdom nor virtue;"* and these two qualities, so necessary to the very existence of society, can only be implanted by religious faith. The prevalence of the Epicurean philosophy did much to destroy the Roman Empire; and, in later years, the teachings of Voltaire and Rousseau removed the only check which restrained the French nation from those frightful excesses which form so dark a picture in the history of mankind. The "Goddess of Reason" has ever been insufficient to direct either individuals or multitudes; and the first step towards the restoration of order in France, was the recognition of the Divine power in the government of the world.

As the cherished sentiments of thousands of our naturalized and alien citizens become known to the American people, it is discovered that we not only have the Romish priest, industriously at work to suppress the Scriptures, but that we have organized societies of avowed infidels and atheists, who openly proclaim that there is no

* Alison.

liberty where even moral, much less religious, restraints prevail, and that the perfection of society is accomplished, when the unregenerated passions of the heart alone control human action.*

The experience of other nations presents warnings to the American, of the necessity of constantly insisting upon the moral training of our youth. We want no dogmas, no "isms," but we want the Scriptures free. That they might be so, our forefathers made a home in the wilderness, and left the heritage to the present generation. Shall we, in the prosecution of our school-system, allow it to be emasculated of its chief strength, because of the demands of the priests of a corrupted religion, or because we are required to do so by foreigners who openly declare war upon religion itself? It is for the Americans who truly love their country to decide.

* See published statements of the principles of various German Societies throughout the Union.

THE POLITICAL POWER OF THE POPE.

"The Romish Church has always ranged herself on the side of Despotism."—Guizot.

It has lately become the fashion for party men and journalists to assert that the influence of the Papal See on political affairs no longer exists; that history proves her power to have been on the wane during many past years; that the march of intellect and spread of education have forced her to relinquish coercive power; and that the resumption of her former influence is impossible. We are constantly told by prelates, priests, and politicians, that the supremacy of the Pope in temporal affairs "is not an established doctrine of the Roman Church; it is simply a *sententia in ecclesia*—an unadjudicated question, without positive authority, and incumbent upon no one's faith; that a Romanist may believe what he pleases on the subject, and be a good Churchman still." Those, on the contrary, who, relying on the authority of the Fathers of that Church, receiving the declarations of the priesthood themselves, and accepting the explanation of the Roman press, maintain a different opinion, are accused of bigotry and intolerance, or stigmatized as enemies to liberty. It becomes us, therefore, to examine these pretensions, and, having seen their import in other ages, to inquire if they have been relinquished, or, as is strenuously urged, become obsolete.

In order to a full appreciation of this momentous question, a glance at the origin and progress of Papal assumption is necessary, so that a full idea of the arrogance of Rome may be realized.

Systems which are longest in their growth, are most lasting in their effects. This is peculiarly the case with that politico-religious organization—Romanism: commencing in the first centuries of the

Christian era—a period when the whole known world was in a state of transition—it has steadily progressed from infancy to robust manhood: accurately observing cause and effect, it quickly learnt to control events, and mould men and monarchies to its will. What was originally conferred as a favor, it quickly arrogated as a right; and, when princes remonstrated, or jurists denied its claims, forgery was resorted to in defence of its usurpations, and absolution and preferment were the rewards of assassins who removed its opponents.

In the struggle between the Eastern and Western Empires, the See of Rome early rejected the Byzantine yoke, thus asserting a right to *resist* governments. In becoming temporal princes, the Popes declared that a union could exist between the temporal and spiritual; and, at the election of Pepin to the throne of France, arrogated the *power of umpires* in political disputes. Thus, gradually establishing authority by precedent, the Papacy matured its policy, until Hildebrand placed a climax on the growth of six centuries.*

This famous Pontiff is regarded by all historians as the master mind of his age, and the architect of the Romish Church. His great antagonist, Henry IV., Emperor of Germany, found the armies of the empire powerless against the Eternal City, and was compelled to listen to the Pope as he fulminated interdicts against his kingdom, and excommunication against himself. Nor did the Papal emissaries confine their operations merely to Germany. In England, they imposed and collected taxes without the consent of the authorities, and frequently raised insurrections by their extortions. So extravagant became their demands in France, that the civil power was forced to interfere, and St. Louis decreed the "Pragmatic Sanction," curbing the power of the Papacy in his kingdom. In fact, monarchy was in rebellion, and what could not be acquired by force, Rome resolved to gain by wiles.

The thirteenth century saw the struggle commence between the people and Feudalism. But the Papacy early understood that Liberty would be death to its pretensions, and therefore allied itself with

* Gregory VII., A. D. 1073.

Tyranny. The Barons, who had extorted MAGNA CHARTA from John, were excommunicated by the Pope, and a war of extermination commenced against the Albigenses. This people, in the enjoyment of political and religious freedom, were under the protection of the Count of Toulouse, who, on his refusal to abet the designs of the Papacy, was excommunicated, and his destruction resolved upon.

Every expedient was resorted to in order to detach their protectors from this unfortunate people; and the Pope showed the policy of Rome towards her opponents, in the following memorable words :

" We advise you, according to the precepts of the Apostle Paul, to use cunning in your dealings with the Count, which, in the present case, should rather be deemed prudence. It is expedient to attack those separately who have broken the unity of the Church; to spare the Count of Thoulouse for a season, treating him with wise dissimulation, in order that the other heretics may be more easily destroyed, and that we may crush him at our leisure when he stands alone."*

But treachery was not the only weapon which Romanism found useful to adopt. Henry VII., Emperor of Germany, was assassinated by order of Pope Clement V., poison being administered to him in the Eucharist, from the hands of his Dominican confessor. But crimes become virtues in a creed which asserts the maxim—" The end justifies the means."

Religion has always given place to policy when Romanism has been forced to an alternative. The Duke of Guise was assassinated by order of his sovereign; yet, notwithstanding his opposition to the Huguenots of France, and his being the leader of the Romanist party, the Pope justified the assassination on the ground of political expediency. But the most memorable instance of Papal duplicity is shown in the treatment of Philip II. of Spain, one of the greatest supporters of the Romish See that history can produce. Rome, however, feared his power, and secretly sought the alliance of Elizabeth

* Pope Innocent III. to the Abbot of Citeaux.

of England, advising her to assist the insurgents against Philip's authority in the Netherlands. When this sovereign had resolved on war with England, the Pope sent information to Elizabeth of the plan forming for her destruction, together with copies of letters he had received from the king relative to the Armada. The whole history of the Papacy is full of such instances as these; and neither succeeding centuries nor the progress of civilization have produced a change.

The history of Westphalia, in 1649, was the triumph of Protestantism and free opinions. The Papacy then ceased to have any direct political influence in the affairs of Europe; henceforward it was no longer to maintain authority by the aid of arms and the civil power; but to struggle for present existence and prospective influence by craft and cunning. It may be said of this system—

"It was not for an age, but for all time."

Romanism has weapons suited to every cycle. It adapts itself to every people; it conforms to and supports every government; but in despotism, monarchy, and republicanism, its aim is still unchanged. Tyrannizing in barbarism, fawning in the sixteenth century, intriguing in the nineteenth. Tolerant where forced, it persecutes where possible. Liberal in England and America, autocratic in Spain and Austria. Truly, "tout chemin mêne à Rome."*

The weapons which the Papal hierarchy now wields in free countries, are admirably suited to the organization of its ministers. Celibacy of the priesthood gave power to the Papacy, and maintains its influence. Family and country have no ties on the Romish clergy, and the Popes have always been convinced that celibacy is the great bond which unites all portions of the Papal dominions. Rome therefore enjoys exclusive possession of every feeling which can render her ministers good subjects or good citizens. Pius IV. comprehended the immense value of an unmarried clergy. Though he violently condemned the administration of the eucharist in both kinds, he relaxed

* "Every road leads to Rome."

the prohibition, at the instance of the Emperor Maximilian, and permitted the cup to be given to the laity in Germany. But on the point of celibacy he was inflexible; for he was justly convinced that it was the great bond by which all the portions of Papal domination were united, and that, if it should be relaxed, the entire edifice would fall in sunder.

A very necessary element of success, is the command of funds; and here the Romish Church is aided by the celibacy of her priesthood. "The clergy is a family which can never perish; its wealth therefore remains with it forever; and, as it is not a family to increase, government should restrict its power of acquiring additional wealth." (Montesquieu.) Rome shows her appreciation of such restrictions, by treating them as sacrilege; and governments, in asserting their independence of Papal tyranny, have found it necessary to first curb its financiering proclivities. A government which neglects legislative enactments on so momentous a subject, will eventually find the Romish Church capable of any resistance, and bidding defiance to the laws.

We are at a loss to understand how men, otherwise far-seeing, can speak of Rome as powerless for evil. Are any of her means of action restrained? Is she less wealthy? Are her followers materially diminished, or less devoted? Is her alliance with governments perilled? Or has she become meek and lowly, and forgotten her former arrogance? In every country we see her bishops and priests leading a strong party, whose alliance is sought, and opinions pandered to, by party-men of different shades of opinion. In England, the Popish Parliamentary league is feared and hated by every ministry. In France, their alliance is gained by the government, in return for almost supreme ecclesiastical power. In Germany, Rome educates in the schools, and Jesuits bear sway in the cabinet. She attempts to arrest the march of freedom in Sardinia, and strives to stifle its rise in Spain. Is it egotism which induces Americans to deny her influence in this republic, and are they blind to passing events in their own country? What, then, is the explanation of demagogues flattering the Papal hierarchy; what the meaning of the riots of our foreign population; and for what purpose is so much property in the hands of the priesthood, and in their hands alone? The fact is obvious, that the means Rome formerly possessed, she has not parted with. She is as powerful for evil as in the days of Innocent III.; and, when the situation warrants it, she will know where to find another Hildebrand.

We are not alone in this conviction. The historian, Macaulay, holds the same opinion, in the following language:

"The Papacy remains—not in decay, not a mere antique, but full of life and youthful vigor. The Catholic Church is still sending forth to the furtherest ends of the world, missionaries as zealous as those who landed in Kent with Augustin; and still confronting hostile kings with the same spirit with which she confronted Attila."

There is a fundamental mistake made by would-be philosophers of the present day, which may lead to very disastrous consequences. Viewing the want of education in Romanist countries, and the unintellectual character of their inhabitants, they imagine the Papal priests to be participators in this ignorance, whereas the contrary is the case. The Romish priests, as a body, are educated, scientific, and refined. They number men among them eminent in every branch of literature, and especially in political philosophy. This fact is one which should cause them to be regarded with greater fear, since they are prepared beforehand for every emergency. Their education is instilled into them with, and becomes a part of, one great controlling aim—the supremacy of their order.

Rome formerly worked by what may be termed physical means. She was a species of equipoise—a political umpire between contending governments. But this influence has departed, and Rome adapts herself to the age. She educates her ministers to meet the times; and her followers are trained to make every action of their lives, every phase of their existence, subservient to a fixed policy. Seated in the midst of the civilized world, accurately marking every change of the political horizon, Rome awaits her moment, and, when the success of one or other political party is wavering in the balance, she throws in the immense weight of her followers, and bears down all opposition. Politicians laugh at our fears, and deride our assertions; yet these same men are courting that party whose influence they deny. Why is it that public men are so courteous to, and apologistic of, the Romish Church? It is because they know it to be an undivided power,—no two policies there, no factions, no North and South, but a party one and indivisible. Whigs and Democrats may contend, "isms" may come in contact, and a "National party" be rent by fanatics, but Rome is unchangeable. There are no divisions there; she commands, and countless thousands obey. No wonder, then, our public men are so deferential to such a power, though at the same time denying its existence to the country. Will America thus be treated by her representatives?

The oft-repeated assertion of the Papal See not claiming temporal supremacy, is one calculated to bring about the most disastrous results. Legislators in this, as in other countries, are unceasing in the propagation of this error; and even Romanists themselves assert a doctrine which is entirely opposed to the spirit and affirmation of their hierarchy. From the ninth century to the nineteenth—from Gregory VII. to Pius IX.—the doctrine of that Church has been, the elevation of the spiritual over the secular. This right is not asserted as *a consequence* of the spiritual power, but as of *divine origin.* Thus Hildebrand, in excommunicating Henry IV., uses the language, "*Ex parte omnipotentis Dei.*" The same Pontiff asserts that "kings and princes are bound to kiss the feet of God's vicegerent. He has a right to depose emperors. His sentence can be annulled by none, but he can annul the decrees of all." Successive Pontiffs were unceasing in maintaining this doctrine, and constantly asserted that governments held their authority from the Romish See. Pope Boniface VIII. addresses Philip le Bel of France in the same arrogant language: "We would have thee to know that in things spiritual and temporal, thou art subject to us." In fact, throughout the whole range of the Papacy, from Hildebrand downwards, such has been the declaration of the so-called successors of St. Peter.

In A.D. 1414, the Council of Constance declares: "The laity have no jurisdiction and power over the clergy." And the Council of Trent, in 1545, asserts: "The exemption of clerical persons has been instituted by the ordination of God, and by canonical institutions." (*Sess.* 25, chap. 20.)

It was in the early ages of the Papacy that Rome found her most critical moments; and such decrees as the above were necessary, not merely to acquire additional power, but to retain what she already possessed. Many national Churches were almost independent of Rome, particularly that of France. Under the leadership of such men as Bossuet and Fenelon, backed by the enormous power of Louis XIV., France successfully resisted the encroachments of the Romish See, and even gave a name to all such opposition, namely, *Gallicanism.* But this independence of Rome is now only history; the Papal hierarchy of the present day is ultramontanist throughout, and the Church recognizes the Pope as infallible and supreme in all matters. Even France herself owns to the annihilation of her national Church. The Count of Montalembert thus speaks, in 1852:

"Let us all labor, according to the measure of our meekness, to maintain her (the Romish See) in this dignity, in this sovereign independence. We are entering upon the age of the regeneration of Catholicism, which will console us for all the outrages, all the defections, it has had to endure since the revival of paganism, four hundred years ago."

The ultramontane doctrine, as enunciated by Bellarmine, and defended by the Jesuits, is now, in fact, the faith of the entire Romish clergy and Church. Bellarmine thus illustrates his position:

"The Pope, as Pope, although he has not any merely temporal power, hath, nevertheless, in order to a spiritual good, the supreme power of disposing of the temporal concerns of all Christians." (*Bellarmine*, chap. vi.)

Again:

"The clergy cannot be punished by political judges, neither be in any way brought before the judicial chair of the secular magistrate. . . The Pope has redeemed the clergy from the obedience due to princes; therefore kings are no more the superiors of the clergy." (*Bellarmine*, chap. 28.)

Another of the Fathers of the Romish Church is even more explicit. Baronius, in speaking of the supremacy of the Papal power, observes:

"All those who take from the Church of Rome, and from the See of St. Peter, one of the two swords, and allow only the spiritual, are branded for heretics." (*Baronius*, Ann. 1053, §14.)

Political partisans and unscrupulous demagogues may assert that the march of civilization has caused Rome to relinquish these claims, but there never was a time when her pretensions have found more numerous or abler champions than at present. The doctrine is triumphant throughout the entire Papacy, and in Protestant countries it is pertinaciously asserted.

To be convinced that this ultramontane power of the Popes is truly the belief of every faithful Romanist, we need only look to the writings of Brownson, in our own country. The opinions of his Review are endorsed by the Romish hierarchy throughout the States, and he therefore speaks the creed of his Church.

"There is, in our judgment, but one valid defence of the Popes, in their exercise of temporal authority in the middle ages over sovereigns, and that is, that they possess it *by divine right*, or that the Pope holds that authority by virtue of his commission from Jesus Christ, as the successor of Peter, the Prince of the Apostles, and visible head of the Church." . . . . . . "As the denial of the spiritual authority soon leads to a denial of the temporal, so the denial of the temporal soon leads to the denial of the spiritual. When we found democracy even by nominal Catholics embraced in that sense in which it denies all law, and asserts the right of the people, or rather of the mob, to do whatever they please, and making it criminal in us to dispute their infallibility, we felt that we must bring out the truth against them, and if scandal resulted, we were not its cause. The responsibility rests on those whose obsequiousness to the multitude made our opposition necessary."

"The Pope has the right to pronounce sentence of deposition against any sovereign, when required by the good of the spiritual order." (*Brownson's Review*, vol. i., p. 48.)

"The power of the Church exercised over sovereigns in the middle ages was not a usurpation, was not derived from the concession of princes, or the consent of all people, *but was, and is, held by divine right*, and whoso resists it, rebels against the King of kings and Lord of lords." (*Ibid.*, p. 47.)

"She (the Church) bears by divine right both swords, but she exercises the temporal sword by the hand of the princes or magistrates. The temporal sovereign holds it subject to her order, to be exercised in her service, under her direction." (*Ibid.*, p. 60.)

"The spiritual is not only superior to the temporal, but is its sovereign, and punishes its law." (*Ibid.*)

We consider this the most open-mouthed, bare-faced assertion of the temporal supremacy of the Popes over free governments and universal suffrage of which it is possible to conceive, and this asserted too in a country which has separated Church and State, fearing the encroachments of the spiritual power. Has this man sworn to maintain the Constitution of the United States? Can Jesuitry reconcile his words with such an oath?

But this doctrine is developed in its utmost elaboration in the Eternal City. The *Civiltà Cattolica* is a journal published at Rome under the auspices of the Pontiff, and its views and opinions are received by the Romanists throughout the world as the effusions of the Holy See. In the course of a late article, this paper thus speaks:

"What are the limits of the power of coercion? There are but two, which, in fact, comprehend all others, namely, *means* and *aim*.... What then are the limits of the Church's means? There are none except the limits of human power, and of the divine assistance by which the Church is comforted. As the Church commands the spiritual part of man directly, *she therefore commands the whole man, and all that depends on man.* . . . . . From the darkness of the Catacombs she (the Church) dictated laws to the subjects of the emperors, abrogating decrees, whether plebeian, senatorial, or imperial, when in conflict with Catholic ordinances. . . . . Did the Christian emperors become insolent? The Church armed against them their very electors. To every rampant heresy the Church knew how to oppose the power either of the peoples or of their princes; and when these supports seemed at last to have been snatched from her by a universal rationalism, behold! there is a sudden turning back of both;—of the nations, fearing an unbridled royal power, and proclaiming the necessity of a supreme spiritual power; of the princes, beginning to understand, at the light of a bloody communism, that *the principles of the Church are a firmer foundation for their thrones than bayonets, which must always be intrusted to a part of the people.* . . . The conclusion is, therefore, that there are no limits to the exercise of the coercive power of the Church, either in view of her means or of her aim." (*Civiltà Cattolica,* No. cxi., 2d Series, vol. viii., Nov., 1854, pp. 273–282.)

This, we take it, is proof positive of the assumptions of Rome in regard to the civil power, but lest our readers should suppose these would not be enforced, we will give a further extract from the same article:

"Petty politicians may conclude that the Church has lost her power, because she does not enlist artillery, cavalry, and infantry; but the truth is, that the artillery, cavalry, and infantry of the Catholics are in the hands of the Church, inasmuch as in her hands are the mind, the reason, and the power of every true Catholic." (*Civ. Cat., ibid.*)

Such is the arrogance, such the declarations of the See of Rome in the nineteenth century; nor is it probable that she will surrender pretensions which have been successfully asserted through ten centuries. It was by this authority, Paschal II., in 1099, deposed Henry IV. of Germany; Innocent III., in 1210, deposed Otho IV.; Gregory IX., in 1239, excommunicated Frederick II., and absolved his subjects from their allegiance; Innocent IV., in 1245, pronounced sentence of deprivation against the same Frederick; Boniface VIII., in 1302, thundered forth against Philip le Bel of France the famous bull *Unam Sanctam*, containing the most extravagant assertions of the power of the Holy See; Paul III., in 1536 and in 1538, deposed and damned Henry VIII. of England, and absolved his subjects from their allegiance; Pius V., in 1570, uttered a bull against Queen Elizabeth, in which, "out of the fulness of apostolic power," he deprived her of "her pretended title to the kingdom," and released her subjects from "all manner of duty, dominion, allegiance, and obedience." In virtue of this same power, Spain is now impeded in her progress of reform, and Sardinia is expecting shortly to be excommunicated.

A bull of the Pope was the death-blow to the revolution of Poland in 1830; like interference caused mischief to the Republics of Florence, Genoa, Venice, and was the origin of the wars of the Sonderbund in Switzerland in 1847. No struggle has ever taken place in favor of popular liberty, in any Romish country, but it has invariably met with opposition from the priesthood.

We are at an utter loss to understand how Americans can be misled by assertions in their own country relative to Rome, when events of such magnitude are passing in Europe. Spain is struggling to throw off the overwhelming influence of the Church, yet Rome abates not one of her pretensions. Sardinia, too, is entering upon her own regeneration and that of Italy, but the Eternal City is straining every nerve in opposition, and the country is daily fearing to be laid under interdict. It is the duty of Americans to keep pace with these events, and the favorers of the Papacy would then meet with small consideration at the hands of our citizens.

The Sardinian government, having become enlightened by the spread of education and free opinion, entered upon a course of beneficent reform under the auspices of the late king, Carlo Alberto. His benevolent designs were frustrated by Austria and Rome, and himself compelled to abdicate. His son, Victor Emanuel, has steadily pursued the policy of his father; but, as is invariably the case, the

Romish Church places itself in opposition to the movement, and Sardinia is all but racked with civil war. The property of the clergy amounts to eighty millions of dollars a year, but is so unequally distributed, that the government has been obliged to pay two hundred thousand annually for the support of the lower orders of the clergy. Between eight and ten thousand monks and nuns, inhabiting more than six hundred monastic establishments, enjoy an annual revenue of nearly half a million of dollars. Such enormous ecclesiastical wealth is felt to be a drain on the prosperity of the country, and the government finding it in the way of reform, has lately legislated upon it. This calls forth the fierce opposition of the clergy, and the Pope thus speaks of the decrees of the Sardinian government:

"We reject and condemn not only all and each of the decrees of that government, hurtful to the rights and authority of religion, of the Church, and of the Holy See, but likewise the law lately proposed. We declare all these acts to be absolutely null and void." (*Allocution of Pope Pius IX., in Jan.,* 1854.)

At the close of the Revolution, the Established Church of England still held ecclesiastical sway over the Episcopalians of America, and John Wesley had direction over the rapidly increasing denomination of Methodists. But the members of these Churches being Protestants, at once followed the example of the government, in separating from "foreign influences," and the spiritual power of foreign ecclesiastics. This was done without injuring the cause of true religion, and was in strict accordance with the spirit of our institutions. The communicants of the Romish Church have alone persevered in their foreign allegiance,—an obedience at war with good citizenship, and, although denominated *spiritual*, is for all practical purposes a political despotism.

We appeal to our readers. Is it patriotic, is it right to abstain from binding this enormous, this ever-increasing power, simply from fear of being accused of religious persecution? When we find the sceptre and the crosier so bound together, that we cannot tell where one begins and the other ends, is it not the duty of every true American to crush such a fearful hierarchy, such an overwhelming influence? We are surrounded by countless thousands of foreign Romanists, who, in their superstition, believe the priest to be a demigod; the priests, in their turn, have no volition apart from their diocesan; and the bishops reverence the Pope as God's vicegerent, in temporal as in spiritual matters. The mind fails to conceive a system more suitable to attain power, and yet we are told that we should not fear the Pope.

While we are thus unconscious of danger, Rome is ever working; her clergy throughout the different States are amassing untold wealth; they are allying themselves with various parties, and rendering assistance to demagogues; they are studying the weak points in our political fabric, and the defects in our constitution; and when they are strongest and we weakest, they will strike with a force, telling us but too strongly, that while we slept, Rome was ever watchful.

NOTE.—See Appendix, "Relations of the Pope to the Civil Power"--a Letter from O. A. Brownson, the chosen champion of Romanism in America.

EVILS OF MILITARY ORGANIZATIONS EXCLUSIVELY OF FOREIGNERS.

"An army, to be efficient, should have but one purpose, encourage but one object. This makes the mass invincible—the individuals, heroes."—ANTHONY WAYNE.

OF the many evils arising from the want of a proper appreciation of the peculiarities of our institutions, one of the most pernicious is the formation of foreign and unnaturalized citizens into military companies savoring of the nationality of the countries from which they have emigrated. Although the tendencies of our government are eminently republican, giving free liberty of action and of conscience, still there are certain obligations, tending to its maintenance untrammelled by a foreign proclivity, which are due to the people at large, and to the laws under which this liberty is guaranteed. The moulding of the minds of our citizens on an American basis, through American surroundings, and by American examples, should be the aim of every one who desires to retain the material which shall insure the perpetuity of our institutions. That material is founded in veneration for habits and customs of a purely American bias, irrespective of the individualities of any other country, and without regard to the sentiments of any other nationality.

The organization of foreigners into separate regiments, and even companies, is entirely subversive of the fundamental principles on which this republic is established. It was in order to annihilate all foreign influence and tyranny, that our country asserted its independence, and took its rank among the governments of the world, not merely as an assemblage of free and independent States, but as one indissolubly united people, bound to each other by the same hostility to tyranny and love of liberty; and actuated by the same principles and motives. It is only in this union, that our republic can hope to exist; and every thing that does not tend to preserve this unity, is disastrous in its nature, and should be resolutely discountenanced. Can it be said that organized bands of armed men unacquainted with our language, will produce the desired result? regiments having foreigners for their component parts, their officers drilling them in a foreign language?

The object for which the militia is formed is, to protect the country from foreign invasion, and from internal riots. Is it likely that in time of war these regiments of foreigners would be of the same service as when all speak the same language? Would they be likely to take up arms against the country of their birth, in the event of our becoming involved in a war with that country? It is well known that numbers of the German population of Williamsburg, New York city, and elsewhere, have threatened to arm themselves, in order to prevent the enforcement of a law which was distasteful to their feelings and opposed to their supposed interests. Would the German companies of those localities obey the summons, if they were ordered to put down this armed resistance to our laws? It is possible that the very men who have made this threat, are those who belong to some military organization, and depend upon the muskets which our authorities have placed in their hands as citizen-soldiers, to enable them to carry their threat into execution.

Thus it will be seen that, if a foreign military organization be inimical in a national point of view, it is positively destructive on social grounds. The peace and order of our country, so long as they exist, are ever at stake; nor can it be otherwise, in the nature of things. The interminable hordes of emigrants who seek our large cities, constantly frequent the same localities, which renders them exclusive; so that an American entering certain neighborhoods, would fancy himself in Germany or Ireland. The denizens have little communication with the outside world,—have their own papers, clubs, and gatherings,—and are practically a distinct people. Laws may be enacted, affecting, as they believe, their rights; these laws they refuse to obey. The municipal authorities order force to compel obedience; but force can be met by force, since military companies exist, composed of the rioters themselves. Thus bloodshed may ensue. We have had painful examples of this fact in late years. It was only on the last anniversary of St. Patrick's Day in New York, that such a probability was freely discussed in the papers, and looked for with forebodings by our peaceable citizens. Is not this sufficient to open the eyes of our legislators to the crying evils of such organizations, and to induce the authorities to constitute them illegal?

Let us, for a moment, strip the subject of its dangerous results, and view it as a matter of taste. The plea of emigration to this country is, tyranny. The tools of power, whether through compulsion or choice, are the soldiers,—who are pleasing to the rulers by their pliant subserviency—and hateful to the people by their uniforms, their badge of office. Accustomed to view the soldier, and his constant presence, with a feeling of dread,—uncertain at what moment his power might be exercised on him,—the foreigner has little of ease or security associated in his reminiscences of their tinselled trappings. In the hovel, the dwelling, or the palatial residence, they are always present; in village, town, or city, they are ever tramping. Their acts are servile, and their impulse tyrannical. Associated in the minds of the people with cruelty and oppression,—bearing on their persons the livery of tyranny, and enforcing its mandates with an undisguised zest,—the foreigner is happy to flee their presence, and escape their power. And yet, in spite of these associations, and the dread inspired by them, they form themselves into volunteer companies, on their arrival here, and adopt the very uniforms which have oppressed them with fear, thus wilfully assuming the badge of tyrants. The folly (we might use a stronger expression) of this taste must be apparent to all who think about the matter, and is one of such peculiar import, that we seek in vain a reasonable excuse for its adoption. It is so much at variance with all our conceived notions of the impulses which govern the human breast, and is so glaring in its inconsistency, that we are forced to reflect upon it with some degree of apprehension, and look with a feeling of dread at its ultimate operation.

These foreign-accoutred regiments are found in every large city throughout the Union. There is not a single petty nationality in Germany but has its military representatives amongst our citizen-soldiers—German in blood, feelings, language, and dress; German in their officers and organization. France has given us fac-similes of those troops who perpetrated the atrocities of the sanguinary demagogues of her first revolution—troops who, in 1848, stormed Rome and annihilated the Italian republic. Austria presents us with the counterparts of those ruffians who, under the butcher Haynau, whipped delicate women to death, and waded knee-deep in blood through the plains of Italy and Hungary. Even contemptible little Hesse—whose hireling soldiery became so odious to our forefathers in the Revolution, and were the laughing-stock of their English comrades—even Hesse has her representatives among our military. But, worst of all, Americans, forgetting the glorious traditions of their country, and relinquishing every claim to self-respect, adopt the livery of a foreign prince—that same uniform which their forefathers used so badly at Saratoga, Trenton, and Yorktown.

We are at a loss to understand how Americans can suffer such outrages of all decency, such contempt for the historical associations of the Revolution. Where is the Executive, that such atrocities are permitted? If these foreigners must become soldiers, why are they not compelled to wear the uniform of the United States—that dark gray and blue, which military men tell us is most suitable for such purposes? But no! our feelings must be outraged to meet the views of political hacks, who pander to the prejudices of these foreign cohorts, for vile party ends. Is the Eagle thus to be insulted in her own eyrie?

There is a motive, an intention in foreigners banding themselves together in military companies. Accustomed in their own country to see the soldiery paramount to the civil power, they hasten to clothe themselves in the same garb of power here, under the impression that they thus elevate themselves above the citizen, perfectly unconscious of the great principle of our government—that the civil power is paramount to all other. Should any question be mooted in coming time, in which their jealousies and prejudices are enlisted against the patriotism of this country, we shall bitterly rue our shortsightedness in placing arms in the hands of men, who cannot appreciate our institutions, and are ever ready to follow demagogues in their insidious attacks on the country and the Constitution. We have, in fact, removed a great incentive to virtue, by giving them the power to commit wrong.

We cannot look upon the armed confederacy of foreigners, clothed in a uniform fashioned upon a foreign model, without, to say the least, a thought of its impropriety, and the entirely anti-American phase which it presents. It is certainly due to the feelings of citizens of this country who guarantee to foreigners the liberties they enjoy under our laws, that some degree of respect should be paid to their sentiments, in the adoption of a uniform (if foreign companies must be formed), which will not insult their vision, nor interfere with their desire of having a citizen-soldiery, entirely American in appearance and feeling, although its individuals may be of foreign birth.

There is a reason of great moment, which characterizes these peculiarly constituted companies as dangerous. By their means priestcraft is enabled to maintain a strong hold upon the mind and impulse of our foreign population, and even to effect results which are contrary to the Constitution and aim of our government. The founders of this Republic wisely ordained that religion and politics should not be associated together. Although no one religion is recognized by our laws as paramount to another, yet no one will deny that this country is essentially Protestant—Protestant in its foundation, in its principles, in its impulse and education, and opposed to all connection of Church and State. Were no other proof of its Protestantism required, it could be found in its liberality towards the religious sentiments of the people, in allowing them freedom of thought and opinion in the matter of sect or tenet. Were it a Roman Catholic country, all other denominations, years ago, would have been, by the thunders of the Vatican, "crushed out," and driven from its face, even though it required the aid of an Inquisition or an *auto da fe.* What then shall we say to the priesthood using the military for church display, and making the Flag of our Union bow in obsequious reverence to the Host? We are at a loss to understand by what authority a mitred priest could command the attendance of regiments at the consecration of the Cathedral of St. Louis in 1834, when, amidst the thunder of American artillery, the Stars and Stripes were lowered in idolatrous veneration. Such scenes as these, not meeting with the merited rebuke from the people that their gravity demanded, are consequently persisted in, and we find a parallel atrocity repeated in the city of Brooklyn, on the festival of *Corpus Christi.*

"The ceremonies took place at the German Romanist Church, located in Montrose Avenue, Brooklyn, in that section of the late city of Williamsburg known as 'Dutch Town.' The neighborhood being almost exclusively German, the characteristics of Fatherland are visible in many respects, of which this is one most prominent. The day wore the appearance of the Sabbath. Labor was at a stand; the holiday-suit was donned, and the principal portion of the people flocked to the church to participate in the services. A military company of the locality, under command of one Captain Maerz, thoroughly armed and equipped, with a full band, was on the ground. At 10 o'clock the church was filled to attend mass, and hear the discourse for the occasion. During mass, and at certain intervals, while the organ was playing, and the choir and congregation chanting, the military company, DRAWN UP IN LINE IN FRONT OF THE ALTAR, presented arms, and then followed in quick succession the roll of the drums, the sound of trumpets inside of the church, and loud discharges of fire-arms outside of the church. This was repeated several times during the services. The church was decorated with evergreens, and the altar with flowers. The edifice was filled to its utmost capacity by the congregation. At the close of the semi-military services, the military were marched into the street, and formed in front of the church. Some further ceremonies, including a discharge of fire-arms at the side of the church, closed the services of the morning. The band of music playing—the military proceeded to their quarters, followed by an immense throng of spectators."*

These are not exceptional instances, but proofs among many others of the determination of the Roman hierarchy to obtain power, and hold influence over the minds of its bigoted followers, by any and every means within its complicated machinery.

The Romish Church is far-seeing—it sows to-day, knowing that a future generation will reap the bitter fruit. Gradually accustoming the public to the spectacle of the military in alliance with ecclesiasticism, they will ultimately claim this innovation as a right, and our soldiers will be looked upon as part of the religious power, and the natural defenders and supporters of the priesthood. This is Rome's aim, and yet our legislators, yea, we ourselves neither complain nor resist. Who are the commanders of these regiments and companies? can it be that they willingly accord their permission to such conduct, and consent to the arms and accoutrements of the State being employed for such purposes? What would be thought of the Episcopalians, Baptists, or Methodists, calling out the military to assist in their religious services, and proclaiming "peace and good-will towards men" at the point of the bayonet? The idea, even, is ridiculous; and yet we permit the Romanists to persist in an abuse which we would immediately and deeply resent in any Protestant denomination.

We contend that such proceedings are not merely in defiance of the feelings of a large majority of the people of the country, but are in direct opposition to the fundamental principles and spirit of our government. The Executive is the only authority vested with power to call out the military, yet here we see a professedly religious body asserting equal power, and forming an *imperium in imperio.* How is it possible to make such regiments lose their national characteristics, surrounded as they are with a foreign, and to them kindred population, and controlled by a foreign priesthood? They have

* See the New York Tribune, June 9th, 1855.

brought the bigotries of Papal Germany with them, and Protestant America, instead of passing laws for the restriction of these military abuses, by her guilty silence tacitly consents to the arrangement.

The wish of all men who have been oppressed, it would be supposed, would be to forget the uniforms and machinery of the land of their oppression, especially its political ones, and to banish from their sight all that can remind them of a former tyrant, most especially when they are the recipients of the blessings of Republican institutions. As long as these foreign organizations exist, the public mind will be kept in a ferment, and we shall be constantly startled by the announcements of disagreements between these foreign troops, and American officers, commanding divisions. Ere we are aware of it, discord will ensue, and blood will be shed,—the fearful consequence of which cannot be comprehended. The evils existing which are complained of, and the terrible catastrophes which loom up in the future, could all be avoided, if every State would pass laws requiring the citizen-soldiery *to wear uniforms sanctified by American associations*—loved, because they have only been worn in defence of freedom, and never disgraced as the livery of foreign potentates or mercenary slaves.

DEMORALIZING INFLUENCE OF DEMAGOGISM.

"For his thoughts were low,
To vice industrious, but to nobler deeds
Tim'rous and slothful; *yet he pleased the ear.*"
MILTON.

One of the most pernicious characters brought forth by the abuse of free institutions is the Demagogue. His business is to obtain office and honors by corrupting the people. This degradation of candidates for office, acts upon the voters. The good and true men are not appealed to; the scramble is to secure the suffrages of the ignorant and licentious, which are always for sale. A controlling minority of the "sovereigns," in this country, acquire a love for adulation, quite equal to that possessed by the rulers of the Old World, and instead of bestowing their favors with judgment and regard to the good of the community, they are to be solicited by gross flattery, or purchased with a given price. The true standard of merit, private worth, and acknowledged capacity, is lost in personal considerations; and the Demagogue rides into office, not because he has shown attention to any useful business, but because he has blown his own trumpet, degraded himself among his constituency, and won the character, among the thoughtless, of being the best fellow in the State. The slime of his contact can be traced among the members of the bar, on the bench, in the pulpit, in our legislative assemblies. The Demagogue is the professed worshipper of the sovereign people. He is a fawning sycophant at the foot of power,—ever grovelling on his knees in the dust, ready to do any act, however debased, perform any service, however wrong, if he can but win the patronage and smiles of his deity. Change the relations of the Demagogue from a republican to monarchical government, and he would still be the same, and, true to his ruling passion, worship the fountain of power. It is the Demagogue who labors to retard the improvement of society, who endeavors to break down the self-imposed restraints so necessary to make a good citizen; who tells the vicious that they are good—the ignorant that they are wise; who, in short, demoralizes society, by always appealing to the passions instead of the reason of the people, who represent the sovereign power.

The lust of office which generally seems to be the strongest in the minds of persons least capable of filling them with honor, gives rise to demagogism; and the people, occupied by the various avocations of life, are apt, as far as the government is concerned, to allow assumed (self-elected) leaders to do their thinking. The sublime privilege granted to freemen, of choosing their public servants is thus trifled with, and hence arise most of the glaring evils in the working of our free institutions. We often witness in members of our legislative bodies, an appalling recklessness with regard to their pledges made before election, and also in their private life. We find at Washington, as well as in our State capitals, an infinitely lower standard of morals among public men, than is demanded of the same individuals in the communities in which they reside.

The regime of the Demagogue is secured through different causes, all, however, subversive of the strength of our free institutions. The neglect of intelligent voters to attend the polls, and a general indifference to the machinery which brings candidates before the people, are perhaps among the most pernicious. Americans who thus trifle with the sacred privileges of their birthright, excuse themselves upon the ground, that the business of politics is distasteful, and the associations around the ballot-box and the unworthiness of candidates cause them to stay at home. The consequences of this criminal apathy are becoming every day more apparent in the acknowledged utter incapacity of a large majority of our public men, and in the disgraceful scenes that attend the carnivals of every legislative body.

The chief source of demagogism, however, is the constant ingress into our country of ignorant foreigners, not always destitute of literary cultivation, but entirely without any practical knowledge of our institutions. The Demagogues proclaim, through the pen and from the stump, that our republican form of government can only exist by virtue of intelligence and morality among the governed, and in the next breath they tell the undisciplined and ignorant immigrant, that he has the capacity and the right, from the day he lands upon our shores, to sit in judgment upon the claims of our candidates for office, and to participate in all the privileges enjoyed by Americans, who add to their birthright and descent the discipline acquired from law-abiding habits, and a life-long practice in the science of self-government. The foreigner may have democratic opinions, but the American has a democratic character as well as democratic opinions; and both these qualities are essential to make a person fit to perform, intelligently, the duties of American citizenship.

The Demagogue, finding that the priest has an uncontrolled power over the immigrants, seeks to secure his influence, that he may obtain the support of his priestly authority at the polls. The proposition is, "Secure me office, and I will secure you the interests of your church." The effect is seen in the action of our legislative bodies, who grant exclusive privileges and enormous donations to the Romish Church, while they rudely deny the same privileges and donations to Protestant denominations. And why? Because no Protestant clergyman can control the votes of his parishioners. No freeman accustomed to judge for himself will submit even to advice, unasked, much less dictated to, in a matter purely political. Innumerable instances might be given of the invidious special legislation referred to, either accomplished or attempted. Our readers will remember the struggle made by this spirit of demagogism, directed by priestcraft, to break up the unity of the public school system of the State of New York, and to throw a large part of the money advanced by tax-payers, and appropriated for the education of all the children of the State, into the hands of foreign ecclesiastics, to be used by them for sectarian and proselyting purposes. The Romish priests obtained a few years ago, from the Common Council of New York city, a grant of thirty-two lots of land without any consideration whatever! while at the same time, a Protestant Benevolent Association, for much less valuable property in the immediate vicinity, was made to pay thirty-eight thousand dollars. When Bishop Hughes opened his Cemetery at Newtown, he obtained a special ordinance, exempting those who used it from the necessity of obtaining "permits" from the City Inspector, such as are demanded from individuals of all other denominations when they bury the dead. This special legislation in favor of Romish priests will be found to have taken place in almost every State. It is the substantial reward which that cunning hierarchy seek, in exchange for their political influence; and they will be able to traffic it off at high prices, as long as the people are too supine to eject the Demagogues from the public service, and to find, and employ in it, only the honest and capable.

But the Demagogue does not confine himself to this quiet tampering with the priests, who hold the reins over so many of the immigrating population. They aspire also to win the "most sweet voices" of the strangers, by appealing immediately to their vanity and their passions. Our immigrant population having never felt in their native land, any other relation towards the established laws, than that of the oppressed to the oppressor, and having been habitually compelled to a blind, yet unwilling obedience, understand therefore by liberty, only the power to set the restraints of the law at defiance, and to violate its commands with impunity. Arriving in the United States, they are at once seized upon by the Demagogue. He flatters them with the wildest delusions as to their value in this country, and as to the motives of their coming, which he impudently perverts, even in defiance of their own knowledge. He informs them, that to them the country is indebted, not only for its freedom, but for its wealth. He ascribes to them and their predecessors in their westward journey, the vast internal improvements of our land; as if, forsooth, Irishmen had dug and built our thousands of miles of canals, and our tens of thousands of miles of railroads, had tunnelled our mountains, and bridged our rivers, out of *pure benevolence and kindness*, to assist our helpless nation! He informs them that their coming here is a voluntary tribute to our republican institutions; that, instead of being accidentally related to our form of government, as, according to the Demagogue, the *natives* are, they, the immigrants, occupy the superior position of those who select with great care the form of government under which they choose to live.

Readily swallowing such pleasant flatteries, the gullible foreigner loses all respect for the men or the institutions of his adopted country. Every necessary prescription of the law is resented; its power, although the legitimate will of the majority, is as odious as if emanating from his European rulers, and never having learned any self-restraints, he neither can nor will make nor appreciate the sacrifices which freemen are daily called upon to make for the sake of the public weal.

Amongst the natives of his own country, our Demagogue does not find so fertile a field for the exercise of his snaky gifts. Yet, even there, as there are always many less wise than the wisest, the Demagogue, although he may not be able to cram his patients with such gross concoctions as he serves up to the degraded foreigner, contrives to accomplish much evil by dexterously gilding the pill he administers. Whatever may be the weakness of his audience, whatever their error; whether they are right or wrong, he preaches their doctrine. *Vox populi, vox Dei*, he cries—the people's voice is God's voice: he demonstrates to them that they must be right, and modestly intimates that his complete conviction of that fact makes him the only fit man to accomplish their will. They may safely trust in him, and in his servile obedience, until there shall appear something or somebody offering a higher bribe.

The American Demagogue is a shameless monster, without parallel, without compeer. He stands alone in the infamy of his conduct, solitary in the sublime prostitution of his intellect, in the utter corruption of his heart. His is the double guilt of the sinner, who sins against clear light. Born in a nation peculiarly founded, and maintained by disinterested patriotism, he considers the love of country only narrow-mindedness, and almost thinks it treason to be proud of being born a citizen of the Republic. In a commonwealth, of which integrity and disinterested public spirit are the very life, he lives without principle or patriotism, whiffling about at every wind of political doctrine, and outwardly bowing with supple knees to the popular idol of the hour, while all the time, careless either of the nation or of right, the secret devotion of all his little selfish heart is expended in the idolatrous worship of his own purposes. Believing nothing, he puts on by turns the semblance of belief in every thing. He manufactures facts, statistics, history, philosophy, religion, to order, to suit his customers. He has passions always at command. Tears or smiles are squeezed out, to suit the occasion, and the doctrine of the day "commands his hearty support and consistent advocacy," as did the doctrine of yesterday, and as also will the doctrine of to-morrow.

At the magnetic touch of interest he flies, like a telegraphic dispatch, back and forth from one end to the other of the longest and most divergent lines of belief. Is a law popular? it is precisely what he always knew was needed. Does it become unpopular? he had always considered it oppressive, unconstitutional, and unnecessary. He would sacrifice the well-being of the nation for an office; the prosperity of the whole commonwealth, and his own conscience into the bargain—no great addition, to be sure—for a better salary or a fat job. He would defame his native land to secure an election; he would spit on the graves of his forefathers to gain a vote. For the base support of foreign priests, the votes of besotted immigrants, he will falsify history, and belie the fame of a thousand heroes. To gain such an object, he can find but one American who was distinguished in our Revolutionary struggle, and he would name as that one, Benedict Arnold! He would announce that the brunt of that fearful strife was borne by foreigners, and that our Revolutionary battles were won for us by the personal prowess of Lafayette, of Montgomery, of De Kalb.

Do our naturalized citizens murmur at any restraints upon their actions, at any laws and legal prohibitions, unusual to them—the Demagogue seizes the occasion, and eagerly strives to ride into office. He inflames the brutal rage of the mob; he goads angry men to murder and sedition; he shrinks not from awaking all the horrors of licentiousness and anarchy, from stirring up whirlwinds of baleful passions, if only his own dear objects may be attained by the crime. It is always easier to persuade to evil than to persuade to good. Poor human nature needs very little impulse in the path of wrong. Our laws and constitutions are not made as iron fetters and shackles are made, to grip and chain the ferocious violence of stubborn felons or murdering maniacs—they are made to guide the wise and congenial conduct of men seeking to do right. The Demagogue takes advantage of this to pervert the privilege of goodness into an occasion of crime; to the downward tendency of all the lower and viler parts of men's nature; to the exaggerated passions and blind brutality, the foolish prejudices and dogged obstinacy, of all the dregs of the community, of the untaught, the vicious, and the lawless; to the fearful momentum of this mass of dangerous and explosive elements, the Demagogue lends all the energies of his being. He throws all his weight to sink the fortunes of his country; he drags downward with all his might, towards the destruction of his native land. With the recklessness of the madman, but with more method in his madness, and therefore more dangerous effect, he "casts firebrands, arrows, and death." He cares not if he witness the conflagration of the whole Republic; for he intends to fill his own pockets by the thefts which he hopes to commit with impunity during the confusion.

God has not left any evil without providing a remedy, although he often leaves men to use it. The dark portrait which we have drawn, is not that of a necessary incubus upon our body politic. The Demagogue, the scourge of republics, only exists by sufferance. When the good and true men of the nation arise and act, this villain is crowded off the stage. It is now as it was in the homely but inspired parable of the Scriptures: "While the husbandman sleeps, the enemy sows tares." It is only when the right men neglect their duty, and leave their posts vacant, that the Demagogue can occupy the scene of action; can perform his fantastic tricks, and concoct his unprincipled schemes; can marshal his foolish regiments, and accomplish his vile undertakings. He lives by sufferance, and although his guilt is his own, yet honest men must remember that upon them rests the responsibility of permitting his sin to succeed. Upon their heads, after all, will lie the fearful responsibility of having, by criminal supineness, permitted the enactment of all the wickedness which Demagogues perpetrate.

WHAT CONSTITUTES THE RIGHT TO VOTE?

"The preservation of the sacred fire of liberty, and the destiny of the republican model of government, are justly considered as deeply, perhaps as finally, staked on the experiment intrusted to the hands of the American people."—WASHINGTON.

ALL human rights are either natural or acquired. They must either reside in the individual, co-equal with his life and the varied faculties of his nature, or become delegated to him by concession, by compromise, or by some specific compact to which he is a legitimate party.

Natural rights are absolute and inalienable: they rely on no presumptions of an arbitrary character, but are fully prescribed and ordained with the existence of man.. Whether exercised or not, a man cannot, by any enactment, be divested of their proper and positive possession. They may be yielded to the unlawful encroachments of other men, but the concession is merely temporary, and cannot be considered to invalidate the individual's privilege of resuming their exercise at such time as he may think proper.

All men, says the Declaration of Independence, are born free and equal; they possess certain inalienable rights, such as life, liberty, and the pursuit of happiness. These are their *natural endowments*, and by no lawful process can they be taken from them. The Bill of Rights, which was adopted by the Colonial Deputies at Philadelphia, previous to the Declaration, declared that the people were entitled to life, liberty, and property; and that they had never ceded to any sovereign power whatever a right to dispose of either, without their consent.

These inheritances, therefore, belong to us by nature. One man possesses them as largely as another. Factitious circumstances cannot enlarge their limits, nor can oppression and usurpation contract them. Wherever a human being is to be found, there these rights of necessity exist. They owe nothing of their strength to conventional usages and laws, nor are they sustained in any fuller force because they may happen to commend themselves to the approbation of enlightened men. They are rooted in the individual, and cannot by any violence be wrested from his nature: they are among the necessary conditions of his being.

Acquired rights exist by a different tenure. They hold their title either by concession, by compromise, or by compact. Their prerogative is more nicely defined. Certain limits bound them, beyond which their progress is forbidden. They are described with accuracy, and secured by due processes of legal enactment. Of such are the privileges of the subject, or the citizen. The former holds his by virtue of a kingly concession or compromise; in either case admitting the subject to rights and prerogatives which he does not naturally possess. The latter enjoys his by virtue of his compact with the general authority of which he is a component part.

It is only of the *rights of the citizen* that we propose to speak in this place—all others being foreign to the subject under consideration—and not of the *natural*, but of the *acquired*, rights of the citizen.

As the human race is constituted, its entire history illustrates the imperative necessity of some method of social organization. Left to themselves, all things would immediately relapse into a condition of misrule and barbarism. Certain powers must be vested in certain individuals, from whom, by a reverse process, all acts of authority are to emanate. Influences which one individual would not permit any indifferent person to exercise over himself and his interests by a consent, either expressed or implied, he freely allows some other person to exert without protest or opposition.

Hence arise forms of government that give character to the deeds of men, and shape the destiny of nations. Hence ensue decrees, edicts, proclamations, and laws. These evidences of authority testify everywhere to the admitted necessity of some ruling and guiding power. They are an expression of the opinion of all men, that a controlling authority of *some* character is demanded by every consideration of human welfare.

There can exist but two general forms of government, let the specific *titles* of the various kinds of authority be what they may. Every government must be either *arbitrary* or *constitutional.* Every thing that tends to usurpation, or that operates to defraud individuals of the enjoyment of their natural rights, no matter in what cause or name professed, belongs to absolutism and arbitrariness. Some governments style themselves constitutional, whose very constitutions are arbitrary in themselves, and do not receive their vitality from any co-operation of the popular will. Their practices give the lie to their professions, proving them what they wish to avoid seeming to be. Principles strike their root much deeper than professions, and by their natural fruits their true character is understood.

Constitutional or voluntary forms of government derive their authority from the immediate consent of the governed; that is the only source of their power. They are but the emphatic expression of the popular will, and, as that will changes its direction, must they alter the direction of their authority.

The American Government is of the strictly constitutional form. No powers reside in it but those delegated by the people, who are its founders. It derives no authority from usurpation, but the whole of it from voluntary cession. Its existence and its strength alike depend upon the spirit and intelligence of those who give it vitality and support. Its powers are every one carefully described and defined. Its prerogatives have a fixed and unalterable limit. The natural rights of man are not invaded by any of its usurpations, but are retained inviolate by the individual, and guarded from aggression with a jealous watchfulness.

Indeed, the question is seriously agitated under this auspicious form of government—How much is it profitable for a man to be governed? How far is it best for him to yield up his own rights in the name of the welfare of the whole? Where shall the dividing line be drawn that is to separate the control of one's self from the control of a voluntarily constructed authority? From the discussion of such a question various conclusions have, at different times, been arrived at; and, among others, that "that is the best government which governs men the least." This seems almost to have become an aphorism; and the spirit of the idea is by no means inoperative in the general workings of our political system.

Under our government no man is a *subject*—all men are *citizens;* because it is never acknowledged that the government, deriving its existence primarily from the individual, is superior in itself to its origin. In the nature of things, it could not be. A citizen is in no manner a subject, nor can a subject be a citizen. However specious may be the reasoning that seeks to make the two characters seem compatible with one another, their differences are too wide to be reconcilable. The subject makes concessions that the citizen would not admit. The subject lacks inherent power, not because he has delegated it to another, but because he never yet was allowed its possession or exercise. By the citizen it has been vested in other hands for the very purpose of its more safe and careful administration; reverting to him after stated intervals, to be again trusted to other depositaries for the same general purpose of a healthful and constitutional exercise.

Citizenship, therefore, implies no ordinary privileges. Its possession argues from the individual directly to the government. It connects the man with all the operations of the laws and the whole scope of public institutions, and associates him in close relations with whatever belongs to the common welfare. It removes the many tendencies to selfishness and egotism in his permitted pursuits, and makes him large, comprehensive, and generous in his conduct and views. It widens the sphere of individual sentiment and action, so that a man may at the same time be true to his own interest, and not forgetful of the vast and complicated interests of the whole.

In fine, citizenship can be enjoyed only where men are *free.* In any other condition, the character of the possession at once is changed, being held on terms that impliedly declare the government to be arbitrary, and the people to be subjects. It belongs only to institutions that are democratic in their nature, and to states of society in which men are the arbiters of their own rights and fortunes.

For the possession of such prerogatives there certainly should be some rigid and absolute qualifications. To put one's self in direct relationship with the moral and social interests of a great nation, it should be insisted that there exist certain preliminary conditions. Such a relationship should not be rashly entered upon, nor without serious thought of the mutual result to both the individual and the mass. The government, relying on the intelligence and understanding of each one of the vast number that contribute to its character, it must be seen that no single violation of the conditions of such a connection can pass without its proper share of wrong to the whole. If the individual forgets his duty as a party to the general compact, the rest are defrauded of that moral and political security for which they had a perfect right to hold him responsible. If he neglect the obligations of his oath and pledge, the rest are so far losers by his act of repudiation. If he be a tool in the designing hands of those who intrigue for the overthrow of political freedom, the entire nation is to that degree involved in the web of fear and insecurity.

The origin of all government is property; the manner in which that property is held determines its form. If the lands of a community have but *one* possessor, it is an autocracy; if partitioned by *a few*, an aristocracy; if the inherent right of the *whole people*, this forms a democracy. *Res-republica*, *common-wealth*, represent, not merely the form, but the basis of government.

Man is entitled to sustenance and protection from that society in which nature places him at birth. There are, however, certain causes which may compel him to forsake one community for another. What relation do his acquired privileges bear to the rights of the new society?

A stranger can only acquire property in a foreign community by permission of the owners—that is, the state. But in acquiring this, is he necessarily entitled to all the privileges of the natives? Because he has forsaken the land of his birth, is the land of his adoption compelled by any law, human or divine, to place him on a perfect equality with her own children? By the political constitution of the new society he may enjoy all their privileges, but, in the nature of things, he has not, and never can have, such a right to them as the sons of the soil. That which is granted as a favor, can never be asserted as a right.

In a republic the power is in the hands of the whole people, for the entire land is theirs. For convenience in legislation they appoint men to represent their interests, hence the representative is the servant of the represented. This is obvious: no man can represent the interests of others unless delegated so to do; this power *conferred* necessarily subjects him to the will of those who bestow the office. Hence no man has a *right* to office, which it may be in the power of others to refuse.

Representatives having to be chosen, there arises a momentous question—What gives the right to vote? We have shown that where the right to property belongs to all, power is universal; therefore, suffrage must be universal. But we must define this, in regard to men who have not a *born-right* in the country, but simply one of tolerance or permission.

Government takes cognizance of the entire property of the country, that is to say, the land and its products belonging to the sons of the soil—the entire community decide (by representation or otherwise) in the general interest. Strangers arriving in their midst receive as a gift a certain portion of that which is the *right* only of the native-born. Is it logical to assert that this gift carries with it the right to vote, or, in other words, to legislate for those who have just granted what it was in their power to refuse? Such an argument is monstrous, yet it is one which we hear constantly asserted.

Escape from the then existing systems of European government, as well as from its religious hierarchies, prompted our forefathers to settle what were termed the American colonies. In process of time they achieved a separate nationality in regard to other countries, a federation of states to themselves, in which each state was independent of the others.

"The character of our people was admirably calculated for setting the great example of popular government. They were accustomed to representative bodies and the forms of free government; they understood the doctrine of the division of power among different branches, and the necessity of checks on each. The character of our countrymen, moreover, was sober, moral, and religious."*

This portraiture forms an obvious opinion on claims set up by demagogues and others in favor of the so-called rights of our foreign population. The entire body of emigrants to this country for many years past, with but few exceptions, never exerted the slightest control over any government whatsoever: are we then to be told that such men can appreciate and properly wield the electoral power in a country, the political constitution of which is so difficult to understand? Besides, is the moral character of these emigrants calculated to remove any fears we may entertain relative to the uses to which they will put this novel power? We take it experience is very much inclined to a negative.

There is no principle in the American Constitution which guarantees land or political power, by vote or otherwise, to foreign citizens. These men do not leave Europe as did the first settlers of this continent; they are, in fact, dissimilar in every respect. Europe disgorges a surplus population—people she can best afford to lose: they arrive *in forma pauperis*, and our authorities permit them to reside. In process of time they begin to have a stake in the country, and maybe lose their ancient prejudices; they are permitted to vote at elections. But they have not, and never can have, the same right, either to one or the other, which a native-born citizen possesses.

At various periods in our history laws relative to naturalization have been passed, exacting, in some instances, but two years of residence in the country. Circumstances might then have justified so short a probation, but, at the present time, not merely has the class of emigrants

* Webster.

changed, but the country itself has been radically modified: it has, in fact, assumed a nationality that it did not formerly possess. Demagogues enunciate a monstrous proposition in asserting this republic to be one of composite races. It is not. The Republic of the United States is Anglo-Saxon in all its bearings: other peoples may arrive, but they must be gradually absorbed, and, in process of time, become amalgamated with, and lost among, the predominant race. Ethnology and history both assert this fact, and the senseless opponents of it are merely perpetuating the evils of *caste*, in pandering to the prejudices of various nationalities. It is the province and duty of the patriot to discountenance such endeavors.

The objection is frequently advanced that in thus debarring a whole class, men are kept out, whose aim in adopting American citizenship is to enjoy a political freedom, which experience tells them can only be found here. But it would be scarcely possible to enumerate all these exceptional instances; suffice it to say, the legislature might be permitted to admit such cases to citizenship, especially where services have been rendered to the country, or additions to its glory. This is fully consonant with the democratic principle; but, in any case, it is much better for the country to lose the advantage of such instances, than to receive with them the immense masses who are fast making universal suffrage a mockery and delusion.

The hordes of emigrants who yearly crowd our shores, seek us, not to obtain a voice in government, but a certainty of life, food, and personal freedom, which they never before enjoyed. If, like the adder warmed into life by the peasant, they get prosperous, and turn upon their benefactor; or, listening to the voice of vile demagogues and designing politicians, they raise tumult and civil discord in the land, then surely native-born citizens have a natural and a constitutional right to curb such disorder, and to legislate so as, in future, to prevent any doubt as to whether an American have a nationality or not.

In America, no man becomes a citizen through the influence of either money or titles. It was a wise act of our forefathers, when they abolished titles, except such only as might be the expression of simple respect; and it has conduced more effectually to the complete political equality of all classes of citizens than many measures about which vastly more has been said. It taught the people the truth, that there was in America *nothing greater* than citizenship itself; and weaned them rapidly from the foolish inclination, that is no part of a high and self-reliant manhood, to bestow honor upon the emptiest of human pretensions.

Citizenship, if it involves the serious responsibilities that exist along with its possession, presumes—or, at least, should presume—certain fixed qualifications. If the elector be ignorant of those responsibilities, assuredly he cannot be supposed to assume them; and if he fails to assume them, it is proper that he be refused the use of the electoral franchise until such time as his ignorance has yielded to a more profound understanding of his obligations. Nothing can be plainer than this. And yet there are Americans, who should know better what is the priceless worth of our institutions, who seek to throw open every means of access to a privilege that should be guarded with so watchful a care, and affect indifference to qualifications of such momentous importance,—men seemingly careless of the true character of the liberty which we profess, and ignorant of the certain consequences of licentiousness and misrule that are to follow close upon any laxity of electoral obligations. Such men need to study more thoughtfully the meaning of our government, and the true spirit and character of its institutions.

Any native-born citizen, on attaining the age of twenty-one years, and having taken the oath of allegiance to the Constitution and fidelity to the laws, is admitted to all the privileges of the electoral franchise. He has the right to vote on all questions affecting the common interest, and by the deposit of his ballot throws his individual influence into the scale of political affairs. He is licensed to assist in the regulation of the highest and the lowest interests that pertain to the welfare of the nation. He may make the power of his influence felt throughout all the affairs of state. Law and order are intrusted to his hands for preservation. The general intelligence will either

12

advance or retrograde, according to the power of his vote and example. The public peace and prosperity depend upon the manner in which his privilege as an elector is exercised. The national character is elevated or depressed, as his own character is made to impress itself upon its existence.

Gaining so exalted a right on such easy terms, unless some steps be taken to secure the elector's intelligent appreciation of his privileges and responsibilities, his individual gain must of necessity be the country's loss. An ignorant and degraded citizen can be only a bad citizen; and a bad citizen, assuredly, is worse than none. We had better all remain peaceful subjects, than become irresponsible and licentious citizens.

What, then, should those qualifications be for possessing and enjoying the electoral privilege? This is the important question that so immediately concerns all the free citizens of America. It presents itself to us at this day, demanding a thoughtful but speedy answer. That there should be certain fundamental qualifications, of a general and disciplinary nature, attached to the privilege of voting, we do not see how any intelligent American can doubt. The more extended the responsibilities, the greater should be the precautions to make them appreciated and understood. The more valuable the character of the possession, the more positive the need of its being impressed on the mind of every one who is admitted to it as a participator.

In the first place, it seems necessary to insist on some degree of familiarity with the principles and working of our constitutional form of government. The native-born citizen acquires this in the course of his education from his youth up. Even if not much given to reflection, and to the habit of tracing results back to their original causes, he nevertheless is placed and kept within the circle of those ever-recurring events which mark the movements of our political system; and even imperceptibly, and unconsciously to himself, he is taught by them lessons of the highest importance to the better understanding of the institutions that surround him. The very atmosphere that he breathes is conducive to his progress in the right direction. All his associations are pregnant with the instruction of which he has so much need.

The alien knows nothing of these things. What acquaintance he obtains with the principles of constitutional freedom, must be had only through the instrumentality of his own studious and persistent efforts. Nothing comes to him by mere force of education, or through the facile medium of early associations. In a strange land, he is himself an utter stranger. He may understand that here his physical condition is susceptible of the largest possible improvement, and yet he may remain in the grossest ignorance of the vital truths and principles by whose agency alone that improvement is so firmly secured. Such strange things present themselves to our observation daily.

Unless the elector has a clear apprehension as well of the character as of the workings of the institutions under which he lives, it can hardly be supposed of him that he is truly capable of exercising the electoral franchise. The possession of that privilege should of necessity presuppose a certain degree of intelligent capacity both to employ and enjoy it. Unless that capacity is present, there remains so much more of ignorance to be overcome by the superior intelligence of the rest, and they are losers to the extent of that ignorance over the popular mind.

In the second place, no man should be an elector, possessing its various powers and privileges, who has not already asserted and proven his decided preference for free institutions over all others, and is not willing to live perpetually under the active operation of the principles in which they are rooted. It may be replied, we admit, that the elector's oath, taken at the time of becoming a participator in the privilege of the electoral franchise, is *prima facie* evidence of such a preference and willingness; yet, as the details of our political affairs have from time to time exhibited themselves on the surface, it is by no means so well established, that behind that solemn asseveration there lurks NO DANGEROUS RESERVATION. We have had abundant proof in our own day, that the oath of the freeman is too often forgotten,—vitiated by the force of secret compacts,—nay, scouted, denied, and derided, by men to whom in safety its administration should have been refused. We have had not a few most melancholy reminders of the insecurity that attends the too free and unguarded gift of its power, to those who had no proper estimate of its use or value. These warnings appeal directly to the cause of liberty and a free government, and have no connection with considerations of mere personal safety or personal prejudice.

It seems to be the most natural and reasonable of all demands conceivable, that he who is about to have a part in the operations of government, should in his heart be firmly attached to that government. Less than this condition, is an abrogation of all conditions. If a man be ready to bind himself, it is presumable that his attachment is beyond question for the object with which he desires to make the engagement. And to attach one's self to a *cause*, instead of a mere *interest*,—a cause the most holy and lofty of all that absorb the thoughts or exercise the emotions of the human race, because it is co-ordinate and co-equal with the great truths of Christianity itself,—is properly indicative of enthusiasm. It is an open confession that the generous impulses outrun the slower movements of calculative reflection, and that the man has grown energetic in behalf of that cause, rather through the quickening warmth of his irresistible convictions, than through the calmer and steadier influence of reasonings which he cannot put aside.

In the next place, all voters should possess at least a fair share of general intelligence—enough, certainly, to enable them to distinguish the difference between the American and other forms of government, and to know the uses and meaning of law, the general rights of individuals, the sacredness of life and property, and the ordinary object and scope of free institutions. Such men are not naturally to be looked for among the masses of those who are not yet able to read and write, nor do they abound in quarters where the controlling influences are anti-American, Jesuitical, and dangerous to liberty. The very object of freedom, we know, is to elevate the character of the masses; yet the necessity is absolute that there should be some degree of elevation with which to begin the experiment.

If it be admitted that intelligence and ignorance alike are to be incorporated into the system of our institutions, it requires no prophet's eye to see that those institutions must, in a fearfully brief space of time, become changed in their character. They are capable of elevating men from the degradations of ignorance, if allowed the influence that was inherent in them at their establishment; but, in an altered condition, they may become the most powerful engines of licentiousness and misrule, by which ignorant and vicious men permit themselves to be moved.

A certain standard of general intelligence ought to be demanded by the popular voice for those who aspire to the privileges and power of electorship. The danger of laxity here is plain to the most superficial observer. It is only tearing away the ordinary safeguards of freedom, opening a road for the aggressions of depravity, paying premiums for the perpetual presence of anxiety and fear, and suffering the general interests and welfare to relapse into the unfathomable depths of degradation. There can be no laxity, with safety, in a state of actual freedom. Vigilance is the corner-stone of the whole fabric.

And, lastly, the participator in a free government, like that of America, ought to have some definite understanding of the true *aims*, and the extended *influence* of the system under which he lives. It is incumbent on him, as a valuable citizen, that he know, not simply the theory of that system, but something, also, of its lofty purposes, its far-reaching influences, and its marvellous power in the great work of regenerating and exalting the human race. If, in such a knowledge as this he has no deficiency, he is secretly conscious that he has risen by progressive steps, from being a mere observer of disconnected facts, to the higher conditions of a true philosopher.

A familiar understanding of these purposes is what every American should possess. He ought to know that a free government exists for some other end than simply what is to be found centering in itself; that its proper aims can never be selfish, and never limit themselves to the elevation of a few over the many; that it has for its scope the welfare of every citizen, however degraded and however humble, within its territorial boundaries; that its object is purely the elevation of the masses, who, in turn, must reflect their character and its varied influences upon its name and institutions; that the perpetuation of truth, and not of falsehood, is the natural result of its manifold operations; and that its works will not cease from their living and spreading influence, till that influence shall have made the peaceful circuit of the world.

These are grand objects to attain, and must excite both the admiration and enthusiasm of all who possess the capacity to comprehend them. And if they belong, of such a plain necessity, to the government that has true freedom for its permanent foundation, what a weighty responsibility attaches to every individual who is permitted a share in the transactions of that government! How earnest ought all to appear in hastening forward purposes which are fraught with such beatific consequences to the whole human race! What a necessity rests on all citizens alike, to see that these grand aims are not perverted by either the ignorance or wilfulness of any, who seek to be admitted to the same free privileges with themselves!

That the true worth of the electoral franchise too often suffers from degrading uses, it is impossible to deny. Proof of it is offered us on every side. It is bestowed where it should have been withheld: it courts the acceptance of the incompetent, instead of demanding that they first qualify themselves for being invested with its inestimable gifts: it is losing its character for dignity, by being literally thrust upon men in no wise fitted for the performance of any of its functions.

The high characteristics of citizenship must manifestly relax their claims to general respect, when ignorant foreign immigrants are made voters before they can so much as understand their relations to the laws or to the people at large. We are undeniably going backwards, when we admit men to be electors, who cannot distinguish between a blind and sullen obedience to statutes, and an active and intelligent co-operation with the principles on which proper restrictive enactments are founded. It is a dangerous policy to make voters of men who think that freedom from European servility should be marked by an irresponsible delirium of license here. It degrades the general standard to which the condition of electorship should aspire to hold itself fixed. Such men grow suddenly exhilarated in the free atmosphere into which they have come, and contract exaggerated ideas of liberty, that are never borne out by the reality of their subsequent experience. Demagogues flatter these naturalized voters, and they are delighted;—if, afterwards, honest men should tell them the truth, they could neither endure them, nor the institutions in whose name they profess to speak.

In itself considered, and setting aside these multiplied abuses to which so priceless a gift as the electoral franchise is subjected, American Citizenship is invested with a dignity that transcends in intrinsic importance, any and all the titles that foreign courts have it in their power to bestow; there is, in reality, no condition that may successfully claim to be its equal.

From the citizen, in his individual character, emanate influences that reach alike the government and the world. By his power, is circumscribed the welfare of associated masses and multitudes. He feels the glory and the shame of his country, for that country has the sources of its existence in him; he stands the immediate representative of the government and the citizen, and happily illustrates the nicely adjusted relationship of each to the other.

By the very name Citizen is fairly implied both honor and honesty, purity and morality. He should fear only what is wrong, and aspire to nothing but what is right. He must be impressed with the number and magnitude of his responsibilities, feeling the weight of the trusts he has received, both from his country and from God. He cannot fail to see that his own free system of government, that degrades none, but seeks to exalt all alike, is the light and illumination of the world; that it most truly represents the cause of freedom and equal rights; that it abnegates selfishness, and has within the reach of its influence the welfare of the entire human race. He must be deeply impressed with the greatness of his mission, knowing it to be the mission of the government in which he is an active participant. His reflections can be in no manner allied to levity, for they must tell him perpetually of a work, whose mighty results are to be carried steadily forward to the end of coming time.

FALLACY OF SUPPOSING THAT AMERICAN INSTITUTIONS NEED NO SAFEGUARDS.

"Eternal vigilance is the price of liberty."

It appears to be an almost universal truth, that those who are in possession of the full desire of their hearts, betray extreme carelessness in securing for that possession an adequate protection. A severe experience seems needed to discipline men into habits of prudence, self-control, and precautionary foresight. Any advantage, if not acquired by personal sacrifice, generally fails to carry with it those impressive lessons of discreetness which are the surest securities against either its invasion or decay.

Americans of the present generation have been peculiarly liberal in relation to their political privileges. Holding them in a measure cheap, because so easily attained, they have hitherto failed to see the need of dispensing them to others with a prudent hand, or of hedging them about with such restrictions as would place them out of reach of questionable influences. Liberty has a tendency to make men's heart's large and generous, and to give the utmost latitude to thought. With a practical knowledge of the manifold blessings of freedom ingrained in their very natures, it is hardly possible for them to desire less ample endowments for those whom they find deprived of them altogether.

The actual aim of our free institutions is universal brotherhood. Whether acknowledged or not as the purpose of our political organization, this, nevertheless, is the vital spirit that imparts all power and energy. And yet it is not to be argued as a consequence of this truth, that so grand an attainment will be reached any the sooner, or that its blessings will be secured in any greater degree, by laxity in the care of these institutions, and a mistaken generosity in extending the power of directing their operation. By indifference of this sort, their character must suffer degradation; and when that result is reached, the true end of their existence is perverted, if not entirely destroyed. Free gifts are assuredly evidences of large possessions; and multiplied acts of generosity are proofs of deep sympathy with those who are so unfortunate as to be destitute. But there are always limits to such deeds, beyond which they cease to be beneficial, and become means of injury or mischief.

If absolutism feels the necessity of protecting itself against the inroads of men who deny the lawfulness of its claims, how much more sensibly must that necessity be felt by the friends and supporters of constitutional freedom. The former fears conspiracies, machinations, and the outbursts of rebellion. The latter have to guard continually against indifference to privileges,—an indifference which soon is followed by licentiousness and riot,—eventually leading to a tyranny far more fearful than that of any one-man power. Liberty is apt to be careless, from its very inclination to generosity. Unsparing in favors to all, it dreams not of ingratitude from its recipients. The law seems to be entirely in its own favor, removing all those sources of anxiety in which absolutism is so prolific; and yet other causes of fear are known to spring up plentifully under a certain complication of circumstances, which nothing but the utmost prudence and firmness can hope to remove.

There is nothing that Americans should guard with so watchful an eye as their country's liberty. They cannot be too jealous in its care. They cannot hope to enjoy freedom and slothfulness together. Liberty has its own unchangeable price, which is vigilance unceasing. It is good to dilate on the blessings of freedom, but the reflections are idle and the words are empty harangues, when freedom has no sentinels on its farthest outposts, and careless defenders in its citadel. If they who hold priceless possessions are indifferent to their preservation, where shall men be found to volunteer protection for that upon which they set, as yet, no value? If the free are not watchful, how can we hope to find a guardian for liberty among the oppressed?

None ought to be so capable of understanding what freedom is worth, as those to whom its riches have fallen by inheritance. A proper estimate of its value is not to be expected from others. To them it is still an unreal speculation—a dim and far-off vision. They have heard, perhaps, of its reality, and come to settle their calm convictions upon its truth. Still, it is practically unknown to them, and from it they have never been able to derive any personal advantage. But Americans have no excuse to plead for their ignorance. Under the protection of free and constitutional laws they are secured in the possession of both life and liberty. Themselves the original power in the State, they impart character and direction to all the operations of government. Holding certain inalienable rights, they are free to attain happiness after their own desires. All pursuits, of a proper character, lie wide open to their ambition in every direction; and they may boast that theirs is the noblest country and the freest nation on the face of the earth.

There are, therefore, no reasons why such large privileges should ever suffer from diminution. If they unfortunately do, the fault lies at the door of those who should have been their most ardent champions. They must rehearse their misfortunes to none but their own ears, and brood in silence over the loss that might have been turned to their immeasurable gain.

Facts are imposing authorities in the disposition of theories and suppositions. Nothing is better calculated to open the eyes of the blind, or to unstop the ears of the deaf, than these most stubborn and irresistible things. Upon them, all reasoning is based; and from them logical conclusions are unerringly deduced. From them alone we are able to understand the real position, both of our free institutions and the dangers by which these are surrounded. They will tell us the plainest truths of our national welfare, and enable us, better than all else, to comprehend the chart by which our national course is guided.

In dealing with this subject, we do not propose to enter very deeply into statistics, yet it may be well to illustrate the points to which we wish to call general attention. We desire to establish three distinct statements; and from their tenor may be inferred the particular dangers to which our free institutions are at this day most threateningly exposed:

I. The foreign voters, who are proved to be *ignorant* and in every way *incompetent*, are admitted to the enjoyment of the electoral franchise.

We, who never knew what a blind and passive obedience to law is, can form no adequate idea of the recklessness and delirium which seize hold of so many foreign immigrants the moment they put foot upon our shores. We admit that some of them are men of intellectual culture, while it will not be denied that too many are persons of the most degraded character, and destitute even of the most meager attainments. The ignorance, however, from which Americans experience the greatest cause for distrust, is that which relates to the nature and spirit of republican institutions. These they do not seem either able or inclined to comprehend. They scout all ideas of obedience, because they claim that here they are free. Liberty and lawlessness are with them one and the same thing. Hitherto, they have never borne any intelligent relation to the existence or execution of law, but have occupied the places of unreflecting persons, accustomed, in passive silence, to bear the burdens with which they were weighed down. Coming to a country like America, and hearing the most exaggerated and extravagant stories of its ample freedom for all men, without a thought of their responsibility to the nation sustaining the fabric of this glorious freedom, they conclude that here the field of license lies open, and that any sort of restraint is powerless and illegal against unbounded indulgence.

Heretofore, all their feelings have been marshalled against government; for it was established upon their oppression, and never exercised its functions for their interests or welfare. They have lost that high and self-reliant sense of manhood, under its operation, which gives to men the clearest ideas of true freedom, and enables them to understand their relation to freedom. The result naturally follows, that these same feelings of antagonism to government and law are brought with them to the land which they have chosen as their future home. They breathe the same spirit of hostility as before, to whatever has a tendency to impose upon their careless action a healthy restraint. Not comprehending the meaning of self-government, they know nothing of the spirit of conservatism by which our free system is upheld, and are ready to enter with recklessness upon any changes which demagogues hold out as beneficial.

Lacking religious sentiment of any description, they become the easiest dupes, as they are the most dangerous fanatics. They are ever ready for change, nay, for revolution, rather than continue in peaceful quiet, obedient to law, and evenly pursuing their own highest interests. As are their sympathies in the lands of their birth, so are they here: as are their hatreds there, so do they betray themselves here. All ideas of law are confounded with mere physical force, and they have no definite conception whatever of the true aim of legal enactments.

Such are the people flocking to our shores by tens of thousands, and admitted, even welcomed, to the privileges of citizenship. The direct tendency of such an addition to our roll of voters, is the unmistakable degradation of the electoral franchise. Such gross ignorance could produce no other result. We have a large proportion of such voters in the country, answerable for the operation of our political institutions, and directly concerned in the character of their influence, both at home and abroad.

In 1832, at the time of the Presidential election, there were supposed to be fifteen thousand foreign voters in America; in 1840, they were computed at fifty-four thousand, comprising one forty-sixth of the whole number of electors; while in 1852, the foreign vote was known with accuracy to be one hundred and eighty-eight thousand, or had risen to *one-seventeenth* of the electoral body. In other words, the foreign vote had nearly multiplied itself by *twelve*, since 1840, while the aggregate vote of the country has not multiplied itself by *three!* The moral lies in the figures.

During the past five years, it is calculated there has been a steady immigration at the rate of three hundred thousand persons a year, or about one thousand per day! Out of each thousand, it is safe to consider at least one hundred and fifty to be voters. The great mass of these men is composed of all the ignorance, poverty, lawlessness, and general degradation, that could be induced to emigrate to America. They come to the ballot-boxes side by side with those who have been bred from their youth to a perfect familiarity with and respect for free institutions, and are too often found ready to become the servile tools of demagogues, even more reckless and unprincipled than themselves. These are the men we permit to help fashion our laws, give tone to general society, infuse energy into the spirit of our political organizations, and protect us and all our dearest interests from destruction or decay. With no knowledge of our Constitution, they never interest themselves to understand its meaning. They do not comprehend what is the scope of law, nor are they conscious of the existence of any check or responsibility that may hold them to its observance.

It is time this threatening danger be averted. The evil increases by continuance, and daily becomes more and more difficult of remedy. Unless efficient and timely safeguards are interposed by the vigilant watchmen of freedom, it will have acquired an imposing magnitude, capable of overawing the most energetic efforts for its subjugation.

II. Our institutions are alarmingly menaced, by the aggressions of the Romish priesthood.

We are well aware that much has been said on this subject; but with the practices and professions of that priesthood before our eyes, we insist that it is impossible to warn the people of America too frequently against the arts by which their liberties are sought to be subverted. It is not for Americans to raise the rallying cry of persecution. Every religious body should be left free to the enjoyment of its own worship, and the publication of its own creeds. Uncharitableness belongs not to the spirit of our system. Interference with the convictions of conscience, is sternly forbidden by the whole history and tenor of our political customs.

But when religion forgets the holy cause of its mission, and, in the name of designing men, is inoculated with selfishness and ambition, and a spirit of arbitrariness in direct conflict with freedom, both of conduct and conscience—when it lays off the unsoiled robes of peace in which it has been clad, and girds on the sword in order to wage worldly conflicts—it seems then as if, with its own pure character, it had divested itself of its former claims to our reverence, and entered the field with all the greedy desires, deceits, artifices, and hot passions, that disfigure the character of man.

If the devotees of the religion of Christ once give over the singleness of their calling for the sake of compassing ends which are purely ambitious and worldly, they deserve to be met with the prompt rebuke that such conduct so richly merits. No reproofs can be too severe for their hypocritical practices. No opposition can be too unbending for their attempted usurpations. They are to be checked at the outset in a career that promises nothing but danger to the free government that affords them its indulgent protection.

That there are truly and devotedly pious members of the Romish priesthood in America, we shall not take it upon ourselves to deny; still their zeal burns only for the Church, whose faithful servants they are, while the tenets and practices of that Church are undeviatingly hostile to freedom. These facts are well supported. The professions of the temporal head of that Church are openly at war with free institutions. His words are swift witnesses of his hostility to any political system that secures liberty of conscience to the worshipper. He insists that the Church, and the Romish Church alone, is the source of all temporal as well as spiritual authority, and that to its tyrannical behests and decrees the State should bow in silent submission. In America, the people form the State; and hence the people must be brought beneath a yoke that takes away every thing like individual freedom, and offers in return nothing but the most degrading servility.

On such conditions, no free State could ever hope to stand. Its history would pass out of the light, into a darkness that would enshroud it from the eyes of the world, forever. The rock on which it stranded would always be marked, but, in the wide waste of the seas, no fragments of the noble structure would afterwards be found. It would be ingulfed in a vast whirlpool, that never gives back to the eye any tokens of the ruins with which its voracious appetite is gorged.

It would be easy to extend beyond the limits of our work, examples of this hostility of the Romish Church to liberty; volumes of confessions might be collected from the lips and pens of both priests and press, all going to establish beyond question their undying hatred to the freedom of the individual. The great writer and defender of Romish doctrines in this country, in his Review, frankly confesses as follows:

"I never think of publishing any thing in regard to the Church, without submitting my articles to the Bishop for inspection, approval, and endorsement." And after this important admission, he declares (with the Bishop's authority, of course,) that "Protestantism of every form *has not, and never can have, any rights* where Catholicity is triumphant."*

Daniel O'Connell, in one of his speeches in parliament, gives like testimony: "I declare my most unequivocal submission to the head of the Church, and to the hierarchy in its different orders. If the Bishops make a declaration on this bill, I never would be heard speaking against it, but would submit at once, unequivocally, to that decision. They have only to decide, and they also close my mouth; they have only to determine, and I obey. I wish it to be understood that such is *the duty of the Catholics*."†

* Brownson's Review.

† Spotskniskay, recently a Romish priest, officiating in Paterson, was denounced as a heretic, and excommunicated by Bishop Hughes, of New York city, because he went to hear a Protestant minister lecture on Popery, a thing the priest declares he could do in Poland without censure, "but could not do it in this land of liberty without expulsion from his Church."

By this kind of evidence of the proscription of all kinds of individual liberty in the individual, the spirit of animosity to American institutions, that directs the action of Romish priests, is laid open to public inspection. It is bitter and deadly in its operation, to the last conceivable limit. It affects to be quiet, when quiet is for its interest, yet never hesitates to trample ruthlessly on all law, and all liberty, when its increased power permits it so to do with impunity. By a process of astonishing accretion, it builds up a power within the State, the ostensible purposes of which are to overshadow every combination of opposing influence, and to subvert and defy all the forces of the civil government. It demands of its votaries a pledge totally vitiating their solemn oaths as freemen, and offers their united political influence to that party which shall show itself most supple to its insinuating address.

Against such a power there is great need that Americans should secure proper protection. Whether it seek to effect its objects by fraud or force, by stratagem or violence, it should be resisted in season, and resisted energetically to the end. The existence of such a power, aiming to reach political advantage under the professions of devotion to religion, is both alarming in its tendencies, and incompatible with the spirit and character of free institutions.

III. We stand in great danger of losing our liberties, from a growing indifference to the exercise of our own rights as voters at the polls.

In itself considered, this point is not strictly to be regarded as of an aggressive nature; but when viewed in connection with *the other two*, it assumes a magnitude and importance calculated to arrest the attention of the most careless and unreflecting. It implies a state of things within, in perfect co-operation with the dangerous designs from without; a previous preparation, that promises more certain success to the destructive plans by which republican liberty is besieged.

It is not necessary to our present purpose, to speculate on the causes of such supreme indifference, on the part of freemen, to the safety of their high privileges; enough that a truth so melancholy is forced on our attention. The fact is palpably plain. The results betray themselves on all sides—in an inferior grade of public functionaries; in the impudent presumptions of demagogism; in the greater abundance of examples of intrigue; and in the general deterioration of that healthy influence which properly belongs to a nation of intelligent freemen.

Many of the best men of America refuse to go to the polls, while the worst never fail to avail themselves of their privilege. It is impossible that this should long remain so, without a gradual change, for the worse, in the character of our government. What is most needed at the polls, is the constant expression of the opinion and will of the discreet and temperate portion of the community. It is only upon the sentiments of the more intelligent and sober citizens, that a republic like ours can hope to build a reputation for extended usefulness; or a renown that will bear its name, like a blessing, to every quarter of the habitable globe. Their common country has a right to demand their most zealous services in her behalf. She appeals to them in the name of that ample protection which her laws afford; she warns them by considerations of fear, of comfort, of happiness, and of obedience to their sincerest convictions of duty. If they give over their efforts on her behalf, what will all other efforts be worth? If they are careless of the safety of her noble institutions, to whom can she look with the hope of ever finding for them either advocates or defenders?

We do not claim that the complete vote of our more intelligent citizens would be capable of paralyzing the force of that ignorance which has of late years been making such astounding progress at the ballot-box. We would not venture, as yet, to hope as much; but the influence of that vote would give an impulse to the cause of enlightened freedom, such as has not been felt since the days of the heroic founders of the Republic. It would awaken loftier resolves in the breasts of many who now but help to confirm the secret decrees of demagogism. It would inspire the masses with more noble sentiments respecting liberty, with the wand of whose living spirit they have hardly yet been touched. It would shake off drowsiness and indifference to matters of the highest concern. It would put the plotting enemies of freedom to rout, and her guilty and silent betrayers to shame. It would work a mighty miracle of renovation in all branches of government—in its character, in its policy, in its influence, and in its world-wide reputation.

Unless the better class of citizens do step forward with alacrity, to preserve our institutions from the fearful evils to which their supineness may expose them, there can remain but little hope for us in the future as a nation of intelligent freemen. Unless they interest themselves individually in all the elections, from those of the highest importance down to those of the lowest, it may not be long before their interference may come very sadly too late. They should see for themselves, what are the fearful penalties of supineness in the cause of their own liberties. They should understand what a crime they are guilty of, when, in disgust with the low party tactics of the day, they relinquish their right to trample the obnoxious system under foot. They must be made to feel that safety was never yet known to be found in inaction; that it is intelligence and virtue alone that can preserve the State; that the ballot-box—so powerful both for good and for harm—carries within itself the most effectual remedy for all evils; and that if they cease to wage perpetual warfare against tyranny, ignorance, and usurpation, there will remain to them but a share in that general misfortune, of which they have been the equally guilty authors, and in which they must abide as silent and uncomplaining sufferers.

It behooves the American people to make seasonable provision against their external dangers and internal fears. Every human heart beating quick at the name of Freedom, calls on us to guard with sleepless vigilance the high trust that is committed to our hands. Untold generations, in the far-off future, implore us to relax no effort, and to forego no exertion, in order to secure its priceless blessings to the people of all coming time.

THE NATURALIZATION LAWS OF THE UNITED STATES.

"Then the chief captain came and said unto him, 'Tell me, art thou a Roman?' He said, 'Yea.' And the chief captain answered, 'With a great sum obtained I this freedom;' and Paul said, 'BUT I WAS FREE BORN.'"—ST. PAUL.

IT is clearly necessary, in order to the preservation of the laws and institutions of every country, that its own citizens, who love and obey those laws, should reserve to themselves the exclusive power of modifying them. If, however, they choose, they may of course admit to the participation in that privilege, any persons born and educated in foreign lands. The obvious condition of such admission is the possession of such qualifications for citizenship as are required of the natives; namely, a good moral character, a certain amount of habituation to the laws of the land, and such a love and respect for those laws as will make the new-comer a citizen not in form only, but in heart and soul; not merely a receiver of favors from the country of his adoption, but a true and faithful adopted son.

In monarchies, where the mass of the people have no influence upon the conduct of the home or foreign affairs of the nation, there is often no mode of admitting aliens to full citizenship; and wherever there is such a mode, it is tedious and formal. Even in England, the freest of European governments, an alien can only be naturalized by a special act of Parliament in his favor.

The United States of America, on the contrary, as if with a benevolent, generous trust in the good-will of the human race, has ever extended the right hand of fellowship to all the world, and has opened the doors of her temple of freedom to all comers, with a liberality wholly without precedent or parallel. The only delay necessary, before admission to the enjoyment of all the privileges of our intelligent and educated native freemen, is that of a five years' residence; the only forms are the reasonable declaration of intentions of naturalization, the obviously indispensable one of abjuring all foreign allegiance, and swearing to be a faithful citizen of this country.

We proceed to give a careful analysis of the Naturalization Laws of the United States, and also of the several States. There is no Constitutional guarantee to aliens of any right to naturalization, although such an impression extensively prevails. The Constitution only says, that Congress may establish a uniform rule of naturalization. It is, therefore, of course, entirely practicable to refuse, if we please, the privilege of citizenship to aliens on any terms, and thus to confine their political capacities within the United States to the exercise of such rights of State citizenship as the several States may choose to give them. But, as has been before remarked, a contrary and very expansively liberal policy has uniformly prevailed in this respect.

The first Naturalization Act for the United States was approved in 1790; and was so liberal in character, as to show the desire then prevailing to attract population to our unsettled territories. It demanded for admission to citizenship, proof before any court of record (that is, any court having a clerk and official seal), of good character, and of residence in the United States during two years preceding the application, and residence in the State where it was made during one year so preceding. In 1795, however, a more stringent law was passed, requiring, "the usual oaths," proof of good character, a declaration of intentions three years in advance of admission, five years' residence in the country, and one year in the State, and also, that the applicant is "attached to the principles of the Constitution of the United States, and well disposed to the good order and happiness of the same." In 1798, the terms of residence were again lengthened to fourteen years in the country, and five years in the State, and the intention of naturalization was required five years in advance; besides that, the forms of record of admission were made more expansive and full, various registrations required, and naturalization was refused to citizens and natives of nations at war with the United States.

In 1802, an act establishing rules for naturalization was passed, which has been so little modified that the law, as substantially in force from that time to this, may be stated together, as in force at present. The alien, then, who now desires to become a citizen of the United States, must appear before a State common law court of record, or a circuit or district court of the United States, or the clerk of one of those courts, at least two years (since 1824, from 1802 to 1824, three years) before admission to citizenship. There he must swear or affirm, that he honestly intends to become a citizen of the United States, and to renounce all allegiance to any other sovereignty.

This preliminary having been performed, the applicant must, at the end of the two years, take the oath or affirmation so promised; and these proceedings are entered by the clerk upon the records of the court. The applicant must also prove, before his naturalization, to the satisfaction of the court, that he has resided in the United States at least five years, and in the State where the court is held at least one year; and that during that time he has behaved like a man of good moral character, attached to the principles of the Constitution of the United States, and well disposed to the good order and happiness of the same. Residence must be proved by the oaths or affirmations of two citizens of the United States; the oath of the applicant being inadmissible. He must, if he has borne any title or belonged to any order of nobility, renounce it, and the renunciation is to be recorded. No applicants from any country at war with the United States are admissible. Minor aliens, residing here three years next before their coming of age, and continuing to reside here after that time, are admissible without the previous declaration of intention, on compliance with the other provisions of the law. Aliens resident here before 1812, and sufficiently proving that fact, and also continued subsequent residence up to application, are also admissible without declaration of intentions. Widows and children of persons having made declaration of intentions, and having died before naturalization, are considered citizens upon taking the oaths prescribed by law; as also are minor children of naturalized persons, if dwelling within the United States; persons born without the limits of the United States, whose fathers were citizens at the time of their birth; and women legally capable of naturalization, married to citizens of the United States.

In only two of the States, Indiana and Wisconsin, does there appear to be any express and separate provision for the admission of aliens to State citizenship. In these States, aliens twenty-one years old, having declared their intention of becoming citizens of the United States, and having, in Indiana, a residence of one year in the country, and six months in the State, may become voters. In the remainder of the States, it is merely provided that those seeking to become voters shall, besides occasional property and other qualifications, have been citizens of the United States, or of the State where the application is made, for terms varying from the instant of their arrival, as in Utah and Wisconsin, and ten days in New York, to two years. Very generally, it may be said that in five years from entering the country, any foreigner may be a voting citizen of the United States.

Naturalization, as we already have stated by implication, is not a right vested in foreigners. No man coming to our shores from abroad, has any natural indefeasible title to the exercise of the voting power, any more than he has to draw a thousand dollars out of one of our banks to get a start in business. It is *a privilege conferred*, not a right conceded. Accordingly, the Constitution, giving Congress, if it chooses, the power to establish naturalization laws, says nothing of aliens, except what is restrictive. It *forbids* aliens from being President or Vice-President. It requires a long citizenship for members of Congress.

The danger to be apprehended from carelessness in this particular, has been foreseen by our best men. The following extract from the writings of Thomas Jefferson, one of the wisest and most farseeing of the great men who have influenced the politics of our country, fully sustains the views here taken of the essential significance of naturalization laws, and of the dangers to our country, from laxity in making or administering them. He says: "But are there no inconveniences to be thrown into the scale against the advantages expected from a multiplication of numbers by the importation of foreigners? It is for the happiness of those united in society to harmonize as much as possible in matters, which they must of necessity transact together. Civil government being the sole object of forming societies, its administration must be conducted by common consent. Every species of government has its specific principles. Ours, perhaps, are more peculiar than those of any other in the universe. It is a composition of the freest principles in the English Constitution, with others derived from natural reason. To these nothing can be more opposed than the maxims of absolute monarchies. Yet from such we are to expect the greatest number of emigrants. They will bring with them the principles of the governments they leave, imbibed in their early youth; or, if able to throw them off, it will be in exchange for an unbounded licentiousness, passing, as is usual, from one extreme to the other. It would be a miracle were they to stop precisely at the point of temperate liberty. These principles, with their language, they will transmit to their children. In proportion to their numbers, they will share with us the legislation. They will infuse into it their spirit, warp and bias its directions, and render it a heterogeneous, incoherent, distracted mass."

Have not these predictions been fulfilled? Have we not already amongst us an Irish nationality, a German nationality, a French nationality, a Dutch nationality, an Italian nationality? Has not our legislation already been "warped and biased" by their influence? Have they not already, to a great extent, "infused their spirit" into it, and are they not trying to make the infusion stronger?

The right and duty of government, enjoyed by the free citizens of the United States, and by them now granted to aliens at the rate of nearly one hundred thousand a year, is one of the most weighty responsibilities imposed upon man. This grave and lofty power, the citizens of the United States have usually shown themselves well able to appreciate and to use. But whether they have done wisely in granting to aliens such free admission to their birthright privilege, may well be doubted. The citizenship of this country should only be conferred upon those who will become useful and reputable citizens. Such was in fact the design of those who enacted our naturalization laws. It was not intended to permit our glorious and free institutions, to be altered at the ignorant pleasure of men brought up under monarchies, and drilled out of self-control. It was intended to admit only those who would make good citizens, and no others; and to admit them on proof of their fitness: five years' residence has hitherto been deemed sufficient, and certain testimony to good behavior and attachment to Republican principles.

1. *The defects of our present naturalization laws.*

The term of five years, with honorable exceptions, is not sufficient to prepare a foreigner to assist in governing this country. The mass of emigrants are from the lower classes of the European populations. To the limited natural powers and low grade of moral and mental nature, which are the results of the depressed physical and social condition of their ancestors for so many generations, they add the unhappy results of a political education, expressly contrived to unfit them for the exercise of such rights as those of our citizens. They are kept from thinking, discussing, or acting. The attempt to do either of these things is punished as sedition—rebellion—treason. So, what is here a right and a duty, is there a crime. Moreover, they learn to hate a law which always forces them from without, and rejoice in the only liberty they can conceive of, which is riot and licentiousness. Coming here, then, not only with the need of learning to be wise freemen, but of unlearning early education, and that most often at an age past the easily moulded character of childhood—when the strength and fixity of adult age has hardened their prejudices and increased their obstinacy;—coming here under such a double and triple disqualification, is it to be supposed that in five years of the life which they lead here, they can understand our institutions sufficient to make their political intelligence and trustworthiness equal to that of Americans born and educated? If the plain statement of such a case as this is not proof enough, no arguments could avail. Without inquiring what term of years is sufficient for the purpose of training aliens to American freedom, it is at least perfectly clear that a longer term should be required than the present one.

The present naturalization law confides to clerks of courts—insignificant assistant officers; men unknown and irresponsible—the important duty of judging upon the fitness of candidates for citizenship. As the law now reads, all the forms of admission may be complied with, either before one of the proper courts, or before the clerk of one of them. It is not well that such vitally important trusts should be confided to such subordinate officials. They are too much tempted to dispatch the business for the sake of the fee, and to admit the voter, for the same purpose, without sufficient scrutiny of him or his qualifications.

2. *Loose modes of administering the law.*

The merest apparent formal compliance with the statutory requirements has, for a long time, been quite sufficient to secure citizenship to the applicant. Few persons need to be reminded how rife are cases of fraudulent admission, in violation even of the residence clause of the law. Impudence and false swearing by the claimant, and frequently a guilty complicity, or at least a guilty sufferance on the part of the admitting authority, have availed to admit thousands on thousands of aliens to the full exercise of the rights of citizenship within a year—nay, of a month—after their arrival on our shores. However satisfactory the usual proof of residence and character may be to clerks of courts, who are intent upon their fees, or securing votes for a coming election, it is perfectly certain that, in very many cases, this proof is such as would be entirely unsatisfactory to a judge, if offered in court, in regular course of law. Nor is the inquiry usually conducted with the care and seriousness which its importance demands. If there be ever any value in forms, it is when they are used to impress upon weak or ignorant minds, the weight of a great truth, or the importance of a solemn duty. The hasty and careless performance of a ceremony, whose hurried administration commonly turns it into mere rigmarole, is not a safe or decent mode of creating citizens for a great republican empire. It degrades and cheapens our national privileges in our own eyes, as well as in those of the recipient. No ignorant man is likely to consider that responsibility very dignified, which he undertakes at the mere solicitation of a politician, by the payment of a few shillings or of nothing at all, and by the swearing of a few indistinct oaths, administered by a careless understrapper, in a side-room or dirty office.

There can, of course, be no reasonable objection to the admission of aliens to the full enjoyment of our citizenship, provided only they be fit for the trust. It would be a sad departure from the lofty ground of benevolent and impartial justice and freedom, upon which our government is founded, to proclaim, that hereafter the accident of birth alone shall determine the political power of all inhabitants of the United States, and that none coming from without their limits, good or bad, shall ever acquire the rights within them which our nation has ever held to be fundamental rights of man. *That* would be an unworthy political bigotry. But it is time that our naturalization laws, and the administration of them, were put upon a safer footing.

Foreigners should be required to show, that they have, at least, been here a sufficient time to permit them to learn the duties of an American citizen. They should be required, not only, as now, to prove the vague generalities of the statute—that they "have behaved as men of good moral character, attached to the principles of the Constitution of the United States, and well disposed to the good order and happiness of the same"—but to give, as in the case of residence, some tangible proof, aside from an oath, that they are capable of intelligent attachment to our institutions. They should be required to show, in the presence of the authority admitting them, that they can *speak and read* reasonably well, the language in which was originally written the Constitution of the United States. And, lastly, the duty of admission, and the attendant examinations, should be confided only to men whose weight and dignity of character, and high official trust, prove them capable of appreciating the importance of the duty, and of performing it honestly. No official of lower grade than the judge of a State court of record, should be allowed to determine upon the qualifications or admissibility of aliens, applying for the important trust of citizenship of the United States.

UNITED STATES AND IMMIGRATION.

"In proportion to their numbers, they will share with us the legislation. They will infuse into it their spirit, warp and bias its directions, and render it a heterogeneous, incoherent, distracted mass."
JEFFERSON.

For three-quarters of a century, a great, steady, and increasing stream of Europeans has flowed westward, across the Atlantic Ocean, into the United States. Commencing at the rate of one or two thousand a year, it now averages four hundred thousand annually.

The causes of this great modern exodus are easily understood. They have always been moderate circumstances, poverty, misfortune, crime, or political offences in Europe; and the hopes of better days, more wealth, peace, ease, freedom, and happiness here.

Of late, special causes have given a great stimulus to the movement. The barbarous evictions of poor cotters in Ireland; political reactions, and consequent oppressive government measures, on the Continent; the unsettled horizon of the European future, which is cloudy with the shadows of continued wars; the organized operations of governments and private individuals to send hither the paupers and criminals who accumulate in their almshouses and jails,—have, for the last few years, powerfully co-operated with the universal instinctive desire after profit, peace, and freedom.

Of European emigrants to the United States, the great majority are from what are there termed "the humbler classes." They are usually agricultural laborers or mechanics, and include only a very small proportion of persons educated, or of easy fortune. There is also among them an entirely disproportionate excess of absolute paupers, hospital patients, and criminals—a fact due to the organized expatriation of such persons, above alluded to.

The statements which follow will furnish a competent general view of the number, character, source, distribution, and moral and educational condition of the foreign immigration into our Union.

There are now in this country about three millions of persons born without the territories of the United States; and of foreigners and their descendants born within the United States, about four millions. Of these three millions, more than four-fifths have come since 1830, and considerably more than half since 1840. The annual addition to the number—which was, in 1790, about two thousand—was, in 1820, nearly five thousand, and after that time rapidly increased, until it ranged at twenty-seven thousand in 1830, eighty-four thousand in 1840, one hundred and forty thousand in 1845, two hundred and eighty thousand in 1850, and rose to its greatest number thus far, during the year 1854—about four hundred and sixty thousand—without any indications having as yet appeared that the maximum has been reached.

Of the four millions of foreigners and their descendants, Ireland has usually sent a larger portion than any other one country, and Germany the next greatest. For the last year or two, however, the German contingent has been fast increasing, and, in 1854, was more than double the Irish, and nearly half of the whole.

These four millions belong, by birth or immediate descent, to the undermentioned countries, in the following round numbers, which are, however, nearly correct: To Ireland, about one million; to England, Scotland, and Wales, more than half a million (making a total from the British islands of about one million five hundred and seventy thousand); to Germany, nine hundred thousand; to the remainder of North America—namely, Mexico, West Indies, and Canadas—about two hundred thousand; to France (including Belgium), seventy-five thousand; to Switzerland, twenty-five thousand; to Scandinavia (Sweden, Norway, and Denmark), twenty-four thousand; to Asia, Africa, and East Indies (about three-fourths of all being Chinese), twenty thousand; to the south of Europe (Spain, Portugal, Italy, Sardinia, Greece, and Turkey) twelve thousand; to South America, fifteen hundred; to Russia and the Sclavonic races, fourteen hundred. Probably seventy-five thousand have entered the country besides, whose birthplaces are not recorded.

Of the immigration during 1854—the largest for any one year thus far—we furnish the following analysis, on the same principle of classification with that just given. It will be observed that, of some nationalities—the Chinese, Scandinavian, and Swiss particularly—a very large proportion has arrived during the year. From Ireland, one hundred thousand; England, Scotland, and Wales, fifty-four thousand (British islands, therefore, one hundred and fifty-four thousand); Germany, two hundred thousand; remaining parts of North America, and West Indies, nine thousand; France and Belgium, thirteen thousand five hundred; Switzerland, eight thousand; Scandinavia, four thousand; thirteen thousand Chinamen; south of Europe, two thousand eight hundred.

The port of New York receives about two-thirds of the entire number of immigrants; New Orleans and Boston half of the remainder; and Philadelphia, Baltimore, and other Atlantic ports, and, for the last few years, California, the rest. Landing in large cities, a great proportion of the whole remain there, to fill almshouses and hospitals—to beg, sicken, and die. Of the immigration in 1850, there remained in our forty largest towns, forty in the hundred of the whole number of Irish, and thirty-six in the hundred of the immigrant Germans. The remainder distributed themselves throughout the country, the Irish especially gathering along the lines of the newer internal improvements, for work, and living a vagrant, rowdy life, which keeps their children from being educated, and themselves from being civilized; while the Germans, and in particular the Hollanders and Scandinavians, devote themselves to trade or farming. The foreign population gather principally into the northern range of States—the Eastern, Middle, and Northwestern; there being about thirteen foreigners in every hundred inhabitants in the first and last sections: while in the Middle States—where the vast congregation in and about New York, however, is the principal cause of the high average—there are twenty foreigners to the hundred inhabitants.

What amount of property the foreign incomers bring to the United States, it is impossible to estimate. The average of their wealth, as well as of their morals, has declined for many years; indeed, nearly as their numbers have increased. There are individuals, and occasionally companies, who bring with them capital enough to establish them in business; but this is an exception and not a rule, and an exception more unfrequent now, when so many actual paupers are sent over, who arrive with no money, no clothing, and hardly any rags, and who forthwith fall a dead weight upon the public and private charities of the land. If, however, we suppose that there has been an average of ten dollars of capital added to that already in the country, by each immigrant, the whole addition of wealth would amount to thirty millions of dollars. But there will be no balance left upon deducting from this, or from twice as much, the expenses, public and private, of supporting and imprisoning the paupers and criminals of the number, and the amounts withdrawn from circulation here, and sent to Europe to help out the poverty at home. What these amounts are it is as difficult to state, as to tell the entire property of the immigrants; a few items, however, will suffice to show that their aggregates must be enormous. In four years, from 1848 to 1851 inclusive, the English Commissioners of Immigration alone, made a return of sums sent back from America, within their knowledge, amounting to a total of fourteen millions of dollars, which up to this time is undoubtedly swelled to at least thirty millions. Considering then what must have been remitted since 1790, not to England only, but to Ireland, Germany, France, and other parts of Europe, it is not difficult to see that even to make this amount good, it would have been necessary for immigrants to bring with them twenty dollars per head, besides earning or paying for their living from the day of arrival. Suppose them to have brought, all told, even a hundred millions of dollars, remittances at the rate of thirty millions to England alone in eight years would soon exhaust that. But besides this, there must be considered the expense of pauperism and crime—items also incapable of satisfactory investigation. Some idea of their extent may perhaps be gathered from the fact, that aside from all public and private charities, the expenditure for public support of paupers of foreign birth, within the United States, during the single year ending June 1st, 1850, even by the imperfect returns gathered, was over one million four hundred thousand dollars.

The paupers so relieved were sixty-eight thousand five hundred in number, while the number of paupers of American birth relieved in the same way was sixty-six thousand four hundred; namely, one seventh as many in proportion to the entire number.

Of the expenses incurred in repressing or punishing the crimes of immigrants, only an extensive and laborious search could supply any account. But criminal proceedings are expensive, and many criminal prosecutions are brought against foreigners. Of the whole number of criminals convicted during the year ending June 1st, 1850, twelve thousand eight hundred were natives, and thirteen thousand seven hundred foreigners; about, as before, seven times as many in the hundred as those of our own population.

That these items of public expenditure, together with the drawbacks already stated, would exhaust more than any amount which immigrants may have brought into the country, is very certain.

Lastly, a few numbers showing the educational comparison between the foreigners and natives, are indispensable in order to a due comprehension of their tendencies and capacities, when domesticated with us. Of the whole number of native whites in the United States, then, one in five is attending school; of the foreign population, only one-third as many—one in fifteen. Of natives, of school age, viz., between five and fifteen, eight in ten are at school; of foreigners of same age, only five in ten. Of the whole number of native whites, about four and a half out of every hundred cannot read or write; of foreigners, nine out of the same number—twice as many. Of natives over twenty years of age, eight and a quarter in the hundred cannot read or write; of foreigners, fourteen and a half in the hundred.

The prospect of future immigration, however, demands some consideration. There seems to be no reason why the exodus from Europe to America should not yet grow and continue. Even if the remainder of the Irish population should stay at home, there are millions and millions on the Continent who will complete the yearly number of immigrants. So far as material interests are concerned, greater and greater inducements are offered by the increasing wealth, enlarged capacity, and demand for labor within our own country. We have abundance of room and of riches. Such inducements have already operated upon so many of the over-crowded and poverty-stricken European nations, that it is quite certain that they will continue to operate. And on the other side of the Atlantic there are not wanting impulses to co-operate with the attractions here. The future of the European nations is stormy and dark. Revolutionary principles are seething under the apparently smooth surface of her political aspect, and before long, despotism, anarchy, and liberty will be struggling together; wars and rebellions exert their disorganizing and unhappy influence, and increasing crowds will flee from the home misery to the foreign peace upon our territory. Europe then, crowded with people, oppressed with poverty, containing much sterile land, and doomed to the horrors of complicated and obstinate wars, will long send vast and vaster yearly bands to share our free peace, our rich and boundless lands, and our quiet wealth. We shall, apparently, also continue to receive the refuse of almshouses, and the felon garbage of prisons, shipped hither wholesale by European governments and societies.

During the periods of ten years, from 1810 to 1850, the successive totals of immigration have arisen from one hundred and fourteen thousand to two hundred and four thousand seven hundred and eighty thousand, and lastly, one million four hundred and forty thousand. Within the ten years now passing, viz., from 1850 to 1860, all the facts and probabilities indicate that we shall receive four millions of European immigrants of the poorest, and most worthless class of the population. What the increase will be beyond that time, we have no means of estimating. But this number is sufficient to show the vast and increasing importance of the movement, and the certainty of the speedy operation of such a mass of humanity upon our own people in some way, either for good or evil.

We have not here the time nor the space to consider fully the significance of this great movement of the European population. But none can fail to see that an annual irruption into this country of half a million people, who are shown by the merest arithmetical computation to be twice as ignorant as we are, and (perhaps in consequence) seven times as lawless, and seven times as helpless and sick, is a movement of great power. Whether its results are or will be good or evil, of what modifications they are susceptible, what means should be used to modify them, are questions which we discuss in another place.

There is, however, one single phenomenon of such vast importance, and so closely connected with our subject, that it may properly be alluded to in this place. This is the *suicidal political action of naturalized immigrants.* Whatever may be the object of foreigners entering our country, and our nation—whether they come for peace, for freedom, or for wealth—it is beneath the protection of our nationality, our Constitution, and our laws, that they seek that object. The whole fabric of that Constitution and those laws was erected, and has been and is maintained by free political action, by the intelligent voice of our people, appointing what they thought good. The laws so established and sustained have raised us to a position of such strength and wealth, that we are able to offer an asylum to the oppressed of all nations. This has been freely accepted, and accepted in the majority of cases, until lately, with thankful hearts, and a proper acquiescence in the established institutions of the land.

But, within a few years, an ominous change in the demeanor of our foreign beneficiaries has appeared. They seem to be steadily seeking to overthrow our own institutions, whenever those institutions happen to conflict with the prejudices or hatreds engendered in their own minds in the darkness of their native despotisms. The wise Sabbath laws which are so general in our commonwealths, are a living evidence of the intimate connection of Christianity with their fundamental policy. That connection is the very basis of their strength and durability. But a band of atheistical Germans, thinking that in this country there is no need, even outwardly, either to fear God or to regard man, get together and call upon the government to abrogate all laws enforcing the observance of the Christian Sabbath.

Our established, wise, and unsectarian mode of distributing State money to public schools, without regard to any religious denomination, is a great obstacle to the Jesuitical views of foreign priests, who desire to control the education of native youth, and unsuspectedly to prepare the way for the complete supremacy of the Romish Church over our free State. All the open and secret arts of the most intriguing class of men in the world are set in motion to secure the discontinuance of this practice, and to effect the distribution of public money to schools distinctly Romanist, for uses wholly sectarian, anti-republican, and anti-American.

This is not the place to enter into any extended exposition of the necessary tendencies and results of such conduct. But the broad fact stands plainly out, that the masses of our foreign population are determined to move steadily forward in a line of their own, without regard to the laws or feelings of the people who have sheltered them. Armed rebellion or secret plot—bribery or bullying—all modes of action or coercion, however wicked, or unconstitutional, are to be unscrupulously seized and remorselessly wielded, to complete their foolish and disorganizing purposes. This suicidal and unaccountable course of conduct, if allowed to be carried through, will sink the vessel that carries themselves and their fortunes. It is the senseless fury of the maniac who attacks his best friend with the same tiger-like ferocity which he displays to his worst enemy. It would necessarily terminate our present glorious and happy era of constitutional law. It would substitute for it one of two things—either an utter anarchy, such as they have striven to create at home, or a centralized despotism, which they have escaped by fleeing hither.

THE CITIZEN OF A REPUBLIC.

> ———— The elements
> So mix'd in him, that Nature might stand up
> And say to all the world, "This was a man."
>
> SHAKESPEARE.

REPUBLICANISM, the noblest form of earthly government, demands the exertion of the highest moral and intellectual faculties of man.

The establishment of a Republic is a work of comparatively easy accomplishment, its maintenance is a struggle of immense magnitude: the former requires but the hand of a warrior or legislator; the latter necessitates the heart and arm of the entire people. Autocracy may flourish with a nation sunk in ignorance and slavery; Monarchy fearlessly surrenders the destinies of an empire to the guidance of a few; but Democracy is the *vox populi, vox Dei*, and only acts when every citizen has spoken.

As FEAR is the controlling principle of Despotism—HONOR of a Monarchy,—so VIRTUE is the mainspring, the life-blood of a Republic. This vital principle of democracy is the individual influence of each citizen upon public affairs: it is not the mere exercise of political power, but the every-day walk and conversation of one whose example causes others to do well; for, "No deed of a good citizen is useless; for even by his attention, his appearance, his nod, his silence, or his step, he may avail something."

This political virtue, so necessary to a good citizen, and without which no republic can long exist, includes patriotism, integrity, and self-denial. In proportion as these principles influence a democracy, the commonwealth is prosperous; but when they are forgotten, the

State becomes a prey to selfish passions, party feuds, and civil commotion, and is fast travelling the road to anarchy and despotism.

Patriotism is not the mere love of country, nor its object the tinsel of present glory. Far nobler are its aims, for its visions are prospective, and its aspirations invoke the future. The patriot lives not for himself, but for posterity; he works not to aggrandize, but to establish; he sacrifices the chances of success, if trammelled by the possibility of failure. He gives "his hand and his heart" to the defence of the republic, without regard to ties of blood or kindred, and never lends his countenance to any, who, through ignorance or passion, propose measures at variance with freedom, or inimical to the peace of the country. He is the uncompromising foe of demagogues.

"An honest man's the noblest work of God." Where shall we find a better illustration of this maxim, than in the citizen of a Republic? Clothing himself in integrity, he cares not if rulers threaten or the masses rage; emulating the virtue of an Aristides or a Cato, neither the eulogies of the multitude, the charms of popularity, the threats of enemies, nor the entreaties of friends can move his decision. His first, his only thought, is for his country: personal motives cannot sway him; patriotism has told him how to act, no consideration can induce the contrary. He refuses the emoluments of office as an inducement to venality; titles and honors he scorns, for he looks not to outward applause, but to inward satisfaction. His aim is, his country: his motto—Incorruptible.

"Luxury is the death of a Republic."* This vice is utterly opposed to the spirit of democracy, for it is the deification of self, and forgetfulness of the general good. The Carthaginians, unconquered by the Romans, fell before the luxuries of Capua. Athens flourished when wealth increased and manners remained virtuous; but the Republic of Solon, Aristides, and Plato, fell, when her citizens sought their individual pleasures, and forgot their duty to the State. Not the immortal eloquence of a Demosthenes, nor the terrors of Philip at her gates, could relight the flame of patriot-

* Montesquieu.

ism, which had shone so triumphantly at Salamis and Marathon. Athens, the beautiful, the glorious, the mother of the arts and literature, the soul of that Greece whose fame will flourish through admiring ages; even Athens, adjudged the penalty of death to those of her citizens who proposed devoting the moneys of the theatres to the defence of the Republic. Rome, the republic of Brutus and Cato—that empire which has given the world the brightest examples of patriotism, integrity, and self-denial—fell through luxury. As Demosthenes in Greece, so Cicero in Rome, found his eloquence powerless against the ambition, the selfish passions of the aristocracy. The empire of the Cæsars inaugurated luxury, and the masculine vigor of her Horatii, her Cocles, and her Cincinnatus forever departed. Well might Tacitus depict the energy, the sobriety, the manliness of the Germans, and describe the certain fall of his country, unless she returned to the ancient virtues of the Republic. Luxury had destroyed every bond of sympathy between provinces and individuals, and Goths, Visigoths, Vandals, and Franks only completed what the Romans themselves had begun.

What then shall we say to those of our countrymen, who, in spite of the warnings of history, the testimony of philosophers, the antecedents of their country, nay, of their allegiance to the Republic, are seeking to introduce the luxury of an aristocracy in our midst? What means this aping of the exclusiveness of courts, this creation of a factitious, privileged class? Does mere wealth confer social supremacy? is the falsity of *caste* consonant with the truth of democracy? The abhorred relics of feudalism, leading America back to the mediæval ages, should meet with the undying hate of the true citizen, and their partisans should be consigned to universal obloquy and reproach. Perish forever such arch-treason to the Republic, for our existence is only possible in equality!

Luxury is not necessarily associated with trade and commerce: a country may safely foster the latter, if due precaution be taken to avoid the former. The mere fact of becoming rich, will not affect the virtue of the citizen, if he still view as a principle above every other consideration the well-being of the community at large. But, when men amass large fortunes, and, retiring from their fellow-citizens into a species of luxurious cliquism, attempt the formation of an upper class in the midst of that equality without which democracy is an impossibility, the ægis of patriotism must be raised against the treason, and hydra-headed oligarchism be met with that hostility which can alone insure the safety of the Republic. The true citizen purges his soul of all selfishness, and lives and labors but for his country.

The true, the only check to luxury is in religion, education, and public opinion, inducing men to seek the welfare and prosperity of the country rather than their own profit and interest, more especially when these two are in opposition. Memorable are such examples in all ages, and bright the instances in our own history. It is disinterestedness which gives the superiority to republicanism over every other government; only in republicanism does this self-denial exist, for there alone is it possible. The object of all religion, whether true or false, is to govern human passions, to mould the human will. Armed with the authority of its divine origin, its province is to subdue human nature—finding mankind in a state of warfare, it seeks to harmonize the discordant elements and bless the world with peace. Society, the association of man with his fellow-man, is the offspring of religion.

Education inculcates the laws of this association, those checks which society has imposed for its own safety. Religion must, therefore, be a necessary part of all education, since man's passions are as inimical to the peace of the State, as they are hurtful to his own happiness.

But religion and education are insufficient to perpetuate unity, peace, and concord. History gives many instances of agitators, honest, but misguided in their intentions: such can only be withstood by the force of public opinion. All attempts, therefore, to control this free expression are hurtful to the freedom of a country. The citizen must avail himself of this power, whenever the national liberties are assailed; his animadversions upon agitators and their measures are the power of VETO, exerted in right of his sovereignty. When the citizen comes in collision with such, he must freely upbraid their fickleness and expose the fallacies of their opinions; nor will he be intimidated from boldly lifting up his voice against all rash or perilous public measures, no matter how much odium he may incur, nor how many outrages he may have to face. "Neither the depraved fury of a threatening populace, nor the frown of an angry tyrant, can move the firm purpose of a just man, who is established in his opinions."

The citizen should beware of all those measures which beget divisions in free States, and endanger harmony and prosperity. He must be in continual remembrance that he is a freeman, and scorn to ally himself with any who have not proved themselves firm friends of the Republic, or shown themselves unwavering supporters of the Constitution. Despising factious opposition, he will yield on minor points, so as not to refuse his aid to the party which, in essentials, is clearly in the right. Socrates was explicit on this subject: "The citizen should endeavor to persuade his countrymen of the views he cherishes himself, if he can; but, if this be impossible, let him follow their commands." The very perpetuity of a Republic depends upon the concord of those in whom the legislative power is vested.

The citizen will submit himself unreservedly to the magistrates. "To show honor to others is often more praiseworthy than to be honored one's self:" he will recognize the power of the commonwealth in the ministration of the judge; and, so far from withholding obedience, he will esteem it an honor to obey. Nor should this reverence be paid from regard merely to the office, but, if possible, through esteem for the excellence of personal virtue, which has elevated the magistrate to power. Therefore, should the magistrate be wise and virtuous in order to be reverently obeyed. "Obedience prepares men for empire."

There are certain acquirements which it is the duty of every citizen to possess. Such is a knowledge of history, for by this he learns the dangers through which his own and other countries have passed, and observes how certain policies inevitably lead to certain results. From history, he finds examples of the good and great in all ages, fortifies his soul with their virtues, and leaves their memory "a rich legacy unto his children." Most especially should he apply himself to the study of the resources of the Republic; acquiring every detail relative to her agriculture, manufacture, and commerce—the capabilities and deficiencies of the State—her relations with foreign powers, the numbers of the people, and the popular feeling on public subjects.

These acquirements the citizen will find indispensable, since otherwise he cannot legislate in the general good: he must reflect that when the Senate assembles, he is responsible for their decrees. Armed with these acquirements, he will be enabled to select those who are most capable of legislating beneficially, and will be prepared at all times to meet and controvert the designs and sophistries of traitors and agitators. There is no higher glory on earth than in a citizen faithfully serving his country: in the eloquent language of Cicero, "Of all things human, there is nothing more glorious or more excellent than to deserve well of the Republic."

"The acquisition of honors is to be esteemed praiseworthy," yet should offices not be sought for, nor refused, unless they exceed the citizen's merit. He must not disdain companionship and counsel in them, nor fall into the mistake that his duty to the country is discharged when his term of office expires. Aristides and the Roman Cato were seldom in office, yet their republican virtues ceaselessly influenced the citizens.

Self-denial is the highest effort of moral courage. The citizen is as likely to err in false modesty, as in following the dictates of ambition. He should, therefore, accurately weigh the advantages which may accrue to the State by his accepting office, and no consideration of self-interest should induce him to refuse that which his countrymen require him to assume. In this respect, he will model himself upon the examples of Cincinnatus, Brutus, and Washington—heroes, who lived but for their country—in whose breasts ambition found no place—men who on their brows bore the proud boast of the Roman orator—"*Mens conscia recti.*"

How shall we sufficiently reprehend the conduct of those of our countrymen who forget the glorious traditions of their native land, and become courtiers in foreign climes? Ansaldo Ceba, the illustrious citizen of the Genoese republic, observes: "With foreign princes we think the citizen will be wise not to cultivate much intimacy. When he happens to meet them, he should certainly show them all honor, by signs of respect and reverence; but this should suffice. Nor should he hold any other language with them, than courtesy or necessity may require. But, at the same time, if accident bring them together, or he be in any manner provoked by them, let him with noble resentment give such gentlemen to understand, that his republic loves liberty, and that he is ready to offer his property and his life to preserve it."

Far different is the conduct of many of our countrymen, when surrounded by all the pomp and circumstance of kings and aristocrats. Unmindful of their antecedents and the precious reminiscences of their distant land; ignoring the slight which they are thus casting on the republic; unobservant of the obloquy which the titled valets of Europe rejoice to cast on democracy, when Americans are thus seen worshipping that system which their ancestors fought and bled to throw off,—these republican-trained courtiers, these bourgeois-gentilshommes and Potiphars, bedeck themselves in the livery of monarchical servitude, and, like Themistocles at Persia, almost turn traitors to their country, quickly losing even the appearance of republican virtue. Returning to their native land, they retain and move in a European atmosphere. Claiming the friendship or acquaintance of this or that noble lackey or aristocratic debauchee, they affect an air of superiority, establish in their salons the etiquette of courts, and smile with ineffable contempt on democratic institutions. Our paintings and sculptures are false to art, because, forsooth, these travelled coxcombs have lounged in the shadow of the Louvre, or played the minion at Florence. Music has lost its charms, since here it is obtainable by all. Our literature may possibly be tolerated, but it becomes secondary to the productions of other people. America is voted vulgar by her own children, and the horrible putrescence of European decay is inoculated into our democratic system.

Not so acted the first envoys of this Republic. In refusing court to monarchs, they gained respect for themselves and alliance for their country. In the utmost simplicity of dress and manner, they demanded and obtained more true esteem than the proudest nobles of Europe—and left behind them the memory of their simple virtues, which our modern diplomats seem careful not to copy.

Americans! will you thus deny your birthright, defame the memory of your fathers, and inspire contempt for their country in the hearts of your children? Oh, distant, immeasurably distant, be the day when such principles shall become general! Where is the divine *afflatus* of those heroes, who, inspired by universal democracy, rose majestically with the people, and towered, giant like, amidst their aristocratic foes? Where are Franklin and Adams—meteors, flashing across the blackness of European diplomacy? Where those ancient senators, whose eloquence, echoing through the forum, found emphasis in the hearts of the people? Where those citizens, who loved the Republic above property, family, yea, life itself; whom agitators dared not use—before whose inflexible honesty, demagogues feared and trembled?

We must recall the ancient days. We must return to first principles, and study models of former years. Our children must be prepared with more than Spartan care, and taught how bright and glorious is their inheritance,—how hollow the joys which are but the gratification of the senses. The standard of republican virtue must everywhere be raised—selfishness be uprooted from every spirit—patriotism no longer remain a high-sounding name; but the maxim be written in every breast—My country, everywhere and at all times,—the Republic, one and indivisible,—America, above all things.

AMERICAN NATIONALITY.

"It is true we should become a little more Americanized."—GENERAL JACKSON.

THE national characters of the leading nations of the world are clearly defined and understood. The sturdy, thoughtful, grumbling Englishman—the lively, fickle Frenchman—the proud and grave Spaniard—the reflective and metaphysical German, are as well distinguished by these titles, as the Indian, the Arab, and the European by their complexions.

This nationality is stamped on the individuals of the nation and on its policy. As are the inhabitants, so are their rulers and their measures; and the home and foreign operations of the government usually take more or less shape from the character of the people who support them.

In the United States there is a distinct individual nationality. The leading characteristic of the Anglo-American is energy: he is the energetic American. His energy is not only continuous in operation, but wise in its aim; his enterprises, whatever they be, are admirably contrived, energetically commenced, obstinately adhered to, and perseveringly supported.

There are other qualities which assist in forming our national character. Of these we need only enumerate,—first, shrewdness in business, enterprise, and skill; the results of which, surpassing the slow business methods of the Old World, lead strangers to stigmatize us as mere money-getters and speculators. Secondly, romance and ideality, which are not merely evinced in our literary pursuits, but have given impetus to the actions of our citizens to no inconsiderable extent. A sentiment of romantic enterprise has, from the first, deeply imbued the minds of our people, especially those pioneers of civilization—the hunter and backwoodsman of the West. Thirdly, hope. Other nations may glory in the Past, but we are the people of the Future. To futurity we look, and as time unfolds the mysteries of promise, surrounding countries behold with astonishment our progress, and even we ourselves are compelled to wonder.

Such are a few of the principal characteristics of Americans. Our nationality is distinct and strong, but, hitherto, it has impressed but little of itself upon the policy of our government.

There is no nation of any considerable importance on the face of the earth, that has not its own distinctive policy. Circumstances may give that policy a shape, but it is the native energy of the nation which gives it emphasis before the world. Great Britain has her policy, which is called British, and France has long entertained her own. The policy of Russia has been traditionary from generation to generation. Even Austria understands the significancy of the term, and puts forth her policy in a shape which puzzles all Europe's diplomacy. The policy of Germany is to keep aloof from a war which threatens to become general. Spain is sullenly determined not to loose her hold on Cuba, and thus her policy is known.

All announce their public purpose but America. With her, the national opinion does not yet seem to have become sufficiently defined to take expression. It has not yet so strongly centralized its many elements, as to assume a name. We are drifting about on an open sea, without national compass or rudder. Circumstances alone define the national character; a predetermined sentiment neither governs it, nor gives it shape. We exist but to study the purposes of other nations, having none to contemplate of our own. A great people, we are unwilling to announce ourselves a peculiar nation. In the front of the world in power, we are yet behind all others in a published policy. Fortune seems to guide us unresistingly on her own course, while we merely profit by the temporary and irregular favors she sees fit to throw in our way. We rather thrive by the mistakes of others, than by any fixed resolutions of our own.

The picture is none too broad for truth. It has been repeatedly drawn by the course of our rulers, and as often silently acquiesced in by the people. The popular mind has long been so wrongly bent, that the question has come to be seriously debated, whether America shall be *American*, or shall become an indescribable fusion of all the nationalities on the face of the earth! Designing and ambitious men, whose care is for themselves before their country, declare that America is for the world; that the sentiment of an enlarged and comprehensive humanity is to put aside and replace the glowing and vitalizing spirit of nationality; that while other countries have been bigoted, illiberal, or tyrannical, there is no room on the soil of America for sentiments like these to flourish; and that we are to announce no particular affection for our country simply for its own sake, and the sake of our fellow-citizens, but to consider that all the world has both equal rights and equal affections here with ourselves.

This is a most specious and hollow-hearted doctrine. It would give but a negative character to any country, and make it the dupe of despots, and the football of the nations. It implies nothing less than a complete abnegation of individuality for a State, and insists on the formation of a composite national character which is neither one thing nor another. They who advocate it with such ignorant zeal, forget that its foreign beneficiaries are armed with a national spirit that refuses through life to be dispossessed of its position. They are insensible to the truth that the emigrants who arrive here never give up their love for their native land, and are never expected to make so unnatural a sacrifice; and that one of the most notable provisions of our noble Constitution, forever shutting out the possibility of a naturalized citizen's reaching the Presidency, was an honorable tribute, on the part of its framers, to a sentiment everywhere to be respected.

It is a false and baseless plea, that if America's mission is for humanity, it cannot, therefore, sustain a separate and distinct nationality of its own. Except through an individual organization of all its various elements, a nation cannot in the first place enjoy any permanent existence; and except, again, through the projectile force of that separate organism, it cannot hope to make the influence of its existence anywhere perceived. Without energy, no nation can even keep its place in history. There must needs be an earnest concentration of all the faith, all the hopes, all the affections, and all the ambition of its people around some particular objects, or the nation falls away from its organic strength, and the desires and hopes of humanity must turn elsewhere for their realization. From a truth so apparent there is no possible escape. That nation only is the truest to humanity at large, which never forgets to be true to both liberty and humanity *in itself*. It may not go abroad in search of objects for its beneficence, until it has first acquired for its own people the power to bestow the coveted blessing.

In the conflict of parties, and confusion of tongues of this present time, there comes to the ear one voice, louder than all others. It speaks with an emphasis, and a meaning that is unmistakable. Every syllable promises the inauguration of a new era. Every word inspirits our faltering hopes. It seems undeniable that the period has arrived in our history, when we are to make a stand for a character and a policy that shall be entirely American. It is indeed a happy omen, and we hail it as we daily hail the glorious advent of the morning sun. The national mind is fully awake. The popular heart beats high and healthily. Patriotism rouses itself from its long sleep of forgetfulness, and liberty once more smiles serenely on her votaries.

This sudden uprising of the popular sentiment, strikes vigorous blows at the slothful inefficiency of character, which our country has succumbed to, under the long-continued lead of partisan administrations. It insists on the establishment and perpetuation of a spirit of true nationality, above the reach of political factions and juntos, and removed from the influence of either fawning or flattery. Something like this was certainly needed. America was rapidly becoming a mark for the opposition and intrigues of other nations, rather than the steady director of an imposing and self-sustaining power of her own. Her liberality was fast degenerating into a patient and good-natured sufferance of all evils, instead of asserting that inherent force of resistance, which at the very first lifted her to rank among the nations. Her generosity was relapsing into a disease, whose ulcerous spread threatened the final health of the entire body politic.

Under these circumstances, any movement on the part of the people to destroy and put out of sight the effete existence of a corrupting partisanship, is one which appeals with an eloquent tongue to the heart of the nation. It must command the profoundest attention, and excite the deepest sensibilities of those whose desires are patriotic. The sentiment of nationality demands, at this juncture, a more strenuous advocacy than it has ever received since the days of the Revolution. There exists an urgent need for impressing it on the hearts of the whole people. This day must we assert an American origin, an American spirit, and an American policy, or the opportunity may be gone forever.

In the first place, we cannot treasure too carefully all those peculiar features whether of character, custom, or opinions, that are so distinctively our own. That which lies around us, we ought to incorporate into our being, so that it may do its natural work. Even our various idiosyncracies of national character are worth preservation, if only because they are American. The recollection of them, may some day suddenly fire a train of patriotic impulses, which will terminate in the most noble deeds.

But, above all, our opinions should receive the tincture of a truly national tone. They should all tacitly refer to the existence of a country, whose grand characteristics we each of us seek to reflect. An Englishman will remain an Englishman as long as he lives; and not more in his habits than in his expressed opinions. France, and her glory, is the touchstone to which Frenchmen undeviatingly apply their thoughts; and these give it a shape and color that characterize it all over the world. So it is with the people of other countries universally. No matter how the national sentiment first took form; it exists, and works by a process as secret as it is difficult of analysis. And so it should be with ourselves. A true American cannot consistently hold similar political opinions with an Englishman; nor ought he at any time to entertain the idle hope of bringing about their reconciliation. Between liberty and any form or degree of absolutism, there is fixed an impassable gulf. It must remain so forever.

If the American's opinions borrow their tone from the institutions of his country, they will be large, generous, and comprehensive, while they lose none of that local spirit which should give them both life and energy. They will stand as the representatives of humanity everywhere, yet never put off the national vestments in which they are clothed. They may belong to the world, and still remain rooted in American soil. They may strike boldly for universal liberty, and still consecrate themselves to the welfare of that particular country whose existence they represent. In all respects they will be original and peculiar, free from the taint of old political systems, and clear of alliance with tyrannies and despotisms.

In estimating the true extent of such a national feeling upon the basis of the records of our more recent political history, the results at which we are forced to arrive are almost too astonishing for belief. If it be seriously inquired whether there is any real need of reviving the sentiment of nationality, our only reply is—"Come and see!" And what do we see? A people patiently submitting to the control of men, who, long ago, have sunk the sentiment of patriotism in the slough of partyism; rulers ambitious always for themselves, but rarely for their country; the government kept artfully in the hands of those whose sworn fidelity to political cabals and factions outweighs the thought of duty to that land, within whose limits all parties and all opinions are tolerated; public men holding high offices of trust from the people, abusing their trust without a blush of shame, and converting the administration of government into a game of chance, in which the players are incited by passion, by unworthy ambition, by lust for individual power, and even by malice and revenge; the wishes of the people forgotten and neglected; the hopes of the nation unnoticed, and the name of America receding from that height of influence to which it once attained, and losing the bright lustre which once radiated in every direction over the civilized world.

Our politics have degenerated into quibbles and personal quarrels. Exalted motives do not enter as an element into their direction. The country has fallen a long way behind the party in the race. Individual success is paramount to the general welfare. The triumph of a faction, through the election of its candidates, is considered before the glory of the nation. Measures receive their full share of discussion, but the great principles of national existence never. The future seems to be unregarded, and the past is wholly blotted out. It has come to be supposed, that public men may be never so selfish, never so destitute of any great national idea with which to inspire their conduct, and never so devoted to the single interests of the political organization to which they have promised allegiance,—and still the nation will take abundant care of itself. Under a popular form of government it cannot be so: a deep and strong national sentiment must correct, combine, and subordinate all other sentiments, or it will inevitably fall back into a secondary position, to be shaped and controlled by them. There is no help against so serious a catastrophe.

We need but to become attentive observers, to discover that there *is* such a national sentiment in the breasts of Americans, God-given with their existence. But it is, as yet, hardly more than the germ of what should long ago have exhibited the proportions of a vigorous plant. It is scarcely more than the love of home, with the untold associations that cluster about its name. It exists, but it needs culture. It must be drawn out, developed, strengthened, and healthily matured. Hitherto, opportunities have not been offered. Circumstances have been extremely unpropitious. The sentiment has broken its strength upon objects unworthy of its attachment, and been fawned upon by sycophants to whom patriotism is a forgotten word. It has been addressed by politicians who failed to comprehend its character, and basely deluded by the appeals of those who sought its aid for mean and unholy ends.

But, distorted and misused as it has been, it still maintains its inherent vigor and virtue. Its surface has been sullied, but with time the taint will wear away. The original sentiment remains intact. As we remarked before, it needs only more propitious circumstances and influences to give it character and definiteness. Such names as Jackson and Clay possess the power to draw it out into expression, because no men have lived who were more American than they. They knew no country save their own. They were of ourselves,—the natives of our own soil,—fresh, large, and original; and to such men the American heart will instinctively attach itself, because in their very persons they worthily represent our country and its noble institutions. This impulsive attachment, therefore, betrays the existence of the national sentiment, and tells too plainly what is required to impart to it energy of action.

When this great national idea takes complete possession of a people, rooting itself so deeply in their hearts as to defy dislodgment, it will not brook even the most trifling opposition on its own soil. It is a power dwelling with the masses, that cannot be provoked or insulted with impunity. It claims an imperial sway, and exacts the deference demanded by despotism. Nothing is so large that it cannot embrace it; nothing so trifling that it cannot invest with undying glory. It stands for its own right, and feels itself strong enough to be secure. Those who underrate its consequence, must fall beneath its power; those who seek to bring it into contempt, shall themselves one day be held up to universal scorn and detestation.

It has been claimed that, as we cannot expect our foreign population to forget the ties that hold them to their native land, and to enter into close relationship with a sentiment for which they possess no qualifications, we ought therefore so far to submit to a modification of our national preferences as to accommodate ourselves to their unfortunate situation. This is the doctrine, though it is not, perhaps, quite so plainly announced. But, by what authority are we bidden to put off our own nationality, and go peddling it about to aliens, strangers, or outcasts? Who commands us to exchange the immortal memories of Bunker Hill, of Trenton, of Saratoga, and of

Yorktown, for the mess of pottage which they bring from other shores? What power is it that dares to exercise such authority—but the shameless and irresponsible power of party, that forgets country, that forgets all things, save only its own selfish success?

Our foreign population, as a body, were never induced to come to American shores from the simple love of liberty, or its institutions. It is no deep attachment to us, or our principles, or to the spirit and genius of our government, that brings them here. They can confess to but one motive; and that, the hope of bettering their fortunes. They come to receive more money for their labor, to provide more liberally for the necessities of their families, to hoard wealth, and to be beyond the reach of tyranny.

And is it not enough, then, that America offers them the free enjoyment of all these privileges? Is it not enough that each family may have a farm in the heart of our rich domains, on the simple condition of their taking possession? Is it not enough that our laws are as efficient to protect their lives and their property, as to protect our own? Is it not enough, that we freely open to them all the avenues to wealth and happiness that lie open to our own citizens? Is it not enough, that we do all this for them, and do it, not in a grudging spirit, but out of a deep sympathy with their past misfortunes and unhappiness?—that henceforth we stand between them and want,—between them and their former oppressors,—between them and all the world?

Must we be expected to surrender our entire nationality to them, and to allow them to inoculate it with their customs, tastes, opinions, manners, and prejudices? Must we be asked to give up all that we hold most dear, because, forsooth, in the nature of things, it cannot be as dear to them? Must our hospitality become the means of its own destruction, and our generosity prevent the noble objects for which it is put forth?

A thousand times, No! We may say to our foreign population, both in sympathy and sincerity, that they are no more than our guests; we neither compelled nor invited them to come among us, and we do not insist that they shall remain; we offer them equal protection with that given to our own citizens, and equal opportunities for improving their condition. But it is for them to assimilate their ways of thinking to ours; not for us to go over to them. If they are dissatisfied with our opinions, they are free to return again whence they came. But they shall never assume the management of our public affairs while they are yet foreign to us in spirit; and we will insist on exercising the right of passing upon their qualifications to a citizenship so fraught with high responsibilities. Short of this point, it is idle to think of stopping. To pause midway, is to invite untold disaster.

In this country, the predominating race is the Anglo-American. It was that invigorating blood, which reddened the battle-fields of the Revolution. That race has stamped its mind upon the nation, and given it permanent character. That mind has built up our liberal institutions, through which passes the course of all our national thought. It is the same heart that sends the life-giving blood through all the members of the vast political body. If other races have united with it, they have, of necessity, merged their individualities in its overpowering current; they have forgotten themselves, and fallen in with the wide stream of American life and manners. It remains for the original Anglo-Americans alone, therefore, to go forward with the work of impressing all national sentiments with their own bold and free peculiarities. They are the dominant race, to whom the possession of the continent has manifestly been delivered. Their native spirit belongs to the soil. It has been strengthened through the storms of war, and it will be nurtured in the long sunshine of peace. Its sceptre will not depart; and it steadily refuses to acknowledge on its own ground any power coequal with its own.

The national policy of our country must, above all things, be decided and strong, since the nature and objects of our commonwealth are so widely distinct from the policies of other nations. As a lonely settler among savages must fortify his home, and keep watch and ward against the insidious foe, so must our Republic preserve itself with scrupulous care against the infectious assaults of foreign elements, incompatible with its prosperity or even with its existence. America demands the careful preservation of whatever has given us our national prosperity. Americans must be Americans; Americans must govern America.

Under ordinary circumstances, a truth so obvious as this would hardly need assertion. But the true basis of our national existence and success, has for some years been studiously ignored and kept out of sight by a set of wily politicians, who, reckless of the means employed, have only sought their private advantage. These agitators have pandered to the violent and lawless tendencies of a brutal foreign immigration, for the sake of their votes. To win them, they have loudly proclaimed that America is the great receptacle for all fugitives; scarcely making a distinction between fugitives from justice, and fugitives from oppression. They have sought to convince these strangers that they had legislative rights in this country; and by such delusive appeals have, to a very great extent, succeeded in managing the foreign vote, which, in the balanced condition of parties, became a preponderant power. These operations have resulted in preposterous assumptions on the part of the immigrant population, in the degradation of the average character of our own rulers, and, to a lamentable extent, in forgetfulness of the true characteristics of our nationality.

But a true nationalism, although not inconsistent with the broadest philanthropy, is altogether opposed to this spurious cosmopolitanism. The laws and foundations of our American freedom are peculiar and separate; nor is any man fitted to govern under them, without an experimental training in them. This fallacious pretence of political benevolence, which studiously avoids mentioning either nationality or patriotism, and which enlarges with many windy generalities upon the human race, the equality of man, and the brotherhood of nations, is the merest sophism. Every man has *some* equal rights, among which are life, liberty, and the pursuit of happiness. But these must be sought by means not inconsistent with the general good. Nor has the criminal equal rights with the lawful citizen. He has forfeited them. Nor has the beggar, who does not own a foot of land nor a suit of clothes, in fact, equal rights with the millionaire. He has not the right to use as much money or estate, until he gets them. He has the right to earn them, if he can, and then to use them. His attempt to use them without that preliminary, is robbery, or swindling. Degrees of intelligence and morality also determine what extent a man's rights shall have, in practice. What rights he is fit to use, he may have. This false cosmopolitanism which would grant equal rights in all respects to the ignorant and the wise, the barbarous and the enlightened—which would at once confer equal political privileges upon the educated, intelligent, and law-abiding American, and upon the foreign pauper and foreign criminal—upon the German, the Irishman, and by parity of reasoning upon the Croat, the Turk, the Chinese, the Hindoo, the Hottentot, the Australian, the Andaman Islander, who crawls on all-fours like a beast, and has neither clothes, language, nor God, cannot meet with too severe a reproof, or too summary a condemnation. As well talk of equal liberty to the philosophic statesman or the lawyer, intrusted with the destinies of millions of men or the interest of millions of capital; and to the idiot, who cannot put his food into his mouth, nor hide his nakedness.

Such dangerous principles, have been so industriously inculcated, and have been so greedily accepted by the foreign population; such a criminal apathy in regard to the preservation of political purity and the election of good men has prevailed among native citizens; and foreign emissaries, lay and clerical, are pushing such extended and powerfully contrived enterprises to grasp the control of our educational centres, our political organizations, all the springs of our national life, by schools, hierarchies, and the filthy dregs of European prisons and almshouses, that a great question is this day up before the people of the United States for determination—new at least in form, if not in substance. Under the guidance of a truly patriotic feeling we must answer it. Clear-minded and true-hearted Americans are to-day called upon to decide a question the most momentous that has ever stirred the heart of the nation, since the struggle at its birth. It is no minor question of dollars and cents, no dispute between sections of the country, no dreaming discussion of abstractions or political theories, no question whether this, or that, or the other political measure will benefit the State; but a question that underlies all these, the decision of which might possibly obviate any necessity of examining them—it is, Are we to have a policy at all? Shall our American Empire, as established with its broad and deep foundations and its noble superstructure, cemented with the blood and the prayers of so many great and good men, yet exist? Or shall it be mangled and corrupted, perverted and defiled, to suit the diabolic ends of lay and priestly plotters, either native or foreign born?

Here is a duty sublime enough to gratify the desires of the noblest. The appeal is made to the true sons of America. Shall our native land become a sink for the pollution of the civilized world? Shall our government, organized with a most complex and delicate machinery, expressly to be directed by the highest grade of intelligence, be controlled by the bungling hands of the foreign boor, or the meddlesome cunning of the foreign priest? Shall its wheels be clogged and embarrassed by shipments of men, sent hither, apparently, for no other reason than the deliberate intention of at once relieving Europe, and embarrassing us?

Let our freemen reflect. The pure stream of our nationality may perhaps endure the infusion of a little foreign matter without perceptible injury. Yet there is *some* injury; and a continuance of this may corrupt the whole. Our power of resisting such influences is doubtless great, but that is no reason for the wanton abuse of it.

What then does the Republic now demand of Americans? The answer is easy. It is not any new or strange doctrine; it is only to restore the principles of action which heretofore have guided our best and greatest men. It is to rule our own country as Washington and the Revolutionary Fathers would have it ruled; to cultivate and develop that strong and good nationality which has already carried us so nobly onward as a nation—to Americanize America.

What were the opinions of the Father of his Country as to the character of foreigners, and the probable consequences of employing them here?

He speaks as follows: "These men have no attachment nor ties to the country, further than interest binds them." "I do most devoutly wish that we had not a single foreigner among us, except the Marquis de La Fayette." "My opinion with respect to immigration is, that except useful mechanics and some particular descriptions of men or professions, there is no need of encouragement."

"It is not the policy of this country to employ aliens where it can be well avoided, either in civil or military walks of life." "It does not accord with the policy of this government to bestow offices, civil or military, upon foreigners, to the exclusion of our own citizens."

Even for outpost service, among the rank and file of the army, Washington could trust none but Americans. "He therefore orders," reads a general order dated Cambridge, Headquarters, July 17, 1775, "that, for the future, none but natives of this country be placed on guard as sentinels on the outposts."

Can any one doubt what Washington would now say, were he alive, as to the demands of an enlightened and nationalized patriotism in the present juncture? And it is well known that his sentiments and apprehensions were shared by his venerable coadjutors in founding this Republic. The profound and wise intellect of Daniel Webster perceived the same dangers, when he said, ten years since, "There is an imperative necessity for reforming the Naturalization Laws of the United States."

There is, then, urgent occasion for the re-assertion of a strong and distinctive nationality by all true citizens of our Republic. In despite of the certain and venomous opposition of the demagogues, who will struggle violently, when "their craft is in danger;" in despite of the anger and bull-headed resistance of the ignorant foreigners who have been trained by demagogues to imagine that the cherished franchises of American freemen are equally theirs; in spite of obloquy and invective, the time has come for the sons of America to stand shoulder to shoulder in the defence of her free and enlightened Constitution, in opposition alike to the open and to the concealed attacks of ruthless foes.

First, and chiefest of all, we must keep the privilege of citizenship as a precious and honorable gift only for those approved worthy of it. Let us not confer it upon the ignorant or the vile. Let us not cast pearls before swine. Why should we lavish upon the rude and vicious stranger the birthright of our free citizens? In so doing, we nourish in our bosoms the viper that prepares to give the fatal sting. When the immigrants are fit for citizenship, then let them have it. Up to that time, let them rest secure in the refuge which we will give them, and be satisfied with their safety. We must educate them first, nationalize them next, but naturalize them only, last of all.

We are also called upon to select and to elect as our rulers, not the men who bluster and prate of their principles and their devotion to the country, or the professional politicians who want office, but the purest and best men, without regard to their situation or business. They cannot, without dishonor, refuse the voice of their country. We can have them if we will. In the exercise of the powers of government by such men, we should soon see the safety of our institutions replaced upon its accustomed basis. Americans would again rule America, as in days gone by; and while our great distinctive political beliefs would mark the character and conduct of our empire, we should continue to offer protection and freedom to all, and citizenship to the best.

We must maintain the peculiarities of our social and civil life. We must maintain our Christian character as a nation. We must still enforce the observation of the Christian Sabbath. We must continue scrupulously to preserve the Church and the State separate from each other. We must again avow and maintain the Christianity of our public education. Shall children be taught here in heathen schools? Shame on the defenders of such a measure!

NECESSITY OF AMERICAN HABITS AND PRINCIPLES.

"This lovely land, this glorious liberty, these benign institutions, the dear purchase of our fathers, are ours; ours to enjoy, ours to preserve, ours to transmit. Generations past and generations to come, hold us responsible for the sacred trust. Our fathers from behind admonish us with their anxious paternal voices, posterity calls out to us from the bosom of the future, the world turns hither its solicitous eye,—all, all conjure us to act wisely and faithfully in the relation which we sustain."

WEBSTER.

AMERICANS are frequently reminded that national sympathies are not to be eradicated; that the Scot cannot be expected to bury those recollections which the songs of Burns so sadly recall; nor can the exiled German shut out from his heart the feelings that will rise and swell at the mention of Fatherland, or the Swiss forget his wild mountain-home. These appeals come with irresistible power to every mind, and with none do they plead more loudly than with an American.

We freely concede the force of these appeals; for our heart would be false to its own instincts if it did not acknowledge their power. We would never ask our foreign friends, who seek amongst us an asylum from tyranny, or a home in which they may better their condition, to forego and keep out of sight any of those endeared associations which give life its chief sweetness, and throw around it the highest charm. These recollections are sacred. They can never be torn from the human heart; and that would be but a wretched profession of liberty which allowed itself to interfere with their existence. Rather would a true liberty feed and foster these deep emotions, underlying, as they do, natures of the finest quality and the noblest capacity.

But is it conceded, as yet, that such sentiments as these ought to supplant principles that embrace the happiness of a world in their comprehensiveness? Do those who plead so touchingly for the exile, believe that he is to make no surrender of any of his feelings, nor even of any of his prejudices, in exchange for the inestimable privileges he here seeks to enjoy? Why has he left home, kindred, and friends, if not to avail himself of an advantage that is to outweigh every other? And are we to expect that such advantages are to be put aside for the sake of ministering to the pleasures of memory?—that our fundamental principles are to be held as nothing, in order that emotions which stir an individual heart may have free course, even to the building up among us of new nationalities? With all due respect to the feelings by which our new foreign friends profess to be so deeply moved, such a course is absurd on their part, and inimical to our interests.

We might, very naturally, discourse of the duty of naturalized citizens to adopt our habits and principles, before we thought of what the advantage would be to them. But our address is not now so much to those foreigners who come into our midst simply for a home and its many untold comforts, as it is to that portion who have become what is termed "naturalized;" that is, who, like plants removed to another soil, are there to take root and thrive in common with all things else which that soil produces. They deliberately declare their intention to throw off all allegiance to, and connection with, foreign potentates, and bind themselves with a solemn oath so to do. As soon as the requisite period of probation has elapsed—which is, indeed, a most indulgently brief one—by complying with certain forms, they are admitted to all the rights, privileges, and immunities of American citizens. From that hour they stand on just the same footing with a native of the soil. Our laws throw around them the same sufficient protection—which, indeed, they did not fail to do before—the same opportunities lie before them for bettering their worldly circumstances, and the same field is allowed them in which to expand and develop their individual characters. Our richly endowed public schools are thrown open to their children, that they may go in with the sons and daughters of our citizens, and become, like them, candidates for any of the public trusts which may in after years be imposed upon them. They find no restraint thrown upon their accustomed modes of worship, but are at liberty to do exactly as their consciences may dictate. In every direction, they find liberty in its largest sense. The single restraint upon it is, that what they enjoy shall in no wise conflict with the enjoyments of others. It is upon this simple principle of concession, of regard for the rights and privileges of our fellow-creatures, that all government exists; and without such mutual concession, a government could not stand for a day.

Such being the position of naturalized citizens, and such the liberality of the gifts bestowed, it may well be inquired whether their very first duty is not to put themselves in the way of acquiring our habits, and obtaining the most intimate knowledge of, and insight into, our principles. The inquiry seems most natural. Indeed, the wonder rather is, why it should be made at all; for, were it not for the strange course that popular events have taken, within a few years in this country, in reference to naturalized citizens, it would seem egregious to ask such a question at all. When an alien relinquishes his obedience as a subject, and puts on the allegiance which we owe our country, he in fact becomes one of ourselves, and is supposed, by the very act, to declare that he admits his duty to be the same with ours.

What else can this declaration which he has made, and this oath which he has taken, be supposed to mean? If it have no meaning, then what the necessity of going through such a ceremony at all? But if the forms are invested with any thing like a purpose; or any intention is thought to lurk within their limits, what can that purpose and intention be? How shall we know, except by means of the very plain language which the alien, who is about to become naturalized, takes voluntarily upon his lips?

We should regard with the utmost aversion a native citizen who openly, or even by his conduct, professed to set at naught the solemn oath by which he bound himself to perform the duties of a citizen. We should brand such a person as a traitor to his country and its interests, and he would receive nothing but the anathemas and execrations of every true patriot. Naturalization is not simply a one-sided case of promising; it is a matter of *mutual* obligation, wherein a citizen receives quite as much as he gives. It is a contract which cannot be dissolved except with the consent of both the parties concerned. Those two parties are—the great public on the one side, and the individual man on the other.

No man understanding the rights and duties of American citizenship, ever could have thought he was at liberty to slight or overlook the requirements of a citizen. To imagine he may proceed so far as he finds it for his interest, but that when he is called on to make some few sacrifices for the sake of duty, he will retreat within his own selfishness, disregard all the demands of the common interest upon him, and still call on government—which is with us but the expression and execution of the common welfare—to protect him intact from harm, is impossible and preposterous. No popular government could ever exist for a day on such a basis. The ground on which our political institutions rest is, that the general interest ought to take the place of that merely individual. Every citizen, freely agreeing to this, is most certainly assured that his private interests will be abundantly protected; and whatever concessions it may be needful for him to make in view of the public benefit, will be sure to return with large interest. All private rights being merged in those of the many, the former acquire a new strength, are able to sustain themselves, and never fear conflict with those of any individual.

We are hardly able to conceive how the majority of our naturalized citizens look at these things in a different light from this. Those of them who may not do so, have yet the alphabet of political freedom to learn. They have still to be taught, perhaps by hard experience, that each individual can be free only where all are free; that respect for others' rights by no means implies a loss of one's own privileges; and that mutual concessions, instead of depriving any of individual liberty, are rather the means whereby that liberty may become larger and more expansive.

When a foreigner, for the first time, styles himself an American citizen, he feels that he has come into possession of certain privileges that were never his before. He is a new man, in more respects than one; he has cast off old alliances, and put on broad and new responsibilities. Henceforth, our schools are his schools; our public halls, our rights at the ballot-box, our claims upon the protection of law,—all are his as much as they are our own. It is but fair to suppose that he has come into this new arrangement, not with the sole idea of personal and selfish advantage, but rather out of love for the principles of our system. He must have an affection for those principles, because they allow him, as well as others, to pursue his own highest happiness without hindrance of any description.

If this, then, be the case—and it most assuredly ought to be with every honest naturalized citizen on our soil—how obvious are the advantages that will grow out of the immediate adoption by those citizens, of our peculiar habits and modes of thought? What a blessing it is to them, to come at once into a close and hearty realization of those principles for which they have professed so much affection! How much richer, and broader, and deeper will be their share of our common inheritance, if they acquire an early possession, undivided by the lines of any selfish reservations, and retained with all the singleness of feeling which belongs to the native born?

Taking the case of our common schools, for example, every naturalized citizen must feel that there is open to him a privilege which no other nation has ever offered to its people. In these schools, so amply endowed at the public cost, he finds instruction from well-qualified teachers for all his children. There they may be taught the necessary branches of an education, which in after-life they can expand to any limit. They sit on the same benches with the children of our most worthy citizens. No ideas of quality or rank are allowed to throw up the least barrier between them. They study from the same books, and are placed in the same divisions and classes. They compete for the same rewards, and are alike honored by the commendation of instructors and the appreciation of the public.

Could any educational system be devised that would give wider freedom, or more extended privileges than this? Is there the least room for any man, however bigoted, to find fault with a plan of such generous comprehensiveness? If a naturalized citizen honestly wish to enjoy the boasted privileges which our institutions extend him, and bringing his children to the same enjoyment with himself, to have their minds educated and adapted to the realization of all our national advantages—both civil and social—by what more easy and direct method can it be done, than by taking advantage of our common schools? If the foreign-born parent was first led, through pure admiration for our country and its institutions, to leave the place of his birth for our more favored land, assuredly he must be doubly anxious to secure for his offspring every one of those inestimable privileges, which, till now, he has never enjoyed. He will be watchful, lest some of them may be accidentally overlooked. Every thing that lies open for the common benefit, he will be specially strenuous to have a share in. Intellectual advantages he will be particularly earnest in his endeavors to obtain; and all facilities for better comprehending the principles and working of our system of government, he will not only take quick advantage of in his own person, but will likewise introduce his children to, at the earliest moment within his power.

So far, we have only looked at the manner in which a naturalized citizen should show himself consistent with the professions made at the time of his assuming citizenship. There is a point beyond this; it is the way in which such a newly-made citizen can acquire an absolute advantage, by instantly conforming to the spirit of our institutions, and to our peculiar modes of thought. If the foreigner have had the sagacity to recognize, previously, the advantages of our system, it certainly cannot be very necessary, at this late day, to rehearse to him what he already knows. Of course it must be supposed he had pondered this matter well before he took the first step; but having once joined the bands of brotherhood with us, he cannot be too forward or too earnest in adapting himself, wholly and heartily, to those institutions, the high blessings of which he seeks to enjoy.

It would seem, too, most natural that a stranger who had determined to cast his lot with ours, should throw all his sympathies into the same channel with our own,—should closely scrutinize our habits, our principles, our institutions,—and show himself behind no other citizen in transfusing the spirit of his new nationality into his own individual feelings and thoughts. He must remember that ours is a government of the people; of that large community he counts but one. All public affairs rest, for their maintenance and security, upon the popular will. If the people are frivolous, thoughtless, guided by any less serious motive than the single one offered by a sober and deliberate judgment, then the general interest must suffer accordingly. As one of the people—as a citizen among his fellow-citizens—our naturalized friend cannot fail to perceive that whatever is done by the popular voice, directly affects himself. Hence he is interested in all our laws, our customs, our habits of thought, and our institutions. He cannot remove himself away from our midst, and deliberately declare that whatever may transpire, is all the same to him. He cannot conscientiously hold himself aloof, and say that he cares neither for this nor that law. As a citizen, he must care for every public transaction that bears upon the general welfare. Having once adopted certain responsibilities—invested at the time of his acquiring citizenship—it is out of his power, so long as he remains a citizen, to lay them aside on any pretence whatever.

The sooner, too, he enters with his whole soul into the spirit of our American life, the sooner he will learn to love the new possession that has become his own. It will be easier for him, then, to note and understand the practical working of many things that before were little better than enigmas. As his interest increases, his affection will deepen. As he feels his own share of the common responsibility enlarge, he will likewise find the confidence of his new fellow-citizens abounding. Instead of being suspiciously pushed aside or overlooked, he will find himself openly welcomed, whilst thousands of generous hearts respond to the anxious beatings of his own.

But let the naturalized citizen keep back these spontaneous impulses of his better nature; let him say to himself, "I will enjoy the full protection of their laws, but never will I subscribe to their spirit or principle," and matters immediately assume a very different aspect. Adopting such a course, he cuts himself off from his own rights, and forfeits every further claim, either to the protection or the respect of all true Americans.

If such a one league with others similarly disposed, and place himself at the direction of any man, or body of men, to compass measures that are calculated to subvert the fair and open workings of our political system; if this new organization, stretching from city to city, and from State to State, bind together its cords, and weave over and over its network of conspiracy, till it is thought that no human power, social or political, can break it in sunder; if these men attack, stealthily, our common-school system, determined, by cajolery, by supplication, by art, or, finally, by force, to overthrow this bulwark of liberty,—we are necessarily compelled to look about us in absolute dismay, hardly prepared for a demonstration of such magnitude and power, and perfectly at a loss to understand what may be the object aimed at. But the reaction will inevitably arrive. It must come, where all men are free; nor can it long be delayed, where the people are the watchful and jealous guardians of their own liberties. It is but the fulfilment of the old law, that "they who sow the wind shall, in due time, reap the whirlwind."

This it is that has called into life the active and repellent spirit of Americanism which is to-day sweeping, with the power and majesty of a tempest, over the length and breadth of our land. Such unnatural and underhanded demonstrations were the only ones that could summon forth this giant resistance to the enemies of American liberty. The naturalized citizen should read the lesson carefully, and ponder it with diligence; for it teaches him but too emphatically what is the deep meaning of those principles which Americans profess, and how completely ingrained they are in every true American heart.

THE RIGHT OF THE MAJORITY TO RULE.

"And sovereign Law, the world's collected will,
O'er thrones and globes elate,
Sits empress—crowning good, repressing ill."

MAN was created for society: the necessity of laws for governing his relations to his fellows is, therefore, co-existent with his nature. No community ever existed, however savage or degraded, which did not acknowledge some of the elements of government. The products of the chase—the earth-hole used as a habitation—even the rude knife and spear, have their acknowledged owners, and any infringement of these rights, results in personal conflict. A little reflection leads us to the conclusion, that we have no individual rights which can be separated from our relations towards others; for if selfishness could swallow up the whole being, then self-government was the original law, and man, in the enjoyment of the purposes of his existence, should live alone, and exterminate those about him; yet this is not the case. The practical effect of such an assumption would result in destruction of the individual; he would be outlawed even by savages, as quickly as he would be arrested and imprisoned among civilized people. A desire then for government grows out of the necessity of our being: it is an appetite as positive as that for food.

The time necessarily occupied by the individual members of every community, in procuring subsistence, suggests, as a matter of economy and expediency, the delegation of the management of government to one or many; and upon this necessity arise, not only the first forms of organized society, but, from the manner in which this authority is delegated, springs every possible form of government.

Numberless absurd theories, sanctioned by "great names," have been proposed to account for the first formation of government. Some declare it to be of Divine origin, and consequently a compact between the people and divinely appointed rulers. Opposed to this proposition, are those who believe it to be simply an agreement among the people themselves.

To say that government exists by Divine power, is true in the general sense of all things existing by the same cause; but we are not to stop at the threshold of inquiry by such a misapplication of a truism. We are to consider how far that same Divine Authority decreed that man should be left to choose and fashion his political relations. The advocates of the Divine origin of government have always been the idolatrous worshippers of absolutism, and no outrage has ever been committed by tyrants upon the people, that has not had the profane endorsement—Divinely chosen rulers can do no wrong. But the wisdom of those fathers of our country who established the American Republic rejected such a theory, finding no Divine sanction for oppression and wrong, and therefore set vigorously to work to extend the blessings of rational freedom, and to build up fortresses against encroaching power.

In the history of nations and individuals which have passed away, the idea that the only legitimate end of government is the public good, was confined to the breast of the philosopher, or announced at the sacrifice of life by the patriot and reformer. The organized power of the oppressor was more than equal to the undiscipled assertors of so great a truth; but in our day, the example the American people have set of the beauty of the practical workings of this truth, has already had the effect to make its adoption almost universal, not only among reflecting minds, but among the governed of the great bulk of every enlightened population. To the people the importance of cherishing this idea, that government is an implied contract, and not a Divine right, can hardly be estimated. Its simple conception is the beginning of political wisdom: a clear and comprehensive idea of it in the mind of each individual, is one of the best safeguards of our own free institutions.

Having decided that government is a compact, its operation, if consistent, must be to effect the greatest good to the greatest number. Hence it is evident that the rule of the majority is the clearest expression of the cherished principle. To say that this rule is an imperative necessity, is harsh and unsatisfactory; but to say that to pursue some determinate plan for a general happiness among the contradictory interests, opinions, and feelings of society—this rule of action is the most admirable, and most in harmony with those great general laws which bind together both the physical and moral world—then we shed light upon the reason of the rule, for that the principle grows out of the very nature of the best form of political existence.

The rule of the majority is the only one calculated to secure the happiness of the whole, for there is rarely an exception in an intelligent community where the majority is not competent to take the best possible care of its own interests; and the minority, having the full benefits of the prevailing laws, will be found, on examination, rather to sacrifice opinions and feelings than things of vital importance. In the practical working of this principle in our government, it is noticeable that however the people may be agitated upon any question—however, for the moment, the minority may feel aggrieved—the majority never becomes permanently fixed; for in the constant changes of our rulers, every possible opportunity is afforded to correct errors or soften opposition, and the clamorous minority of to-day in a few short months finds itself triumphantly borne along on the breeze of popular favor. The keen and searching inquisition under which every scheme of public policy passes in a republican government, before it becomes "a law," may be said to test its value and practicability before it has a vital application. A universal agreement of opinion would soon degenerate into apathy, and apathy would pave the way for the foot of the oppressor. The opposition, therefore, of the minority is just as essential for the full understanding of our rights, as is the approbation of the majority necessary to give them legal force. The clash, in fine, of the minority and the majority, so far from marring the great design of civil institutions, contributes directly to advance it.

In its every-day workings, we find society insensibly separates into three divisions—the very rich, the people made comfortable by daily industry, and the poor. Now the majority must ever be found among those who are successful laborers, and it will never yield to the assumptions of the wealthy, nor to the unreasonable desires of the very poor. Here then we find the rock against which vainly beat the pretensions of the parvenu, and the distinctions among those who would even demolish society for personal gain. And it will be found, that notwithstanding the public mind is occasionally clouded by threatening storms, or suffers from absolute outbreak, the solid interests of all are carefully guarded; for this conservative majority is constantly recruited from the ranks of those who, but a short time previously, were among the poor; whilst the pretensious rich, in the vicissitudes that attend the holding of property when no exclusive privileges are granted, sink out of sight before they can do any material injury by the misapplied use of their wealth.

It is remarkable that a government of the majority has constantly set limitations upon the exercise of its own authority. The ruler, therefore, of a republic is constantly surrounding himself with restraints; while the ruler of a monarchy, a single individual, is constantly extending the gratification of his powers, and thus affords the best illustration of the fitness of the majority to rule. Constitutions, however, when majorities govern, are after all only written checks and limitations upon the actions of men, and are created by their powers without reference to the fact, whether they shall in the future fall into the party in the majority or in the minority. This conduct, so magnanimous, has its moral effect upon the minds of men, for it is rarely that a faction attempts to violate the fundamental law; or if ventured upon, it quickly retraces its steps. There are always in every majority a large number of persons who will not sacrifice to party what belongs to the country, and these individuals are ever ready to abandon an oppressive majority, and by going over to the minority, restore the balances of the written con stitution.

In the history of our government it will be found that repeated attempts have been made by the legislatures of our States to violate their respective constitutions, and even that of the Federal Government. Every instance has proved abortive. So many people have instantly resented such an attempt, and abandoned the presumptuous party in power, as to render it incapable of doing injury, and the sober second thought of these revolutionists themselves, has caused them finally to seek redress only through the legitimate channels of the laws.

In the Federal Government the advantage afforded the minority is permanent. Much as the States may differ in relative size or population, they are equal in the Senate. The veto of the Executive operates as a check in favor of the minority, for its immediate effect is always to defeat the will of the majority of the legislature. Another class of checks grows out of the distribution of the government into departments, thereby separating interests which are common to all its parts from those which are exclusively local. Another very important security against excessive accumulation of power is the confinement of the Federal Government to the exercise of such powers as are expressly given to it by the constitution, and the retention of the remaining portion of sovereignty in the hands of the State Government.

Such are a few of the most prominent instances of the radical importance and effective character of the checks or limitations which our majority constantly imposes upon the exercise of its own authority. They are yet more strongly illustrated in the formation of the constitutions of the new States, which, though founded upon the principle of universal suffrage, yet judiciously impose limitations upon the power of the majority, wherever believed to be necessary for the public weal.

Yet all these checks and limitations, however wisely contrived, skilfully arranged, and harmoniously operative, are mere machinery.

Notwithstanding the wisdom of its arrangement, and the applicability of its construction, the instrument requires a judicious and energetic hand to wield it. Indeed, its very complexity and delicacy make the proper handling of it an impossibility to the ignorant. Neither our own, nor any other free government, could flourish or exist, unless controlled by checks and restraints exterior to, but necessary to the well-working of its machinery. The real safety of our government—its true security against oppression on the part of the majority, or rebellion from the minority—is no mere contrivance, no balancing of class against class, no reliance in selfish interests. It is something stronger, safer, wiser than any or all of these: it is the uprightness and wisdom of an educated and Christian nation insuring the justice of the majority's decision, and the acquiescence of the remainder in their judgment. This, therefore, requires wisdom in our statesmen; it is this makes our country peaceful, happy, and prosperous, and prevents the wanton abuse of the constituted forms of government by a victorious majority. It is these moral checks which remove any apprehension on the part of the minority, and obviate any vindictive or illegal action, or even a passive resistance to measures honestly intended to promote the well-being of the whole community, however much they may fail to meet the views of a part. Such measures must be maintained or opposed, not from sinister or selfish motives, but from the unfeigned conviction that their retention or alteration will be for the good of the greatest number.

Such is the course of every true citizen whose patriotism is not a mere name. A contrary action on a question pregnant with such mighty results, is certain to lead eventually to anarchy and revolution. From parallel scenes of civil discord—the oppression of the weak, the tyranny of the many—there is a certain and dread alternative,—an alternative destroying every hope of liberty, blighting the virtues of the soul and the powers of intellect, enthralling man in all the darkness of mental slavery, but an alternative in which relief may still be found—an irremediable, a hopeless despotism.

FREEDOM FROM FOREIGN INFLUENCE.

"Our virtues
Live in the interpretation of the times."
SHAKSPEARE.

It is a preposterous assumption that any single class of our citizens are exempted from their civil responsibilities by reason of the religion which they may happen to profess. We are not able to understand why all the members of our vast commonwealth are not equally bound and equally interested in the preservation of the general safety. We cannot comprehend the rule by which one man must offer all his resources for the public good, while another, because of a different religious profession, may remit every exertion on the same behalf, as to him alone seems equitable or agreeable. American citizens should permit no religious creed to teach them forgetfulness of their common country. They should spurn alliance with every cause which leads them to forego their love for the equal rights of all men. If they cannot stand together upon the broad platform of liberty for the whole human race, there is no hope left that humanity shall be benefited.

Strange times, indeed, have we fallen upon, that demand of us a demonstration, to any portion of the American population, of the necessity of the duty of their most zealous support of the free system of government under which they live. Mighty revolutions must assuredly have been wrought in public sentiment, when American citizens are discovered to be forgetful of their obligations to the sacred cause of republican truth, and wilfully derelict to the high duty they owe to the country whose sufficient protection they are proud everywhere to claim. No domestic influence, germinating here on the blessed home-soil, could ever have been potent to produce a state of things so alarmingly fraught with mischief. It could have arisen from the operation of none of those healthy principles with which our fathers wisely set in motion this comprehensive system of peace. Alien hatred is its real author, and foreign interference is its malicious progenitor. It was produced on a distant soil, and it is diligently sought now to be domesticated on this. It bears the brand of foreign iniquity on its forehead, and stands confessed a monster of too hideous a mien to be the product of the clime whose breezes all whisper of freedom.

We will not pause to undertake the proof of what is already so transparently obvious, namely, that both Catholic and Protestant Americans are bound by an equal engagement to sustain the liberties of that country whose appointed guardians they are. It is a duty from which, while members of the great body of freemen, they can neither ask nor expect a release. The obligation is stamped too deeply on their souls; it is ingrained with their nature, by the process of their early education; and he must, in truth, cease entirely to be an American—openly cast off his allegiance altogether, and forswear both the rights and the privileges of citizenship—who hopes, by any method, to absolve his conscience from the religious duty he owes to the country, either of his birth or adoption.

But consenting, for the moment, to set the question of duty aside, we are left to estimate the measure of interest that should lead every citizen, of whatever religious creed, to strive to maintain American freedom intact from the taint of foreign influence. Interest is sometimes a powerful advocate, when duty cannot find a tongue. Fear often persuades, and moves to action, when a loftier motive feels its power paralyzed and gone.

The better to understand the nature and extent of this common interest, it is necessary first to study the character of that influence from abroad, by whose threats and usurpations our free institutions are subjected to peril. The grounds of fear must be accurately ascertained, before the alarmed heart instinctively puts forth all its energies for preservation.

No nation can achieve either character, influence, or power, unless it be founded and compacted on some particular principle. Monarchy builds on the principle that one man is better than his fellows, and possesses therefore an hereditary right to rule. Republicanism cherishes the heaven-born idea that ALL MEN ARE EQUAL, and not only equal, but free—capable of self-control, and the safe direction of their own concerns and interests; and, so dearly has this grand idea been cherished, that it has become an incorporated *principle* in the political system, and been employed as the corner-stone of the entire edifice of republicanism. Here, at the commencement, all absolute forms of government are at open issue with democracy. There is a fatal incongruity between them from the beginning. And not only so, but it is not possible for the influence of one of them to falter in its active progress, until it shall have finally succeeded in outrooting the other from existence.

Foreign potentates are not blind to truths of such magnitude, looming ominously from the lessening horizon of their future. They understand that inactivity is destruction; that silent acquiescence is worse than destruction; for it is a humiliating confession of wrong, to the syllables of which they have never fashioned their lips. They start up with awakened fears and renewed energies. Watching the constant changes that occur in the political sky, they draw themselves secretly into closer companionship, each hating the other with the full measure of his heart's power, but hating the new influence even more. Considerations of safety weigh down thoughts of mere policy, and they swear to forget the smaller evils in the face of one they esteem far greater. It is selfishness that is working at the bottom; but this selfishness is destined to perform an important work,—for it will be the most active element in the destruction of every system of government where Church and State are connected. The prophecy, even now, is in the progress of a literal fulfilment.

Opposing republicanism on grounds like these, it is little to be expected that foreign powers will abate a jot or tittle of the intensity of that spirit of hatred which uniformly characterizes their action.

Nor do they at any moment give evidence of its relaxation. If America but crosses the Gulf-Stream, their swiftest ships are on her track. If she treats with a nation like Texas, they are there to whisper words of disaffection and discouragement. Our name is employed as a term of ridicule and reproach abroad, and our soil is considered only a fit lazar-house for the reception of all cases of political disease. We are styled the Botany Bay of the world, accepting every ingredient that is offered to help build up a wild and incongruous nation; and into our lap are poured the paupers, the convicts, the lazaroni, the assassins, and the vermin-eaten rabble, whose presence is a source of peril to governments whose duty it is to make proper provision for them. We contribute of our bounty to famishing nations, and yet are styled the most avaricious and grasping of any on the face of the earth. Our march forward is one of peace alone; yet are we charged with a spirit of piracy which befits only a nation wholly barbarous. If our representatives abroad convene to confer upon the highest interests of their common country, spies dog their steps, falsehoods hunt down their true purposes, their government is spoken of as an outlaw, and secret pledges are circulated to destroy its growing influence by whatever means, and at however great a hazard.

But this is only a superficial view of the matter. It is not altogether abroad—it is even on our own soil that foreign powers seek chiefly to do the work, the performance of which they have undertaken. Knowing that if a battery is to be silenced it must be carried by a vigorous assault, and that in order to destroy a fortification a breach must first be made in the walls, they direct all their secret forces against that government which stands sponsor for free and liberal institutions. To cripple its power, to weaken its energy, to obstruct and overthrow its matured purposes, to turn its very forces against itself, and thus give it the name of an insane suicide,—these are the objects that are sought with such an unmistakable eagerness, and the accomplishment of which would fill the world with the jubilations of tyranny.

To carry forward so gigantic a purpose, there is need of the co-operation of an equally gigantic power. Such ends are wrought but through the aid of mighty instrumentalities. Secrecy is likewise required to insure success, to mask the almost resistless energies of an attempt of such magnitude. Where was a power endowed with qualifications of so peculiar a character to be found? At whose bidding would it start up, mailed in its coat of impenetrable armor, and exclaim—"Here am I!"

The needed power was already in existence. It was the ultramontane party of the Romish Church, whose Pope and prelates sprang forward with an alacrity that showed how welcome was the work. That Church holds almost complete ascendency in the Old World; her emissaries are prowling everywhere; she sustains an army of secret laborers—sappers and miners of true freedom—whose toils are never relaxed by favor, and never relieved by sleep; her temporal head is ambitious only of rule, and her myriad children are commanded only servile and unqualified obedience. Her whole history is at war with free aspirations of any kind or grade. Her principles are those of high-handed usurpation. The rack and the thumb-screw have been her barbarous instruments of discipline,—the bloody Inquisition has been the secret but terrible source of her power,—and the Confessional still remains the silent engine of its perpetuation.

Foreign rulers, as a body, acknowledge the supremacy of that gigantic despotism. It is one which engulfs all others, making their assumptions appear even trifling in comparison with its own. Hence they consider its decrees inviolable. From its high court they expect no appeal. They, therefore, have plotted with it, and the fruits of their machinations they promise to the Mother Church. The head of that Church understands the plan, and forthwith sets himself to divide and conquer the fair realms of Liberty. The means are ample, and are all ready to his hand. Emigrants are coming in long and unbroken processions to America, all, or nearly all, the sheep of his fold. This vast mass will he secretly and silently congregate on our soil, not for the pure and lawful purposes of religion, but for the more easy and rapid spread of his power, and the gratification of the foreign potentates who form the bulwark of his sovereignty.

He delegates faithful messengers, who are appointed shepherds of his spreading flocks. Patiently and quietly they go about their work, carefully avoiding any irritation of the popular mind, seeking no conflict with any existing power, enduring in silence whatever reproach or contumely may overtake them, and striving continually for the attainment of a single end, the political as well as the spiritual supremacy of the Pope. This countless array of immigrants, though they may hate their former rulers never so intensely, nevertheless acknowledge obedience to the Pope and his prelates. That connection it is not even thought of dissolving. Yet the rulers are but ready instruments in the hands of this Pope,—the Arch-Priest who is skilfully intriguing for the perpetuation of their power, as well as his own. The connection which holds their interests together, is one that cannot be dissevered.

By such a complex process is the overthrow of our institutions sought to be compassed. Tyranny first drives its beggared population from the land, to inhabit one of the fairest and freest promise: the Pope is the ally of tyrants, because it is through them alone that his ambitious ends are reached; and adherence to the Church of which the Pope is the visible head, is the first condition needed to bring the success of both Popery and tyranny to its desired culmination. They are joined in an indissoluble league, and the same principle vitalizes both. In that union they will stand or fall together. Popery is a political system; cunningly constructed, and energetically kept in ceaseless operation. Its ambition enclasps the globe. Its aims circumscribe all nations and all people. It works secretly, when openly might be dangerous; but for evermore *it works.* Its efforts know no relaxation. It is a gigantic scheme of despotism; first sapping the course of free thought, and then appealing to the superstitious fears of the heart, whose sentiments are rendered unhealthy by its enchaining wiles.

No wonder that the foreign powers who seek our destruction,

should apply for aid to the head of a system like this. They must have been forgetful of their own purpose, if they had passed it by. No wonder that they consent so unanimously to do the Pope's bidding, if he will but engage to perform a service in which they crave his effective assistance. He serves, by this means, both himself and them. He strengthens their power, and adds enormously to his own. If he can but rule in America, his supple minions will be no less satisfied than himself. They do not desire a new empire; they care nothing for further self-aggrandizement, or the baubles of an authority that cannot fail to prove troublesome rather than profitable; they do not seek to erect a new despotism, whose head they may, some day, become themselves: they only wish that there may be no America. This beacon-light of the world does but throw into deeper shadow the realms over which they bear rule. They would have it extinguished forever; and Popery has seriously undertaken the task, determined here, on American soil, to make its final stand, and fight its last battle. That great conflict, we firmly believe, is to be fought out in our own day.

This is the nature of that foreign influence, exerted on our soil, which has awakened such alarming fears in these present times. The mask has been torn away; the monster stands exposed before us. So far as Romanism is only religious, it has equal rights with every other form of worship, and every other creed in existence; but the moment its aims become political, and it seeks aspiringly to bring the State in subjection to the Church, that moment it deserves, as a system, to be scouted from existence, and its pharisaical leaders to be deprived of that freedom whose interests they have so basely been laboring to betray.

To check the inroad of such a system of despotism, Americans of all creeds are urged, by every possible consideration of safety, to apply themselves without delay. American Catholics may enjoy their religion, but they should never allow themselves to be used for the betrayal of their freedom. They must see, as the rest of us, that the reign of Romanism in this country through its deputed representatives, is a relapse into the power of the self-same tyranny from which they have escaped. It must be plain, that whatever might be the loss to Protestants by the overthrow of our liberties, it would certainly be an equal misfortune to Catholics. Their interest is a common one with ours. We have no rights to lose by so appalling a misfortune, the privation of which would not cripple and injure them as well. All are bound up in one common destiny. All must know that they are to rise or fall together.

The words of Washington burn in our memories at thoughts like these: "Against *the insidious wiles of foreign influence*, I conjure you to believe me, fellow-citizens, the jealousy of a free people ought to be constantly awake; it is one of the most baneful foes of a republican government." And the expressed fears of Jefferson must not be forgotten: "I hope we may find some means, in future, of shielding ourselves from foreign influence,—political, commercial, or in whatever form it may be attempted. I wish there were an ocean of fire between this and the Old World." And Madison added: "Foreign influence is a Grecian horse to the republic; *we cannot be too careful to exclude its entrance.*" Warnings like these are not to be passed lightly by. Events have abundantly shown the far-seeing sagacity of the fathers of the republic, and irrefragably prove that their fears were founded in wisdom. Americans must at this day give such warnings due heed, be their creed what it may. When liberty is menaced from without, it should arouse us all like the sound of a fire-bell in the night.

THE ORIGIN OF POLITICAL POWER.

"For what is freedom, but the unfettered use of all the powers which God, for use, has given?"
COLERIDGE.

NATIONAL prosperity arises necessarily and only from intelligent freedom. Nations have ever been prosperous and strong, in proportion to their appreciation and wise use of *liberty*. All the Divine teachings, whether by revelation or by human example, have shown that the true basis of civil and political liberty—the true source and organization of civil and political power—are divinely ordained. The greatest happiness is always attained by those who live in closest observance of all the divine laws of life; and this is true of the divine law of political organization, as much as it is of the divine laws of bodily health or social happiness.

To fulfil these conditions of happiness, men must *think*. Just as much as they are left to their own guidance, just so much they need to possess and to use the power of quickly discerning between right and wrong, truth and falsehood. From this truth it follows that we Americans, who live in the enjoyment of a freer exercise of our faculties, and under less restraints than are experienced by any other nation, need more than any other the full possession, and constant and active use of a thoughtful and foreseeing intelligence.

The true basis of political power is the consent of the people governed; and in proportion to the wisdom of that consent is the wisdom of the government, and the happiness and prosperity of the whole. It is a melancholy fact which might be adduced in reply to this statement, that so vast a majority of the human race has dwelt contentedly in darkness and chains. But though true, it does not militate against our argument. It only shows that their consent has not been wisely given. Nor has any such nation ever attained to a true prosperity, or a true happiness. It is the consent of the governed which has upheld all human governments, and the refusal or withdrawal of it has always overthrown them. As the nation, so is the government. The men have always made the ruler—not the ruler the men. The ruler has held his place by virtue of being an exponent of the national spirit; by being such a man that the national mind found in his actions its fullest and freest expression. This expression of the national mind, which has always controlled even the direst tyrannies, has found its freest, safest, and most dignified manifestation in our republic, the best form of government yet established on earth,—which arose, by the force of necessity, above forms and precedents, and whose vigor and vitality are sustained by a stern adherence to the original principle upon which it was constructed,—where the majority speaks for the whole, without tyranny, and the minority acquiesces without rebellion—and the glorious result is a peaceful and happy unanimity.

That the will of the governed, according to the design of the Almighty, should constitute the substance of the government, is proved by the fact that aspirations after political freedom are an integral part of the human mind as created by God. Ignorance, as we have remarked, may obscure this glowing thought, and may apparently quench its light; but the capacity for desiring and enjoying liberty is yet alive, and the innate longing sometimes bursts forth, like an unsuspected volcano, beneath the very feet of the tyrants who think that they have trodden out every spark of the sacred fire. We need not prove this assertion to Americans. Every American feels the truth of it, and will recognize the principle in full operation as he looks into his own heart, or observes the actions of his fellow-citizens.

But God has revealed the truth of free political principles in other ways than by this indistinct and feeble natural light. The revelation is implied often and necessarily, throughout the Biblical history of the Jewish constitution and its workings; and it is once, at least, absolutely commanded to be proclaimed regularly, in so many words. No allegiance was sworn to any human ruler. The code revealed by God to Moses, was submitted to the people, according to the forms of pure democracy, and by them accepted and deliberately agreed on. "All that the Lord hath said," was their promise, "we will do, and be obedient." At the semi-centennial jubilee, there was a ceremonious constitutional proclamation of freedom. At those periods it was expressly commanded, in words whose noble meaning and associations are sacred in our own land, to "proclaim liberty throughout all the land, unto all the inhabitants thereof."* The whole Mosaic code was essentially popular in character. It was calculated to develop individual well-doing, and to permit only a minimum of litigation.

The country was subdivided into the same sort of local jurisdiction as constitutes our "townships," and which is well known to be the strong and essential basis of all the machinery of our own republican government. The people elected their own "selectmen," or municipal rulers. "Judges and officers," ran the command, "shalt thou make thee in all thy gates." There were captains of tens, and of fifties, and hundreds, and thousands; and important disputes, upon appeal, were only occasionally, and in the last resort, to be decided by the leader of the nation. The general scheme of government, aside from their municipal authorities, consisted of the leader for the time being, a chief magistrate or judge, like Joshua; the great Sanhedrim, or assembly of the princes, instituted by Moses and discontinued under Herod; and the great Assembly of the People, which wielded a supreme and predominating power. Popular movements even controlled the divinely appointed leader, thus nullifying the divine command. The Israelites forced Aaron to make them an idol. They all refused to enter Palestine, upon the report of the spies, although Moses desired them to do so.

When three of the tribes appeared to be designing to secede and establish a new commonwealth, the rest of the nation assembled at

* These words were cast upon the old bell that hung in the State-House, in Philadelphia, at the time of the Declaration of Independence.

Shiloh, and in their governmental capacity sent Phineas and ten princes to treat; preparing for immediate war in case of their failure. Joshua's last public act was to convene the assembly of the people, and to make a covenant with them before the Lord. When the Levite's wife had been abused by the people of Gibeah, the "whole congregation of Israel" met, and resolved upon war against the tribe of Benjamin.

It is true that brief directions were early given for the conduct of their king, but with a cautious avoidance to recommend such an officer. And when the nation at last demanded one, Samuel earnestly and displeasedly remonstrated, with a forcible and careful explanation of the nature of the government they were requiring. And he only ceased at the command of God, who distinctly attributes their monarchical tendency to the spread of irreligion, asserting that they were not rejecting the authority of Samuel, but of himself, Jehovah; and he orders the prophet to comply with their foolish wish, saying, "Hearken unto the voice of the people," but only after solemn protest. Even then, it was the nation, assembled in convention, that chose Saul, as they afterwards chose David. So they repudiated the heir, Rehoboam, who refused to agree to the sort of Magna Charta which they demanded of him, and chose Jeroboam instead.

The whole organization, indeed, of the Israelitish government, as intended by God, was of the very freest and most popular kind. God told them to be free, gave them the means of being free. In proportion as they remained free, they were happy; the chronicles of their kings are red with blood, or black with crime. Yet among their kings, David and Solomon who were selected, one by God and the other by his father, on the ground of individual merit, and not by the hereditary right which afterwards prevailed, were the best of the kings. The surrender of this freedom which God had given to the Jews, was substantially the surrender of their prosperity and virtue. At once they ceased to be freemen, and to be virtuous. Moses and Samuel, in foretelling to the nation the evil results of the renunciation of their liberty, emphatically stated that God would be displeased at the measure, and would not hear them; that such renunciation was especially hateful to him; that it aggravated all their guilt since they came out of Egypt. The Hebrews were often and long in the practice of the true principles of civil liberty. Their Creator was their teacher, and their souls were elevated and purified by the virtue and prowess of their valiant chiefs and inspired prophet-poets—Moses, Joshua, Gideon, Samuel, David, and Solomon. When they forsook those principles, courage and success failed them together; and they were conquered and dispersed into endless exile, by Assyrian and Babylonian armies.

Thus it appears, both by the prosperous obedience and the fatal disobedience of the Jews to the divinely given free organic law of their national existence, that God revealed plainly and emphatically the truth, that the will of the people constituted the government; that precisely as that will was upright and wise, or degraded and foolish, the government was good or bad, and the commonwealth prosperous or unprosperous.

The whole of profane history is full of examples proving the same point. By the actual choice of the nations, or by their satisfied acquiescence, have the great majority of rulers been chosen. The Spartans chose their kings by vote for their ability to govern, to lead in war, to conquer. The Athenian, and, indeed, all the Greek States, elected their ordinary rulers, and likewise the leaders who commanded their armies in extraordinary emergencies. Romulus was elected, as were his immediate successors. And when Tarquin undertook to govern despotically, Brutus and his fellow-freemen taught the tyrant a lesson, and established the Roman Republic. The popular will of the Romans chose not only their annual consuls, but also a dictator, putting the whole government for the time being into the hands of a Camillus or a Scipio, because only such a man could perform what the nation desired. The Franks and the Saxons, the Goths and Vandals, chose their leaders on the field of battle, or in the camp; selecting the men who could lead most successfully the national army, and so guide the popular will to fulfilment. The great Tartar tribes, the Huns who came into Europe, and the enormous hordes who from time to time have ravaged and conquered Asia, all in like manner chose their leaders on account of their fitness so to administer the concerns of the nation as to fulfil its wishes. The Turks and Saracens, while they made conquests, were commanded by chiefs chosen by the nation, or acquiesced under as suitable to govern it. The French dynasties have repeatedly perished for incapacity, and stronger men have founded others, with the consent of the people. Neither Meroveus, Pepin, nor Hugh Capet, could secure the inheritance of their throne to incapable men. All the warlike leaders who descended upon the west and south of Europe, from Scandinavia, during the early part of the Middle Ages, were appointed by their followers, as were, indeed, the kings of the Scandinavian kingdoms. But the citations of individual cases would be endless. Always it has been either the actual selection of the people, or their satisfied acquiescence, which has supported the government. This popular appointment or permission may most often have been injudiciously made,—the acquiescence may have been that of the most stupid folly or sottish cowardice,—but such has been the case.

Emperors, kings, hereditary and usurping rulers, the governors of republics and monarchies and oligarchies alike, all have rested upon the support of the people. Whenever the government has become sufficiently disagreeable to the people to excite them to the proper point, it has fallen helplessly before their wrath. The thrones of tyrants are proverbially unsafe. Most true was that bitter and famous jest of Dionysius with his flatterer : the sword hangs over the tyrant's head by a single hair.

Freedom and intelligence have ever secured strength and respect to nations and to their members. The close phalanx of the Greeks, few in numbers but strong with the generous discipline of freedom, mowed down as grass the great Persian hosts. It was for such a reason that Cyrus the Younger trusted more in this ten thousand Greeks, than in all his Asiatic hosts ; and in that immortal retreat of which Xenophon was first leader and then historian, through a thousand miles of hostile country not an enemy ventured to oppose them in battle array. The proud consciousness of such powers stimulated Agesilaus, with only thirty-six Spartans, and neither money nor influence, to levy war against Artaxerxes, the monarch of all Asia. Such powers carried Alexander and his Greeks conquering through a continent. Such power enabled the small Swiss republics to beat off the repeated attacks of the Austrian empire, and made the Dutch victorious over the veteran Spanish infantry, although commanded by the best generals in Europe. Such power has made England the first among the nations. Such power enabled the Old Thirteen Colonies to resist her; and is making the empire of which they were the nucleus, first her rival, and then her superior. Free nations have never been conquered or resisted but with the extremest difficulty. No monarch could overcome Greece or Rome, as long as Greece and Rome were free. But with their loss of freedom declined their power; and in proportion as they became enslaved and debauched at home, they were impotent abroad. The Romans, who trode down more kingdoms than any other single people, in losing liberty lost both vigor and virtue, and lived ignobly, content with *panem et circenses*—"bread and the circus."

Thus liberty has not only strengthened the strong, and fortified the souls of the valiant, but it has always and everywhere breathed courage even into the timid, and supplied the feeble with strength.

We have shown, then, that God, in three revelations, has revealed the truth, that government is properly the free exercise of the will of the people:

I. By the consciousness of the truth, existing in the soul of all.

II. By express inspired revelation to the Jews, and by definitely establishing such institutions among his own chosen people.

III. By revelation to human reason, through the lessons of history.

Man, therefore, was created by God to be free. As He created man upright, so He breathed this principle of freedom into his soul. And every disuse or loss of its exercise is owing, as all of our human imperfections are owing, to the "many inventions" that men have "sought out." Liberty is a right given by God to every individual man. Free political institutions are of immediate divine origin. They are God's appointed means of insuring the utmost freedom of each citizen, together with the utmost prosperity and peace of the State. They are the gift of God; and when men refuse that gift, they suffer the consequences. Freedom is the life and strength of the individual and of the State. Its prosperous exercise demands intelligence and union. Many causes have retarded its extension. Physical force has predominated in the earth. The apostles of freedom have been silent or destroyed. Yet the basis of freedom exists in every human heart; and wherever human nature is elevated, morally and intellectually, to a sufficiently lofty position, there free political institutions must necessarily follow.

Free government is the legitimate government of the world. It is the one form of State authority which is founded upon the everlasting justice of God, which appeals to the universal conscience and consciousness of men. By virtue of the immortality of truth, we are bound to hope and expect that it will finally become the sole and universal government which shall exist on earth.

MEXICO AND THE SOUTH AMERICAN STATES.

"Progress, the growth of power, is the end and boon of liberty. Without this, a people may have the name, but want the substance and spirit of freedom."—CHANNING.

THE republics of Mexico and of Central and South America, when compared with the great Anglo-American republic, instead of presenting any analogy, exhibit a striking contrast in their political, social, and moral aspects. The question naturally suggests itself, What has produced this marked dissimilarity? What have been the procuring causes that have rendered those States, possessing territories more extensive and more fertile than those of the United States at their original settlement, so weak and powerless? The problem is not of difficult solution.

Avarice and rapacity marked the career, in South America, of the colonial system of Spain. The interests of the colonists were sacrificed; the spiritual tyranny of the Inquisition suppressed all freedom of thought or action; and crushing monopoly stifled all attempts at domestic industry or commerce,—for it even denounced death against all who were detected in trafficking with foreigners,—whilst the vines and olives of Mexico were rooted out, that its inhabitants might be compelled to draw their supplies from Spain; and the wheat which the colonists were forbidden to export, was applied to fill up the marshes. Not only did the Romish priesthood control the bodies and souls of the Mexicans, but the crafty policy of old Spain kept them in the grossest ignorance and degradation.

"Still promising
Freedom, itself too sensual to be free,
Poisons life's amities, and cheats the soul
Of faith, and quiet hope, and all that lifts
And all that soothes the spirit."—COLERIDGE.

It was remarked by the Duke of Wellington, that, in all his experience with Spanish official men, acquired during the Peninsular war, he met with hardly a single man whose abilities rose above the meanest order of mind. If this be their national characteristic, no wonder they prefer to perpetuate ignorance.

The specious and subtle policy of Spain failed, however, in great part, of its accomplishment. Much of the precious metals became diverted to other countries, as fast as they were robbed from the natives of Hayti, Mexico, and Peru. Yet vast were the treasures that flowed into the exchequer of the haughty and sanguinary Spaniards. The cupidity of Spain seems only to have been equalled by her perfidy and cruelty. In order to retain conquests, the natives were exterminated. The spirit of her government was tyranny; the discipline of her Church, persecution; her moral of trade, monopoly. The long duration of these fallacies rendered them, in Spanish wisdom, venerable. The Spaniards believed the precious treasures of the New World exhaustless. They imagined their power invincible: their ambition and pride exceeded all limits. But her haughty spirit was doomed to quail before her rivals; and the pomp and chivalry of Spain, like her wealth and power, became the sacrifice required of her political crimes.

In order to a right estimate of Mexican character, it will be necessary to refer to the characteristics of the Aztec race prior to the conquest of Cortes.* Our historian, Prescott, here comes to our aid. After speaking of the romantic and legendary features of the conquest, he remarks:

"Yet we cannot regret the fall of an empire which did so little to promote the happiness of its subjects, or the real interests of humanity. Notwithstanding the lustre thrown over its latter days by the glorious defence of its capital, by the mild munificence of Montezuma, and the dauntless heroism of Guatemozin, the Aztecs were emphatically

* The ancient Mexicanos were descendants of the Aztecas; they assumed the name of Mexicos, from Mexictl, that of their chief idol. Prior to the arrival of the Spaniards, they lived under a kind of oligarchical government.

a fierce and brutal race, little calculated, in their best aspects, to excite our sympathy and regard. Their civilization, such as it was, was not their own, but reflected, perhaps imperfectly, from a race whom they had succeeded in the land. It was, in respect to the Aztecs, a generous graft on a vicious stock, and could have brought no fruit to perfection. They ruled over their wide domains with a sword, instead of a sceptre. They did nothing to ameliorate the condition or in any way promote the progress of their vassals. Their vassals were serfs, used only to minister to their pleasure, held in awe by armed garrisons, ground to the dust by imposts in peace, by military conscriptions in war.

"The Aztecs not only did not advance the condition of their vassals, but, morally speaking, they did much to degrade it. How can a nation, where human sacrifices prevail, and especially when combined with cannibalism, further the march of civilization? How can the interests of humanity be consulted, where man is levelled to the ranks of the brutes that perish? The influence of the Aztecs introduced their superstition into lands before unacquainted with it, or where, at least, it was not established in any great strength. The example of the capital was contagious. As the latter increased in opulence, the religious celebrations were conducted with still more terrible magnificence—in the same manner as the gladiatorial shows of the Romans increased in pomp with the increasing splendor of the capital. Men became familiar with scenes of horror, and the most loathsome abominations. Women and children,—the whole nation,—became familiar with and assisted at them. The heart was hardened; the manners were made ferocious; the feeble light of civilization, transmitted from a milder race, was growing fainter and fainter, as thousands and thousands of miserable victims, throughout the empire, were yearly fattened in its cages, sacrificed on its altars, dressed and served at its banquets! The whole land was converted into a vast human shamble! The empire of the Aztecs did not fall before its time."

"The American Indian has something peculiarly sensitive in his nature. He shrinks instinctively from the rude touch of a foreign hand. Even when this foreign influence comes in the form of civilization, he seems to sink and pine away beneath it. It has been so with the Mexicans. Under the Spanish domination, their numbers have silently melted away. Their energies are broken. They no longer tread their mountain-plains with the conscious independence of their ancestors. In their faltering step, and meek and melancholy aspect, we read the sad characters of the conquered race."

The earliest insurrection of modern Mexico against Spanish rule, occurred in 1809, headed by Hidalgo and Allendo. Its real object was not, however, the establishment of a republic, but an abortive attempt to reserve to Ferdinand VII. a portion of his dominions, whose sovereignty in Spain had been alienated to France. Subsequent commotions took place, when something like a democratic basis of government was projected, but rejected by Iturbide, who, in 1822, was declared emperor by the people, but who, before a new order of government could be organized, was, as he deserved to be, deposed and banished;—he was but a military usurper.

In 1824, Mexico became a republic, and a federal constitution was adopted. General Victoria was elected the first President, and he has been succeeded by such men as Pedraza, Guerrero, Bustamente, Santa Anna, Herrera, and Paredes, as Presidents or Dictators, at best, with scarcely an exception, rival military adventurers. Actuated by no higher motives than those of personal aggrandizement, they manifested no patriotism above party purposes, and but little conscience above self-interest. Having no hold upon the affections of the people, they relied upon no security except military rule, and this was made subject to the greatest treachery, or to the greatest cunning.

We have a glimpse of her political condition in the following:

"The unfortunate, miserably governed Mexico, when she emerged from her revolution, had in her history nothing of representative government, habeas corpus, or trial by jury; no progressive experiment tending to a glorious consummation; nothing but a government calling itself free, with the least possible freedom in the world. She had collected, since her independence, three hundred millions of dollars, and had unprofitably expended it all in putting up one revolution and putting down another, and in maintaining an army of forty thousand men, in time of peace, to keep the peace."*

The pictures we have of social life in Mexico are revolting to contemplate. The Mexicans are, as a people, a nation of swindlers, thieves, and murderers. Their vacillating government has proved false to every sacred trust, has impoverished the country, debased the people, countenanced crime, engendered civil war, and tolerated treason. It has ignored all progress, neglected education, and discouraged domestic industry. The only party that thrives in the midst of all this moral desolation, is the Romish priesthood. To them belongs a large portion of the real wealth of the country. There are in the city of Mexico alone, some eight hundred secular, and about two thousand regular Romish clergy. They take care of the money, and do their utmost to get it, even from the most abject, at the expense of suffering need. It is said there is more gross licentiousness and vice in Mexico than in any other country on the globe. The Romish Church has nowhere so corrupt a priesthood. What moral lesson are we to gather, then, from the republic of Mexico? Is it not surprising that it has existed so long—so racked with discordant elements, and so *effete* and demoralized with crime?

Peru is believed to have been founded about the middle of the twelfth century, by Manco Capac, the first of the race of the Incas. The Peruvians were in advance of other aboriginal tribes, having acquired some proficiency in architecture, sculpture, mining, agriculture, etc. They knew something of the arts, for they constructed suspension bridges over frightful ravines, although they had no implements of iron; but their forefathers could move blocks of stone as huge as the sphinxes and Memnons of Egypt, and had an acquaintance with astronomy, several of the useful arts, and various domestic manufactures. They were pagans, and the ruins of their numerous temples and palaces are yet to be traced. The great Tem-

* Daniel Webster.

ple of the Sun at Pachacamac, the palace and the fortress of the Incas, were connected together, so as to form one great building, about a mile and a half in circuit. Their code of civil and religious laws were favorable to morals; and they did not, like others, sacrifice human victims to propitiate their deities. On the arrival of the Spaniards, in 1524, Huana Capac, the reigning Inca, and the fourteenth of his order, was made prisoner and perfidiously put to death by Pizarro, the discoverer of the country, although the poor captive had paid, according to the stipulation, as much gold for his ransom as would fill the place of his confinement! Although Pizarro founded the city of Lima, and had thought himself secure, yet several insurrections ensued with various success, until the surrender and execution of the last of the Incas, in 1562, when the Spanish rule was established.

The State founded by Pizarro remained a dependency on the Spanish crown until the year 1782, when an outbreak occurred, and the standard of independence was reared, around which the natives rallied with great spirit, and in great numbers. For two years the war continued with alternate success; the enterprise, however, finally suffered defeat. But these efforts were triumphant in 1817, under General San Martin; and in July, 1821, the independence of Peru was solemnly proclaimed, with San Martin as Protector. This office he resigned, after constituting a Congress; but its inefficiency soon became apparent. In 1823, the patriots were defeated, the Congress dissolved, anarchy predominated, and Lima again surrendered to the Spanish troops. They were, shortly afterwards, partially dispossessed by Bolivar, and the Chilians; but Peru, though freed from Spanish subjugation, was like a vessel tossed by every casual wave, unsafe, and exposed to conflicting dangers.

The history of Upper Peru, better known as Bolivia, a name it derives from its great deliverer—Bolivar—is briefly told. Previously to the battle of Ayachuco, in 1824, it formed a part of the viceroyalty of Buenos Ayres; but General Sucre, at the head of the republicans, having then defeated the royalist troops, the independence of the country was effected; and in the following year, at the request of the people, Bolivar drew up its constitution. Soon, however, domestic factions sprung up, the purity of his motives were questioned, and he was suspected of aiming at a perpetual dictatorship. He gave, however, a noble denial to these unjust imputations, by quelling the disturbances that affected the State, and then retiring to private life. For a time he was recalled to the exercise of the chief authority, till 1830, in which year his death occurred. The government is still in the hands of a President; and it may be said this republic is, of all those of South America, the best as to its internal quiet and prosperity, for most of them are, indeed, republics but in name.

It is needless to fatigue the reader with historic details of the several independent States and Confederacies of Central and South America. Grouping them together, we may sum up the whole by saying, that they have been but experiments towards freedom, and, without exception, unsuccessful experiments. Knowing comparatively little of the sweets of real liberty, they seem to be not very ambitious for its attainment; but a sluggish supineness renders them insensible to its value. An amusing illustration of this occurred not many years ago at Chili. At a dinner given to some officers of an American vessel on the fourth of July, one of our officers gave as a toast, "General Washington," when a Chilian followed with "The hundred Washingtons of South America!" In the republics of South America, which preserve the blood and the indolent pride of the Spaniards, constitutions are destroyed hourly, by the will of some Dictator; and the people, after a transient appearance in the career of civilization, fall back into the darkness of barbarism, and are not even conscious that they have been free for a day. Society, in short, stumbles at the first step it attempts to take forward, and falls helpless at the entrance of that path in which modern civilization springs forward, radiant and proud, to the goal.* While we, in common with the civilized world, have been constructing our railroads and steamships, many of the natives of these States pursue the barbarous custom of travelling on the back of a man, or of a mule, and thus pursue journeys of several

* Malte-Brun.

days across a stony and rugged country. Every species of social and moral degradation seems to prevail. The principal occupation of the wealthier class consists in doing nothing; that of the majority something worse—surrendering themselves to filthiness and vice.

It has been already intimated that the superior progress in civilization of the United States is the fruit of the Protestant faith. It is to the refining, elevating, and hallowing influences of a pure Christianity, that we trace the high developments of social and civil order to which Protestant America has attained. The Bible is the bulwark of a nation's safety and success. Need we proofs, we have the fact amply illustrated in the comparative civilizations of the northern and southern portions of our own continent.

A few men land, one by one, on the shores of North America, poor, humble, and unknown; they bring with them but one book, the Bible; they open it on the rocky strand, and begin immediately to construct their infant community or commonwealth in accordance with its sacred order, subordinating all to its claims. Their sympathies and aims are one in the common faith, and hope of its teachings. Amid the frosts of winter, and on a rugged, sterile soil, yet are they all undismayed.

"See the calmness and boldness of these men: we discover in the constitution of this rising empire, the fire of Luther united with the coolness of Calvin. Fancy pictures the scene all glowing with Christian beauty and heroism; with the sound of the axe and hammer, mingles the chant of a psalm. Their firm faith in the favor of their God renders them indifferent to dread of the desolate wilderness. The light of Heaven sanctifies their toil; and by a sort of social miracle the wilderness, and the solitary place, is made to blossom as the rose. Where once was the rude wigwam of the savage, we now behold thousands of cities, towns, and hamlets, filled with the abodes of peace and plenty.

"Look we on another picture. The proud monarchy of Spain sends her stately viceroy and armament, accompanied with the sanctions and pomp of Rome, to a country and a clime of luxuriant fertility, and which is known to abound in the precious metals. As if to render the contrast of circumstances the more convincing, nature herself seems to echo to her Maker's voice. In order that the test may be the more decisive, every physical advantage seems to be in favor of the mission of Romanism. But while all around is grand and gigantic, glowing with exuberant life and fertility, man is here in weakness, imbecility, and vice. He is under the vassalage of a spiritual thraldom, which effectually prevents the development of his moral and intellectual nature. To all the noble incentives to action he is alike indifferent; he is the victim of supineness, indolence, and immorality.

"What means this wondrous sterility in a new world, except that the idea brought thither had given elsewhere all its fruit; that Romanism, essentially conservative during three ages, has lost power of impulse—the creative spirit; and that, henceforth, she is incapable of giving to the wide expanse the word alone pregnant of a new social world; that her soul, imprisoned in the cathedrals of the mediæval ages, has no longer the strength of divine tempests to purify chaos and baptize continents.

"Let these nations of the South do what they will, they end inevitably by realizing in their government the ideal which they have inscribed on their state religion, that is, absolute power. All they can do is to change dictators, and thus we see them succeed in nothing but in tightening the bands of their thraldom. Progressive punishment! South America lies as it were at the foot of a vast upas-tree, ever distilling its torpor, while the trunk, rooted in another continent, remains visible."*

"The Spaniards, in spite of unexampled barbarities, which have covered them with lasting shame, have not succeeded in exterminating the Indian race, nor even in hindering their sharing their rights. The Americans of the United States have attained this double result, with a wonderful facility; quietly, legally, philanthropically, without bloodshed, without violating, in the eyes of the world, any of the great principles of morality."†

* M. Quinet. † De Tocqueville.

If respect for its laws be the test of the morality of a country, the South American States will be found miserably bankrupt in this particular: for hardly a day passes that is not the witness of the execution of some political offender, while "the United States of North America," writes M. De Tocqueville, "is, I think, the only country upon earth, where, for the last fifty years, not a single individual has been put to death for political crimes. There is not a single manufactory in Buenos Ayres that takes advantage of the products of the soil: thus the country grows poorer and poorer.* It is the same in all the republics of South America. The laws are wholly inoperative to suppress crime, consequently vices of the most hideous and revolting character obtain to an alarming extent. The social relations of life are in a state of moral putrefaction—the most extreme licentiousness prevails, and society exists only in name; its phases are as dark and degraded as in pagan lands. What a fearful responsibility, then, must attach to that pretended system of religion which, having absolute will over the minds and property of the people, can sanction and perpetuate such a state of things!

The South American "republics" teach the people of the United States the evils of a corrupt religion connected with the State, and the fearful consequences of intestine broils. Every month witnesses a revolution in some one of these distracted countries; and in the objectless struggles, neighbors and relatives imbue each other's hands in fraternal blood. Military executions constantly take place, and the patriot, and the ignorant victim of designing usurpers, are shot like dogs, and consigned to the earth. The imagination cannot comprehend the future of these countries; they seem every year to fall lower and lower in the scale of civilization. Arts, commerce, and the fruits of peace are decaying away. Nothing flourishes, but the processions—the feast-days—the pomps and ceremonies of the Roman Church.

* M. D'Orbigny.

AMERICA, THE THEATRE OF THE GREAT DEMONSTRATION.

"Into the full enjoyment of all which Europe has reached only through such slow and painful steps, we sprang at once, by the Declaration of Independence, and by the establishment of free representative government; government, borrowing more or less from the models of other free States, but strengthened, secured, and improved in their symmetry, and deepened in their foundation, by those great men of our own country, whose names will be as familiar to future times as if they were written on the arch of the sky."—WEBSTER.

It must strike every reflective mind, that ours is no history of mere chance, or even of simple fortune. This gigantic country, stretched between so many parallels of latitude, its shores washed by the two great oceans of the world, its past so wonderful, its present so great with mighty promises,—this America does not exist without a purpose, as if the careless hand of Chance had originated it, with no designed place among the other countries of the world, and no grand promise to perform for the regeneration of mankind. It is not possible, even for him who affects to disbelieve in the providence and the power of a God, to imagine that an existence like ours ever sprung out of the chaos of accident, or was the unlooked-for fruit of circumstances which never felt the guidance of a Supreme, controlling hand.

That we are specially deputed to begin and to carry out successfully the greatest social and political problem in the world's destiny, is enough to fill the breast of every man with hope-felt determination, for it commands our thoughts, our energies, and our faith. The sooner our citizens recognize this feeling, the speedier and the more energetic must be the steps in that great demonstration in which we are certainly the accredited principals. If individuals have a destiny marked out for them, suited to the inclinations and endowments of their natures,—must it not be equally true that *nations*, made up of vast masses of individuals, with all these same endowments and inclinations, have as large a share in the plans of that Providence which both rules and loves the world?

In our country, all things are new; and we ought heartily to thank God for having cast our lot, with this mighty experiment, too, in our keeping, in a locality where the fetters that belong to an old and effete society are not known. We often speak of our vast virgin soil, hiding nutriment enough in its bosom to sustain the entire population of our globe; but have we not as good cause to boast of that fresh and virgin-like way of thought, and that childlike and impulsive style of sentiment, which hitherto has made the despots and proud nobles of the Old World regard us with ineffable disgust, but which is now beginning to challenge real respect and admiration everywhere?

Yes,—let us thank God that with us, in this experiment on which we have entered, all things are new. Let us sing praises that we are neither hemmed in by any other tyranny than what we are free to impose upon ourselves, nor made timid by any of those eternal suspicions which rob older nations of their energy and their peace.

It is sufficiently apparent to even the least attentive observer, that the masses of Europe are fast growing restive under the old yokes and dominions; that the instinctive sentiment of manhood is rapidly rising and overgrowing every other idea in the breasts of the governed; that the millions of silent subjects in Europe are expectant of a dawn that shall call on them to rise from their sleep to the freedom of a glorious day. Who can tell how much of this is the natural result of our own quiet and dignified example? Or who will say how much these events in the world have, under God, been hastened by the steady and silent illumination which we have been offering for now three-fourths of a century? Such things as these are evidences enough of the depth of the sentiment of freedom, native in all breasts; as well as of the strength of that influence which our own country must of necessity exert wherever her institutions are generally known.

The past history of the world points with an unerring finger to America as the nation where all its old, and bloody, and unhappy experiences, are to be spoken of only as things belonging to darker times, to clouded intellects, and corrupt hearts; where what was bad is forever to be put behind us, and what is good is forever to allure us along; where oppression shall cease to be the law, and freedom no longer be the exception; where those true and lofty sentiments which belong to the human race, are henceforth to be allowed room for indefinite expansion; where government is to cease to be a crushing process upon the integrity of the heart and intellect, but is to take its very root and sustenance in the intelligent consent of those who are governed; and where the great truth, that peace is the natural political condition of the human family, and love is the loftiest and most absolute law, is to be not simply propounded, but proved.

Such are the important truths to the existence of which we, as a people, are to testify. This is the time for us to bear willing testimony, as we are the nation to whom the responsibility has been intrusted. Whether we will or no, our destiny, our history, our nature, our geographical position, our very inclinations,—all conspire to point us to our duty.

If we will but take the map and glance at the present geographical boundaries of our country, we shall see in a moment what a wide field for carrying forward this great political experiment we are in possession of. We people a variety of climates, such as no other nation on the face of the earth ever held direct ownership in. Our soil is calculated to furnish all the productions needed for the comfort and sustenance of man. We lie between the extreme latitudes of the temperate belt of the earth's surface,—a position of infinite consequence, when considered in connection with the world's past history; for it has been said with truth, that in none but temperate climates have the great deeds of human history been performed. The statement is well worth serious thought: it is, that nations only that are occupants of the *temperate* regions of the northern hemisphere, ever governed the world.

Let us see how such a statement is supported by facts:

Below the tropic of Capricorn, there is hardly enough of Africa to attract notice. South America lies chiefly between the two tropics, and has never brought forward any special claims either on the world's notice or admiration. Within the Arctic Circle, there is no better hope held out to the world; nor, in fact, has it ever been at all different through the whole course of history. Only one almost eternal winter reigns, against the long torpor of which men have but a very brief time to make provision, and during which term, all life, whether physical or spiritual, seems wrapped in fatal lethargy.

Now, if we leave these two extremes of the earth's surface, and come within the limits that geographically form the *temperate* zone, we find, in the first place, Asia, with a population of from five to six hundred millions, swarming, like bees in a busy hive. What great events in the drama of the world's history has not Asia brought forth? On her prolific soil was set the cradle of mankind; there Christ was born, there he delivered his message of love to mankind, and there was he at length crucified. There, too, were the great and powerful cities of antiquity; there lived and reigned David and Solomon; there spake the Apostles and the Prophets. The arts first saw their existence there—and science, and learning, and religion. In Asia, commerce first made men restless and energetic, and drove them to seek shorter routes to the parts of the world beyond them.

In Europe, the illustration is still more complete. There, exists a population numbering about two hundred and fifty millions, of various races and languages. In resources of every description—physical, intellectual, or purely spiritual—that population is astonishingly rich. We need but rehearse their deeds, to convince our reader of the vast native superiority of such a people over all others of the Old World. We have only to mention the names of Greece and Rome, to start in every mind the right thoughts on this subject. Of the world's great poets, who has not heard of Virgil and Homer? Of her orators, to whom are not the names of Demosthenes and Cicero familiar? Who has not yet heard of Plato? of Socrates? of

Aristotle? of Alexander? And to whose ears are not the sounds of both Cæsar and Brutus like "household words?"

But such an historical recital is needless. Every intelligent American citizen is well aware of the truth of these things, and how forcibly they bear on the point which we design to illustrate. All tend to show that over this belt of the temperate zone have passed, from the beginning, the power, the energy, and the promise of the world's final exaltation and redemption.

Exactly within this same favored limit, lies our own country. The United States of North America form a new nation in the history of the world. We are a people, likewise, whose government, both in its form and principles, is wholly peculiar. Nothing like it has the world ever seen or known before. In developing the details of such a form of government, we certainly have shown ourselves, thus far, both apt and energetic—shrinking from no responsibilities, and rising to the heights of heroism itself by the mere force and fulness of faith in our destiny. Having sprung from a race peculiarly educated, by means of the experiences of the generations gone before, we were first fitted, by this wise dispensation of Providence, for the reception of the broad and deep principles which pertain to our civil existence.

We have, then, to say, in the first place, respecting ourselves, that though perhaps as yet behind some of the European countries in particular fields of science, or literature, or general learning, we may, nevertheless, challenge the whole world in fair comparison with our people for general intelligence, for intellectual activity, for practical learning, for bold and comprehensive thought, and for striking and energetic action. The Americans combine elements in their character that no people, as a whole, ever possessed before. No sooner does a new or progressive idea become born in their brain, than it is forced into the notice and approbation of the world.

See how we cut the waters of rivers thousands of miles long, and plough our way majestically across the stormiest ocean of the globe. Count up the almost interminable lines of railroad over which steam is made to whirl us every day, and destined yet to lace a continent many times across. See with what overwhelming yet steady energy we tunnel mountains, skirt fearful precipices, fly over rolling prairies, and drive on with a noise of thunder to the extreme boundaries of the broad continent. All this, too, the work of a small cycle of years. And our experiments with electricity—what amazing wonders have been wrought in the briefest breath of time! The world may well look on astonished, though it hardly fills us at home with the same emotion. We comprehend now the answer to the sublime question put to Job: "Canst thou send lightnings, that they may go, and say unto thee, 'Here we are!'" And we feel that this is all but an experiment as yet, and so toil earnestly on after new victories, and the achievement of still grander successes. We are not yet content with this; we are content with nothing. Our action is fully up with our national motto, that watchword of the future—"Onward!"

We have conquered earth, air, water, and lightning successively. We have taught mankind how all things were at the first designed for their happiness and comfort, and that nothing was wanting but ingenuity and energy to unlock the hidden treasures of a globe. Our material greatness is not paralleled by that of any nation in existence. Wealth has flooded our coffers, and enabled us generously to offer a helping hand to the less fortunate ones of the world. Power has consequently increased, until we are acknowledged to be one of the great nations of Christendom—a nation on which are fixed the eager eyes of all mankind. And, to carry out the point still further, our population has increased in a ratio that seems really incomprehensible. The mind itself is hardly rapid enough to keep pace with the facts thus presented. It cannot be very long, at the present ratio of increase, before we shall have a population on our soil denser even than that which makes old China the standing wonder of the earth. And this crowded and busy people, alive to the vanquishment of time, space, and matter, must be the people from whose midst will go forth the manifold influences that are to subjugate all men and all things to their high sway. We do not contend that this new government will be in any way related to the tyrannies that have hitherto cast nothing but gloomy shadows over the hearts of mankind; nor that it is to seize hold of men and compel them to obey, or even to believe; but that in such a government will reside the spirit and essence of freedom, more than any other element,—that it will bring all men eventually out of political darkness into a world of mental light,—that it will succeed everywhere in establishing and vindicating individual manhood,—and that, with their native rights restored to them, men will at once feel new responsibilities, and assert their true claims to all that is high, and great, and holy in their nature.

This is plainly our mission. Is it not one of unsurpassed grandeur, both in itself and its results? Power for ages has gradually been moving westward, exactly through this geographical belt of the earth. Each successive step has been attended with still more important results. Every westward remove of this power has been marked with the burning of a still brighter light, and has left behind it a still more luminous track for mankind to gaze upon. It has now struck the Atlantic shore of North America, and, in a space of time almost incredible, has pushed its rapid way to the Pacific boundary. When it leaps that ocean, it gets back on its old ground again, and thus in its course the highest form of civilization has girdled the world.

Young and vigorous as America is, its youth and vigor are not to be wasted in dreams. Nor is there much fear, either, that such will be the case. Some timidly caution us against going "too fast," professing ignorance of where our destiny may lead us. That, however, seems plain enough to a mind possessed of true faith. Our course is clear; our mistakes are soon corrected by the aid of experience; our successes overwhelm the warnings of the hopeless, and bid us on.

We see, then, that the United States offer the field for the fair trial of this great experiment of man. The experiment is,—to learn whether men are of more worth than things; and if autocracies, and monarchies, and all tyrannies,—disguise them as you may,—are not violent usurpations of the very laws of existence. Upon our fortunes rests the destiny of the world. Our success and our example are making all peoples restive; our moral strength is more powerful than fleets, more dreaded by tyrants than unnumbered men in arms. We are to conquer, but not by the sword. We are to subjugate, but not by violence. All nations are to come under the sway of our principles, but never are they to pass under any yoke. All is to be freedom and light, and the eye is to see as clearly as at the noonday. Whatever is done, will be done in the direction of a single purpose: and that is, the *emancipation of our race.* We are not working for mere wealth; nor position; nor social consideration; but while laboring for all these, we are insensibly helping on the great cause, and solving the grand problem of a world's freedom.

America—not even yet thinly populated—is the battle-field where the contest is waged between the armies of freedom and tyranny. Every sign points to this imposing fact. Here the last great onset must be made by the phalanxes of darkness, bigotry, illiberality, and bondages of all descriptions; and, under God, if Americans are but true to themselves and their principles, here will occur a glorious victory for freedom and truth—a victory having the regeneration of man for its object, and the happiness of the universe for its result.

SECRET POLITICAL ASSOCIATIONS,

THEIR USE AND ABUSE

"A proper secrecy is the only mystery of able men: mystery is the only secrecy of weak and cunning ones."—CHESTERFIELD.

"A fool's mouth is his destruction."—SOLOMON.

A GREAT outcry has, of late, been raised against the use of Secrecy in political organization and action. It seems to be taken for granted that a secret mode of operation is sufficient to condemn the operator and his work, with all honest men. The prevailing mode of discussing the question is so very shallow and insufficient, that we shall here attempt to put it in its proper light, by considering the principle of secrecy in human action, and secret practices in American politics.

Very little argument is needed to prove, in general, that Secrecy, in itself, is of an indifferent quality, neither right nor wrong; and that it is only the use or abuse of it which renders it good or bad. Christ himself expressly enjoined secrecy in the performance of good deeds, with a force which he could not express, except by the Oriental hyperbole of commanding that the left hand should not know the doings of the right. Neither such actions, nor the personal religious exercises of his disciples, were to be spoken of or known farther than was unavoidable. Such concealment was practised by the Great Master himself. Again; how many human beings would like to be deprived of the use of secrecy? What would become of the shrewd enterprises of business men, if they could not keep their secrets until they are ripe? How endurable would it be to men in general, to know that all their memories and all their hopes—the faults they would fain forget, and the plans they would fain pursue—were to be seen and known of all men? As long as there are individual interests and human imperfections, so long must secrecy be an indispensable ingredient of human life. If the world were perfect—which would make it heaven—secrecy would be needless. Until then, it is not only proper and useful, but absolutely indispensable; although, like every thing else, it may be perverted to wrong uses.

Without further inquiry into a truth so abstract, and so unlikely to be denied, the proposition may now be laid down, that *Reforms* (real or pretended) *directed against powerful existing interests, begin with Secrecy.* Secrecy was the cradle of Christianity—the greatest Reform movement the world ever saw. Christ himself trusted in his Divinity; and knew that before his time no hands would be laid on him. Yet how often did he conceal himself from his enemies, once even by a direct exercise of miraculous power? And after his death, it is a fact as notorious as any in the whole range of history, that without a practice of concealment more elaborate and profound, perhaps, than any other ever known, the new-born faith would have been exterminated from the face of the earth, simply by the murder of every professor of it. For years and years together, every discoverable Christian had forthwith to choose between apostasy and death. The reason is clear. Christianity was held to be at enmity, first with the established religion of the Jews, the most ferocious and unrelenting of bigots, and afterwards with the Roman Imperial Power, the greatest existing interest on earth.* At the beginning, the weak young twig had to be hidden from the destruction with which all the powers of the earth menaced it. But as it grew up into a noble tree, it threw off its cloak of secrecy. It retains it, however, even to the present day, in countries under the domination of savage Paganisms, or scarcely less savage Romanism.

The lesser reform movements before the great Protestant Reforma-

* De Quincy, Hist. and Crit. Essays, vol. ii. Secret Societies, p. 338.

tion in the sixteenth century, and indeed that Reformation itself, took more or less refuge in secret investigation and secret communion; and for the same reason, viz., that open profession would have endangered the whole movement. Luther, proclaiming aloud his earliest doubts of the Romish doctrines, would have suddenly and silently disappeared. Indeed, it was only a like disappearance into the friendly concealment of the Wartburg, that saved him from the actual gripe of the iron-handed Church of Rome. Wicliffites and Hussites, wherever they could be hunted out, followed the fiery path to Heaven trod by their bold teachers, whose Reformations were substantially quenched in blood.

The Romish Church is a secret organization. It distinctly claims, and always attempts (and has too often succeeded), to over-influence and thoroughly control and direct all civil governments. For this purpose, as well as for the purpose of retaining a good hold upon the people at large, its constitution has always been essentially secret. It has operated through mystic forms. It uses an unknown tongue in its ritual. It wields a secret influence through the confessional. It centralizes its power in the hands of one man, and so proceeds that the masses of lay members, who are the basis of that power, are utterly ignorant of the mode of its use. The two great instruments, moreover, of the Romish Church—the two griping talons which serve it as his two great claws serve the lobster, to seize, hold, and crush its victims—are the Jesuits and the Inquisition. The Jesuit claw is for governments and nations, the inquisitorial claw for individuals. It is unnecessary to show how secrecy is the very life and breath of these wicked engines. They could no more live or work without it, than a fish could breathe without water.

This secret plotting of the Romish Church, and the secret manœuvring of its two ministering spirits, have become so notoriously and undisputedly believed, that they serve to supply some of the commonest and most forcible words of the English tongue. Seek out a name for some false and treacherous proceeding; for some revoltingly tyrannical piece of oppression under forms of legal inquiry; or for the man guilty of such things;—the proceedings, you say, are a Jesuitical plot; or they are an Inquisitorial proceeding. The man is a Jesuit; a crafty, Jesuitical fellow. Fasten those names on him or his schemes, and whatever an ill name can do, is done.

Yet notwithstanding this secret character—perhaps we should say, according to it—the Romish Church has invariably sought to destroy all secret organizations not professedly subordinate to it, by arms spiritual and temporal—sometimes by cursing, and sometimes by burning. The Freemasons were excommunicated by a Bull of Clement XII. Freemasonry has been the crime for which many victims of the Roman Inquisition have died in the fire, or suffered torture and confiscation. The purely literary or philosophical Illuminati and Rosicrucians in Germany, the Carbonari in Italy and France, the Freemasons and Odd-Fellows everywhere, have operated under open opposition, and even actual persecution.

To leave organizations distinctively religious—The Illuminati and Rosicrucians, although they proposed only philosophical investigations, or the moral and intellectual improvement of their members, yet used doctrines so liberal as not to be orthodox in the estimation of established governments; and therefore necessarily worked secretly, as long as they existed. The United Irishmen, who aimed at establishing an independent government in Ireland, worked in the profoundest secrecy; were a terrible bugbear to the English government, and were finally suppressed by it. The Italian Carbonari, as well as their successors who are yet seeking the freedom of Italy, held their lives in their hand. They existed, as they yet exist, only because the Romish despots of the Peninsula could not find them. Patriot Republicans, seeking the freedom of Hungary, yet live amidst the oppressive and penetrating espionage of Austrian soldiers and Austrian pettifoggers, solely by secrecy. The bullet, or the hangman's rope, would be their portion within the day of their discovery.

But it is needless to multiply instances. In religious, politico-religious, and political movements alike, for purposes good or bad, in every case when they have directly or indirectly opposed strong constituted interests, secrecy has been an element. Especially, it is hardly possible to name an important political enterprise, successful or not, which has not been nursed under a secret shadow. Our own history informs us, that the *Convention which framed the Constitution of the United States sat with* CLOSED DOORS from the 25th of May, to the 17th of September following.

Few words, indeed, are more familiar to the reader of history, than *plot* and *conspiracy*. We barely suggest the English Revolution of 1688; the Irish revolutionary efforts from 1780 to 1848; the various French Revolutions; the Hungarian Revolution; the Italian, German, and other Continental Revolutions of 1848; the periodical pop-gun revolutions of Mexico and South America; and our own Revolution of 1776. The beginnings of such enterprises, according to the Greek fable, must be hidden, as the baby Jupiter was on Mount Ida, otherwise they will be swallowed up by the powers that be; as Saturn, the constituted authority of the period, swallowed up all Jupiter's little brothers and sisters; and for a like reason. The old monster knew that it was foretold that one of them should supersede him. But when the new-born power has strength enough to proceed openly, it does as Jupiter did—it vigorously assaults and dethrones the wicked Titans.

In the political management of the present day, more peaceful phases of the spirit which operated the bloody plots of old times, yet prevail. Secret political machinations are perhaps as numerous, and as harmful, in our free nation, as in any other. Our parties originate in secret scheming, and are managed by secret scheming. Who knows the *facts* of the political life of any leading politician of the present century?—how he secured a nomination; arranged with the "friends" of this or that rival; secured the support of this or that leading newspaper? Mackenzie's notorious Collection of Letters is a series of confidential communications passing among the set of New York politicians, of whom Martin Van Buren was one. It furnishes a great mass of details relating to the mingled threads of their personal and political fortunes, as unreservedly discussed among themselves. That collection, embracing many documents referring to the lives and fortunes of Van Buren, Hoyt, Swartwout, B. F. Butler, Cambreleng, and the numerous tribe of their allies and followers, furnishes the best illustration ever yet published, of the spirit and practice of American politicians. And throughout the long and tortuous series of transactions of which it treats, it is secrecy always, and inviolable, which is assumed to be the cloak and necessary medium of all the enterprises and combinations.

Was it open management that organized the opposition that latterly arose against Washington's administration, under the name of the Republican party? Was it open management that nearly made Aaron Burr President of the United States? Is it open management that at the present day presents candidates for the suffrages of American freemen? Did open management nominate Polk or Pierce for the Presidency? Who knows, indeed, how his own State Governor was nominated and chosen; how many sly bargains and private schemes were contrived and executed to complete the present organization of any State Legislature? Who knows even the precise mode in which were selected and appointed the municipal government of his town or city, and the business committees under it, or even the officers of his school district? Who knows precisely how are originated and carried through such measures as the Nebraska Bill; the Collins Mail Appropriation; or any other of the public or private measures that yearly are enacted by Congress? Who knows how the State Legislature is guided; or how the vote in town meeting or city council, for or against a sewer or a park, is arranged? It is not claimed that *nobody* knows, by any means. A few know; and these few take very good care *not to tell. The main body of voters* DO NOT KNOW *how or why the men for whom they vote, were set up for suffrage.*

It is true that the old political parties, in their "nominating conventions," proceed with open doors; speeches are made, and resolutions adopted, but all this machinery amounts to nothing more than the mere publication of the acts of secret committees, the moving cause and reason for the resolves being unknown and unseen. When the great elections are pending, does not each party have its secret agents in Washington—meeting in dark conclave—flooding the country with sealed packages? And does not the party in power carefully keep the key of the Post-office? Is not then the finger pressed on the lips? "Say nothing!" "Keep dark!" These and other cabalistic words, with all the mysterious inuendos of conspiracy, are uttered with low tones and smothered breath; and all justified, commended, practised, and applauded. What, then, is there so strange in the practice of the American party, desiring to keep its own secrets?

Secret management, by the retention of these "State secrets" in the hands of a few astute men, who handle the caucus and convention machinery, the parties through it, and the nation through the parties; is the whole essence of political operations in the United States. Indeed, our political parties belong to the most perfect species of secret organizations, because the rank and file of the army do not know its leaders.

The conclusions thus far reached in this chapter are these:

1. Secrecy is indifferent in itself, and good or bad according to the use which is made of it.

2. Secrecy is often necessary in the beginnings of reformatory enterprises which interfere with established interests.

3. Secrecy is an established and universal element in the usual course of American politics.

The American Party is young. It has grown to its present stature by the spontaneous gathering of the people to its standard, rather than by the efforts of any apostles. Its strength has come voluntarily from either of the two great parties, or from the increasing host of political sectarians or neutrals. The active enmity of all these it naturally would and did incur. The masses of these established organizations were not altogether opposed, as the success of the new-comer shows, to its principles: but the leaders of them were in the unhappy case of a sleeping cur whose tail is pinched. They jumped up in a fury, and barked at all creation. But they did no execution, because they did not know where the trouble came from. Under such irritating circumstances, it is perfectly natural that they should indulge in condemnations of the very practices which are the basis of their own influence. People seldom relish being attacked with their own weapons. Their editorial yokefellows were in the same difficulty, and were further annoyed at the slight put upon their professional importance. They could not discover the facts about this new movement, either for their personal gratification, for paragraphs and editorials in the paper, or for the use of "the party." They considered that they had a prescriptive right to know every thing first, and to tell it or not, at their discretion; and here was something of which they seemed doomed to know nothing, first or last, except by its results. So they very generally joined in the outcry. It was to be expected that editors, shut out from all participation, would revile an organization that they knew nothing about; and that politicians, with their legs knocked from under them by invisible blows, should cry out in distress as they fell into the pit which their own hands had prepared.

No one doubts, however, that the safety ensuing upon this mode of action has, in fact, saved the American Party from very great dangers, if not from destruction. It has confounded and confused all measures of opposition. If there had in the beginning been open proselyting, importunate grasping after disciples, and all the ordinary "advertising department" of new enterprises, would not the usual party discipline have sufficed to keep the new party down, and the old ones together? There would have been a great blustering show of argument for some, and of threats and promises for others. But these accustomed weapons were useless, because the enemy was invisible. There may have been very many errors in the practical details of the plans adopted to secure this secrecy. It is not necessary to claim perfection for human productions. But this secret mode of operating, if the history of our political parties is authority, is in itself proper and defensible.

Secrecy is not a necessary constituent principle of the American Party. Secrecy is an old abuse—an established vicious practice of the old parties. It was a temporary necessity of the new party. But if the American Party has any mission in this respect, it is to break up the secret mode of operating, and to introduce a new and open mode of political action. It proposes to destroy the old irresponsible despotism which has been exercised over the masses of the people, and to introduce the present generation, for the first time, to a free democratic practice in self-government. The American Party proclaims the New Era of Government by the Intelligent Action of American Freemen. This is now, in effect, a new principle. This Intelligent Action *is* a necessary constituent principle of the new party. And by just so much as the members of it are more intelligent, by as much the permanent maintenance of the secret mode of operation is less practicable. Accordingly, the approaching end of this state of things is shown by the many and significant secessions, and threats of secession, which are already dividing the Party in various States. Now, therefore, the American Party needs carefully to consider whether henceforward an open activity—a new thing in American politics—is not its necessary condition of success. This "unprecedented attraction" will be much more potent than the veil of a concealment which, after all, is enticing to the weak-minded rather than attractive to the wise.

The American Party has not been organized to take advantage of secrecy, as if it were a newly discovered method of political operation. It has been organized to work *against* secret political organizations, namely, the old political parties, and the Romish Church. It does not attempt to introduce an unjustifiable *new* mode of political management; it proposes to destroy an unjustifiable *old* mode. It is already contrasted with the old parties by its free and bold avowal of that secret mode of operation which they used *without* avowing it. It now has an opportunity to cast away even this avowed secrecy, and to enlist our voters into a great and new party—a united, intelligent, free and open organization of American freemen, expressing their own views and wishes as to the government of their own country; when *that* shall have been accomplished—America will be redeemed, not from Popish Jesuits only, but from political Jesuits as well. Then will be inaugurated the dominion of true political freedom; of which there is practically none, to-day, in these United States.

THE AMERICAN REPUBLIC, THE HOPE OF THE WORLD.

"The preservation of the sacred fire of Liberty, and the perpetuation of the Republican model of government, were considered by its founders as finally staked on the experiment intrusted to the hands of the American people."

WASHINGTON.

OURS is a period in the world's history, when great and important events crowd on the attention almost too rapidly to admit of properly studying them, or of estimating their consequences. The Present seems to be in league with the Future, to put to open shame the deeds of the Past. Events have run together so hurriedly for the last half century and more, that it would appear as if the time had arrived for their unravelment. Where the torpor of indifference has lain with its benumbing influence, symptoms are now beginning to be perceptible of returning consciousness and animation. The oppressed, whose energies have long been worn with the chain, are ready to herald the first ray of light in their prisons, with peans that shall reach the heavens. The weary-hearted are once more recruiting their strength, with the hope that the beautiful dream of their souls is about to find its happy realization. The blind are again groping about in their cells, calling for the aid of their deliverers. All things are made to feel the influence of the new spirit that rules the age.

The nations of the earth seem to be hurrying forward for the adjustment of accounts long overlooked and forgotten. All are eager to present their claims, and to receive, as soon as may be, the share that in equity is their own. Topics are now in discussion, that, but a short while ago, were left out of the category altogether. Interests that, till now, never presumed to thrust themselves from the oblivion in which they were buried, are now openly canvassed. Rights now find a tongue, that heretofore have been unnoticed and unknown, for want of any one to advocate and plead for them. The times are wonderfully changed. A revolution has been wrought. The sword has not done it, though the sword has been sheathed but little during this long interval; but it is the silent work of awakened and intelligent public opinion, which no power is able to withstand. It cannot be cajoled from its position; it cannot be bribed; once fixed, it cannot be driven from its place by either force or fear.

For years, the continent of Europe has been the theatre of revolutions, succeeding one another with a rapidity truly astonishing. France seems, from the beginning, to have been the furnace in which all the fires have originated. One ruler has given place in Paris to another, till it has become difficult to keep the various changes in mind. Thrones have been erected and overthrown, as if they were but the baubles and playthings which the greater Napoleon affected to consider them.

Italy has given signs of regeneration. Throughout her line of States, from time to time, encouraging voices have been heard in the name of liberty, and now and then her people have risen upon their usurpers, to wrest from them the power they have so wrongfully exercised. From far-off shores, the flame has been seen burning in that classic land; and hopes have been entertained that it was a bright and lasting illumination. But such hopes have all been cast down. With Austrian swords at their throats, and French bayonets at their breasts, it was scarcely to be expected that the people of Italy could succeed in so unequal a contest. A guard is quartered now in every house; but no military surveillance can imprison those expansive ideas, or the spirit of those vital principles, that spread so mysteriously over the face of a land. No power is sufficient to overawe those deep and scarcely audible mutterings, which presage the earthquake by which all things are destined to be shaken.

The struggle of Hungary for independence adds a new and bright chapter to the book of the world's history. It was an unsuccessful effort; and some may conclude that its failure established the worthlessness of the cause contended for: but the very unhappiness of the issue has had the effect to draw upon that people the sympathies of liberty-loving hearts everywhere, and their example has been recorded as one worthy of imitation, wherever the sound of freedom has been heard. Hungary reposes; but we believe that hers is the rest which recruits the strength, and precedes other and more earnest efforts in the cause for which her energies have been exhausted. She fell by treachery, more than by the combination of foreign enemies; and when her tattered ensigns are lifted again from the dust, the wish of all American hearts will be, that they may lead on her armies to the speedy and successful achievement of her freedom.

The German States from time to time have felt the throes of this mighty convulsion. Of all others, they seemed the least likely to resist the current of liberal ideas. They were the earliest to hail the light that came dancing over the earth, and welcomed it with hearts that had been tutored to the love of liberty. Great things were expected of them, and great things should have been performed. But the spirit was not universal. It had not yet struck deep root in the common heart. The masses had not yet gone far enough in that school of bitter experience which inculcates high resolves in man. The existing order of things carried a preponderating influence which was hard to overcome. The ancient and time-honored barriers it was difficult to remove; but another and a far mightier obstacle was, the close and compact union of absolutism in its own defence. Monarchy was made to feel that upon this one effort might forever depend its existence. The conspiracy was successful. The weary ones, whose faith had been so enduring in behalf of their holy cause, succumbed to the pressure they could no longer resist, and took up their abode in foul prisons,—wandered, sad-hearted, abroad, to eat the bread of exiles,—or laid down and died, desponding forever of freedom.

If we scan the history of Europe for the last few years, it will offer us little else than a confused record of struggles and repulses, of efforts and disappointments, of hopes and fears, of popular outbreaks and tyrannical usurpations. Sometimes, indeed, the rulers, trembling for their immediate safety, have granted concessions, in order to appease the popular clamor; but on regaining power, all these concessions have been blotted out, and tyranny has become more exacting than ever. In this, absolutism was only true to its own nature. As soon as it was safe to lay aside the mask, it never failed to exhibit its true character in all its hideous proportions. Not once has it offered gifts to the people, which it did not, at the time, resolve to take back again, with usurious interest.

Austria, Prussia, Russia, France—what else can the eye fasten itself upon in scanning the history of their more recent acts, but records of murder, of imprisonment, of fines and confiscations, of banishment, of leagues against liberty, of cruelty and tyranny in all their multiplied forms? Where is the hope to-day that their people are making themselves ready to go forward with the conflict that will reward them with freedom? How many of the population of those empires are languishing abroad at this moment, dying lingering deaths far from home and friends, rather than swear away the freedom of their consciences at the dictation of crowned conspirators! Who shall tell the number, or the acuteness of their sufferings? Who shall estimate the depth of that grief which seems able to consume both body and soul together?

Europe is now a seething caldron. The great game of the kings, carried on so long with impunity, at last appears to be completely blocked. The rulers are at a stand. Events have mastered ambitious men; and the extended laws of cause and effect, running silently through a course of centuries, at length seem about to vindicate their supreme authority. Politics is now another name for confusion. Ministers study and scheme how they may extricate their royal masters from their dilemma, and give over their efforts with exclamations of mortification and despair. The rulers grasp their sceptres more firmly, fearing that it cannot be long ere they must give them up forever. Cabinets have grown timid, and dare not assert with former boldness the policy of their several courts. There is a manifest want of confidence everywhere. Armies are called into service, till there are scarcely any men left to recruit them. The treasuries are depleted by enormous drafts, and bankruptcy and ruin threaten nations that but yesterday were prolific in resources.

But in the midst of this inextricable confusion, certain signs are beginning to betoken the increasing interest which foreign countries take in our national welfare. We see, from time to time, symptoms of a more decided leaning to republicanism. Here and there sturdy words are spoken—at the right time and in the right place—in our behalf. The spirit and principles of our government find admiring friends where it was least to be expected. Our institutions are criticised and commented on in an appreciative temper, and without that rancor and prejudice which was once so certain to be excited, by the mere mention of our name.

It is too important a truth for any of us to overlook, that the American Republic is the home of Liberty, and the final hope of the world. Through the efficacy of her example and her teachings, must redemption finally come. We hold the treasure in our own keeping; we are the trustees of a possession that is to enrich mankind. On our soil dwells that living spirit, which is, in time, to overthrow error, tear away the deceits of usurpation, deprive tyranny of its power, and everywhere animate the human soul with the belief that freedom was coeval with its birth.

If the world may not hope in us, then all hope is in vain. The experiment of a free government is one with which we have made ourselves familiar. With the institutions which belong to such a form of government, we have an acquaintance that is practical, and thus the more valuable. Their spirit has infused itself into our habits, our customs, and our ways of thought. If these privileges are worthy to be perpetuated, none ought to be more eager and earnest in the performance of such a work, than we who have so freely enjoyed them; and it should therefore be a labor of love with us, to publish their blessings to the world.

Foreign rulers no doubt regard us with jealousy, convinced that our system is incompatible with the secure existence of their own. It must be so, in the very nature of things. The work of Republicanism is a silent one, because it deals with the understanding alone. Other systems put forth military power, to crush out opposition by brute force, and to secure acquiescence by fear. But true Liberty has no such murderous weapons in her armory. The means by which she works are those that soonest disarm tyranny, and bring usurpers to confusion. She appeals not to prejudice, but to reason. She overcomes opposition, not with opposition, but with the teaching of sublime truths that cannot be resisted.

Americans should not forget their invaluable trust. They should be as true as their forefathers to the hope which is committed into their keeping. Through menace, and artifice, and open opposition, they should walk undaunted; holding their way with the resoluteness that will take them out of the reach of fear, and vindicating by every act of their lives those immortal truths which form the broad basis of our national existence.

Above all things, *sectionalism* is to be frowned upon as the worst enemy known to the republic. Let it come from what quarter it may, the heart that harbors the thought of it without fear, and without regret, is nowise worthy of the stamp of the American name. They who cherish it with the hope thereby of raising their individual fortunes, will certainly be classed with the Arnolds and Iscariots of our race.

It is a monstrous thing, that after so many years of national prosperity, the men can be found who dare openly excite one portion of our people against the other. Honest differences of opinion are to be looked for, and open expressions of those differences are a necessary consequence; but to excite treason, to inflame sectional prejudices, to build up barriers between one State and another, to breed a swarm of pestilential sentiments that threaten to infest the land like a plague,—is to put one's self without the pale of honorable American citizenship, and beyond the reach of honest men's consideration.

If we are to possess a nationality of our own, we must become one people. There can be no strength to the national character, if its forces are dissipated by domestic divisions. Unless we are able to stand together, we must straightway fall in pieces. The moment unity begins to relax, disease and death set in with all their ravaging train. Differences should exist only as spurs to efforts of greater patriotism. If they take hold on the character of citizenship itself, qualifying its value and demeaning its rank, they become mischiefs instead of aids, and ought to be silenced, even at the cost of the greatest sacrifices.

In so vast an area as that comprised within the limits of the United States, it would not be at all strange if there were a great diversity of interests. It is to be expected that, on numberless subjects of local concern, the inhabitants of the different sections should entertain directly opposite opinions. Nothing is potent to counteract the effect of these divisions, and to draw together the widely separated interests of our extended country, but some sentiment that shall take a deeper root in the heart than mere interest, and control all other influences by its superior power. We look in vain to any other sentiment for the performance of this work, than that of love for one's country. Once fixed in the heart, there is no supplanting it. It is strong enough to shape all the affections and interests that are recorded in the list of our common humanity.

And if other people are to be found whose hearts beat quick at the mention of their country's name, Americans have reasons a thousand-fold stronger for laying all their nobler feelings on the altar of patriotism. We are addressed by considerations such as appeal to no other people on the face of the earth; we have entered on an experiment without a parallel in the history of the world; we are seeking great and hidden truths; we hold the hopes of all liberty in our hands; and the wise men of other nations are watching the course of our star with both jubilant and prayerful emotions. Surrounded by such stern realities, and weighed down with these vast responsibilities, imposed by Heaven itself, he must utterly fail to understand his true relations to his fellow-men, or even to discern the meaning of his own existence, who remains indifferent to the great circumstances that beset his situation.

There is no safety for us, except in unity of feeling and harmony of action. We must learn to consider the whole country as dear to our hearts as any single part of it; to forget the too ready feelings which promote distrust and alienation; to cherish every true and noble sentiment that enfolds within its embrace the welfare of the whole of our common country; to cultivate feelings of brotherhood and peace; to hold steadily up to contemplation the one idea of our high American name and nationality.

No consideration should be allowed to take precedence of a spirit of patriotism. Our country before all things, should be both the sentiment and the motto. Union as well as liberty, should be on every one's tongue. Nationality as well as freedom, should vitalize the thought of every one's heart. No great good can be permanently secured, except by generous and oft-repeated sacrifices. No human institutions can hope for stability, unless they are founded in the deepest human conviction of their necessity, and sustained by the perpetual heroism of those to whom their value is apparent. We must either be brethren, or become aliens to the memories of the past. We must sink jealousies in nobler considerations, or lose sight of all the promises of our glorious future. We must earnestly determine to be nothing but AMERICANS,—knowing no greater name, and resolved that there shall be no greater nation,—and at once the bright inheritance becomes ours, and our grandest hopes leap forward to their swift realization.

Appendix.

I.

SECRET SOCIETIES AND OATHS.

Judge Gayle, of Alabama, formerly a Whig member of Congress, and a prominent man in his State and elsewhere, has written an able letter to some of his personal friends, from which we make the following extracts, bearing upon the political topics of the day. After considering and endorsing the platform of the American party as maintaining the great principles of free government, he gives reasons which ought to commend his views to all good citizens.

This remarkable party was formed some eighteen months since, to correct the flagrant abuses which had crept into public affairs, and which threatened the most serious consequences to the union of the States and the government. The arts of demagogues, and the corrupt practices of the two great parties of the country, had trained the public mind to regard with indifference, if not with approbation, the advancement of men without merit to the high and responsible trusts of the government, which had hitherto been reserved as the reward of experience, of wisdom, of tried patriotism, and of elevated and enlightened statesmanship.

Each of these parties professed to have some good principles, it is true, but all observing men witnessed, with disgust, the total disregard and abandonment of these principles in disgraceful and revolting scrambles for office.

The extraordinary increase of the foreign population had been witnessed with concern by all considerate Americans. Tides of immigration had wafted to our shores, in almost countless numbers, the people of all nations and all countries —of all grades, classes, and conditions—from the haughty Briton to the grovelling, besotted Chinaman; from the high-toned, educated gentleman, to the ignorant serf and convicted felon: all demanding and all alike admitted (none are ever rejected) to the privileges of the ballot-box, thereby filling our halls of legislation with men of their own choice, and exerting a commanding influence in the passage of laws for the government of this American country of ours.

They had seen these people occupying, as they are constantly doing, extensive districts of country in large communities to themselves—having but little intercourse with our citizens, without which they can never acquire the true American impression of our government, or imbibe the true spirit of our laws.

They had seen them form separate societies and associations, and organizing into large military bodies, to the exclusion of our people, showing an aversion to incorporate with them, or to assume the American character, and evincing a preference for the manners, habits, customs, and institutions of their respective nations.

They had seen them convene in large political assemblies, and with characteristic arrogance demand changes in our constitution and laws to suit the peculiar views in which they had been trained and educated from infancy.

And above all, and worse than all, they had witnessed the degradation of the country in our national legislature, by the passage of laws conferring upon unnaturalized foreigners the full right of suffrage in the territories, and all the other rights, privileges, and immunities which form the priceless heritage of the native-born citizen, in total disregard of the Constitution, which confers on Congress the power to pass uniform naturalization laws only.

The allegiance of these aliens is wholly due to the crowned heads of the countries from which they emigrated. They have no right to claim the protection of our government, or to petition for a redress of grievances. In case of war with the nations to which they belong, as alien enemies, they would be liable to be seized under the laws of Congress, to have their goods confiscated, and themselves imprisoned or sent out of the country. And yet it is upon these people, composed, as a large majorirty are known to be, of the vicious dregs of European society, that authority is conferred of controlling the ballot-box, and of exercising the high and responsible functions of our territorial governments. The right of suffrage has also been conferred on aliens in some of the States.

Now, if the foreign population has, at this early period of our history, acquired such commanding influence in our national and state legislatures, it requires no prophetic sagacity to predict that the day is not distant when they will control the destinies of this great republic.

This idea has strongly and universally impressed itself upon the public mind, and given rise to that truly noble and patriotic sentiment that "Americans shall rule America." This sentiment proclaims the existence of that intense American feeling and love of country which is a surer safeguard of our liberties than all our constitutions, and which can never more than partially animate the bosom of the foreigner, because nature has given him the same inspiration for his own native land.

The correction of these and other abuses, to the dangers of which no one can be indifferent, was the principal inducement to the formation of the American party. They saw that they had their origin mainly if not entirely in our naturalization laws. A million and a half of American voters have banded together in one great political brotherhood to cause these laws to be repealed or modified; and roused and animated as they are by the feeling just stated, you can no more defeat them, in their purposes, than you can suppress the feeling itself.

The feature of this remarkable American party that has been deemed most assailable, and accordingly has been attacked with the greatest violence and rancor, is the secret or private character of its organization. Jacobin club, secret conspiracy, underground party, dark-lantern party, and such like epithets, have been unsparingly applied to it. These are very ugly names, intended to awaken popular prejudice, and to render an object hideous which is otherwise comely enough.

The party is composed of numerous societies or councils, dispersed through the country, and established at localities to suit the convenience of its members. These localities are made public, the times of meeting are made public, their membership is public, and, what is of more importance, the result of their deliberations is made public. These councils, or societies, to accomplish the great objects of their institution, went sedulously to work, and their joint efforts, in an incredibly short space of time, have enabled them to lay before the public, the great principles, to the support of which they stand pledged before the American people. Their consultations, as to the details of their platform, were necessarily private; but when their great work was done, they submitted it to public inspection, and if well done, the public will not take the trouble to inquire into the process by which it was accomplished.

The simple question is, are these private associations, formed for great public purposes, hostile in their tendency, as they are asserted to be, to the free institutions of our country, and to the true spirit of the Constitution?

The right of the people peaceably to meet together and to consult upon public affairs, whether their meetings are private or public, whether in the form of private societies or public assemblies, has never before been questioned in this country, even during periods of the highest political excitement and exasperation.

As evincive of the jealousy and apprehensions of the fathers of the republic, they classed the right of the people peaceably to assemble (privately or publicly and without restraint) with the right of petition, religious freedom, the freedom of speech and of the press, and in the first articles of the amendments of the Constitution, prohibited Congress from passing any law to abridge them in any manner whatever.

These have always been revered by the enlightened friends of free government, as among the great elements of human liberty, and it is to be regretted, that, without reflection it is hoped, they or any of them should be denounced by persons of standing and character, as hostile to our free institutions.

If there is truth in history, private political societies have ever proved themselves the natural enemies of tyrants, and the natural and indispensable allies of republics. In despotisms they are resorted to by necessity, and in free governments through choice, as being more efficacious and convenient in compassing the objects proposed, whether they look to the improvements in government or to the correction of abuses. Since the accession of the house of Brunswick to the English throne in 1714, these private associations for all purposes, whether political, commercial, religious, or any other, have been of universal prevalence. They are so interwoven with the business of the people, in all its branches, that they have become a part of their social organization, and if any attempt were made to restrain them, a blaze would be kindled throughout England that it would be difficult to extinguish.

But of all countries in the world, they are most prevalent in the United States, especially those of a political character. They are the peculiar and exclusive machinery which have kept our political parties in motion during the entire period of our existence as a nation. This will be acknowledged by all, and denied by none. All the platforms that have ever been formed by these parties have been the result of private and secret meetings, of secret consultations and deliberations; and the mere matters of detail employed in their formation are never known, and never sought to be known, except at the instance of impertinent curiosity.

Pending our presidential elections, these societies are formed throughout the country under the name of clubs. They are as numerous as the cities, towns, villages, hamlets, and neighborhoods of the whole country, and all affiliated in a common brotherhood. The information of each is rapidly and secretly communicated to the others, and all their schemes, plans, and contemplated movements are as carefully withheld from the public as are the plans of hostile armies from each other. These periodical organizations are very much on the plan of those of the American party, and they are quite as secret in their character. No one has ever blamed or censured them for this, for it is obvious that without them success would be hopeless. It is therefore too late in the day to denounce private political associations, and anathemas come with a bad grace from those who invented, and have always resorted to them.

But the American party administer oaths to their members. This, in the opinion of its enemies, is very horrible, and the Billingsgate vocabulary is too meagre to supply appropriate epithets for its condemnation. It is, they say, anti-republican and anti-democratic. This accusation has been as inconsiderately made as that against the secret character of the order. If oaths are taken to bind men to a course of conduct that is moral, charitable, and benevolent in its purposes, or if they are taken to bind them to the support of the great principles of liberty as contained in the Constitution of the United States, such oaths cannot be regarded as either wicked, immoral, or unlawful. They are required to be taken by all public officers to support the Constitution, and it is not perceived that there is any thing wrong in requiring the members of a political party to come under the obligations of an oath to support the great principles contained in the same instrument, such as the right of petition, the liberty of speech and of the press, the purity of the ballot-box, &c., which are among the cardinal principles of the new party, and it is devoutly wished that they may be faithfully maintained, even if it be by the instrumentality of oaths.

But it is said that the members are required to swear that they will be governed by the decisions of the majority, and particularly in the nominations of candidates for office. The answer to this is, that any member dissatisfied with any of the principles or regulations of the party is at liberty to withdraw from the order, and he becomes immediately released from any oath he may have taken.

The charge of religious proscription is not to be combated by argument or inferences. It is a fact to be determined by the platform itself. Conspicuous among the articles of that instrument is—"the protection of all citizens in the legal and proper exercise of their civil and religious rights and privileges, and the maintenance of the right of every man to the full, unrestrained, and peaceful enjoyment of his own religious opinions and worship."

Thus, gentlemen, you have my views and opinions briefly and hastily expressed, though deliberately formed, of the character, principles, and objects of the American party. They have been derived entirely from its own publications, and conversations with its members. I am not a member of the order, and have no connection with it beyond a lively sympathy in its efforts to establish and maintain the great conservative principles it has adopted.

I am respectfully your obedient servant,

JOHN GAYLE.

II.

RELATIONS OF THE POPE TO THE CIVIL POWER.

Letter from O. A. Brownson.

Boston, *Tuesday, June* 12, 1855.

My dear Sir: I have received this moment yours of the 7th instant, with its inclosure. I am a little at a loss to determine what course to take. There are no numbers of my Review wherein I have maintained the civil authority of the Pope in this country; but as there are several numbers in which I have discussed the relations of the two orders—temporal and spiritual—I think I shall, upon the whole, best answer your wishes by sending them. I will therefore order my publisher to send you all the numbers of 1853 and 1854.

You will find in the articles entitled the "*Two Orders*," January, 1855, "*The Spiritual not for the Temporal*," April, and "*The Spiritual Supreme*," July, of the same year, the statement of my doctrine on the subject; and in "*You Go too Far*," January, 1854, "*The Temporal Power of the Popes*," April, 1854, and "*Uncle Jack with his Nephew*," for October of the same year, my explanations and defence of my doctrine.

May I ask you to read these articles in the order in which I have named them? If you will, although you will doubtless find much which, if a non-Catholic, you will object to, I am sure you will find no such doctrine as I am accused of holding. The subject I treat has been much obscured by controversy, and I am liable to misapprehension by those who have not studied it somewhat profoundly from the Catholic point of view. I treat the subject only under certain aspects, and for Catholics, and many of the terms I use have in Catholic theology a technical sense, which those not familiar with that theology may misapprehend. I say this in excuse of those who have misrepresented me.

I claim—and never have denied for the Pope, out of the Ecclesiastical States of which he is the temporal sovereign—no temporal or civil jurisdiction, power, or authority, properly so called. The only power the Pope has in this country, is his power over Catholics as the spiritual head of the Church. It is purely a spiritual power, and can be exercised only for a spiritual end, and even then only over Catholics, for the Church does not judge those who are without.

Mr. Brownson is here asserting the usual doctrines of his Church in those countries in which his creed is in the minority. *The Church* DOES *judge those who are without*, else wherefore the Athanasian curses?

In matters purely temporal, I, as a Catholic, owe no obedience to the Pope, because he has received from Jesus Christ no authority as a temporal sovereign over me. He cannot make or unmake the rights of the sovereign or the duties of the subject—abrogate the former or absolve from the latter.

This paragraph is entirely annulled by the succeeding portion of the letter, and history stamps falsehood upon such assertions.

Thus far, all Catholics, whether the so-called ultra-Montanes, or the so-called Gallicans, are agreed. The dispute lies not here. All agree that the State is supreme and independent in its own order—that is to say, in the temporal order. *But what I maintain is, that the temporal order is not supreme and independent, but, in the very nature of things, subordinated to the spiritual, since the end of man —the end for which God made him, directs and governs him by his providence— lies in the spiritual, not in the temporal.* Every man who believes any religion at all, whether Catholic or non-Catholic, does, and must admit this; for it is only saying that we must obey God rather than man, and live for the Creator rather than the creature. This premised, I think I can state to you, in a few words, the doctrine I do really hold.

The italics are Mr. Brownson's own. The inference drawn from them immediately after, is worthy the followers of Loyola, but Protestants cannot, will not admit it. If "the State is supreme and independent,"—what does the writer intend by its being "subordinated to the spiritual?"—"Much learning doth make thee mad."

Inasmuch as the temporal order is subordinated to the spiritual, it follows that the State is under the laws of justice, consequently the prince holds his powers as a trust, not as an indefeasible right, and therefore forfeits them when he abuses them, and loses his right to reign. This is the common doctrine held by all of us Americans, and all Catholic doctors teach and always have taught it. It lies at the foundation of all true liberty, and is the only doctrine that can ever justify resistance to the temporal powers. This right of resistance of power, when it becomes tyrannical and oppressive, I take it for granted, is held by every American.

But here is a difficulty. The Church, following the Holy Scriptures, makes civil allegiance a religious duty, and says with St. Paul (Romans viii. 1, 2): "Let every soul be subject to the higher powers, for there is no power but from God. Therefore, he that resisteth the power resisteth the ordinance of God, and they that resist purchase damnation to themselves." Here you see I am forbidden by the law of God to resist the power, and commanded, on peril of damnation, to obey. Here is my conscience bound to obedience, and my conscience as a Catholic can be released only by a declaration of my Church, as the divinely appointed director of conscience, that the prince of tyranny and oppression has forfeited his right, fallen from his dignity, and ceased to reign. What I claim for the Pope, as visible head of the Church, is the power to release my conscience from this religious bond, and to place me at liberty to resist the prince become a tyrant. This is all I understand by the dispensing power.

The power itself, everybody, not a tyrant or a slave, asserts. The American Congress of 1776 asserted it, and deposed George III. *The only difference is, some give it to the people, some to the individual; and I claim it for the Church, and the Pope as head of the Church.*

So that the Church has, necessarily, "an indefeasible right" to control the secular power, as seemeth it best; and constitutes itself a judge in all matters between the State and the ecclesiastical power. Mr. Brownson claims the same right to resistance on behalf of his Church, which the whole body of Americans possess; but he forgets that the right to resistance, when invested in a whole nation, is scarcely so liable to abuse, as when the sole prerogative of one man—be he Pope, or aught else.

The Pope does not in this exercise a civil power or jurisdiction, and it is called his temporal power only because it is a power exercised over temporal sovereigns, or in relation to the obligation of the subject to obey the prince. But even here the Pope does not relieve from *civil* allegiance, for that the prince had forfeited by his tyranny. He releases the subject only from the spiritual or religious obligation, superadded by Christianity to the civil, and this only in case of the Catholic conscience.

The Pope is the proper authority to decide for me whether the Constitution of this country is or is not repugnant to the laws of God. If he decides that it is not, as he has decided, then I am bound in conscience to obey every law made in accordance with it; and under no circumstances can he absolve me from my obligation to obey, or interfere with the administration of government under it, for the civil government is free to do according to its constitution whatever it pleases, that is not repugnant to the laws of God or to natural justice. That it is free to do more than that, I presume no man in this country will pretend.

Again the italics are the author's. We forbear to criticise, but we say to our fellow-countrymen—behold these opinions, the *sanctioned* tenets of the Romanist party in our republic; for Mr. Brownson "never publishes any thing, until he has first submitted it to the bishop." There is a sword hanging *in terrorem* over our heads, and it merely awaits the verdict of a mitred prince, to raise civil war in our midst, and desolate the Union throughout its wide extent.

I have made these remarks to aid you to understand the doctrine of the articles to which I have called your attention.

You are a stranger to me, but I take you to be a serious-minded man, and a lover of truth and justice; as such I have addressed you. I have no doctrine or opinions that I wish to conceal. I am a Catholic. As such, I aim to be true to my God, and to my fellow-men.

I have the honor to be your obedient servant,

O. A. BROWNSON.

HUGH J. DAVIS, Esq., Warrenton, N. C.

III.

FOREIGNERS AND THE ELECTIVE FRANCHISE.

Less than ten days since, we had occasion to notice the manifesto of the Louisville Branch of the "Free German" Union, and to point out the dangerons tendency of such anarchical organizations. We did not then anticipate that the effects of the principles they hold, aided by Irish violence at elections, would be so speedily and fatally felt in that city. It will not be possible, until more accurate details shall have been received with regard to the bloody occurrences that have disgraced Louisville, to decide adequately in what proportion the guilt of murder, arson, and riot is to be divided between the native and foreign population. If the telegraphic reports prove to be accurate, a general understanding must have existed between the Germans and Irish, previous to the election, that they would go armed during the day, and prevent Americans, by every means, from approaching the polls. The first outrage was committed by a body of Irish or Germans, as early as nine o'clock in the morning. The next attack was made upon Americans, several of whom were wounded, by Germans, who fired upon them from their houses and a brewery in which they had intrenched themselves. It is not stated that any provocation was given; but exasperation —perhaps inflamed by drink—at the defeat of their ticket, was probably the main cause of the violence which these ruffians had recourse to. They reaped, however, bitter fruits from their mad folly. A crowd of Americans assembled, burned the brewery, and after a conflict of considerable duration, sacked several houses. Up to this time, although some persons had been wounded, it does not seem that any one was killed. The scene of slaughter commenced in a different part of the city at a later hour, and was again initiated by a gang of Irish. From this time the riot assumed the dimensions of a street battle. The Irish, who had been guilty of the last assault, intrenched themselves in houses, where they were besieged by a crowd of Americans, infuriated at the crime that had been committed, and the tumults of the night did not end until a large number of lives had been lost, and several blocks of houses had been burned. On the day after the election, the excitement still continued, and at the last accounts yesterday, renewed outbreaks were feared during the coming night. Many foreigners were, however, leaving the city, and there is little doubt that a complete victory has been gained over them by their antagonists.

Pitiable is the lot of most foreigners that land on our shores. They emerge suddenly from subjection to tyrannical rule, and habits of slavery that generations have stereotyped, into that paradise of the depraved and unthrifty, the possession of active political rights. The story is familiar to every one, of the Irishman, who, after regarding for some time with wonder a threshing machine, cried out, "Ye're bloody sthrong, but ye can't *vote*." The Irish, alas, *can* vote; so can the Germans, and between them they are acquiring, in the hands of demagogues more iniquitous than themselves, a control of elections in many of our States, of which it is time that Americans should be wearied and ashamed. Eight months ago, the subject of amending our Naturalization Laws was brought before Congress, by Senator Adams of Mississippi. Reference was made, at the time, in our columns, to the able speech which he made on that occasion, and hopes were entertained that the measure he proposed would be dispassionately discussed, and, with some necessary amendments, adopted by Congress. It fell, however, to the ground. Politicians are afraid to meet boldly, either in

Congress or the State Legislatures, the embarrassments which this question, so important for the future interests of the country, presents. They dread the local opposition which advocacy of manly and patriotic measures of reform would subject them to, and shrink from being ostracised by foreigners, whose opposition at the polls might prevent their re-election to office. The wisdom of the proposal that the term of residence of aliens should be prolonged, before they are permitted to enjoy every right of Americans born, is recognized by provident, far-sighted Americans of all parties; but this cowardly fear of losing votes, on the part of aspirants for office, opposes more than any thing else an effectual obstacle to proper legislation. The indiscreet manner, too, in which foreigners have been confounded by many with the power they wield, and the intermingling of religious elements in all Native American parties that have hitherto existed, have tended to delay, if not totally hinder, an impartial examination of the question, what rights it is expedient to bestow upon persons born abroad.

It is the duty of the people and government of the United States to welcome to our shores those who come here with a claim upon our hospitality, and to the home for themselves and education for their children, which we can so easily afford to bestow. It is also a bounden obligation to act towards them the part of kind protectors, shielding them by our laws, permitting them to hold property, and to transfer it to their children, and even to acquire such control over the soil as they can secure by the labor of their hands. These privileges, however, which the immigrant has a right to look for, and which our laws theoretically give, are poisoned, and rendered practically nugatory by the premature addition, indiscriminately, of the right of suffrage. The poor Irishman or German encounters, as he lands in our seaports, a monster who is legally authorized to obstruct with a frequently impassable barrier his pathway to the happy home to which he is entitled, and where he might enjoy abundantly the products of the soil, and become a frugal, sober, and industrious denizen of the land. This monster is *political temptation.* The hard-handed, humbly-conditioned Irish laborer, as well as the clodhopper socialist from Germany, both sink into corruption by our own fault, more than by theirs. They are at once instructed that they may vote in six months, a year, or less, if fraud is employed to attain the object. They are taught to consider themselves an army of political invaders, are enlisted either in infidel associations, or under the banners of rum-selling middle-men, and made to reinforce the vast floating condottieri between parties, which often at elections turns the scale in favor of the highest bidder or the latest payer, and wrests pledges from candidates in favor of infidel encroachments, or impunity to do wrong. Foreigners who—if their consciences were not drugged by the fatal right to vote before they know the A B C's of our political alphabet, or can distinguish between liberty and license, excitement and disorder, or comprehend the secret of acquiescing in the will of the majority—might become eventually themselves, or through their children, good citizens, are enticed by the glitter of golden bribes to remain in large towns and cities, where they spend freely what has been easily got, acquire habits of debauchery, and a ternate between riotous indulgence, the alms-house, and our prisons. The neglected offspring of such, brought up with their heads in the public-school, and their bodies in the gutter, ripen into that unnaturally shrewd, depraved, dangerous race of infidel bullies, fearing neither God nor man, whose vocation is to seduce others to sin and misery, and increase as widely as possibly the realms of moral ruin.

Every little while, some solemn warning, like the recent riot at Louisville, troubles the minds of thinking men, and points forward to that period of civil discord by which we may some day be convulsed, if a remedy is not applied to the evil created by our present naturalization laws; but unfortunately the age is too peculiarly one of excitement for any single event to leave a lasting impression. Yet if citizens will look back twenty-five years, to a time when disorders that are common now were regarded as impossible, and will then reflect upon the consequences of a like decline, for another quarter of a century, they will be convinced of the danger of delay, and of the rapidity and strength that anti-American influence is acquiring in the country.

New York Journal of Commerce, Aug. 5, 1855.

IV.

RELIGIOUS TOLERATION—HERETICS AND ROMANIST GRAVE-YARDS.

P. Sharkey, Esq., of Jackson, Miss., writes to the *Southern Mercury* as follows, giving an incident of the War of 1812–15, in which he served:

July 25, 1855.

To the Editor of the Mercury:

As there has been a great deal said about ancient Catholicism, and old files hunted up to prove their hostility to the Protestants, and as I am a man of but little ancient reading, and a little on the Young American order, I will content myself by referring back to 1815, after the battle at New Orleans.

I belonged to the Mississippi Militia, and was encamped on a French Catholic farm above New Orleans. After the battle was over, several of our men died by wounds and sickness, as they had been placed at Chef Menteur, where there was not one foot of dry land to stand or lie on, only as they would gather flags and make beds to lie on. We were some distance above New Orleans, and having no way of conveyance to a grave-yard, we proposed to bury our dead on the back or out-post of the farm. Went to dig a grave, without knowing the hostility the Catholics had to heretics. The owner of the land came down and forbid us from burying our corpse. He appeared to be very much enraged, crying out, "Sacre fungas! de American heretic no be put on my land." We said we must bury the man. He replied—"Me no care; dere is de Mississippi river; throw him in de river." We soon made him leave, and when we went to bury our dead we always had our guns. Jo. Templeton was one of our Warren soldiers who shared the fate of the balance that were buried there. We were discharged at that place, and came home. Letters followed us from our friends, stating that as we left all the dead were taken up and put in the river by the owner of the land; as though a dead heretic could hurt a live Catholic.

Now I refer to any man that was belonging to Hinds' Dragoons, or the Mississippi Militia, for the facts of this and the report that followed us. I will refer to a few by name: Esq. McDonald, of Madison; Richard and Battle Harrison, of Jefferson; Haley Cotton, of Leake, as they were there, and know the facts as well as myself.

P. SHARKEY.

The above letter is from one of the most substantial and well-known citizens of the State of Mississippi, and what is the fact developed? This: a lay member of the Romish Church is so fired with hatred towards Protestants, that he denies a burial-place to the brave and patriotic men who came from an adjoining State to repel an invading foe. Men who died in battle in defending the home of the Romanist, have their bones dug up from their mother earth, and thrown contemptuously into the Mississippi, as if their dust defiled the land. Innumerable examples, where the Romish priests have undisputed sway, displaying the same feeling, constantly occur all over the world.

V.

MILITARY IN THE CHURCH.

The enthusiastic in the faith that American institutions need no safeguards, contend that the illuminating influence of Protestantism will, in this country, destroy the pagan rites of the Romish Church so common in Europe. We find, however, that this is not the case. The heathen custom of inaugurating statues, so common among the Greeks and ancient Romans, maintains its place in a church claiming to be Christian, and situated in enlightened America, and in the city of New York.

At the Church of the Redeemer (German Romish), on Sunday, the 12th of August, 1855, "a statue of the Virgin was inaugurated with the celebration of High Mass. Some time before the hour for the commencement of the services, the body of the church was densely crowded, but the gallery was attainable to the lucky possessor of a sixpence, and was very comfortably roomy. Occupying the front central seats was a military band, and behind them a company—one of the German rifle companies, we believe—in uniform. Up the side aisles, at short intervals, were the banners of various Catholic and benevolent societies. Festoons of flowers and leaves, arranged very tastily, ran from pillar to pillar all the way up the church, each bearing the name of a saint.

"The large altar-piece was decorated, to use the choice expression of the announcement, 'in a manner particularly beautiful.' Flowers and leaves were profusely used from top to bottom, and over all ran a *cordon bleu*, inscribed with the prayer, '*Regina sine labe concepta, ora pro nobis.*'

"In the centre of this high altar-piece, in a white-draped niche stood the statue of the Virgin, bearing the infant Redeemer in her arms. The material is not mentioned, and of course could not be distinguished: we suppose it is of wood. The announcement above quoted, says it is 'of exquisite beauty.' It is very brilliantly painted. The robe is blue, fringed and starred with gold. The statue was encircled by a halo of gas-burners, arranged in star-shaped groups, and all the candles were burning at its feet. Mass was celebrated very finely. There is, or was on Sunday, a fine choir at the church, and the band assisted."

Here we have the introduction of foreign military companies, as part of the pageant of a professedly religious ceremony. We would have every reflecting American to ask himself, What is the meaning of this association? and what right have troops, organized by the State, to connect themselves thus with the church?

VI.

AMERICAN NATIONALITY.

The "stars and stripes," the glorious emblem of the Union, form a parallelogram, with six white and seven red parallel stripes, denoting the union of the original Thirteen Colonies, with a blue square in the upper corner, next the flag-staff, cutting off four red and three white stripes, and containing thirty-one white stars, representing the number of States in the Union, combined in one large star, symbolizing the "many in one" of the national motto, "*E pluribus unum.*"

The great Union Flag was hoisted on the 2d day of January, 1776, at Cambridge, by General Washington. Lieut. Carter wrote from Charlestown Heights,

January 26th, 1776: "The King's speech was sent by a flag to them on the 1st. In a short time after they received it, they hoisted a Union flag (above the Continental, with thirteen stripes) at Mount Pisgat; their citadel fired thirteen guns, and gave the like number of cheers." And Gen. Washington wrote from Cambridge, on the 4th of the same month, to Col. Joseph Reed: "The speech I send you. A volume of them was sent out by the Boston gentry, and, farcical enough, we gave great joy to them, without knowing or intending it; for on that day—the day which gave being to the new army—but before the proclamation came to hand, we had hoisted the Union flag, in compliment to the Colonies. But, behold! it was received in Boston as a token of the deep impression the speech had made upon us, and as a signal of submission. So we hear, by a person out of Boston, last night. By this time, I presume they begin to think it strange that we have not made a formal surrender of our lives." Thus we have an acknowledgment of the presence of the stripes, and a device resembling the British Union Jack. This latter, instead of being *above* the stripes, was probably in the place now occupied by the blue square and the white stars. From this it would appear that the Great Union Flag of the Colonies was the British flag modified by drawing six white stripes through the red field, thus making thirteen red and white stripes, representing the rebellious Colonies in Union. This flag probably was originated by the Committee of Conference, appointed by Congress, and composed of Dr. Franklin, Mr. Lynch, and Mr. Harrison; and the idea of such a modification of the British flag is not only simple but certainly a very natural one, when we consider the circumstances and history of the times.

The necessity for a change of the emblem of union was apparent; and the thirteen Colonies readily suggested the idea of a constellation of stars. Consequently we find that the constellation Lyra was actually under consideration, and was used on passports. June 14, 1777, Congress passed the following: "Resolved, that the flag of the thirteen United States be thirteen stripes, alternate red and white: That the union be thirteen stars, white in a blue field, representing a new constellation." It appears that the first act of Congress changing the flag was on the 13th of January, 1794, when it was enacted, "That from and after the 1st day of May, A. D. 1795, the flag of the United States be fifteen stripes, alternate red and white; that the union be fifteen stars, white in a blue field." The stars were arranged in a circle indicating eternal union. This was the flag of the United States during the war of 1812–14. In 1818, the flag of the United States was again altered, and, as we are informed, on the suggestion of the Hon. Mr. Wendover, of New York, a return was made to the thirteen stripes; as it was anticipated the flag would become unwieldy if a stripe were added on the admission of each State; and, moreover, by the plan proposed, the union of the old thirteen States, as well as the number of members composing the existing Union, would be presented by this flag of the United States. Mr. W. also proposed the arrangement of the stars in the union in the form of a single star. In this there was a departure from the original design, as the perpetuity of the Union ceased to be indicated by the flag, as it had previously been in the circle of stars, except so far as indicated by the several stars forming one large star. The resolution of 1818 was as follows: "That from and after the fourth day of July next, the flag of the United States be thirteen horizontal stripes, alternate red and white; that the union be twenty stars, white in a blue field. And that, on the admission of a new State into the Union, one star be added to the union of the flag; and that such addition shall take effect on the fourth day of July next succeeding such admission."

VII.

AMERICAN ELECTIONS.

There was a time, we remember, when the good order and decorum of American Elections was a common proverb, at home and abroad. That time, we fear, has passed, or is passing away. Not that the American people have grown, or are growing less attached to the principles of peace and propriety, nor less capable of self-government, nor the government of their passions and prejudices, but rather because of the introduction into our popular contests of a strange element, that is inherently inimical to Americanism in every leading impulse and aspiration. This pestilent influence, within a very few months past, has been fearfully provocative of bloodshed and strife, in some of the most populous cities of the Union. New Orleans, St. Louis, Cincinnati, and places nearer home, have, each in its turn, been made the scene of a sanguinary strife, generally growing out of nefarious attempts by Irish and Germans—but chiefly Irish—to interfere with American meetings, and American freedom of speech, in cases where it so happened neither those meetings nor that speech were shaped to accord with the sentiments, opinions, or beliefs, of a set of men, who are, of late years, but too prone to acknowledge the civil and political privileges they enjoy here (but which they never were permitted to enjoy "at home") by shooting down Americans in their own streets, and blowing their brains out, whenever they have the audacity to assemble together. Louisville, in Kentucky, it is grievous to see, is now passing through the same ordeal.—*N. Y. Express.*

VIII.

WHAT CAUSES ELECTION RIOTS

Is the low education of our foreign population. The musket and the bayonet are the exponents of the law in foreign cities; and what we bow to here, in deference and obedience, as "law"—as *the will of the majority*—in other countries is bowed to under the prick of the bayonet. Hence, when among such a people, the prick of the bayonet is removed, the law, or the will of the majority that makes the law, is resisted by riot, row, or murder. In Louisville, Kentucky, for example, the Americans beat on election-day; but the foreigners there, instead of doing as Americans do, submit to the majority, in the absence of the bayonet, shoot from their houses Americans in the streets! If the division in Louisville had been between Whig Americans and Democratic Americans, the moment the result was known it would have been acquiesced in, with general submission; but the indignant foreign population in Louisville do, just as they would do—when they dare—in Paris, or Berlin, or Vienna; that is, appeal to the musket and fight.

It is this spirit of resistance to law, to the majority, and to the declared will of that majority, which makes republican government almost impossible over sea—a minority that will not submit to a majority, but prefers a fight, as in Louisville; and hence a result so deplorable.

These numerous riots that we are having, wherever American interests come into political conflict with the interests or passions of foreigners, only go to show that government is a trade, which a foreign population cannot learn by instinct, but must be educated in by long training. *Voting* is a very simple act, but it means and embodies the idea of government, and government is a science, which an Irishman, who cannot read, or a German, who knows not our language, and customs, and traditions, cannot learn in a single day. Indeed, the education of our foreign population is far easier, if we may so express ourselves, than their *uneducation*. To unlearn what they know is their first duty; and it takes years and years, but it is much harder work to *unlearn* than to *learn*. Jury trials, habeas corpuses, &c., are all Greek to them; but all these they can learn. What they have to unlearn, however, is harder than Greek, and that is, armed resistance to law, to government, to majorities. The prick of the bayonet is not half so formidable to an American as the writ of the constable; but this necessity of feeling the prick of the bayonet before they yield, they must all unlearn. Revolutions are wrought here, not in arms, but with bits of paper in the ballot-boxes. Minorities have no rights against laws constitutionally passed, and constitutionally expounded and executed, while majorities, even, have no rights, under laws unconstitutionally passed, or unconstitutionally executed. These are very hard problems for foreigners to solve, but we Americans solve them. We often learn, too, that submission to wrongs is oftener wiser than armed resistance by force. When we are whipped election-day, we lament our bad luck, and try it again, but seldom or never fight, unless attacked by force. The loss of the anti-American candidate for Congress, in Louisville, led to shooting Americans in the streets, and, of course, to the subsequent fearful retribution.

Foreigners, if they were wise, would, themselves, call for a long training for their countrymen, before they gave them the right of governing at the ballot-boxes. Men can no more be good soldiers after a day's enlistment, than good voters without training. Government is a curious piece of human mechanism, which untaught fingers may spoil, but which they can never safely touch. A foreigner may be as wise as Humboldt in philosophy, but as ignorant as a babe of the mechanism of the government of the United States of America. Twenty-one years are wisely demanded of us Americans to live, to think, to look on, to hear, and to talk, and to see, and to study, before we vote. Thousands of foreigners vote fraudulently who have been in the country scarcely a year, and hundreds of thousands that cannot read the Constitution of the United States in the language in which its makers wrote it.—*N. Y. Express, Aug.* 10, 1855.

IX.

GOLDEN MAXIMS OF WASHINGTON.

"Let us have a government by which our lives, liberties, and properties, will be secured."

"The government of the United States, though not actually perfect, is one of the best in the world."

"It is among the evils, and perhaps not the smallest, of Democratic governments, that the people must *feel*, before they will see: when this happens, they are roused to action."

"If we mean to support the liberty and independence which it has cost us so much blood and treasure to establish, we must drive far away the demon of party spirit."

"As there can be no harm in a pious wish for the good of one's country, I shall offer it as mine, that each state would not only choose, but absolutely compel their ablest men to attend Congress, that public abuses may be corrected."

"The preservation of the sacred fire of liberty and the destiny of the republican model of government are justly considered as deeply, perhaps as finally staked on the experiment intrusted to the hands of the American people."

"There are four things which I humbly conceive are essential to the well being—I may even venture to say, to the existence of the United States as an independent power:—

"1. An indissoluble union of the states under one federal head.

"2. A sacred regard to public justice.

"3. The adoption of a proper peace establishment.

"4. Prevalence of a pacific and friendly disposition among the people of the United States, making them forget their local prejudices and politics, &c."

"As avenues to foreign influence in innumerable ways, such attachments are particularly alarming to the truly enlightened and independent patriot. How many opportunities do they afford to tamper with domestic factions, to practise the arts of seduction, to mislead public opinion, to influence or awe the public councils! Against the insidious wiles of foreign influence, I conjure you to believe me, fellow-citizens, the jealousy of a free people ought to be constantly awake, *since history and experience prove that foreign influence is one of the most baneful foes of republican government.* But that jealousy, to be useful, must be impartial, else it becomes the instrument of the very influence to be avoided, instead of a defence against it. Excessive partiality for one foreign nation, and excessive dislike for another, cause those whom they actuate to see danger only on one side, and serve to veil and even second the arts of influence on the other. Real patriots, who may resist the intrigues of the favorite, are liable to become suspected and odious, while its tools and dupes usurp the applause and confidence of the people to surrender their interests.

"The great rule of conduct for us in regard to foreign nations is, in extending our commercial relations, to have with them as little political connection as possible. So far as we have already formed engagements, let them be fulfilled with perfect good faith. Here let us stop.

"Europe has a set of primary interests which to us have none or a very remote relation. Hence, she must be engaged in frequent controversies, the causes of which are essentially foreign to our concerns. Hence, therefore, it must be unwise in us to implicate ourselves by artificial ties in the ordinary vicissitudes of her politics, or the ordinary combinations and collisions of her friendships or enmities.

"The unity of government which constitutes you one people, is a main pillar in the edifice of your real independence, the support of your tranquillity at home, your peace abroad, of your safety, of your prosperity, of that very liberty which you so highly prize. But as it is easy to foresee that from different causes, and from different quarters, much pains will be taken, many artifices employed, to weaken in your minds the conviction of this truth—as this is the point in your political fortress against which the batteries of internal and external enemies will be most constantly and actively (though often covertly and insidiously) directed—it is of infinite moment that you should properly estimate the immense value of your national union to your collective and individual happiness; that you should cherish a cordial, habitual, and immovable attachment to it; accustoming yourselves to think and to speak of it as a palladium of your political safety and prosperity; watching for its preservation with jealous anxiety; discountenancing whatever may suggest even a suspicion that it can in any event be abandoned; and indignantly frowning upon the first dawning of every attempt to alienate any portion of our country from the rest, or to enfeeble the sacred ties which now link together the various parts.

"For this you have every inducement of sympathy and interest. Citizens by birth or choice of a common country, that country has a right to concentrate your affections. The name of American, which belongs to you in your national capacity, must always exalt the just pride of patriotism more than any appellation derived from local discriminations. With slight shades of difference, you have the same religion, manners, habits, and political principles. You have, in a common cause, fought and triumphed together. The independence and liberty you possess are the work of joint counsels and joint efforts, of common dangers, sufferings, and success.

"But these considerations, however powerfully they address themselves to your sensibility, are greatly outweighed by those which apply more immediately to your interest. Here, every portion of our country finds the most commanding motives for carefully guarding and preserving the union of the whole."

X.

MAXIMS AND OPINIONS OF EMINENT STATESMEN, ETC.

"Hearken not to the unnatural voice, which tells you that the people of America, knit together, as they are, by so many cords of affection, can no longer live together, as members of the same family; can no longer continue the mutual guardians of their mutual happiness; can no longer be fellow-citizens of one great, respectable, and flourishing empire. Hearken not to the voice which petulantly tells you that the form of government recommended for your adoption, is a novelty in the political world; that it has never yet had a place in the theories of the wildest projectors; that it rashly attempts what it is impossible to accomplish. No, my countrymen; shut your ears against this unhallowed language. Shut your heart against the poison which it conveys. The kindred blood which flows in the veins of American citizens, the mingled blood which they have shed in defence of their sacred rights, consecrates their union, and excites horror at the idea of their becoming aliens, rivals, enemies. And if novelties are to be shunned, believe me, the most alarming of all novelties, the most wild of all projects, the most rash of all attempts, is that of rending us in pieces, in order to preserve our liberties, and promote our happiness.

"But why is the experiment of an extended republic to be rejected merely because it may comprise what is new? Is it not the glory of the people of America, that, whilst they have paid a decent regard to the opinions of former times and other nations, they have not suffered a blind veneration for antiquity, for custom or for names, to overrule the suggestions of their own good sense, the knowledge of their own situation, and the lessons of their own experience? To this manly spirit posterity will be indebted for the possession, and the world for the example, of the numerous innovations displayed on the American theatre, in favor of private rights and public happiness."—*James Madison.*

"When your lordships look at the papers transmitted to us from America; when you consider their decency, firmness, and wisdom, you cannot but respect their cause, and wish to make it your own. For myself, I must declare and avow that in all my reading and observation (and it has been my favorite study, I have read Thucidydes, and have studied and admired the master-states of the world), I say I must declare, that for solidity of reasoning, force of sagacity, and wisdom of conclusion, under such a complication of difficult circumstances, no nation, nor body of men, can stand in preference to the General Congress at Philadelphia. I trust it is obvious to your lordships, that all attempts to impose a servitude upon such men, to establish despotism over such a mighty continental nation, must be vain, must be fatal."—*Extract from Mr. Pitt's speech in the British Parliament, Jan.* 20, 1775.

"What is patriotism? Is it a narrow affection for the spot where a man was born? Are the very clods where we tread entitled to this ardent preference because they are greener? No, sir, this is not the character of the virtue; and it soars higher for its object. It is an extended self-love, mingling with all the enjoyments of life, and twisting itself with the minutest filaments of the heart. It is thus we obey the laws of society, because they are the laws of virtue. In their authority we see, not the array of force and terror, but the venerable image of our country's honor. Every good citizen makes that honor his own, and cherishes it not only as precious, but as sacred. He is willing to risk his life in its defence, and is conscious that he gains protection while he gives it. For what rights of a citizen will be deemed inviolable when a state renounces the principles that constitute their security? Or if his life should not be invaded, what would its enjoyments be in a country odious in the eyes of strangers, and dishonored in his own?"—*Fisher Ames.*

"The imperishable records of our grand crusade against despotism are emblazoned upon the scroll of Time, and are unsurpassed by the loftiest exploits of Roman or Grecian heroism. The entire world watched with intensest interest the successes of our revolutionary progress, and that which many had considered problematical, has long since become matter of historic truth. To the people of the United States has been assigned the glorious work of effecting and proclaiming the triumph of freedom. More than half a century has tested its stability and its power, affording a sufficient augury of its brilliant future."—*Webster.*

"It cannot be denied, but by those who would dispute against the sun, that with America, and in America, a new era commences in human affairs. This era is distinguished by free representative governments, by entire religious liberty, and by improved systems of national intercourse, by a newly-awakened and an unconquerable spirit of free inquiry, and by a diffusion of knowledge through the community, such as has been before altogether unknown or unheard of. * * * If we cherish the virtues and the principles of our fathers,

Heaven will assist us to carry on the work of human liberty and human happiness."—*Ibid.*

"The spirit of union is particularly liable to temptation and seduction in times of peace and prosperity."—*Ibid.*

"If we are true to our country in our day and generation, and those who come after us shall be true to it also, assuredly we shall elevate her to a pitch of prosperity and happiness, of honor and power, never yet reached by any nation beneath the sun."—*Ibid.*

"The spirit of liberty, growing more and more enlightened, and more and more vigorous from age to age, has been battering for centuries against the solid battlements of the feudal system. All that could be gained from the imprudence, snatched from the weakness, or wrung from the necessities of crowned heads, has been carefully gathered up, secured and hoarded, as the rich treasures, the very jewels of liberty. The popular and representative right has kept up its warfare against prerogative with various success: sometimes writing the history of a whole age in blood, sometimes witnessing the martyrdoms of Sydneys and Russels: often baffled and repulsed, but still gaining on the whole, and holding what is gained with a grasp which nothing but the complete extinction of its own being could compel it to relinquish."—*Ibid.*

"The first object of a free people is the preservation of their liberty; and liberty is only to be preserved by maintaining constitutional restraints and just divisions of political power."—*Ibid.*

"Under the present Constitution, wisely and conscientiously administered, all are safe, happy, and renowned. The measure of our country's fame may fill our breasts. It is fame enough for us all to partake in *her* glory, if we will carry her character onward to its true destiny. Not only the cause of American Liberty, but the cause of Liberty throughout the whole earth, depends in a great measure on upholding the Constitution and Union of these States. Let it be a truth engraven on our hearts, let it be borne on the flag under which we rally in every exigency that we have *one country*, *one Constitution*, *one destiny*."—*Ibid.*

"This glorious Liberty—these benign institutions, the dear purchase of our fathers, are ours—ours to enjoy, ours to preserve, ours to transmit. Generations past and generations to come hold us responsible for the sacred trust."—*Ibid.*

"I have no fears for the permanency of our Union, whilst our liberties are preserved. It is a tough and strong cord, as all will find who will presumptuously attempt to break it. It has been competent to suppress all the domestic insurrections, and to carry us safely through all the foreign wars with which we have been afflicted since it was formed, and it has come out of each with more strength and greater promise of durability. It is the choicest political blessing which, as a people, we enjoy, and I trust that Providence will permit us to transmit it, unimpaired to posterity, through endless generations."—*Henry Clay.*

"*The Constitution of the United States.*—Like one of those wondrous rocking stones reared by the Druids, which the finger of a child might vibrate to its centre, yet the might of an army could not move from its place, our Constitution is so nicely poised and balanced that it seems to sway with every breath of opinion, yet so firmly rooted in the hearts and affections of the people, that the wildest storms of treason and fanaticism break over it in vain."—*R. C. Winthrop.*

"A divine right to govern ill, is an absurdity: to assert it, is blasphemy. Pretensions to a *divine right* have been generally carried highest by those who have had the least claim to the Divine favor. Liberty is to the collective body what health is to every individual body. Without health, no pleasure can be tasted by man; without liberty, no happiness can be enjoyed by society."—*Bolingbroke.*

"Which is the most perfect popular government? 'That,' said Bias, 'where the laws have no superior.' 'That,' said Thales, 'where the inhabitants are neither too rich nor too poor.' 'That,' said Anacharsis, 'where virtue is honored and vice detested.' That is the the best government which desires to make the people happy, and knows how to make the people happy. Neither the inclination nor the knowledge will suffice alone, and it is difficult to find them together. Pure Democracy, and pure Democracy alone, satisfies the former condition of this great problem. That the governors may be solicitous only for the interests of the governed, it is necessary that the interests of the governors and the governed should be the same. The interests of the subjects and rulers never absolutely coincide till the subjects themselves become the rulers; that is, till the government be either immediately or mediately democratic."—*Macaulay.*

"Our own country, though happily exempt,—and God grant that it may long continue so,—from the troubles of Europe, is not exempt from the influence of the causes that produce them. We too are inspired, and agitated, and governed by the all-pervading, all-inspiring, all-agitating, all-governing spirit of the age. What do I say? We were the first to feel and act upon its influence. Our revolution was the first of the long series that has since shaken every corner of Europe and America. Our fathers led the van in the long array of heroes, martyrs, and confessors, who have fought and fallen under the banner of liberty. The institutions they bequeathed to us, and under which we are living in peace and happiness, were founded on the principles which lie at the bottom of the present agitation in Europe. We have realized what our contemporaries are laboring to attain. Our tranquillity is the fruit of an entire acquiescence in the spirit of the age. We have reduced the action of government within narrower limits, and given a wider scope to individual liberty, than any community that ever flourished before.

"We live, therefore, in an age, and in a country, where positive laws and institutions have comparatively but little direct force. But human nature remains the same. The passions are as wild, as ardent, as ungovernable, in a republic, as in a despotism. What then is to arrest their violence? I answer in one word, *Religion.*"—*Edward Everett.*

"Let no one accuse me of seeing wild visions, and dreaming impossible dreams. I am only stating what may be done, and what will be done. We may most shamefully betray the trust reposed in us—we may most miserably defeat the fond hopes entertained of us. We may become the scorn of tyrants and the jest of slaves. From our fate, oppression may assume a bolder front of insolence, and its victims sink into a darker despair.

"In that event, how unspeakable will be our disgrace—with what weight of mountains will the infamy lie upon our souls. The gulf of our ruin will be as deep as the elevation we might have attained is high. How wilt thou fall from heaven, O Lucifer, son of the morning! Our beloved country with ashes for beauty, the golden cord of our Union broken, its scattered fragments presenting every form of misrule, from the wildest anarchy to the most ruthless despotism, our "soil drenched with fraternal blood," the life of man stripped of its grace and dignity, the prizes of honor gone, and virtue divorced from half its encouragements and supports—these are gloomy pictures, which I would not invite your imaginations to dwell upon, but only to glance at, for the sake of the warning lessons we may draw from them.

"Remember, that we can have none of those consolations which sustain the patriot who mourns over the undeserved misfortunes of his country. Our Rome cannot fall and we be innocent. No conqueror will chain us to the car of his triumph—no countless swarm of Huns and Goths will bury the memorials and trophies of civilized life, beneath a living tide of barbarism. Our own selfishness, our own neglect, our own passions, and our own vices, will furnish the elements of our destruction. With our own hands we shall tear down the stately edifice of our glory. We shall die by self-inflicted wounds."—*G. S. Hilliard.*

"We less need new laws, new institutions, or new powers, than we need on all occasions, at all times, and in all places, the requisite intelligence concerning the true spirit of our present ones; the high moral courage under every hazard, and against every offender, to execute with fidelity the authority already possessed; and the manly independence to abandon all supineness, irresolution, vacillation, and time-serving pusillanimity, and enforce our present mild system with that uniformity and steady vigor throughout, which alone can supply the place of the greater severity of less free institutions.

"To arm and encourage us in renewed efforts to accomplish every thing on this subject which is desirable, our history constantly points her finger to a most efficient resource, and indeed to the only elixir, to secure a long life to any popular government, in increased attention to useful education and sound morals, with the wise description of equal measures and just practices they inculcate on every leaf of recorded time. May we not all profit by the vehement exhortation of Cicero to Atticus: 'If you are asleep, awake; if you are standing, move; if you are moving, run; if you are running, fly!'

"All these considerations warn us—the gravestones of almost every former republic warn us—that a high standard of moral rectitude, as well as of intelligence, is quite as indispensable to communities, in their public doings, as to individuals, if they would escape from either degeneracy or disgrace."—*Levi Woodbury.*

"The prosperity of the United States is the source of the most serious dangers that threaten them, since it tends to create in some of the confederate states that over-excitement which accompanies a rapid increase of fortune; and to awaken in others those feelings of envy, mistrust, and regret, which usually attend upon the loss of it. Yet the Americans of the United States must inevitably become one of the greatest nations in the world. The continent which they inhabit is their dominion."—*De Tocqueville.*

VALUABLE

NATIONAL STANDARD WORKS

PUBLISHED BY

EDWARD WALKER,

114 FULTON-STREET, NEW YORK.

I.

A VOICE TO AMERICA;

OR, THE MODEL REPUBLIC, ITS GLORY OR ITS FALL; WITH A REVIEW OF THE CAUSES OF THE DECLINE AND FAILURE OF THE REPUBLICS OF SOUTH AMERICA, MEXICO, AND OF THE OLD WORLD; APPLIED TO THE PRESENT CRISIS IN THE UNITED STATES.

One volume, 12mo., about 400 pages, cloth gilt, $1.25.

CONTENTS OF THE WORK:

The United States—Retrospective and Prospective.
The Ancient Republics—Early Civilization.
Sparta and Athens.
The Fall of Rome.
Italian Liberty in the Middle Ages.
The Anglo-Saxon Race and Freedom.
The Heroes of the Founders of Liberty.
The Boundaries of Countries—how established.
Romanism and Freedom.
The Effects of Romanism and Protestantism on Civilization.
The Rights of Conscience.
Religious Toleration.
The Bible, the Charter of Liberty.
The Principles and Perils of our Common Education.
The Political Power of the Pope.
Demoralizing Influence of Demagogism.
Evils of Military Organizations exclusively of Foreigners.
What Constitutes the Right to Vote?
Fallacy of supposing American Institutions need no Safeguards.
Naturalization Laws of the United States.
United States and Immigration.
The Citizen of a Republic.
American Nationality.
Necessity of American Habits and Principles.
The Right of the Majority to Rule.
Freedom from Foreign Influence.
Origin of Political Power.
Mexico and the South American Republics.
America the Theatre of the Great Demonstration.
Secret Societies—their Use and Abuse.
The American Republic the Hope of the World.
Appendix.

This work is written in an earnest American spirit, by able and experienced writers selected for their eminent fitness for the task, and will be found worthy the attentive perusal of the whole American people. It condenses a prodigious amount of most valuable information relating to our social and political economy, and the dangers to which our civil and national liberties are exposed, together with illustrations drawn from the history of the classic and modern republics. This production will long be regarded as *the great text-book for American citizens.* It is so thorough in its investigations, and of such deep, stirring interest, that it cannot fail of making its direct appeal to the hearts of the people.

II.

NATIONAL HISTORY OF THE UNITED STATES;

COMPRISING THE COLONIAL, REVOLUTIONARY, AND CONSTITUTIONAL RECORDS OF THE COUNTRY; BASED UPON AND INCLUDING THE DOCUMENTS OF THE FEDERAL GOVERNMENT, &c.

By Benson J. Lossing and Edwin Williams.

In two volumes, royal 8vo., illustrated with numerous fine engravings on steel and wood, muslin gilt, $7.

It is a work unique in its character, and of intrinsic value as a standard authority for the statesman, historian, and general reader; and no less important as the exponent of the political ethics and progress of the Confederacy. It will be regarded as *the* National History of our country during its three great epochs—Colonial, Revolutionary, and Constitutional—condensed from the national archives; including impartial biographical memoirs of the Presidents of the United States, from the times of Washington to the present, their administrations, etc., and a mass of highly valuable national documents never before presented to the public in a collective form. The claims of this truly national work will, it is believed, be at once apparent, since it is not only designed as a standard authority of reference, but also as the best work for all who desire to become thoroughly acquainted with the theory and working of our Constitution, its institutes and laws. Comprising, as it does, the great essentials of our national history, it will necessarily become of imperishable value to the American people. The two well-known names which appear on the title-page, afford a sufficient guarantee for the manner in which the work has been produced—its general excellence, comprehensiveness, and accuracy—Mr. B. J. Lossing, the author of the "Pictorial Field-Book of the Revolution," and Mr. Edwin Williams, editor of the "Statesman's Manual," and other valuable statistical works.

The numerous illustrations which accompany the volumes, are beautiful specimens of art, and include exterior and interior views of the Senate of the United States, and House of Representatives, Government Buildings, Capitol, Custom-Houses, Mints, Forts, and a series of newly-prepared portraits of all the Presidents, &c. A copious analytical index is affixed to the work.

III.

THE STATESMAN'S MANUAL;

CONTAINING THE PRESIDENTS' MESSAGES—INAUGURAL, ANNUAL, AND SPECIAL—FROM THOSE OF WASHINGTON TO THE PRESENT TIME: WITH THEIR MEMOIRS AND HISTORIES OF THEIR ADMINISTRATIONS. ALSO, VALUABLE DOCUMENTS AND STATISTICS.

Compiled from Official Sources, by Edwin Williams.

The new edition brought down to the present time.

4 vols. 8vo., with Portraits of all the Presidents, cloth, extra gilt, $10.

This great national work has received the highest commendation from the Press throughout the country, as well as from some of the most distinguished personages connected with the Federal and State governments. It is *indispensable* to all persons in any way connected with official or governmental affairs. A full analytical Index accompanies the work, by which immediate reference can be made to any great question—political, social, or legal.

THE STATESMAN'S MANUAL — CONTINUED.

EXTRACTS FROM NOTICES OF THE WORK.

"We can say no more, and ought to say no less, of this work, than that it is the most complete constitutional history of the United States that exists, or that can be constructed within the same space. It is indispensable to the library of every American scholar, as a book of reference; and, as its title indicates, it is, and always must be, the *Statesman's Manual*."—*New York Evening Post.*

"An indispensable work of reference to all persons engaged in public affairs, and others who study the history and practical operation of our government."—*President Taylor.*

"A very valuable work for reference."—*Hon. Henry Clay.*

"An exceedingly useful and valuable work."—*President Polk.*

"Many hours of idle discussion and senseless debate might be spared to heated partisans, were this book at hand for appeal."—*Democratic Review.*

"It is a *vade mecum* that has no competitor among the books of this country."—*Louisville Journal.*

"This is the most important contribution to American political history ever published. Certainly, no work can compare with this in condensed comprehensiveness, in accuracy, and in all the features which make such a book valuable."—*N. Y. Courier and Enquirer.*

"It is emphatically a national work. No American library, however small, is properly made up, in which a copy of this Statesman's Manual is not found."—*New York Express.*

"It presents information nowhere else to be found in a combined form, of the utmost importance to every American."—*Boston Post.*

"It is a work of the utmost utility and value."—*Boston Recorder.*

"This work is the best help to the study of the history, administrative and diplomatic, of the United States, that exists in the language. It should be in every library, and form a *vade mecum* to every one who aspires to take part in the legislation of this country."—*New Orleans Picayune.*

"It is, in truth, the best historical narrative of our political statistics that has ever been published on the science of government, of any description whatever; for it furnishes, throughout, the varied and interesting development of the action of a free and enlightened government on the multifarious interests of society, and demonstrates that the latter are more perfectly guarded under the ægis of republican institutions than any other. This work is well written, well printed, and well bound, and must, sooner or later, enter into every library."—*Home Journal.*

"This publication is invaluable, not only to the politician, but to every citizen. No American library will be complete without it."—*New Orleans Bulletin.*

"No library should be without the book, and if any man has got a house without a library, let him purchase these to begin one. We take it for granted that a work of such unusual interest will be universally called for."—*Graham's Magazine.*

"Few productions of the present day have emanated from the press with stronger claims upon the public patronage than this. It is a noble attempt to present to the great body of the American people, in an available and popular form, the documentary history of the executive government from its commencement under Washington to that of Taylor, together with the details of each administration, in consecutive order, and a mass of important statistical matter not elsewhere to be met with."—*Boston Courier.*

"It is indeed a work worthy of its title—*national.* There can be no doubt of its taking its place permanently among works of the highest value."—*Boston Register.*

"To say that these elegant and important tomes deserve a conspicuous place in every private and public library, is not all that should be said—they are indispensable to every lawyer, politician, or intelligent, patriotic citizen."—*Boston Witness.*

IV.

A NEW AND ENLARGED EDITION (THE 20TH THOUSAND) OF

DR. DOWLING'S HISTORY OF ROMANISM.

COMPILED FROM ROMISH AUTHORITIES; WITH SUPPLEMENT, BRINGING THE HISTORY DOWN TO THE PRESENT TIME;

WITH FIFTY ENGRAVINGS.

1 vol. 8vo., 800 pages, cloth gilt, $3.

This valuable production, which, by common consent of the Press, literary, religious, and secular, throughout America and Great Britain, has been pronounced the standard authority upon the subject of which it treats, has already attained a circulation in this country of upwards of *thirty* thousand copies. The great characteristic merit of this work, consists in the fact of its being based almost entirely upon Romish authorities—for the most part inaccessible to Protestant readers. It is the result of immense research and labor, and is the most comprehensive and reliable work of its class extant.

☞ The Prelates and Priests of the Romish Church are earnestly invited to give this work their candid perusal, as it contains no unjust strictures upon their Church, but is catholic in its spirit.

"It is a *history*—veritable, authentic history—not a series of declamatory tirades against what the Romish Church is *supposed* to be by those who discard her doctrines and authority—but a plain, unvarnished history of what she is actually by her own admissions and practices; a faithful and impartial exhibition, from her *own* archives, of her recorded and attested opinions and usages."—*Protestant Churchman.*

"This work is admirably adapted to the times. Its circulation would do incalculable good in making known the system, tactics, errors, and dangers of Popery, and thus most effectually put us on our guard. We trust its beautiful appearance will secure it an introduction where its stirring appeals and thrilling facts will tell upon the consciences and hearts of the people."—*National Protestant.*

"Its contents form a rich storehouse of historical instruction, which should be placed within the reach of every family."—*N. Y. Christian Intelligencer.*

"It abounds in facts and incidents, and *is better adapted to furnish a vivid and impressive portraiture of Romanism as it is, than any other book we know of.*"—*New York Evangelist.*

"An able work, comprising the results of extensive reading and research, and well adapted to fill an important chasm in our literature."—*Lutheran Observer*

V.

THE AMERICAN AND ODD-FELLOWS'

LITERARY MUSEUM.

COMPRISING GEMS OF LITERATURE CONTRIBUTED BY MANY OF THE MOST EMINENT AMERICAN WRITERS.

Illustrated with upwards of Thirty fine Steel Engravings. Two elegant volumes. Price—muslin, extra gilt, $5; gilt edges, $6.

This beautiful work is of itself a library of choice, entertaining, and instructive reading—prose and verse—consisting of essays, sketches, tales, and historic and descriptive narratives, etc. It is alike adapted for the social and the solitary hour, and peculiarly suited for the family circle. It contains nearly two hundred original contributions, by esteemed and popular American writers.

www.ingramcontent.com/pod-product-compliance
Lightning Source LLC
LaVergne TN
LVHW020101110826
845151LV00001B/45

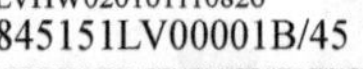

* 9 7 8 1 4 2 5 5 4 3 7 8 5 *